WESOŁA, KLEPARZ, AND BISKUPIE
Pages 128–151

Old Quarter

WESOŁA, KLEPARZ, AND BISKUPIE

OKÓŁ AND STRADOM QUARTERS

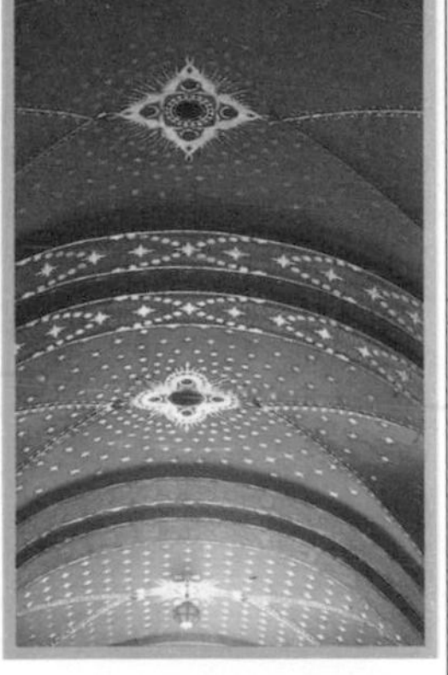

OKÓŁ AND STRADOM QUARTERS
Pages 74–87

KAZIMIERZ QUARTER

KAZIMIERZ QUARTER
Pages 118–127

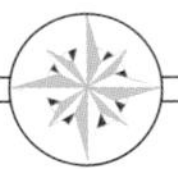

EYEWITNESS TRAVEL

CRACOW

ANTYKI

EYEWITNESS TRAVEL

CRACOW

MAIN CONTRIBUTOR: TERESA CZERNIEWICZ-UMER

LONDON, NEW YORK,
MELBOURNE, MUNICH AND DELHI
www.dk.com

Produced by Wydawnictwo Wiedza i Życie, Warsaw

MANAGING EDITOR Ewa Szwagrzyk
SERIES EDITOR Joanna Egert
DTP DESIGNER Paweł Pasternak
CONSULTANT Jan Ostrowski
PRODUCTION Anna Kożurno-Królikowska

CONTRIBUTORS
Teresa Czerniewicz-Umer, Andrzej Betlej, Piotr Krasny, Robert Makłowicz, Craig Turp

PHOTOGRAPHERS
Andrzej Chęć, Wojciech Czerniewicz, Piotr Jamski, Dorota and Mariusz Jarymowicz

ILLUSTRATORS
Andrzej Wielgosz, Piotr Zybrzycki, Paweł Mistewicz

Reproduced by Colourscan, Singapore
Printed and bound by South China Printing Co. Ltd., China

First published in Great Britain in 2000 by
Dorling Kindersley Limited
80 Strand, London WC2R 0RL

Reprinted with revisions 2003, 2007

ISBN 978 1 40531 937 9

Front cover main image: Wawel Cathedral, Cracow

The information in this Dorling Kindersley Travel Guide is checked regularly.

Every effort has been made to ensure that this book is as up-to-date as possible at the time of going to press. Some details, however, such as telephone numbers, opening hours, prices, gallery hanging arrangements and travel information are liable to change. The publishers cannot accept responsibility for any consequences arising from the use of this book, nor for any material on third party websites, and cannot guarantee that any website address in this book will be a suitable source of travel information. We value the views and suggestions of our readers very highly. Please write to: Publisher, DK Eyewitness Travel Guides, Dorling Kindersley, 80 Strand, London WC2R 0RL.

CONTENTS

The side arcade of Cloth Hall

INTRODUCING CRACOW

Icon of the Virgin of the Rosary in the Dominican Church

◁ Houses around Cracow's Market Square

Cloth Hall (Sukiennice) by night

CRACOW AREA BY AREA

Musicians wearing regional Cracow costumes

TRAVELLERS' NEEDS

SURVIVAL GUIDE

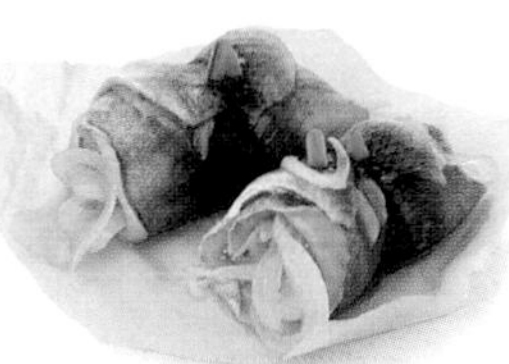

Pickled herrings

Cracow Cathedral on Wawel Hill *(see pp64–5)*

HOW TO USE THIS GUIDE

This Eyewitness Travel Guide is intended to help you make the most of your stay in Cracow. It provides detailed practical information and expert recommendations. *Introducing Cracow* tells you about the geographical location of the city, establishes Cracow in its historical context and guides you through the succession of cultural events. The section on *Cracow at a Glance* takes you through the tourist attractions in the city. *Cracow Area by Area* describes the most important sights with photographs, maps and illustrations. It recommends short excursions out of Cracow and offers three walks around the city. Information about hotels, restaurants, shops and markets as well as cafés, bars, entertainment and sport can be found in the section called *Travellers' Needs*. The section headed *Survival Guide* has advice on everything from posting a letter to using public transport to getting medical assistance.

HOW TO USE THE KEY INDICATORS

Each of the six quarters has been colour coded for your convenience. Each section gives an introduction to the area, its history and character. The *Street by Street* map shows the most interesting parts of the quarter. Finding your way round is made easy by the numbering system. This follows the order in which the descriptions are presented.

Each area has its colour coded thumb tabs.

1 Area Map

For ease of reference, sights in each area are located and numbered on the area map. Sights of particular interest are listed together: churches, museums and galleries, streets and squares, historic buildings, parks and monuments.

Locator map

A locator map places you in relation to the surrounding area.

A suggested route takes you through the most interesting streets in the area.

2 Street-by-Street Map

The most interesting part of each sightseeing area is given from a bird's-eye view. On the area map the most interesting sights are indicated and given a full description on the following pages.

Stars indicate the features that no visitors should miss.

CRACOW AREA MAP

This colour-coded map *(see pages 16–17)* indicates the six main sightseeing quarters described in this guide. Each of these quarters is more fully covered in the *Area by Area* section *(pages 56–151)*. In *Cracow at a Glance* this same colour coding allows you to locate the most interesting places. You will also be able to orientate yourself during the three suggested walks *(page 164)*.

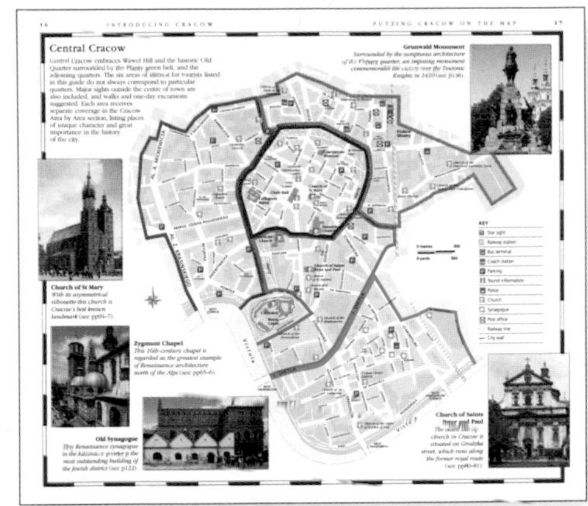

Numbered circles locate the listed sights on the area map and within the descriptive section.

Practical information provides everything you need to know to visit each sight. Map references pinpoint the sight's location on the *Street Finder* map *(see pp228–37)*.

3 Detailed Information

Each of the most interesting sights is described in depth. You will find them listed in order following the numbering on the area map. Practical information, including map references, opening hours and telephone numbers is also provided.

The visitors' checklist provides useful information you may need to plan your visit.

The boxes contain detailed information on a particular subject relating to the sight.

Stars indicate the most interesting sights as well as architectural details and the most important works of art.

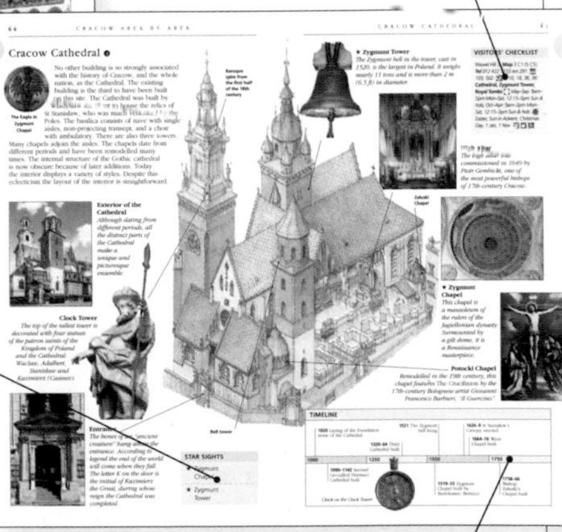

4 Cracow's Main Sights

Historic buildings are dissected to reveal their interiors. Museums and galleries have colour-coded floor plans enabling you to find important exhibits.

A timeline indicates important dates in the history of the building.

***The Prussian Homage* (1882) by Jan Matejko** ▷

INTRODUCING CRACOW

FOUR GREAT DAYS IN CRACOW

There are three themes that define the most visited city in Poland – its royal past, Judaism and culture. Some of Cracow's most important sights are along the Royal Route to the Wawel Castle, while the Kazimierz district, home to the city's Jews since the 14th century, is seeing a welcome revival after the tragedy of the Holocaust. As Poland's cultural capital, many museums here house artistic treasures. Cracow is also a surprisingly green city, full of grottoes and parks particularly suited to children. These four days are designed to uncover the city from these different viewpoints, while page references lead you to more details on the main sights. The price guides include travel, food and admission charges.

The Great Seal of Cracow

WALKING THE ROYAL ROUTE

- **Explore Cracow's Old Quarter**
- **Great views from the Town Hall Tower**
- **Authentic Polish cuisine**
- **Impressive churches and a cathedral**

TWO ADULTS allow at least 300zł

Morning

Starting early to avoid the crowds, especially in summer, there is no better way to enter Cracow's Old Quarter than through the 700-year-old **St Florian's Gate** *(see p111)*, one of the few remnants of the city's original defences. Stroll along **Floriańska Street** *(see p114)*, once Cracow's main commercial thoroughfare and still very much a thriving bazaar where artisans and hawkers sell all sorts of souvenirs – look out for watercolours depicting the best of the Old Quarter.

St Florian's Gate

Cracow's **Market Square** *(see pp98–101)* is both the geographical and spiritual heart of the city, and is surrounded on all sides by historic treasures; **St Mary's** *(see pp94–7)* and **St Aldabert's** *(see p93)* churches are worth a look. Climb the **Town Hall Tower** *(see p93)* for superb panoramic views and wander around the market inside the 14th-century **Cloth Hall** *(see pp102–3)*. For lunch, enjoy some classic Polish dishes at Cracow's oldest restaurant, **Wierzynek** *(see p192)*.

Afternoon

One of Cracow's oldest streets, **Grodzka** *(see p78)* is a cobbled route of different, but harmonious, architectural styles. Admire the **Royal Arsenal** *(see p79)* and the modest but charming **Church of St Giles** opposite *(see p79)*. A little further down, don't miss the **Church of St Martin** *(see p79)*, set slightly back from the street, or the impressively preserved Romanesque **Church of St Andrew** *(see p78)*. Take a look inside the **Church of Saints Peter and Paul** *(see pp80–81)*, an early Baroque masterpiece. At the end of the Royal Route is **Wawel Hill** *(see pp60–61)*, and late in the afternoon, after the majority of visitors have gone, you can stroll the hill at leisure. Be sure to visit the wonderful **Cracow Cathedral** *(see pp64–9)*, and to wander around the inner courtyard of the **Royal Castle** *(see pp70–71)*.

Interior of the Old Synagogue

JEWISH CRACOW

- **The history of Cracow's Jewish population**
- **Great kosher food**
- **World War II Jewish ghetto**
- **The famous Schindler factory**

TWO ADULTS allow at least 300zł

Morning

Start your day at the **Old Synagogue** *(see p122)*, damaged during World War II, but now restored to its original 16th-century design. The exhibition inside serves as a good introduction to the history of Jews in Cracow. Nearby are two cemeteries: the **New Jewish Cemetery** *(see p123)*, created in the 19th century as a resting place for the city's wealthiest Jews, and **Remu'h Cemetery** *(see p122)* in the courtyard of the Remu'h synagogue. For a kosher lunch head to **Klezmer Hois** *(see p192)*.

Afternoon
Stroll over the Powstańców Slaskich bridge to the Podgórze area. The Nazis moved the Jews here from Kazimierz in 1941, squeezing them into the area around Bohaterów Getta and Rynek Podgórski. One Polish man, Tadeusz Pankiewicz, owner of the Pharmacy Under the Eagles at Bohaterów Getta 18, stayed on in an attempt to help the city's Jews. Here today, an exhibition portrays life in the ghetto. At Lipowa 4 is the former Schindler factory, featured in the film *Schindler's List*. An exhibition dedicated to Oskar Schindler is planned; meanwhile the original Schindler gates remain.

CITY OF CULTURE

- **Artworks by the Great Masters**
- **Visit the former home of Pope John Paul II**
- **Explore the Collegium Maius**
- **Beautiful Secessionist architecture**

TWO ADULTS allow at least 250zł

Morning
Begin your day of culture on the first floor of the **Czartoryski Museum** *(see pp112–13)* whose main claim to fame is Leonardo da Vinci's *Lady with an Ermine*, the only Leonardo in Poland. There are also works by Rembrandt and other masters in the gallery, which is worth at least an hour's visit. Next, head over to the **Wyspiański Museum** *(see p110)* to admire the talents of Stanislav

Jagiellonian University

Flowers in bloom in Planty Park

Wyspiański, Poland's leading Secessionist painter. Jump on the No. 124 bus for the short ride to the **Archdiocesan Museum** *(see p82)*, home of Poland's finest collection of ecclesiastical art. Today the building is also popular with pilgrims interested in the life of Pope John Paul II; he lived in the building in the 1950s. For lunch head to **Smak Ukraiński** *(see p189)* for outstanding Ukrainian food.

Afternoon
A walk through the southern part of **Planty Park** *(see pp168–9)*, past the statue of Copernicus, to the Jagiellonian University and Museum in the **Collegium Maius** *(see pp106–7)* is the perfect post-lunch stroll. Enjoy the glorious courtyard and take the 30-minute guided tour of the building, then take a quick peek inside the **Church of St Anne** *(see pp108–9)*. If you have an appetite for more art, head to the **"Bunker of Art"** *(see p105)*, home to cutting-edge exhibitions. Next pay a visit to the **Słowacki Theatre** *(see p115)*. It is officially closed unless there is a performance on, but the doorman may just let you in to admire the lovely Secessionist interior. Round off this cultural day with dinner at **Jazz Club U Muniaka** *(see p205)*, Cracow's best jazz café.

A FAMILY DAY

- **The magical and mysterious Dragon's Lair**
- **Picnic lunch in the park**
- **Shopping in the Cloth Hall**
- **Cycle round the city**

FAMILY OF FOUR allow 350zł

Morning
Few children will fail to be intrigued by the **Dragon's Lair** *(see p63)* on Wawel Hill, a warren of tunnels, nooks and crannies. They can then shop for chocolate at **Wawel** *(see p199)* before you head next door to the deli to buy bread, sausage and cheese for a picnic lunch. Then visit the **Cloth Hall** *(pp102–3)*, which sells excellent wooden toys.

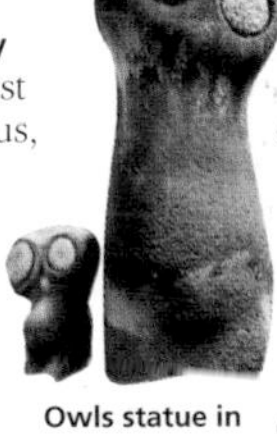

Owls statue in Planty Park

Afternoon
Trams 15 and 18 will take you out to the family-friendly Jordan Park, where you can enjoy your lunch while the kids can take a paddle-boat on the lake. After an afternoon of relaxation, head back to town for an early dinner at the Wild West-themed **Sioux Steakhouse** *(see p192)*. If you still have the energy take an evening bike tour around the sights of Cracow – children over seven are welcome. The tour meets at the southern end of Kanonicza nightly at 7pm.

Putting Cracow on the Map

The old part of Cracow (Kraków), with the Royal Castle on Wawel Hill, is regarded as a fascinating historic town rich in heritage. The historic quarters constitute only a small part of present-day Cracow, the largest urban development in the Lesser Poland (Małopolska) region. The geographical position makes Cracow an ideal base for excursions to the Polish mountains, Auschwitz or the picturesque Cracow-Częstochowa Valley. The town is also well positioned for international connections to Prague, Brno, Bratislava, Vienna and L'viv.

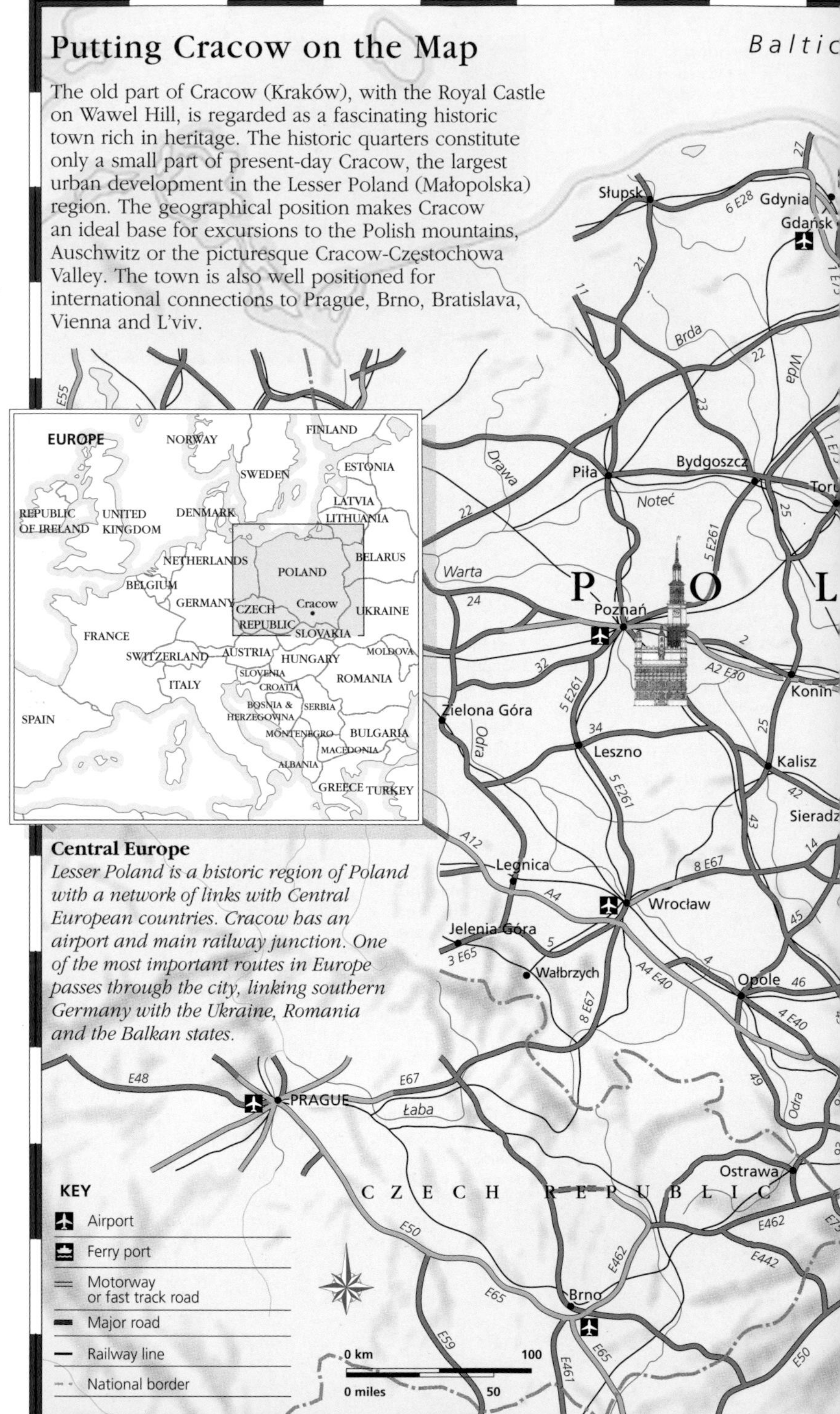

Central Europe

Lesser Poland is a historic region of Poland with a network of links with Central European countries. Cracow has an airport and main railway junction. One of the most important routes in Europe passes through the city, linking southern Germany with the Ukraine, Romania and the Balkan states.

For additional map symbols *see back flap*

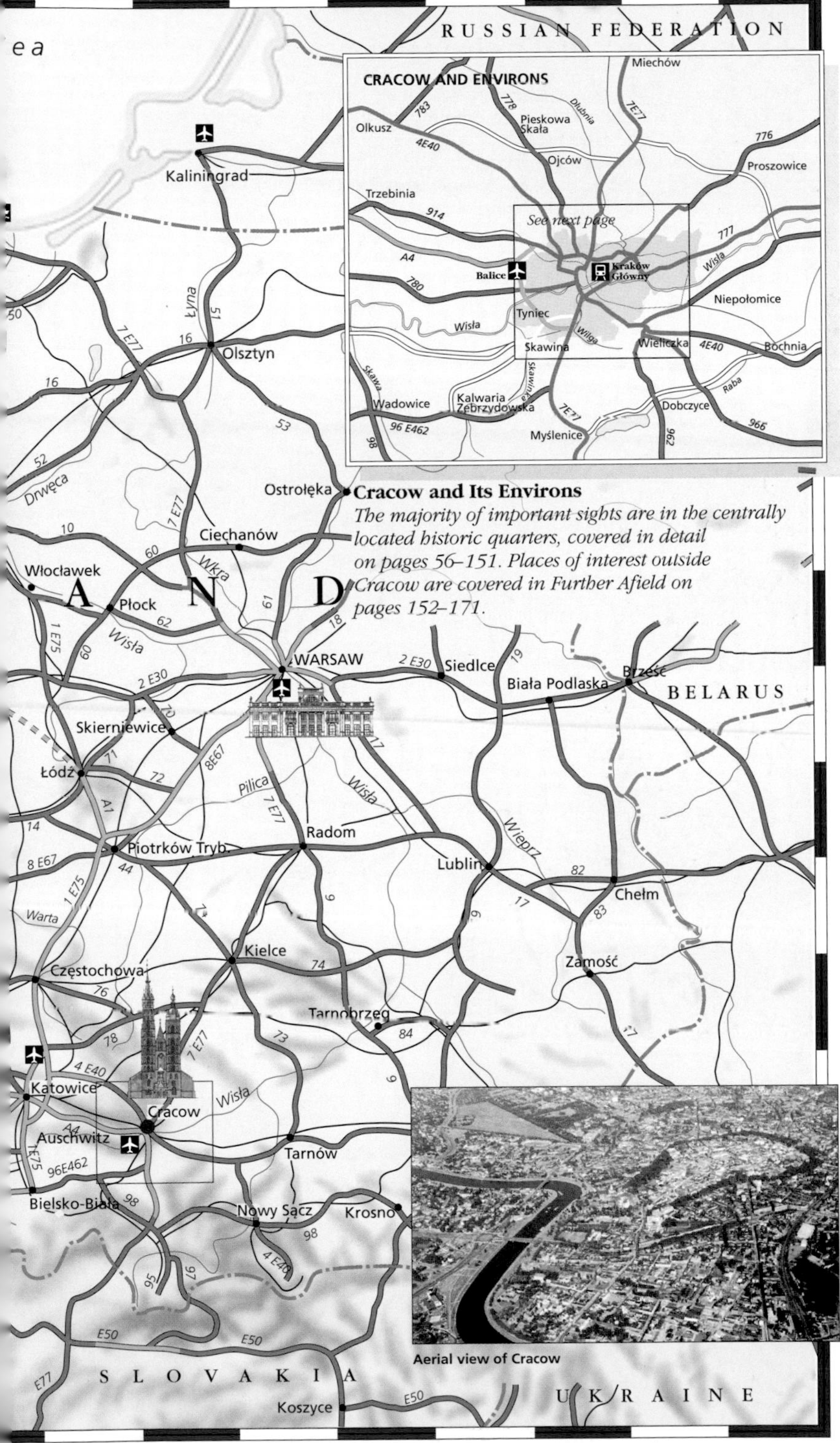

Cracow and Its Environs
The majority of important sights are in the centrally located historic quarters, covered in detail on pages 56–151. Places of interest outside Cracow are covered in Further Afield on pages 152–171.

Aerial view of Cracow

Cracow and Its Environs

Until the early 20th century the conurbation of Cracow occupied a relatively small area on the banks of the Vistula (Wisła) River and was made up of several small towns (Kleparz, Kazimierz, Garbary and Podgórze). Greater Cracow was established in 1910 after the incorporation of the extensive lands of Rakowice, Prądnik, Czarna Wieś, Krowodrza, Bielany, Dębnik, Płaszów and Prokocim. A new industrial district of Nowa Huta was constructed outside Cracow after World War II. Long walks in Cracow are always interesting as all the historic quarters have their own unique character.

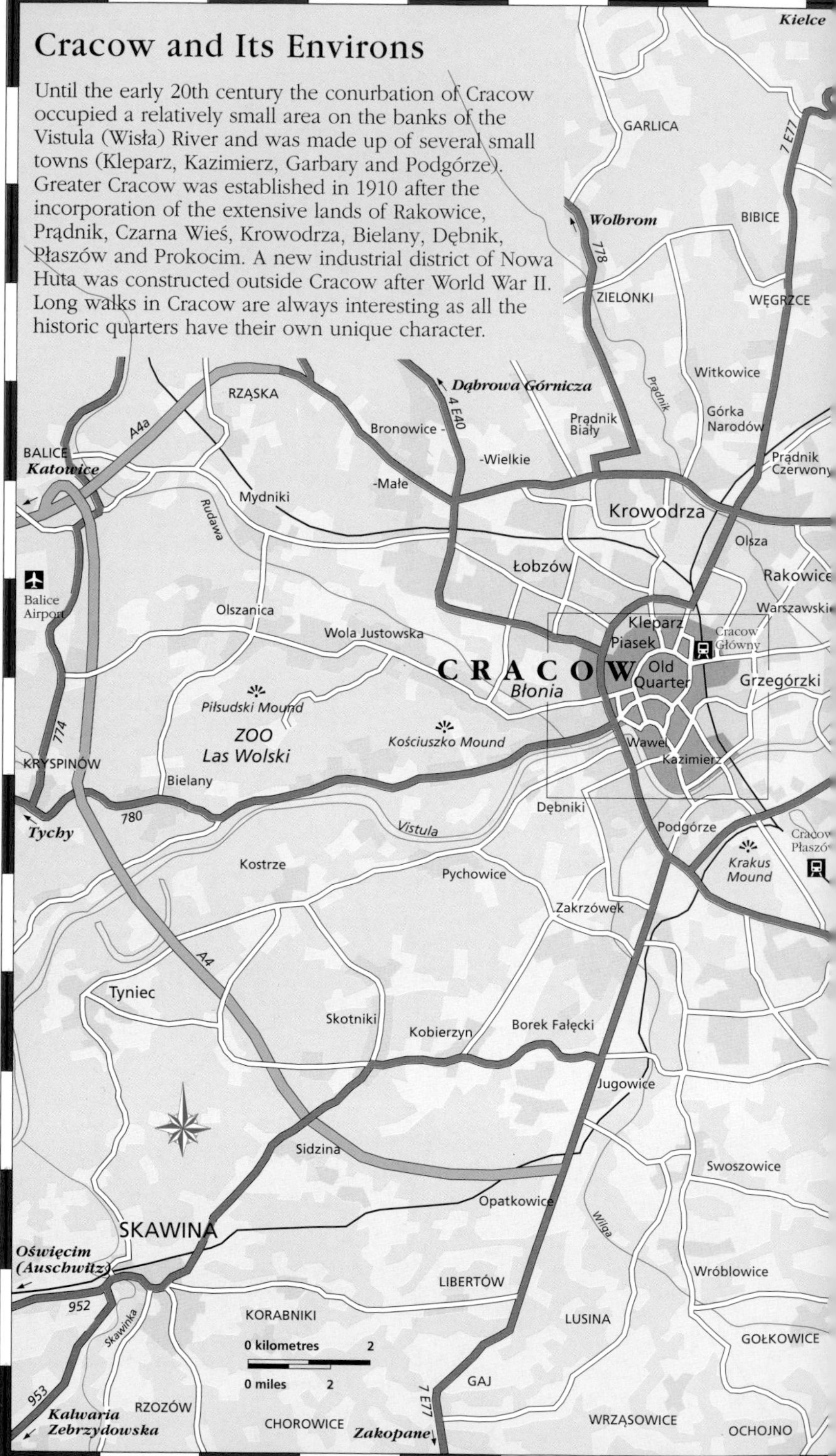

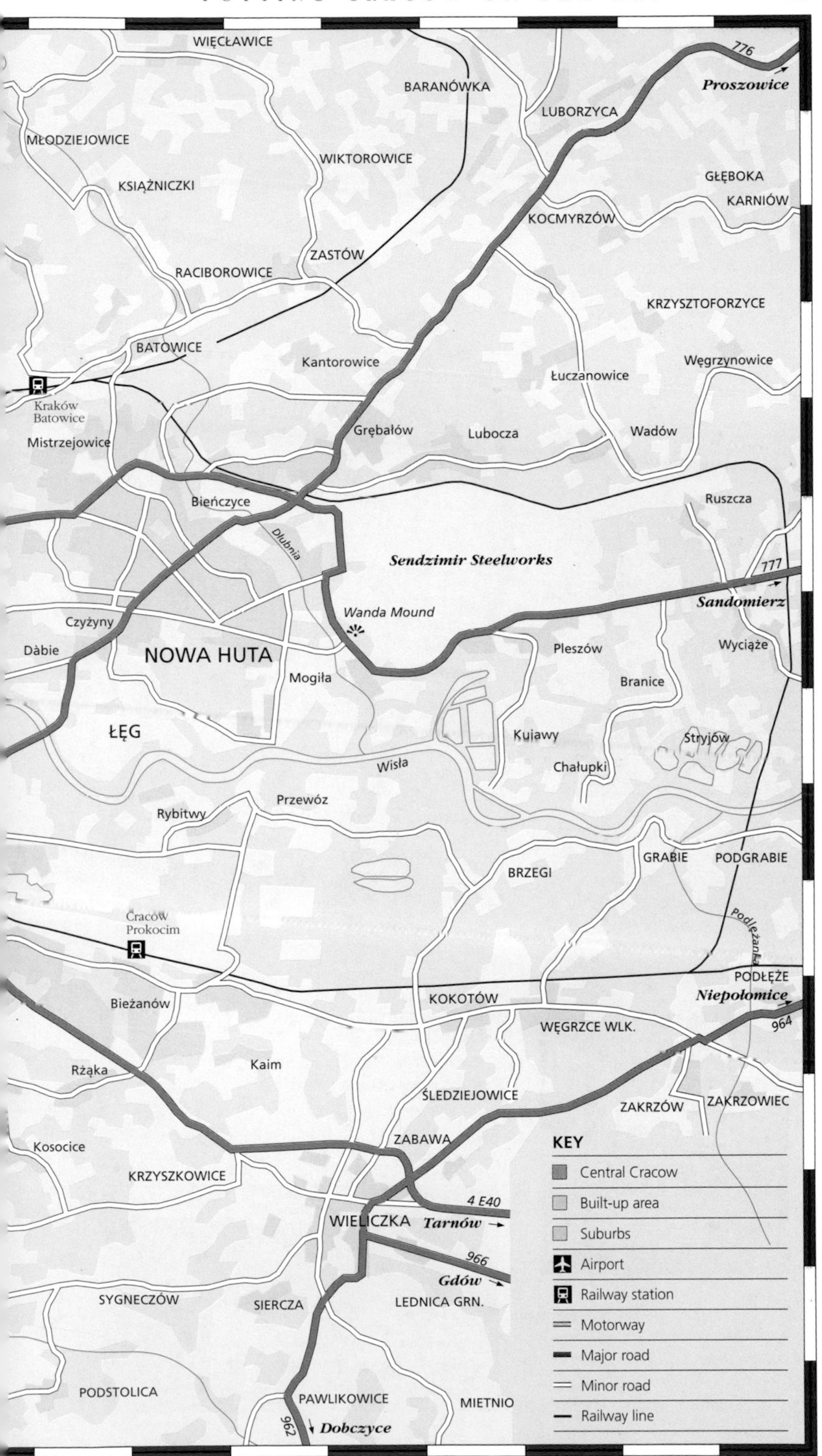

WIĘCŁAWICE
BARANÓWKA
776
Proszowice
LUBORZYCA
MŁODZIEJOWICE
WIKTOROWICE
KSIĄŻNICZKI
GŁĘBOKA
KARNIÓW
KOCMYRZÓW
ZASTÓW
RACIBOROWICE
KRZYSZTOFORZYCE
BATOWICE
Kantorowice
Węgrzynowice
Łuczanowice
Kraków Batowice
Grębałów
Lubocza
Wadów
Mistrzejowice
Bieńczyce
Ruszcza
Dłubnia
Sendzimir Steelworks
777
Sandomierz
Wanda Mound
Czyżyny
Pleszów
Wyciąże
Dàbie
NOWA HUTA
Mogiła
Branice
ŁĘG
Kujawy
Stryjów
Wisła
Chałupki
Przewóz
Rybitwy
GRABIE
PODGRABIE
BRZEGI
Cracow Prokocim
Podłężanka
PODŁĘŻE
Niepołomice
Bieżanów
KOKOTÓW
WĘGRZCE WLK.
964
Rżąka
Kaim
ŚLEDZIEJOWICE
ZAKRZÓW
ZAKRZOWIEC
Kosocice
ZABAWA
KRZYSZKOWICE
4 E40
WIELICZKA
Tarnów
966
Gdów
SYGNECZÓW
SIERCZA
LEDNICA GRN.
PODSTOLICA
PAWLIKOWICE
MIETNIO
962
Dobczyce
KEY
Central Cracow
Built-up area
Suburbs
Airport
Railway station
Motorway
Major road
Minor road
Railway line

Central Cracow

Central Cracow embraces Wawel Hill and the historic Old Quarter surrounded by the Planty green belt, and the adjoining quarters. Major sights outside the centre of town are also included, and walks and one-day excursions suggested. Each area receives separate coverage in the Cracow Area by Area section, listing places of unique character and great importance in the history of the city.

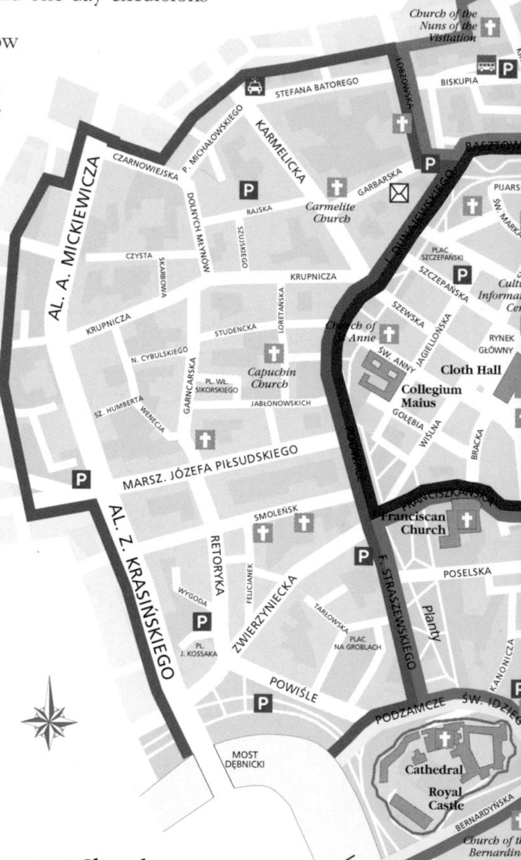

Church of St Mary
With its asymmetrical silhouette this church is Cracow's best known landmark (see pp94–7).

Zygmunt Chapel
This 16th-century chapel is regarded as the greatest example of Renaissance architecture north of the Alps (see pp65–6).

Old Synagogue
This Renaissance synagogue in the Kazimierz quarter is the most outstanding building of the Jewish district (see p122).

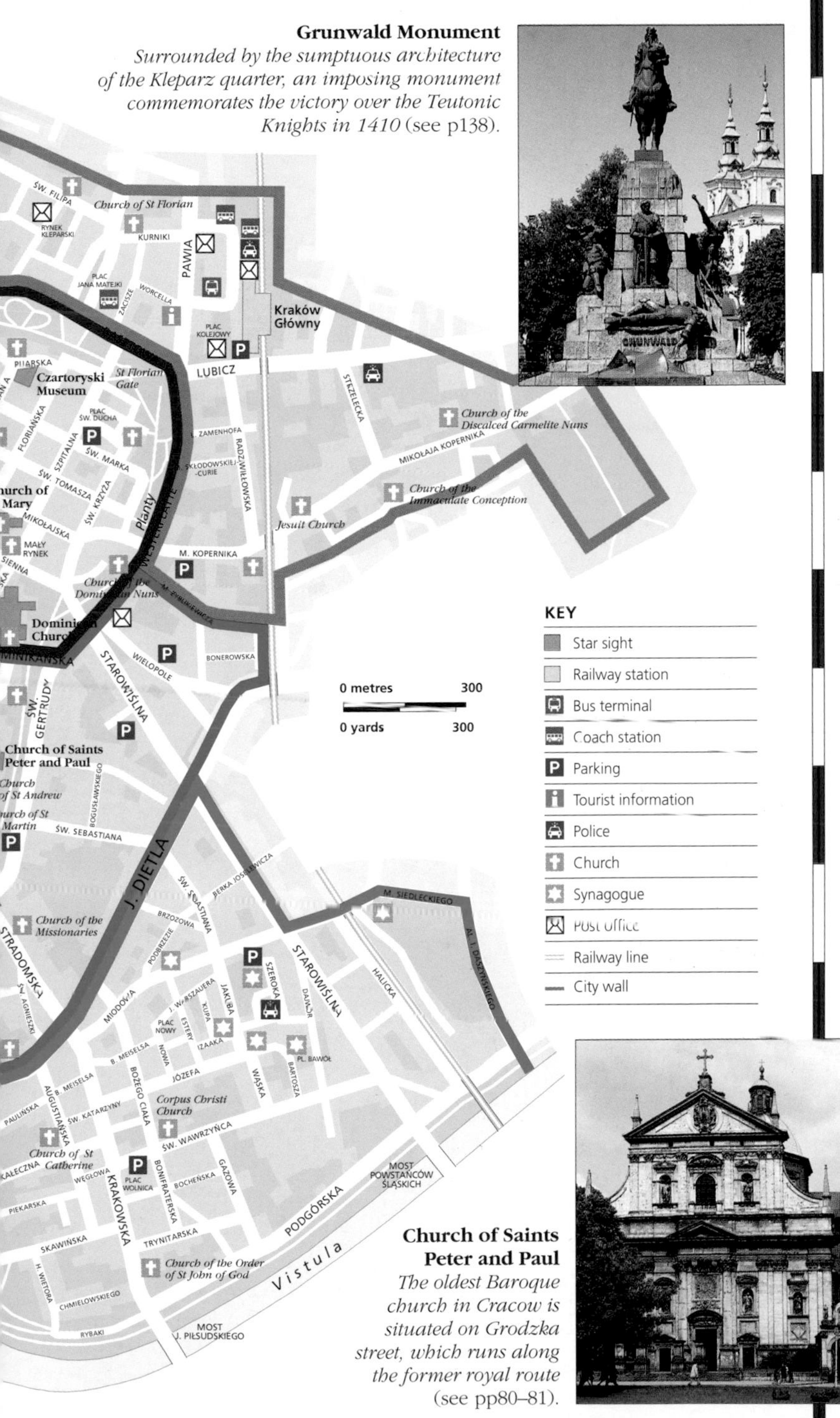

Grunwald Monument
Surrounded by the sumptuous architecture of the Kleparz quarter, an imposing monument commemorates the victory over the Teutonic Knights in 1410 (see p138).

Church of Saints Peter and Paul
The oldest Baroque church in Cracow is situated on Grodzka street, which runs along the former royal route (see pp80–81).

THE HISTORY OF CRACOW

For manly centuries Cracow was the capital of Poland and the country's largest city. Polish rulers resided at Wawel Castle. The royal court moved to Warsaw in 1609, after parliamentary sessions and the election of kings began to take place there. Until the collapse of the First Republic, however, Cracow continued to be regarded as the official capital. Deprived of her former status Cracow suffered a deep crisis in the 18th and 19th centuries.

The coat of arms of Cracow

Despite all the past upheavals, Cracow has retained her magnificence. It is more than 400 years since Cracow ceased to be the seat of national government, and yet she maintains her leading role in preserving Polish national identity. Wawel, the seat of Polish kings, the Cathedral that bore witness to their coronations and houses their tombs, as well as the Paulite Church "On the Rock" in whose crypt prominent Poles are buried, belong to the most treasured national heritage. The 600-year-old Jagiellonian University, formerly known as the Academy of Cracow, is the oldest and one of the most important universities in the country and a pillar of Polish culture. Bearing in mind the small population of Cracow (approximately 760,000), visitors may be surprised by the great number of theatres, cabarets, concert halls and art galleries, which are always popular with regular audiences.

Polish historic cities suffered badly during World War II. Luckily, Cracow's losses were minimal. For those interested in old Polish art, Cracow, with her rich heritage, is certainly the place to go. For many years Cracow's architectural treasures were in a state of neglect, hidden beneath peeling plaster, cracking paint and layers of dirt caused by pollution. In recent years, however, many buildings have been renovated and returned to their former splendour.

Cracow is different from some other large European towns in which historic inner cities have been transformed into open-air museums. The medieval Market Square remains at the heart of today's city. It is the venue for some of the most important events and the traditional meeting place for locals and visitors alike, all of whom enjoy Cracow's unique atmosphere and heritage.

View of Cracow with the Kościuszko Mound (in the foreground), a 19th-century lithograph, Museum of Cracow

◁ *Tadeusz Kościuszko Taking the Oath on Market Square* by Michał Stachowicz (detail), Museum of Cracow

Cracow's Origins

Cracow is one of the oldest cities in Poland. The archaeological findings provide evidence of a Palaeolithic settlement, as well as those from the Neolithic period, and the Bronze and Iron Ages. The Celtic people and invaders from the east, namely the Scythians and Huns, also left important artifacts. In the early centuries AD Cracow and Lesser Poland bordered and traded with the Roman Empire. Written accounts date only from the 9th century and pertain to the Vistulan settlers who, by the end of the same century, came under the rule of the Great Moravian Empire. The Polish rulers from the House of Piast regained power only at the end of the rule of Mieszko I (around 992).

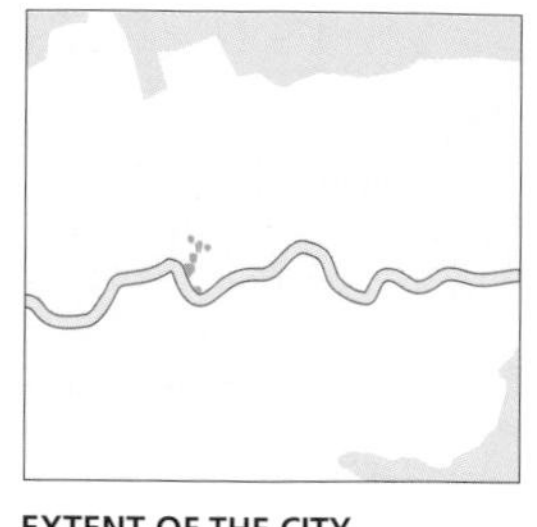

EXTENT OF THE CITY

AD 1000 Today

King Krak
The legendary founder of Cracow is believed to have lived in the early 8th century.

An imaginary view of Wawel Castle

The cave in Wawel Hill

THE DRAGON OF WAWEL

This woodcut comes from Sebastian Münster's *Cosmographia universalis* of 1544 and shows the legendary dragon and his slayer, the cobbler Skuba, below Wawel Castle.

Earthenware with String Ornaments
These earthenware containers were among the 1st-century artifacts excavated at Nowa Huta while constructing the new town.

TIMELINE

c. 200,000 BC Earliest evidence of settlements in the Cracow area

c. 50,000 BC Evidence of a settlement on Wawel Hill

c. 1300 BC Lusatian culture flourishes in Lesser Poland

1st – 4th century AD Cracow settlers trade with the Roman Empire

Palaeolithic stone tool

200, 000 BC | 20000 | 0 | AD 200

Saints Cyril and Methodius
Methodius and his brother Cyril are two of the three Patrons of Europe. The former failed in his attempt to convert the prince of the Vistulans from paganism to Christianity. Soon after, their land was conquered by the Great Moravian Empire.

WHERE TO SEE PREHISTORIC CRACOW

Very little has survived from prehistoric times in Cracow. There are, however, two mounds worth a visit: the Krak Mound dominating the southern quarters, and the Wanda Mound near Mogiła village. The Archaeological Museum *(see p83)* houses many interesting artifacts from southern Poland, and the Cracow region in particular. The figure of the four-faced pagan idol Światowid is of special interest.

The Krak Mound *contains, according to legend, a tomb of Krak, the ancient ruler of Cracow. In reality it was more likely to have been used as a religious site of the Celts.*

Wawel means a hill surrounded by marshes

Światowid
This statue represents a four-faced idol holding a cornucopia. Evidence of ancient pagan cults has been found at the Wawel and other sites.

Iron Treasures
Iron objects in the form of elongated axes found at Wawel Hill were used as a form of payment in the 11th century.

600–1000 Vistulans establish their state, possibly with Cracow as the capital

965 Ibrahim Ibn Yaqub, an Arab traveller, comments on Cracow as a Czech city

400 | 600 | 800 | 1000

Early medieval earthenware vase

before 885 The Vistulans' state loses its independence. Cracow becomes part of the Great Moravian Empire

before 992 Mieszko I adds the former state of the Vistulans to his other territories

Cracow in the Early Middle Ages

Romanesque capital

Following the establishment of the bishopric in 1000 and the construction of the cathedral, Cracow became one of the most important centres of the Polish state. After the destruction of other centres in Greater Poland (Wielkopolska) by the Czechs in the first half of the 11th century, Kazimierz the Restorer and his successors made Cracow their main seat. Following the death of Bolesław the Wrymouthed Poland was divided into duchies, and the Dukes of Cracow gained suzerain position. From 1138 to 1320 the dukes aimed to unite the remaining provinces. Despite the Tatar invasion in 1241, this period saw Cracow flourish.

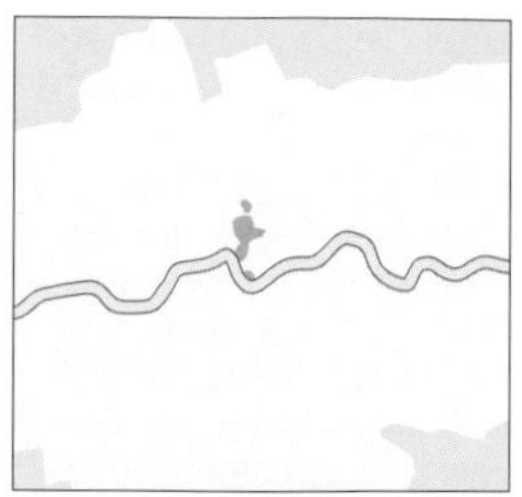

EXTENT OF THE CITY

1253 Today

Bishop Stanisław in prayer

Szczerbiec
According to legend this is the sword of Bolesław the Brave with which he struck the Golden Gate of Kiev on entering the city in 1018. The sword was actually made in the 13th century. Today it is housed in the Crown Treasury as one of the most treasured regalia.

Denarius of Bolesław the Brave
Following the establishment of Cracow's bishopric in 1000, Bolesław made this city one of his seats.

TIMELINE

1000 Bishopric of Cracow established

1020 Construction of first Cathedral in Cracow begins

c. 1038 Kazimierz the Restorer makes Cracow the capital of Poland

c. 1044 Benedictine Abbey at Tyniec is established

1079 Martyrdom of St Stanisław

1079–98 Construction of St Andrew's Church

1090–1142 Construction of second Cathedral at Wawel

1000 | 1025 | 1050 | 1075 | 1100

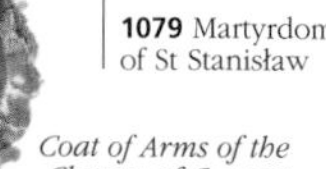
Coat of Arms of the Chapter of Cracow

The Supposed Mitre of St Stanisław
This ornate 13th-century mitre decorated with pearls, sapphires and rubies testifies to the riches of metropolitan Cracow, one of the most important bishoprics in medieval Poland.

King Bolesław the Bold

Kazimierz the Restorer after Jan Matejko
It can be said that Cracow owes her capital status to this ruler, who settled here around 1038 and established a central administration.

THE DEATH OF BISHOP STANISŁAW

The conflict between Bishop Stanisław of Szczepanów (later canonized) and Bolesław the Bold ended with the murder of the bishop in 1079 and the exile of the king. Both events contributed to the weakening of Poland. The cult of St Stanisław began in the 15th century. This scene decorates a 16th-century chasuble (priest's vestment) commissioned by Piotr Kmita.

WHERE TO SEE ROMANESQUE CRACOW

Cracow is rich in Romanesque architecture. Most buildings have survived in their original form, though they have often been enlarged and refurbished. The Church of St Andrew *(see pp78–9)* dates from this period, as does St Adalbert's *(see p93)* and the remains of the earliest buildings at Wawel, including the Rotunda of the Virgin Mary *(see p63)* and the little church of the Holy Redeemer *(see p168)*.

The Church of St Adalbert *was, according to legend, consecrated by Adalbert before his missionary journey to Prussia in 997.*

The Crypt of St Leonard *is a remnant of Cracow's second cathedral. It was built by Władysław Herman between 1090 and 1142.*

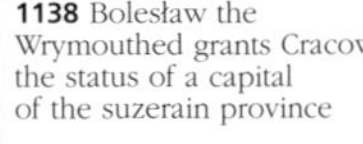

1138 Bolesław the Wrymouthed grants Cracow the status of a capital of the suzerain province

1173 Bolesław the Curly is the first Piast to be buried at Wawel

Cloister at the Dominican Church

1241 Tatars led by Batuhan destroy Cracow

1150	1175	1200	1225	1250

1141–1320 Polish dukes fight for Cracow

Benedictine Abbey at Tyniec

1250 Consecration of the Dominican Church

Gothic Cracow

Detail of the high altar at St Mary's

The Charter granted to Cracow in 1257 facilitated urban development and allowed for a new and more structured plan. A Gothic defence wall surrounded the city, and Cracow began to flourish anew following the coronation of Władyslaw the Short in 1320. The new satellite towns of Kazimierz and Kleparz both received municipal charters. The architectural panorama of Cracow was substantially transformed by the building of many new churches and the Cathedral in the 14th and 15th centuries. The foundation of the Cracow Academy, and its subsequent renewal, contributed greatly to the development of culture and intellectual activities. The ideas of Italian humanism were known in Cracow early on.

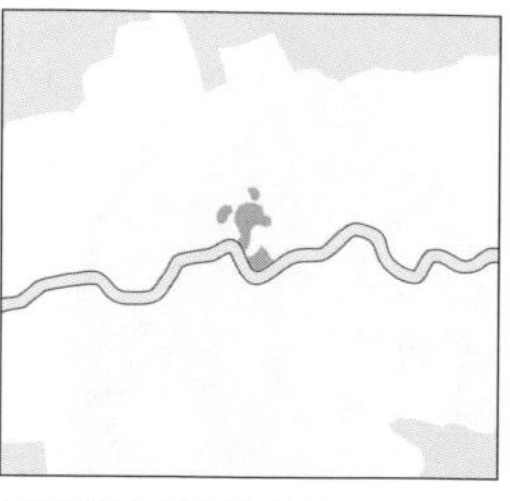

EXTENT OF THE CITY

1370   Today

The Diptych Reliquary
A double leaf Gothic reliquary containing the relics of saints is decorated with the image of the Virgin Mary and that of Christ.

The coat of arms of the Piasts

Saints Stanisław and Wacław shown standing on the battlement walls are patron saints of Cracow's Cathedral and the Kingdom of Poland.

A View of Late Gothic Cracow, 1493
This townscape from the 15th century World Chronicle *by Hartmann Schedel is the earliest known view of Cracow.*

TIMELINE

1250 | **1275** | **1300** | **1325** | **1350**

1257 Duke Bolesław the Chaste grants Cracow her Charter on 5 June

1285 Construction of Cracow's defence walls begins

Coat of Arms of Kazimierz

1312 Revolt of German burghers, led by Albert

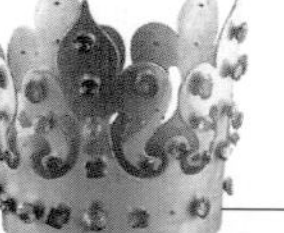

Crown of Kazimierz the Great (replica)

1335 Kazimierz the Great grants Kazimierz its Charter

1340 Construction of Corpus Christi Church begins

1364 Cracow Academy founded by Kazimierz the Great

1366 Kleparz (Florencja) receives its Charter

Cracow's Charter
The municipal status granted to Cracow was modelled on the Magdeburg law and contributed to uniform urban development.

The Coats of Arms shown on both sides of the gate are those of Bolesław the Chaste who granted Cracow her Charter.

Krużlowa Madonna
This beautiful Madonna with Child is an interesting example of the influence of International Gothic on wood sculpture of Lesser Poland in the 15th century.

SEAL OF THE ROYAL CITY OF CRACOW

The 14th-century Great Seal of Cracow (shown here with the image reversed) features the emblem of Poland, thus stressing the role of Cracow as its capital.

WHERE TO SEE GOTHIC CRACOW

Some of the biggest attractions in Cracow are the Gothic buildings, such as the Barbican *(see p114)*, St Florian's Gate *(see p111)*, the Collegium Maius *(see pp106–7)*, and large churches such as St Mary's *(see pp94–5)*, the Dominican Church *(see pp116–7)*, St Catherine's *(see p126)* and Corpus Christi *(see p123)*. Some smaller churches, such as the Holy Cross *(see p115)*, are equally interesting. The works by Veit Stoss are gems of Gothic art.

The Cathedral (see pp64–9) *is the burial place of kings and the seat of the local*

The Church of the Holy Cross *has a single nave whose interior is covered with palm*

1386 Grand Duke Jogaila of Lithuania becomes King Władysław II Jagiełło of Poland

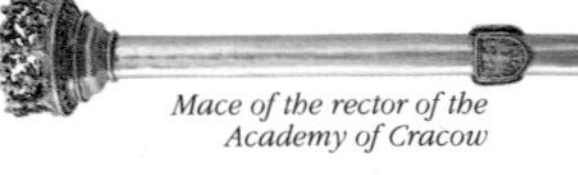

Mace of the rector of the Academy of Cracow

1473 First Polish printing house of Łukasz Straube issues a calendar

1400 | 1425 | 1450 | 1475 | 1500

efore 1400 Collegium Maius is established

1400 Władysław Jagiełło re-establishes the Cracow Academy

Coat of Arms of the Jagiellonians

1477–89 Veit Stoss works on the high altar at St Mary's

1492 Kazimierz Jagiellończyk dies

Renaissance Cracow

Eagle on the cover of Anna Jagiellonka prayer book

Cracow, the capital city, rapidly developed economically and began to change in appearance. The Cloth Hall, the city landmark, was remodelled in the Renaissance style, and the rich merchants of Cracow also began to modernize their houses. The art and culture of the Italian Renaissance was assimilated by the royal courts of King Aleksander and King Zygmunt the Old and his second wife Bona Sforza. Bartolomeo Berrecci, Giovanni Maria Padovano and other outstanding Italian masters established their workshops in Cracow during this time.

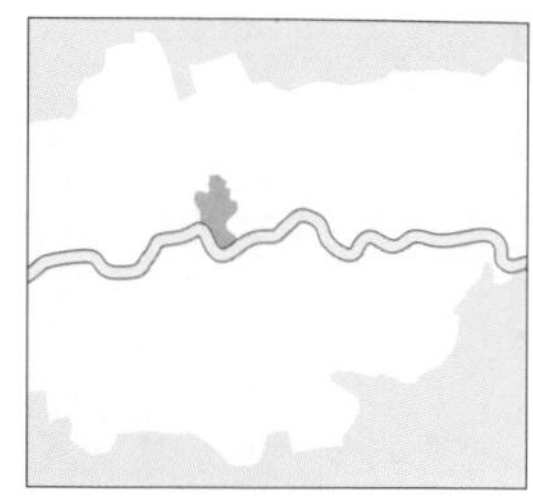

EXTENT OF THE CITY

■ *1572* □ *Today*

"The Sword Makers" from the Baltazar Behem Codex
This Codex of 1505 contains laws and privileges of the town guilds and is illustrated with 27 illuminations showing craftsmen at work.

A Tapestry with Satyrs
This is one of 160 tapestries commissioned in the 16th century by Zygmunt August for the Wawel Collection.

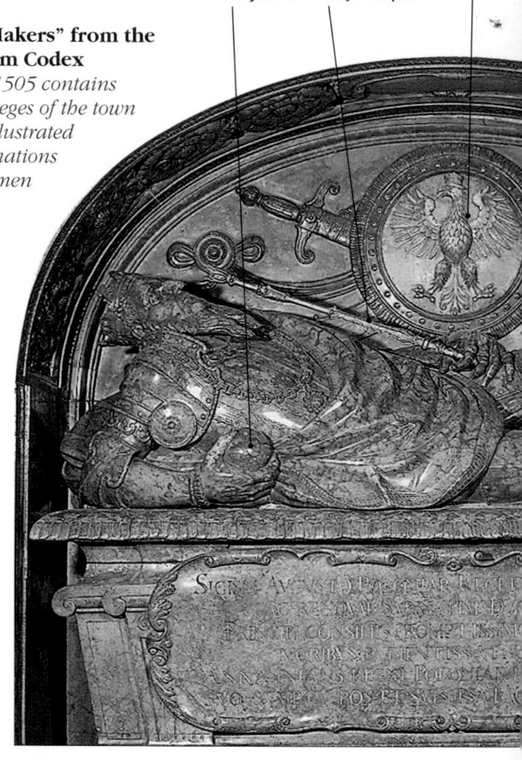

TIMELINE

1502–5 Erection of King Jan Olbracht's monument, the first work of Renaissance art in Poland

1504 Rebuilding of the Wawel Castle starts

1505 Baltazar Behem Codex made

1513 First Polish book in print from the Ungler House

Head in the Hall of Deputies

1519 Bartolomeo Berrecci begins work on Zygmunt's Chapel in the Cathedral

1521 Zygmunt's Bell is hung

1525 Homage paid by the Prussians to the Polish King in the Market Square on 10 April

1543 The treatise *De revolutionibus* by Copernicus is published

1500 | 1510 | 1520 | 1530 | 1540

NICOLAI CO
PERNICI TORINENSIS
DE REVOLVTIONIBVS ORBI-
um cœlestium, Libri VI.

Detail of the title page from Copernicus's treatise

A Renaissance Portal
The first post office in 16th-century Poland, serving the Cracow-Venice route, was situated in the house of Prospero Provana. Today the building houses the Hotel Pod Różą.

Cock of the Marksmen's Brotherhood
This gilt masterpiece, made in 1565, belonged to the members of the Brotherhood whose aim was to support soldiers responsible for the defence of the town.

Oval recess with Renaissance decoration

MONUMENT OF ZYGMUNT AUGUST

King Zygmunt August was a patron of the arts. It was through his commissions that the Royal Castle at Wawel was enriched with an outstanding collection of tapestries. The king's monument was made by Santi Gucci between 1574 and 1575, in Hungarian red marble.

WHERE TO SEE RENAISSANCE CRACOW

Renaissance architecture was introduced by Italian masters during the rebuilding of the Royal Castle at Wawel in the early 16th century. The Zygmunt Chapel *(see pp64–9)*, the Montelupis Monument at St Mary's Church *(see pp94–5)* and a number of houses at Kanonicza Street *(see p79)* are among the finest examples of Renaissance art and architecture in the city.

The arcaded courtyard *at the Royal Castle at Wawel is one of the most beautiful in Europe* (see pp70–71).

The Renaissance Cloth Hall (see pp102–3), *topped with a characteristic parapet, displayed the prosperity of Jagiellonian Cracow.*

Tomb of Stefan Batory

after 1550 Santi Gucci comes to Poland

1556–1559 Giovanni Maria Padovano rebuilds the Cloth Hall

1569 Polish-Lithuanian commonwealth established

1574 Coronation of the first elected king, Henri de Valois

1586 First secular secondary school is opened

1595 Santi Gucci works on the tomb of King Stefan Batory

1595 Archconfraternity of The Passion established

1596 Royal court moves from Cracow to Warsaw

1550 | 1560 | 1570 | 1580 | 1590

Baroque Cracow

The 17th and 18th centuries saw the decline of Cracow. After the king had moved his residence to Warsaw, he was followed by the noblemen who held high office. Foreign incursions and occupations, wars and the First Partition of Poland in 1772 all added to the city's woes. Despite a number of attempts at reform towards the end of the rule of Stanisław August Poniatowski, Cracow became a provincial, underdeveloped frontier town, though the atmosphere was enlivened by royal coronations and funerals. The failure of the Kościuszko Insurrection of 1794 and the subsequent Third Partition of Poland in 1795 brought an end to Cracow's prominence.

Coat of Arms of the House of Vaza

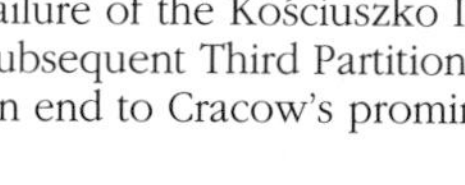

EXTENT OF THE CITY

1700 Today

Hood of the 1669 Coronation Cape
The eagle (the emblem of the Commonwealth) on the cappa magna *of Bishop Tomicki, made for the coronation of Michał Wiśniowiecki, was embroidered with pearls and sapphires.*

Epitaph of King Władysław IV
The monumental and sombre interior of the Vaza Chapel in the Cathedral is decorated with black marble and features splendid memorial plaques of the Vaza dynasty.

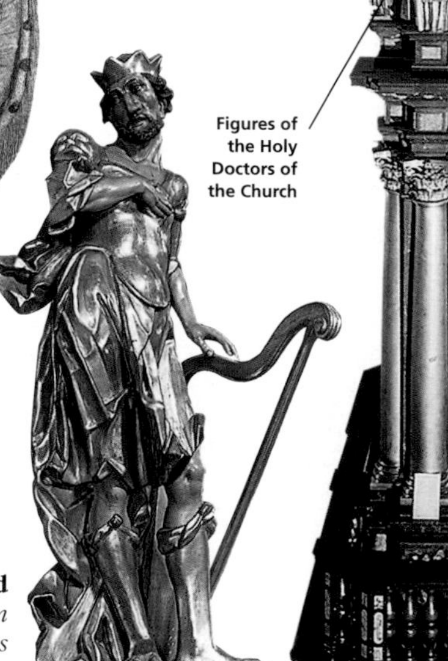

The Evangelists with their symbols: eagle, angel, lion and ox.

Figures of the Holy Doctors of the Church

King David
This late Baroque dancing figure in the Corpus Christi Church was made by Anton Gegenbaur in the second half of the 18th century.

TIMELINE

1626–9 Canopy of St Stanisław is erected in the Cathedral

1619 Church of Saints Peter and Paul is completed

1661 First Polish newspaper "Merkuriusz Polski" published by Jan Alexander Gorczyn's Press

Title page of "Merkuriusz Polski"

1600 | 1620 | 1640 | 1660 | 1680

1609 Zygmunt III Vaza finally abandons his Cracow residence in favour of Warsaw on 25 May

Zygmunt III Vaza

1655–7 Swedish, then Transylvanian, armies occupy Cracow

1676 University Press is established after the Academy buys Piotrowczyks' Press

1664–76 Vaza Chapel in the Cathedral is completed

Memorial Plaque of Bishop Denhoff
Memorial plaques of bishops in the cloister adjoining the Franciscan Church date from different periods. This plaque was made in the early 18th century, probably to a design by Baldassare Fontana.

A silver sarcophagus with the Bishop's mitre and crozier is a reliquary of St Stanisław.

Kołłątaj's Panoramic Map of Cracow
Hugo Kołłątaj led the reform of the University. In 1785 he also created this precise map of Cracow, which shows all the land owned by the city.

CANOPY OF ST STANISŁAW
This canopy in the Wawel Cathedral was inspired by a number of unexecuted designs for the great baldachin in St Peter's in the Vatican.

WHERE TO SEE BAROQUE CRACOW

The earliest Baroque church, that dedicated to Saints Peter and Paul *(see pp80–1)*, as well as much later churches including St Anne's *(see pp108–9)* and the Church of the Order of St John of God *(see p126)*, represent the best of Baroque architecture from Tylman von Gameren and Kacper Bażanka, among others.

The Church of Saints Peter and Paul *is one of the finest early Baroque churches in Central Europe.*

The façade of the Church of the Missionaries *was inspired by Roman Baroque architecture* (see p85).

Medal of Virtuti Militari

1734 Coronation of August III Wettin, the last to take place in Cracow, on 17 January

1791 Kazimierz and Kleparz are incorporated into Cracow

1768–72 Confederates of Bar fight for Cracow

1794 Tadeusz Kościuszko takes his oath in the Market Square on 24 March

00 | 1720 | 1740 | 1760 | 1780 | 1800

1705 St Anne's Church is consecrated

1702–05 Cracow is invaded several times by the Swedes

Hugo Kołłątaj

1777–8 Hugo Kołłątaj reforms the Cracow Academy

1788 Astronomical Observatory established

1798 First permanent theatre building established in Cracow

Cracow in Galicia

In 1772 Austria occupied the southern part of Poland, called Galicia. After a period of Austrian occupation, Cracow was briefly incorporated into the Duchy of Warsaw. The Russian occupation followed. In 1815 the Republic of Cracow, which included the area round the city, was established, but by 1846 Cracow was under Austrian rule again. After a period of suppression, Galicia received extensive autonomy from the 1860s onwards. During the 19th century Cracow was the only Polish territory to enjoy relative freedom. It embarked upon a mission of safeguarding traditions and past historic successes, thus becoming the spiritual capital of Poland.

EXTENT OF THE CITY

1818 Today

Sarcophagus of Prince Józef Poniatowski
Of all the famous Poles who died abroad, Józef Poniatowski was the first to have his body brought back to receive a solemn funeral, which transformed itself into a patriotic demonstration.

A beggar woman receiving alms

Emperor Franz Joseph

***The Opening of the Sarcophagus of Kazimierz the Great* by Jan Matejko**
An accidental discovery of the remains of the king prompted his second funeral in 1869, which became an event on a national scale, reminiscent of the glorious past.

THE ENTRY OF EMPEROR FRANZ JOSEPH IN 1880

Franz Joseph was a popular ruler with the people of Cracow. He was believed to be behind the development of the city and its autonomy. A series of watercolours by Juliusz Kossak (1824–99), such as this one, depicts his stay in Cracow.

TIMELINE

1800 Royal Castle at Wawel made into army barracks

1813–15 Cracow occupied by the Austrians

Ruins of the fire-damaged Dominican Church

1846 Cracow Uprisin[g]; Cracow becomes pa[rt] of Austri[a]

1800 | 1810 | 1820 | 1830 | 1840

1809 Cracow incorporated into the Duchy of Warsaw

1810–14 City walls demolished

1815 "Free, independent and strictly neutral city of Cracow" and her region established as the Republic of Cracow

1820–3 Kościuszko Mound constructed

Coat of arms of Galicia

House of Jan Matejko
Jan Matejko, whose particular genre of history painting imprinted in the nation's mind an image of its past, lived in this house (see p114).

Inhabitants of Cracow greeting the Emperor

Design for the Mickiewicz Monument
This model by Antoni Kurzawa was never fully executed. It is held at the National Museum.

The Cracow Uprising
The uprising of 1846 was intended to spark a revolt in all parts of partitioned Poland, but was suppressed by the Austrians.

WHERE TO SEE 19TH CENTURY CRACOW

The architecture of Cracow in the 19th century was eclectic. The Renaissance Revival style predominated (for example the Academy of Fine Arts, *see p138*), and was often influenced by the monumental architecture of Vienna, the place where many of Cracow's architects trained. The University buildings are a good example of Gothic Revival in which the historic style is blended with vernacular features.

The Church of the Felician Sisters *is one of the few buildings in the Romanesque Revival style* (see p144).

The Collegium Novum *is a prestigious Gothic Revival building designed by Feliks Księżarski* (see p104).

1866 Local government established in Cracow with Józef Dietl as Mayor

1854 Society of Friends of Fine Arts established

1872 Academy of Skills established

1876 Czartoryski Collection opens to the public

1883–7 Collegium Novum built

1850 | **1860** | **1870** | **1880** | **1890**

1850 Great fire of Cracow

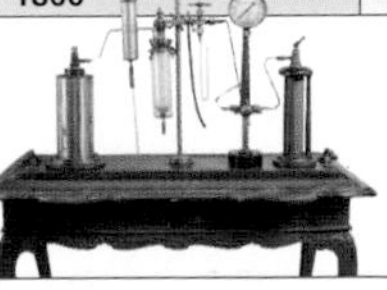

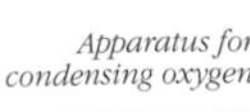

Apparatus for condensing oxygen

1883 Two Cracow scientists, Z. Wróblewski and K. Olszewski, condense oxygen

1893 Słowacki Theatre opens

Modernist Cracow

Bust of Wyspiański decorating the Palace of Art

At the end of the 19th century Greater Cracow was established and became a place of mass excursions from other parts of occupied Poland. People came to see the newly re-established University and the repossessed Wawel, which was then undergoing restoration. It was the period of "art for art's sake", and Cracow became a mecca for Polish artists. Modern life concentrated around artistic cafés, such as the Paon and the Jama Michalika, which were also venues for cabarets. The latter café housed the Zielony Balonik Cabaret. The ambience in Cracow was that of melancholy and decadence but life, permeated by patriotic Neo-Romantic symbolism, was lived here to the full. The outbreak of World War I put an end to this unique bohemian era.

EXTENT OF THE CITY

1900 Today

Stańczyk
This painting by Leon Wyczółkowski portrays the court jester, Stańczyk, in pensive mood, playing with marionettes of historic Polish characters.

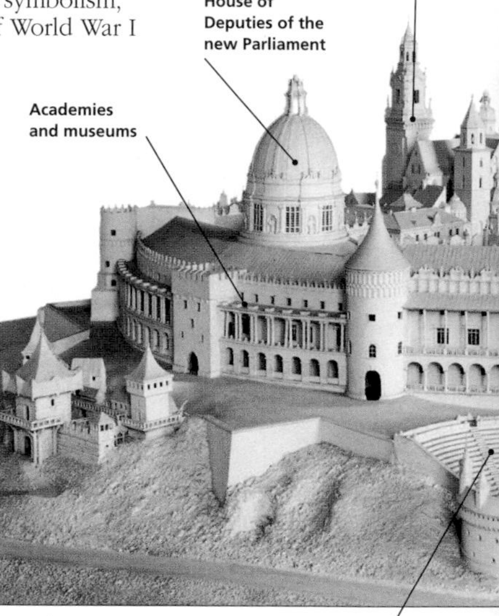

"Życie"
This is the masthead of the magazine of the Polish Modernist movement. The contributors were the leading authors of the time.

TIMELINE

1895 | 1897 | 1899 | 1901 | 1903

1895 Adam Mickiewicz's statue is unveiled

1897 "Życie" weekly is established

1898 Stanisław Przybyszewski arrives in Cracow

1898–1900 Stanisław Wyspiański decorates the Franciscan Church with murals and stained glass

1901 Palace of Art, the seat of the Society of Friends of the Fine Arts, is built

1901 Premiere of *The Wedding* by Stanisław Wyspiański

1903–5 Old Theatre (Teatr Stary) rebuilt in the Art Nouveau style

Wyspiański's Art Nouveau murals in the Franciscan Church

Poster by Stanisław Wyspiański
This poster announces a lecture by S. Przybyszewski followed by a play by M. Maeterlinck.

Marionettes from the Zielony Balonik Cabaret
This cabaret and New Year's satirical show, staged by Karol Frycz, ridiculed the narrow-mindedness and hypocrisy of the Cracovians.

Reconstructed churches of St George and St Michael

Stadium modelled on Roman architecture

POLISH ACROPOLIS BY STANISŁAW WYSPIAŃSKI

The idea behind this design for the rebuilding of the entire Wawel Hill was to transform the Royal Castle into a political, social, academic and cultural centre of the liberated Poland. Its architecture was intended to reflect a synthesis of Polish history.

WHERE TO SEE MODERNIST CRACOW

Modernist Cracow was, above all, a city of literature and painting. Architecture from this period is scarce. There are, however, some magnificent buildings, such as the House "Pod pająkiem" *(see p151)* and the Palace of Art *(see p105)*. Art Nouveau interiors of exceptional beauty can be found at the Franciscan Church with its stained glass and murals, designed by Wyspiański *(see pp86–7)*, the Society of Physicians building *(see p132)* and the prestigious Chamber of Commerce and Industry *(see p139)*.

During the rebuilding of the Old Theatre (Teatr Stary) *in the Art Nouveau style its façade was decorated with a stucco floral frieze* (see p105).

The façade of the Church of the Discalced Carmelite Nuns, *with its elaborate decoration, is in sharp contrast to its austere interior.*

1906 Cracow sports clubs, Wisła and Cracovia, established

1907 Stanisław Wyspiański dies

1910 Riflemen's Union formed by Józef Piłsudski

1912 First cinema opens in Cracow

A late 19th-century armchair

1907 | **1909** | **1911** | **1913** | **1915**

1906 Building of the Chamber of Commerce and Industry completed

The sphere at the top of the Chamber of Commerce and Industry Building

1910 Grunwald Monument unveiled

1914 First Cadre Brigade of the Polish Legions marches out of Cracow on 6 August

Cracow in the Years 1918–1945

When World War I ended in 1918, Poland regained her independence after 146 years of foreign occupation. In the period between the two World Wars Cracow became a source for political, administrative and army staff for the whole of the Republic of Poland. Above all the city was a cultural and academic centre. The Modernist traditions were still present in the arts but soon gave way to a new generation of artists, such as the Formists, Capists (the Polish variant of Post-Impressionists), the avant-garde Cracow Group and the Cricot Theatre. During World War II the German Governor General had his headquarters in Cracow, and this was reason enough for the city to be spared destruction.

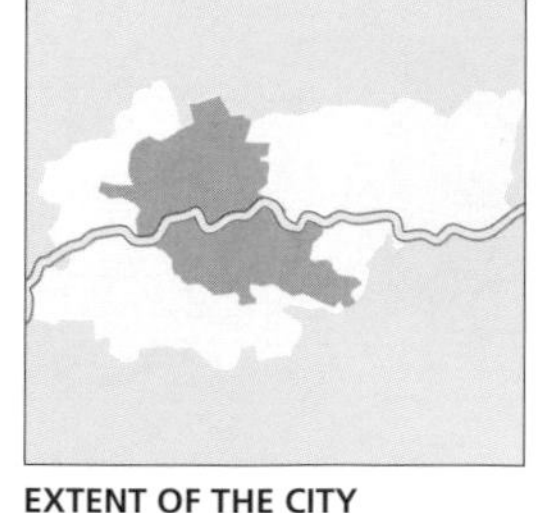

EXTENT OF THE CITY

1938 | Today

Józef Piłsudski
The Commander *by Konrad Krzyżanowski portrays well the personality and character of this uncompromising Polish soldier and politician.*

Portrait of Nena Stachurska
This portrait is by S.I. Witkiewicz, who was one of the most unconventional artists of the 20th century. He called for the utopian ideal of "pure art".

Figures decorating the Academy of Mines and Metallurgy Building
The first school of its type in liberated Poland was established to educate specialists for the industry in Silesia.

TIMELINE

1918 Austrian Army disarmed in Cracow. Polish Liquidation Commission created on 31 October

1919 Academy of Mines and Metallurgy established

1921 Jesuit Church at Wesoła consecrated

1923 Workers' unrest in Cracow

1925 Tomb of the Unknown Soldier blessed

Banner which was raised in liberated Cracow

Jagiellonian Library

1927 Juliusz Słowacki's remains brought to Cracow and buried at Wawel

1930–9 Jagiellonian Library completed

1918 | 1921 | 1924 | 1927 | 1930

Funeral of Marshal Piłsudski
The funeral of the Commander, who was buried at Wawel in 1935, was the biggest state event in interwar Poland.

Demolition of Mickiewicz's Statue
During the German occupation all monuments of importance were demolished, including those of Mickiewicz, Kościuszko and Grunwald.

A military band gallops at the head of the troops.

THE CAVALRY PARADE

The parade of the cavalry of the Second Republic took place at Błonie on 6 October 1933. Wojciech Kossak, member of a distinguished Cracow family of artists, painted this grand event.

AUSCHWITZ (OŚWIĘCIM)

The name Oświęcim may have little meaning for most foreigners but the German name, Auschwitz, raises the spectre of death. During World War II the Nazis established Auschwitz *(see pp160–61)* and the nearby Birkenau (Brzezinka) *(see pp162–3)* concentration camps. Nearly 1.5 million people were put to death in these camps. The Auschwitz camp was set up in 1940 to subject Poles to terror and extermination. Before long the Nazis rounded up and transported people from the whole of Europe, and from 1942 Auschwitz and Birkenau became the largest extermination camps for Jews. A cynical inscription over the gate leading into the Auschwitz camp reads *"Arbeit macht frei"* ("work makes you free").

It was in the Auschwitz Death Block that Maksymilian Kolbe, a Franciscan priest, gave up his life for another inmate. Kolbe (who was later canonized) was sentenced to death by starvation.

In the old barracks of Auschwitz there is an exhibition telling the history of the camp *(see pp160–61)*. Temporary displays are also organized. In Brzezinka, 3 km (1.8 miles) away, only some of the original 300 barracks remain, along with the loading platform. New prisoners were unloaded from railway wagons and segregated here.

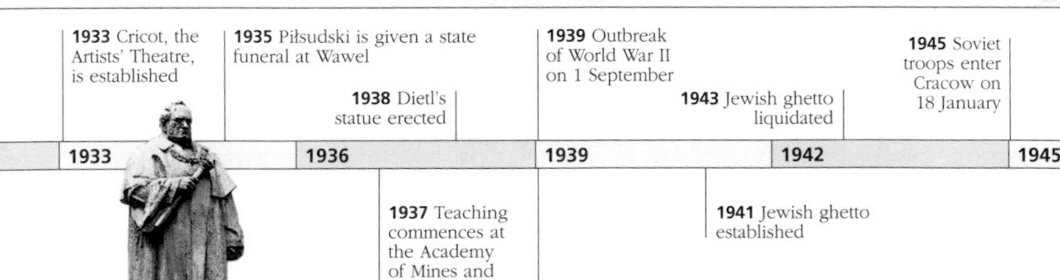

1933 Cricot, the Artists' Theatre, is established

1935 Piłsudski is given a state funeral at Wawel

1938 Dietl's statue erected

1939 Outbreak of World War II on 1 September

1943 Jewish ghetto liquidated

1945 Soviet troops enter Cracow on 18 January

1933 | 1936 | 1939 | 1942 | 1945

1937 Teaching commences at the Academy of Mines and Metallurgy

1941 Jewish ghetto established

1939 Cracow occupied by the Nazis on 6 September

Statue of Józef Dietl

Cracow after 1945

After World War II ended Cracow did not willingly accept the new Soviet-imposed regime. In 1946 the celebrations of the 3 May Constitution turned into clashes with tragic consequences. Soon after the Communist referendum was rejected, in order to "punish" Cracow, a new industrial suburb of Nowa Huta was established with immense steel mills *(see p154)*. The intention was to counterbalance "the reactionist social classes" of the old Cracow. The style of Socialist Realism was adopted for the new architecture. While local authorities struggled to preserve historic buildings, pollution caused by this vast industry damaged many monuments in Cracow, and still remains a major problem.

Statue of Cardinal Adam Sapieha

Tadeusz Sendzimir Steelworks
Formerly known as the Lenin Steelworks, the mills were expected to become a bastion of the Communist proletariat. Paradoxically, they became one of the main centres of opposition.

Banner of the Vatican

Papal high altar

HOLY MASS DURING THE POPE'S VISIT

The political transformation of Poland which took place after 1989 was welcomed in Cracow. The Mass celebrated in 1991 by Pope John Paul II in Market Square attracted unprecedented numbers of worshippers.

Mistrzejowice Church
Built between 1976 and 1983, the church was decorated with sculptures by Gustaw Zemła.

TIMELINE

1946 Bloody suppression of 3 May celebrations

Builders' Brigade *by H. Krajewska*

1956 Piwnica pod Baranami Cabaret established

1967 Construction of the Ark of God Church in Nowa Huta begins

1945 | 1950 | 1955 | 1960 | 1965 | 1970 | 1975

1949 Construction of Nowa Huta begins

1950 Nowa Huta becomes a borough of Cracow

1956 Cricot 2 Theatre established

1957 Celebrations of the city of Cracow's 700th anniversary

1964 600th anniversary of the Academy of Cracow

John Paul II

Demonstrations in Nowa Huta
During the period of martial law, street demonstrations in the workers' suburb of Nowa Huta often ended in riots.

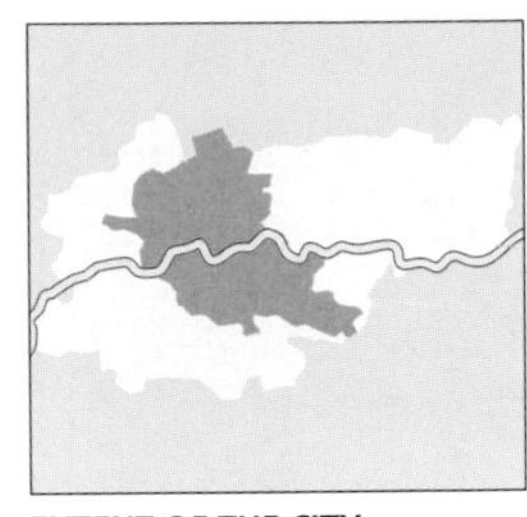

EXTENT OF THE CITY

1945 *Today*

Nobel Prize for Wisława Szymborska
The Cracow poet was awarded the 1996 Nobel Prize for Literature.

St Mary's Church

Polish banner

Sculpture Decorating the Tomb of Tadeusz Kantor
The theatre of Tadeusz Kantor (1915–90) had a Polish, as well as a European, dimension. This sculpture on his tomb was originally designed for his play Wielopole, Wielopole.

WHERE TO SEE MODERN CRACOW

Very few postwar buildings in Cracow deserve notice. However, some examples of ecclesiastical architecture, namely the Abbey of the Fathers of the Resurrection designed by Dariusz Kozłowski, and two churches in Nowa Huta – the Ark of God and Mistrzejowice Church, are exceptional. In recent years an extensive programme of building renovation in old Cracow has been undertaken and many new projects started, including the Japanese Centre of Art and Technology.

The Ark of God Church in Nowa Huta (see p154) *is an example of modern ecclesiastical architecture, rich in impressive forms and symbolic content.*

1978 Cracow included in the UNESCO World Heritage List

1980 Solidarity established

1981 Martial law declared in Poland on 13 December (lifted on 21 July 1983)

1991 International Cultural Centre established

1992 European Month of Culture celebrations take place in Cracow in June

1996 Wisława Szymborska is awarded the Nobel Prize for Literature

2005 Pope John Paul II dies in Rome

1980	1985	1990	1995	2000	2005	2010

1981 Citizens Committee for the Rescue of Cracow established

1978 Karol Wojtyła, the Metropolitan of Cracow, elected as Pope John Paul II

1993 Czesław Miłosz, the winner of the Nobel Prize for Literature, becomes an honorary citizen of Cracow

MIŁOSZ

A book by Czesław Miłosz

2004 Poland joins the European Union

NON
BIS·DO
NON
BIS·SED·NOMIN

CRACOW AT A GLANCE

Cracow was one of the few Polish cities to be saved from major destruction during many wars which devastated the country. The city has preserved not only her monuments but also her specific "antiquarian" atmosphere. Already in the 19th century Cracow was a destination for tourists from other countries as well as different parts of Poland. Cracow and Wieliczka were included on the very first UNESCO World Heritage List. The section *Cracow Area by Area* describes many places of interest. To help make the most of your stay, the following 14 pages are a guide to the best Cracow has to offer. Each sight has a cross-reference to its own full entry. Below are the top ten tourist attractions to start you off. Take a journey back in time and enjoy sites of historic interest and beauty.

CRACOW'S TOP TEN TOURIST ATTRACTIONS

Royal Castle at Wawel
See pp70–73.

Cathedral
See pp64–9.

Kościuszko Mound
See pp168–9.

Church of St Mary
See pp94–7.

Market Square
See pp98–101.

Church of St Anne
See pp108–9.

Planty
See pp166–7.

Collegium Maius
See pp106–7.

Remu'h Cemetery
See pp122–3.

Cloth Hall
See pp102–3.

◁ Zygmunt's Chapel at Wawel

Cracow's Best: Museums and Galleries

Cracow has dozens of museums, which are very varied in character. The Royal Castle at Wawel is the best known, offering visitors the chance to see collections housed in the royal chambers which date from the time when the Polish kings resided here. The Czartoryski Museum is the best place for Western art. The National Museum has rich collections of Polish art housed in a number of branches in the city centre

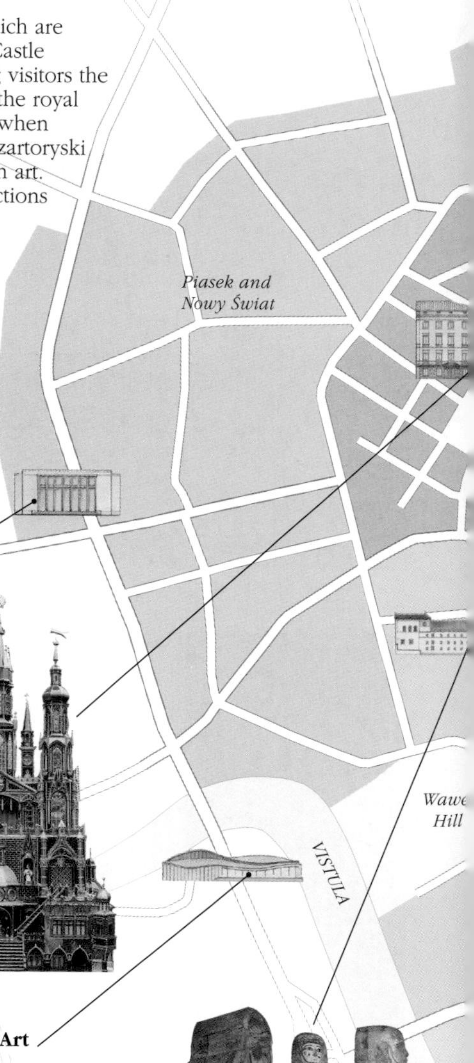

Piasek and Nowy Świat

National Museum Main Building
One of the best collections of modern art in Poland is housed here. The collection of Modernist art is particularly rich, and includes excellent sculptures by Konstanty Laszczka.

Museum of Cracow
This museum is devoted to the history of the city. Cracow is famous for her portable Christmas cribs and the collection housed here is of great beauty.

Wawel Hill

VISTULA

Japanese Centre of Art and Technology
This modern building houses a collection of works from the Far East, much of which was donated by Feliks Manggha Jasieński. The netsuke *(a kind of button) shown takes the form of a tiger.*

Archaeological Museum
Many archaeological finds from the Lesser Poland area, as well as Egyptian mummies, are displayed here.

0 metres 500

0 yards 500

Czartoryski Museum
This karacena *which belonged to Stanisław Jabłonowski, one of the leaders in the Battle of Vienna in 1683, is one of the exhibits recalling Poland's once glorious past.*

House of Matejko
In the family house of Jan Matejko, some of his works, including this study for Joan of Arc, as well as his extraordinary collection of "antiquities", are brought together.

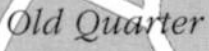

Wesoła, Kleparz and Biskupie

Old Quarter

Cloth Hall Gallery of 19th-century Art
In 1879 Henryk Siemiradzki presented the National Museum with its first gift, his painting The Torches of Nero.

Okół and Stradom Quarters

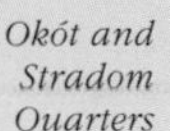

Kazimierz Quarter

Jewish Museum
A collection of Judaica, one of the best in Central Europe, is housed in this Renaissance synagogue.

Royal Castle in Wawel
This royal residence houses an outstanding art collection which includes paintings, sculptures, gold work, arms and Oriental art. The tapestries are of particular interest.

Exploring Cracow's Museums and Galleries

Eagle on a 1918 banner, Museum of Cracow

Cracow's museum collections tell the history of the city and Polish culture in great detail. There are also a few specialized foreign collections. A visit to all the many museums would require several weeks but it is possible to concentrate on just the most important collections and still get to know the city well. Many Galleries, including the Starmach Gallery and Mleczko Gallery, display contemporary art.

St Stanisław's Reliquary, Cathedral Museum *(see p62)*

THE HISTORY OF POLAND AND CRACOW

The former residence of Polish rulers, the **Royal Castle** at Wawel is the best known of Cracow's museums. Outstanding tapestries and paintings are among the exhibits. The Armoury and Treasury are also open for visits. The latter houses the coronation sword *Szczerbiec*. Worth a visit is the archaeological display "Lost Wawel", which shows the Rotunda of the Virgin Mary (Cracow's first church). A computer-generated model of Wawel gives visitors an overview of the early 10th-century construction. The Gregorian chants sung by the Dominican Friars can be heard while viewing the programme.

The history of the former capital of Poland is told at the **Museum of Cracow**. The collections here include the insignia of municipal governments and those of guilds, seals featuring Cracow's coat of arms and many townscapes showing Cracow in the past.

The Jagiellonian University Museum is housed in the **Collegium Maius**, the oldest of the university's buildings. The museum brings together scientific equipment, of which some items are unique, as well as memorabilia left by former professors. Many rooms have retained their original furnishings.

The borough of Kazimierz was inhabited in the past mostly by Jews. This part of the city became a centre for their culture. The **Jewish Museum**, with its rich collection of Judaica, including liturgical objects, is dedicated to the Jewish heritage.

The election of the Archbishop of Cracow, Karol Wojtyła, to the pontificate was an important event in the history of the city. A room, recreated in the **Archdiocesan Museum**, commemorates the years spent by Karol Wojtyła in Cracow.

Deputies' Hall in the Royal Castle at Wawel

The altar by Jerzy Nowosielski, St Vladimir's Foundation, devoted to the Orthodox Church

POLISH ART

In 1879 Henryk Siemiradzki presented Cracow with his painting *The Torches of Nero*. He thus initiated the establishment of the **National Museum**. Poland was then still an occupied country and the intention was to raise patriotic awareness and morale of the Poles. Only Polish art and works relating to the history of Poland were included. As a result the museum has no Western collection. The Polish collections, however, give a good insight into Polish artists and those who worked in Poland. The museum has a number of branches throughout the city. Pride of place in the museum

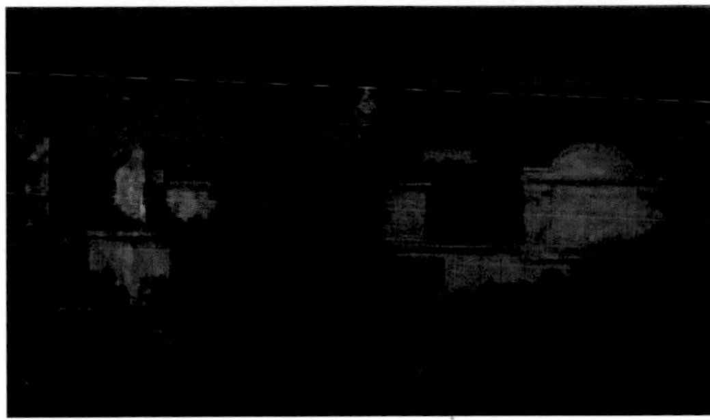

Italian Landscape by Adam Chmielowski, National Museum

goes to the large and outstanding collection of medieval and Renaissance painting and sculpture. This collection will move to 17 Kanonicza Street where a new Museum of Polish Art up to 1794 is planned to open in 2007. Nineteenth-century Polish art, housed at the **Cloth Hall Gallery**, is also of great interest. Twentieth-century painting and sculpture can be admired in the Main Building. The museum has a programme of temporary monographic exhibitions concerned with the life and work of great Cracow artists such as Jan Matejko, Stanisław Wyspiański and Józef Mehoffer. These exhibitions, highlighting the careers of artists who made a great contribution to Polish culture, are always worth a visit.

The **Cricoteka** is a museum of the Cricot 2 Theatre in which works by its founder, Tadeusz Kantor, are displayed.

The collection at **St Vladimir's Foundation** is devoted to the culture of the Orthodox Church among whose faithful were the Ruthenians who lived in the eastern borderlands of Poland. The collection features parts of iconostases and single icons from the 16th to 20th centuries.

Contemporary art can be seen not only at the National Museum but also in a number of galleries, including the **Palace of Art**. The **"Bunker of Art"** also runs a programme of interesting exhibitions of Polish and foreign artists.

The **Archdiocesan Museum** has a magnificent collection of Polish sacred art. The museum also organizes exhibitions of works on loan from leading church treasuries throughout the country as well as other countries.

FOREIGN ART

Those interested in Western art should visit the **Czartoryski Museum**. *The Lady with an Ermine* by Leonardo da Vinci and the *Landscape with the Good Samaritan* by Rembrandt are two celebrated masterpieces, but there are many other fine works here too. Romanesque gold work from the Maas region, Italian Renaissance majolica, and porcelain from the Meissen factory are also in the museum's collections.

The Manggha **Japanese Centre of Art and Technology** covers Japanese art. A bequest of objects from the Far East presented by Feliks Manggha Jasieński constitutes the core of the collection, which also includes works by contemporary artists.

Tin-glazed majolica plate (c. 1545) from the collection of the Czartoryski Museum

LOCAL CULTURE AND NATURAL HISTORY

The **Archaeological Museum** displays important objects found in the 19th century in Galicia *(see p28)*, which was then under Austrian occupation. One of them is the statue of Światowid fished out from the Zbrucz River. Other objects found during the construction of Nowa Huta and renovation works at Kanonicza Street were added to the collection. There is also a notable collection of Egyptian mummies.

The **Ethnographic Museum** houses a large collection of folk art from the Lesser Poland region. Temporary exhibitions, which take place at the Krakowska Street branch, are always of interest.

An extremely well preserved rhinoceros *(coelodonta antiquitatis)* from the Ice Age is a highlight of the **Natural History Museum**.

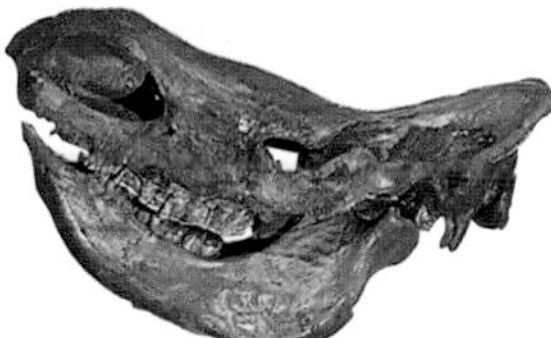

Skull of *coelodonta antiquitatis*, Natural History Museum

FINDING THE MUSEUMS AND GALLERIES

Cracow's Best: Churches

The skyline of Cracow is dominated by churches. There are some 40 churches within the historic centre alone. It must be remembered, however, that a number of churches were destroyed or dismantled in the 19th century. The surviving churches bear witness to the splendour of Cracow. The interiors are surprisingly rich in furnishings and house a variety of works of art in different artistic styles.

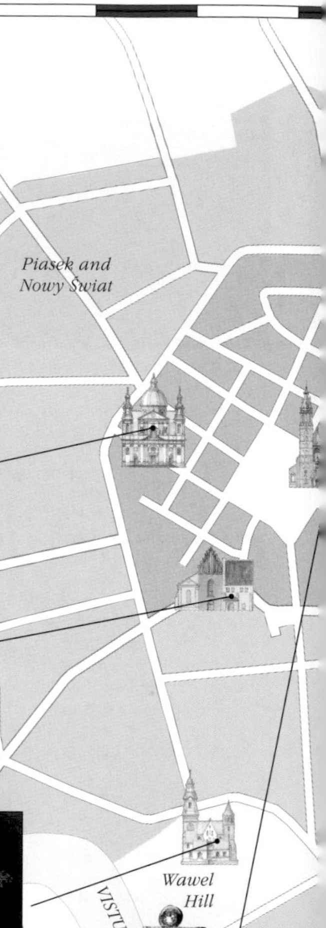

Piasek and Nowy Świat

Church of St Anne
This church was created by two outstanding artists at the end of the 17th century – the architect Tylman van Gameren and the sculptor Baldassare Fontana.

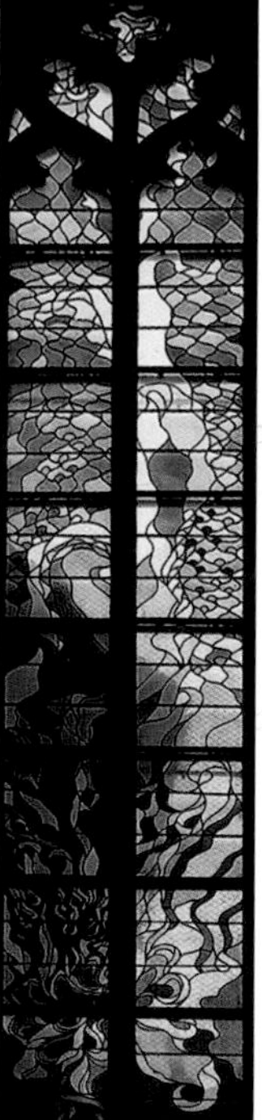

Franciscan Church
Magnificent murals and stained glass by Stanisław Wyspiański decorate the Gothic interior of this church.

Wawel Hill

VISTULA

Cathedral
This Cathedral is a place where the history of the Polish state meets that of the Church and national memorabilia are treasured.

Church of St Mary
The most important church in the centre of historic Cracow, St Mary's is famous for its retable, made between 1477 and 1489, and its interior decoration, which dates from later years.

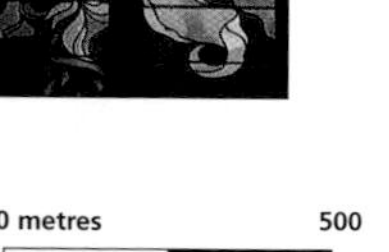

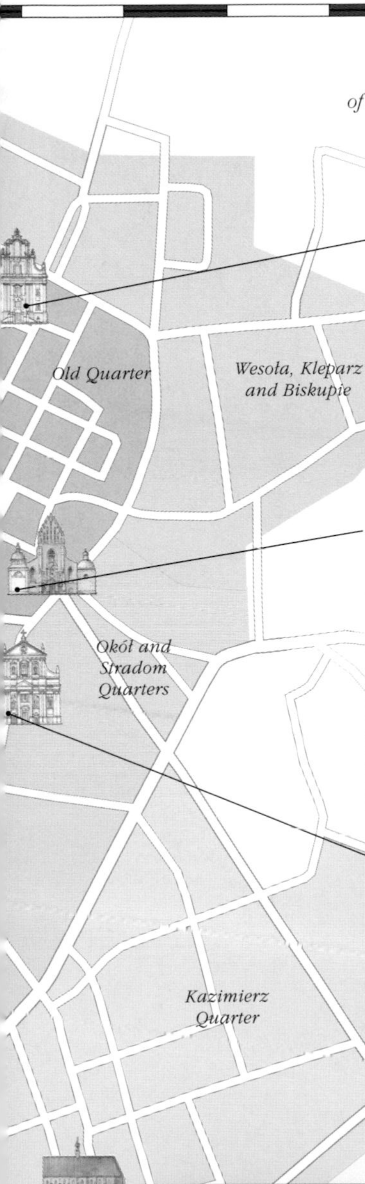

Piarist Church
The Rococo façade of this church is flat but is richly decorated.

Old Quarter

Wesoła, Kleparz and Biskupie

Dominican Church
This memorial plaque of Callimachus (Italian humanist, secretary to the Royal court), made after 1496 to the design of Veit Stoss, is to be found here. The remaining furnishings are mostly Neo-Gothic.

Okół and Stradom Quarters

Kazimierz Quarter

Church of Saints Peter and Paul
This is the finest early Baroque church in Poland, one which can easily rival Roman architecture from the leading architects of the late 16th century.

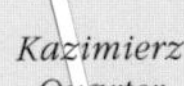

St Catherine's Church
While visiting this church one should not miss the south porch decorated with stonework and tracery.

Exploring Cracow's Churches

Statue of St Peter

Cracow's churches represent many different styles, from the Romanesque and Gothic through Baroque and later eclecticism to the modern. Fortunately the majority of churches were saved from wartime destruction and have not been damaged. Today their splendid interiors impress visitors. However, Cracow's churches are not only tourist attractions but also places of pilgrimage. The relics of a number of saints and blessed, as well as many pious figures who enjoy a local cult, are laid to rest in the city's many churches.

St Andrew's Church

PRE-ROMANESQUE AND ROMANESQUE

The earliest stone churches in Cracow date from the second half of the 10th century. They were built on the site of today's **St Adalbert's Church** and at Wawel, where the remnants of a number of rotundas have been found. Today the reconstructed Rotunda of the Virgin Mary *(see p 63)*, originally from the late 10th century, can be visited. Built around 1079, **St Andrew's** is exceptional among the Romanesque churches. The **Church of the Holy Redeemer** dates from around the same period. The Crypt of St Leonard beneath the Cathedral is a remnant of the second cathedral built between 1090 and 1142. The remnants of the Church of St Gereon and the Chapel of St Mary of Egypt are also at Wawel.

GOTHIC

Slender silhouettes of Gothic churches enhance the city. Some buildings were, however, demolished in the 19th century during the programme of "tidying up" the old architecture. The **Franciscan Church** is the oldest to have survived. Its irregular plan of a Greek cross with an asymmetric nave is unusual. The **Church of the Holy Cross**, begun around 1300, is worth visiting for its palm vaulting supported by a single pillar. **Cracow Cathedral** is certainly a major attraction. This three-aisled basilica with a transept and ambulatory, surrounded by chapels, was constructed between 1320 and 1364. The Monastery, **Church of St Catherine** and the **Corpus Christi** were both founded by Kazimierz the Great, while the **Dominican Church** was rebuilt during his reign. All three churches share the same structural and stylistic characteristics and were probably constructed by the same stonemasons, who moved from one site to another. **St Mary's** the city's main civic church, is also Gothic. It was under construction from the end of the 13th century until the late 15th century.

Gothic vault in the nave of the Corpus Christi Church

TOWERS, DOMES AND SPIRES IN CRACOW

The outlines of many church domes and spires dominate the skyline of old Cracow. They also bear witness to the historic and artistic changes which the city has undergone. The Gothic spires of St Mary's and Corpus Christi are among the tallest and most picturesque. Baroque domes are more common and include the Church of Saints Peter and Paul, St Anne's and the Cathedral Clock Tower.

Towers of the Church of St Andrew

Slender Gothic spire of St Mary's Church

Baroque dome of St Anne's Church

RENAISSANCE AND MANNERIST

There is no complete church in Cracow in either the pure Renaissance or Mannerist styles, but the Zygmunt Chapel, built from 1519 to 1533, is regarded as the greatest example of Italian Renaissance north of the Alps. The chapel, with its spatial design and decoration, provided a model which was followed faithfully throughout Poland for many years.

Renaissance monuments by Jan Michałowicz of Urzędów and Giovanni Maria Mosca ("Il Padovano") can be seen in a number of churches. The career of the Italian Mannerist Santi Gucci, an equally fine artist, spans the last decades of the 16th century.

BAROQUE

Although in the 17th century Polish kings no longer resided in Cracow, many new ecclesiastical foundations were undertaken. The Jesuit **Church of Saints Peter and Paul** was the most magnificent. The church was completed by the royal architect Giovanni Battista Trevano in 1609–19. The imposing Zbaraski Chapel in the **Dominican Church**, built between 1629 and 1631, is another fine example of early Baroque. The Canopy of St Stanisław and the Vaza Chapel, both in the Wawel **Cathedral**, exemplify the best of the High Baroque style. In the first half of the 17th century the interiors of a number of Gothic churches, such as St Mark's *(see p110)* were remodelled in the Baroque style. The century that followed brought about further architectural masterpieces, including **St Anne's Church**. A mention must also be made of the **Church of the Missionaries** whose exterior and interior were both modelled on Roman architecture, the **Piarist Church** with its airy façade, and the **Church of the Order of St John of God** whose façade displays dynamic articulation.

Baroque façade detail of the Church of the Missionaries

NEO-CLASSICAL AND ECLECTIC

The late 18th-century choir and the high altar in the Church of the Norbertine Nuns are the only examples of ecclesiastical Neo-Classicism in Cracow. No building activity was undertaken until Galicia became autonomous, and new churches were only constructed in the second half of the 19th and first half of the 20th centuries. The **Church of the Felician Nuns** was built between 1882 and 1884 to designs by Feliks Księżarski, and the **St Joseph's Church** (1905–09) was designed by Jan Sas Zubrzycki. The **Jesuit Church** designed by Franciszek Mączyński and decorated with sculptures by Xawery Dunikowski and Karol Hukan, is an outstanding example of 20th-century architecture.

Decoration of the porch of the Jesuit Church

Late Baroque Clock Tower of the Cathedral

Neo-Gothic spire of St Joseph's Church at Podgórze

Modern spire of the Ark of God Church in Nowa Huta

MODERN

A variety of designs were applied to modern churches of the second half of the 20th century. Interesting are the **Ark of God** in Nowa Huta (architect Wojciech Pietrzyk, 1967–77), the Church of St Maksymilian Kolbe in Mistrzejowice (architect Józef Dutkiewicz, 1976–83) and the Church of St Jan Kanty at Bronowice Nowe.

FINDING CRACOW'S CHURCHES

Exploring Cracow's Cemeteries

Tomb in the Church of St Barbara

All over Europe the cult of commemorating the dead resulted in the establishment of many large cemeteries, with beautiful sculptures often decorating the tombs. Cracow is no different in this respect. Numerous cemeteries and mausolea in church crypts have been established here over the years. They were already regarded as tourist attractions in the 19th century and continue to be visited by tourists to the city.

The Jerzmanowski Mausoleum, Rakowicki Cemetery

CHRISTIAN CEMETERIES

At the end of the 18th century a Cracovian noted that "Every time one looks through the window one cannot but see graves and crosses in the centre of the city". At that time the cemeteries used to be located near the churches. The one at St Mary's was the largest. It was relocated at the end of the 18th century and the original burial site transformed into Mariacki Square. Many tombstones and epitaphs, often medieval, which commemorate those who died centuries ago, have survived on the exterior walls of the churches of St Mary and St Barbara. A number of mausolea, built as chapels by the patrician families of Cracow, also survive on the former site of St Mary's Cemetery.

The **Rakowicki Cemetery** was established outside the city in 1803 and is the oldest cemetery in use. It occupies a vast plot and its layout is transparent. Many old trees give the place a park-like appearance. Some tombstones, especially those made around 1900 by the best Polish sculptors of the time, are true works of art.

In 1920 a **Military Cemetery** was set up by the Rakowicki Cemetery (they have since merged). Polish soldiers who fell in the years 1914–20 and in September 1939, as well as British airmen who lost their lives in World War II, all rest here.

The **Zwierzyniecki Cemetery** is a far more modest place with no great monuments, but rather smaller tombstones decorated with small-scale but nevertheless interesting bas-reliefs. It is, however, a lovely place, picturesquely situated on a high hill and rich in varied fauna. One of the best times of year to visit Cracow's cemeteries is a few days either side of 1 November, when they glow under candlelight at night.

The graves of British airmen, Military Cemetery

JEWISH CEMETERIES

For many centuries Jews constituted a substantial part of the population of Kazimierz, the so-called

MONUMENTS AND TOMBS

The monuments in Cracow's cemeteries show different ways in which people wished to commemorate the deceased. The medieval monuments show a stiff figure lying on a death bed placed under a canopy. The canopy symbolizes Heaven awaiting the soul. Elements glorifying the deceased were introduced into Baroque monuments. Female figures with attributes personified the virtues. Neo-Classical monuments were influenced by ancient sculpture. Fine sculptures and symbolic content are characteristic of the monuments in the Art Nouveau style.

Monument of Kazimierz the Great (died 1370) in the Cathedral

Sarcophagus of Kościuszko in the Cathedral crypt (1818)

Sarcophagus of Jan III Sobieski in the Cathedral (1760)

Jewish city. They were interred at the **Remu'h Cemetery**, established in 1533. This small plot, squeezed between buildings, has many layers of tombs which have been placed here over hundreds of years. The tombstones are engraved with Hebrew inscriptions and symbolic images that identify the religion and social rank of the deceased. The dense accumulation of tombstones within a tiny and bare space contributes to the unique character of this Jewish cemetery.

The **New Jewish Cemetery** is different. It was established in the 19th century and given, like other cemeteries, a park-like appearance. Tombstones are scattered randomly and surrounded by luxuriant vegetation. This is one of a few Jewish cemeteries in Poland which is still in use.

View of Remu'h Cemetery

CRYPTS WITH TOMBS OF GREAT POLES

During the Partitions period (1795–1918) a number of celebrated Poles received state funerals. These events were intended to raise the patriotic feelings of the Polish people.

Church crypts were open to the public and transformed into pantheons of Poland's greatest men. The **Cathedral's Crypt** contains the most solemn royal tombs of all. The crypt is divided into galleries in which Polish rulers, leading poets and national heroes rest. Tadeusz Kościuszko and Prince Józef Poniatowski were interred here during the occupation of Poland. The funerals of Józef Piłsudski and Władysław Sikorski took place in the 20th century.

The **Crypt in the Paulite Church "On the Rock"** is a resting place for those who made great contributions to the arts and sciences. The eminent historian Jan Długosz was buried here in the 15th century.

The Angel of Vengeance on the Monument to Victims of the 1848 Bombardment of Cracow (1913)

The Vaza Crypt in the Cathedral

MONASTIC CEMETERIES

The crypts beneath monastic churches are unique to Cracow. Their character reflects the unusual burial practices of particular religious orders.

The corpses in the **Crypt in the Church of the Reformed Franciscans** have been mummified naturally owing to the crypt's construction and ventilation. One can see here the corpses of poor friars lying on sand with their heads resting on a stone, as well as lay people in rich clothes resting in elaborate coffins.

The **Camaldolese Catacombs** beneath the church in Bielany are different. Here, the corpses are laid at first in niches cut out in a wall and then bricked up. Some years later the bones are removed and placed in an ossuary with the exception of the skull, which is taken by one of the monks for the purposes of contemplation. The Camaldolese crypt strikingly shows that in the face of death all are equal.

Mummified monks in the Crypt of the Church of the Reformed Franciscans

FINDING CRACOW'S CEMETERIES

Camaldolese Catacombs *p170*
Cathedral's Crypt *pp66–9*
Crypt in the Church of the Reformed Franciscans *p110*
Crypt in the Paulite Church "On the Rock" *p127*
New Jewish Cemetery *p123*
Rakowicki Cemetery **Map** 2 E1, 2
Remu'h Cemetery *p122*
Zwierzyniecki Cemetery *p169*

Cracow's Best: Personalities

Many leading personalities of Polish academic, cultural and public life were born in Cracow. Eminent scholars were educated at or drawn to the Jagiellonian University, which was sometimes called "a gem of all knowledge". Famous artists and writers chose to live here, attracted by the unique atmosphere of the place enlivened by old traditions. The cult of such great figures as Adam Mickiewicz, Juliusz Słowacki, Tadeusz Kościuszko and Józef Piłsudski, all buried in Cracow, is still alive.

Andrzej Wajda (born 1926)
A leading film and theatre director, Wajda was educated in Cracow. He was the main instigator of the Japanese Centre of Art and Technology, one of the city's best museums. Wajda won an Oscar for Lifetime Achievement in 2000.

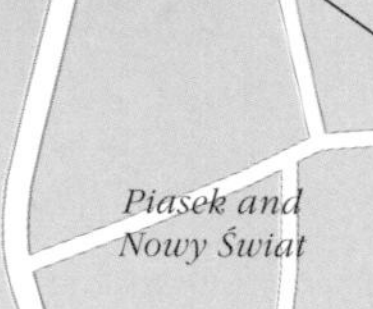

Piasek and Nowy Świat

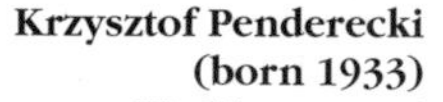

Helena Modrzejewska (1840–1909)
This famous actress began her career at the Old Theatre (Teatr Stary) She is buried in Cracow.

Krzysztof Penderecki (born 1933)
World-renowned composer and conductor, Penderecki was educated in Cracow. He was a Professor and Rector of the Music Academy.

Wawel Hill

VISTULA

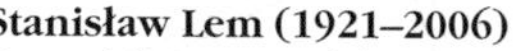

Stanisław Lem (1921–2006)
One of the most widely read science-fiction authors in the world, Lem was also an essayist and critic.

Wisława Szymborska (born 1923)
A prominent poet who was awarded the 1996 Nobel Prize for Literature, Szymborska's links with Cracow span over 50 years.

0 metres 500

0 yards 500

Jan Matejko (1838–93)
The most renowned Polish painter of the 19th century, Matejko's vision of Polish history has influenced many generations.

Sławomir Mrożek (born 1930)
An outstanding playwright and satirist, Mrożek began his career in Cracow as a journalist. After many years abroad, he returned and settled here in 1996.

Czesław Miłosz (1911–2004)
A poet, translator, Nobel Prize winner and honorary doctor of the Jagiellonian University, Miłosz was made an honorary citizen of Cracow in 1993.

Tadeusz Kantor (1915–90)
One of the foremost European artists and theatre directors, Kantor established the world-famous Cricot 2 Theatre.

Stanisław Wyspiański (1869–1907)
Best known for his play The Wedding, *Wyspiański was a dramatist, painter, and designer. His great artistic visions are embedded in the Polish perception of national identity.*

John Paul II (1920–2005)
Before his elevation to the papacy, Karol Wojtyła was Suffragan Bishop, then Archbishop of Cracow from 1963 to 1978.

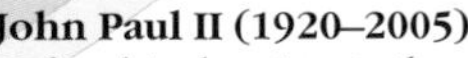

CRACOW THROUGH THE YEAR

Beautiful and magical, Cracow is a city where old traditions are maintained. The bugle call that echoes at hourly intervals from the tower of St Mary's Church sets the rhythm of life. And life is lived here slowly, for one should not hurry when surrounded by stones a thousand years old. Embraced by the Planty, which had replaced the medieval walls, the old quarter remains at the heart of the city. It is not an open-air museum that visitors vacate at night. Although no longer the capital of Poland, Cracow is a cultural centre and one of the oldest university cities in Europe. There is something for everyone here. Press listings and other local media, as well as tourist agencies, are good sources of information.

Gingerbread heart from a church fair

The Emmaus Fair in Zwierzyniec on Easter Monday

SPRING

In Podhale, the region at the foothills of the Tatra Mountains, vast fields of crocuses announce the arrival of spring. In Cracow, the opening of street cafés and people spilling onto the pavements heralds the new season.

MARCH

International Festival of Alternative Theatre, Rotunda Club. The oldest event of its kind in which alternative theatres and fans of theatre are brought together.
Jazz Juniors, Rotunda Club. This international jazz festival for young musicians.
Festival of Organ Music *(Mar-Apr)*.

EASTER

Palm Sunday *(Sun before Easter)*. The blessing of palms in churches. A competition for the largest and best decorated palm takes place in Lipnica Murowana village, 41 km (25 miles) east of Cracow.
Holy Saturday is a day when baskets with food are taken to the church for a blessing, and symbolic tombs of Christ are venerated.
Easter Sunday is the most important Catholic feast.
Easter Monday. The Emmaus Fair takes place in Zwierzyniec and people are splashed with water *(Śmigus-dyngus)* throughout the city.

APRIL

Paka Cabaret Festival. Amateur and professional satirical performers, Polish and foreign, all take part.

MAY

3 May Constitution Day celebrates the first Polish Constitution of 1791 with a Mass said in the Cathedral followed by the laying of wreaths at the Tomb of the Unknown Soldier. Afterwards, there are fairs and picnics.
Procession from Wawel to the Paulite Church "On the Rock" *(first Sun after 8 May, Feast of St Stanisław)*. The Primate and bishops lead the procession and carry the relics of the patron saints of Poland, joined by the faithful in regional costumes.
Juvenalia. Cracow is ruled by students for a couple of days.
International Short Film Festival *(May-Jun)*. The oldest film festival in the country.
Cracow Spring Ballet Festival Słowacki Theatre, *(May-Jun)*. Leading ballet companies of the world take part.

ARCHCONFRATERNITY OF THE PASSION

Since 1595 the Good Friday processions of the Archconfraternity of The Passion have taken place in the Franciscan Church. The Brothers wear black habits with hoods covering the face. The ritual has remained unchanged for centuries. The Archconfraternity had the right to pardon those condemned to death.

Brothers in Procession

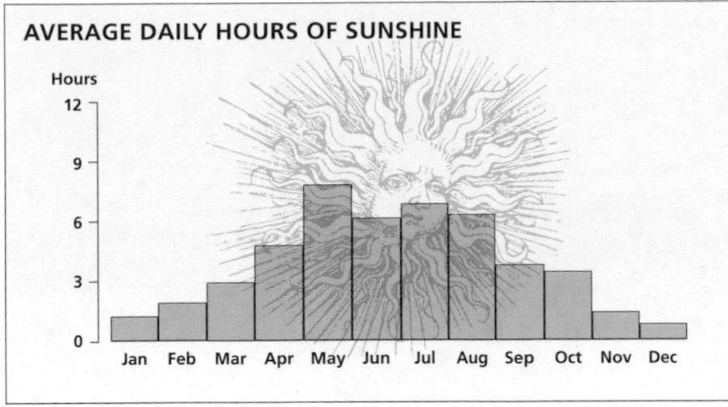

Sunshine Chart
May is the sunniest month of the year in Cracow, but June, July and August are usually also sunny. December is the gloomiest month.

SUMMER

Summer heat may be difficult to bear in Cracow. This is because of the city's location in a valley and its humid microclimate. Many bars, cafés and restaurants in the Old Quarter are open and busy till the early hours of the morning. Crowds of tourists are attracted not only by the heritage but also the nightlife and cultural events. Organ Recitals at the Benedictine Abbey at Tyniec are among the most famous events.

JUNE

Corpus Christi (Boże Ciało) *(Thu in May or June)*. A great procession proceeds from Wawel to the Market Square. On Thursday a week after Corpus Christi *Lajkonik* (the Khan) canters around the town *(see p92)*.
Enthronement of the "king" Marksman, Market Square. The Marksmen's Brotherhood has existed since the Middle Ages. Its members are burghers who are members of craftsmen guilds. Their leader is the winner of the annual shooting competition. The outgoing leader passes the silver cock to the new "king" during a colourful ceremony.
Midsummer's Eve (Wianki) Sat preceding the eve of St John's Feast *(24 Jun)*. Candle wreaths are set adrift on the Vistula by Wawel and there are fireworks displays.
International Music Festival of Military Bands features gala shows of drill, parades in period uniforms and many concerts.

JULY

Summer Early Music Festival. Concerts are held in historic houses.
Summer Opera and Operetta Festival.
Cracow Jazz Festival (Stary Jazz w Krakowie) *(Jul-Aug)*. A real treat for fans of traditional jazz.
Jewish Culture Festival *(early Jul)*, Kazimierz.

Poster announcing events during the Jewish Culture Festival

Outstanding Jewish performers from all over the world take part in this festival.

AUGUST

The Assumption of the Virgin Mary (Święto Wniebowzięcia Matki Boskiej) *(15 Aug)*. A Solemn Mass is said in the Cathedral. This is also the national holiday of the Polish Soldier, commemorating the 1920 victory over the Bolshevik Army. There is a military guard of honour by the Tomb of the Unknown Soldier.
International Festival of Music in Old Cracow *(15–31 Aug)*. One of the most prestigious events in Cracow, with recitals and concerts of orchestral and chamber music in the magnificent historic buildings of the Old Quarter.
The Highlander Folk Festival (Folklor Górali Świata), Market Square. Concerts given by the world's leading groups after taking part in the Zakopane Festival.

Enthronement of the "king" Marksman in the Market Square

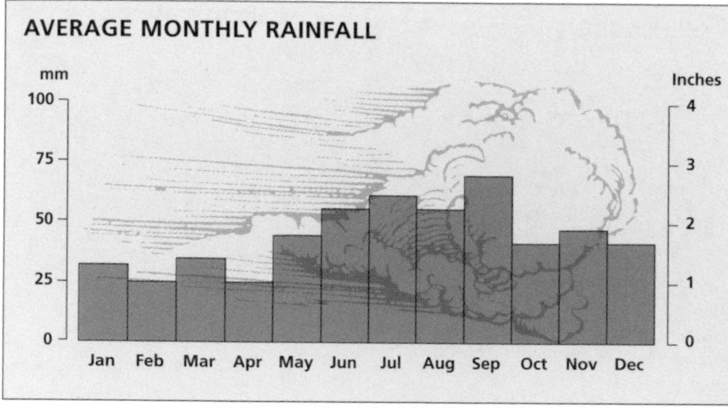

Rainfall
September is the wettest month in Cracow. Storms and cloudbursts may occur in summer. February and April are the driest months.

AUTUMN

On dry and sunny autumn days Cracow is beautifully shrouded in colours; the Planty chestnut trees turn golden and market stalls display baskets full of wild mushrooms from the woodlands of the mountain foothills.

Students return to Cracow by the end of September to take part in the inaugural celebrations of the new academic year. The hymn *Gaudeamus Igitur* can be heard sung at many colleges, and in particular at the Jagiellonian University, Poland's oldest university, established in 1364.

SEPTEMBER

Folk Art Fair (Targi Sztuki Ludowej), Market Square. Demonstrations and sale of local arts and crafts.

OCTOBER

"Etude" International Film Festival (Międzynarodowy Festiwal Filmowy Etiuda). Short films by students of art and film schools from all over the world.

International Festival of Forgotten Music (Międzynarodowy Festiwal Muzyka Utracona) is dedicated to archaic songs of the Slavs and people from the Baltic regions, performed by country folk groups. Seminars and

All Saints' Day

workshops also take place.

Early Music Festival (Festiwal Muzyki Dawnej) *(Oct–Nov)*. Organized simultaneously in a number of cities, the festival presents mainly the music of the Renaissance and Baroque performed on old instruments.

International Biennial of Architecture (Międzynarodowe Biennale Architektury).

NOVEMBER

All Saints' Day (Dzień Wszystkich Świętych) *(1 Nov)*. Many Cracovians visit cemeteries to lay flowers and light candles on the graves. The views of the old Rakowicki Cemetery or of the beautifully located cemetery on the Hill of the Holy Redeemer (św. Salwator) are unforgettable. It is an old custom of Cracow to be able to buy, on this day only, so-called Turkish honey (caramelized sugar with walnuts or pistachios) at the entrance to cemeteries. Children, especially, look forward to this event.

Independence Day (Święto Niepodległości) *(11 Nov)*. After a Mass at the Wawel Cathedral, wreaths are laid at the Tomb of the Unknown Soldier by the Grunwald Monument in Matejko Square.

Inauguration of the academic year at the Jagiellonian University

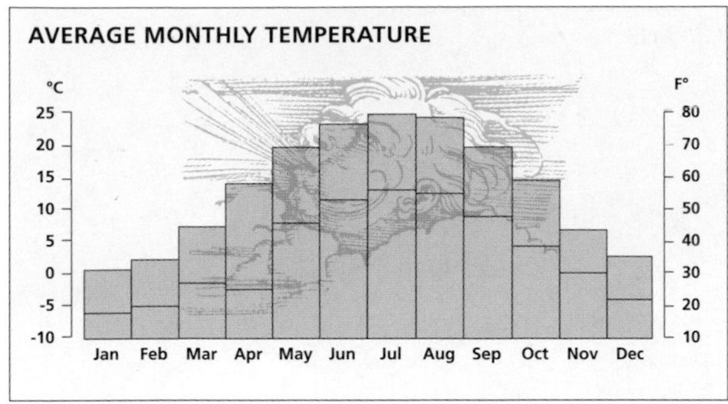

Temperature
Average maximum and minimum temperatures are shown here. July and August are the hottest months with the temperature often exceeding 20°C, sometimes even reaching 30°C. Winter is cold and damp. The average temperature in January is -5°C.

All Souls Jazz Festival (Krakowskie Zaduszki Jazzowe). Oldest jazz festival in post-communist Europe, with concerts in the Philharmonic hall and jazz clubs.

WINTER

Cracow under a blanket of snow is a wonderful sight, but winter also brings misty and bitingly cold days.

Every year on the first Thursday of December a competition for the best Christmas crib *(szopka)* takes place by the Mickiewicz Monument in Market Square. The winning cribs are later displayed at the Museum of Cracow. The tradition of making Christmas cribs, unique to Cracow, goes back to medieval Christmas plays.

Nativity scenes at churches are also worth visiting. The one outside the Franciscan Church, with real people and animals, is best known. It can be seen only on Christmas Eve and Christmas Day.

Stalls selling hand-made Christmas decorations and traditional delicacies fill the Market Square during the Christmas Fair.

Carol singers in traditional costume in Floriańska Street at Christmas time

Nativity play being staged at the Franciscan Church

DECEMBER

Christmas Eve (Wigilia) *(24 Dec)*. The evening begins with a meat-free meal. Midnight Masses are said and the Zygmunt Bell rings at Wawel.

Christmas (Święto Bożego Narodzenia) *(25 and 26 Dec)* and the day after are public holidays. Masses are celebrated in all churches.

New Year's Eve (Sylwester) *(31 Dec)*. A crowd, several thousand strong, gathers in Market Square to see in the New Year. The Wielopolski Palace, the seat of local government, is the venue for one of the grandest balls in Poland. Distinguished guests arrive from all over the world, and the proceeds go to charity.

JANUARY

New Year's Day (Nowy Rok) *(1 Jan)*. Public holiday. A month of balls and parties begins on this day.

FEBRUARY

"Fat Thursday" (Tłusty czwartek) *(last Thu before Lent)*. Everybody eats doughnuts. The *Gazeta w Krakowie*, the local supplement to the *Gazeta Wyborcza*, rates the bakeries to help people choose the best doughnuts in Cracow.

Shrovetide (Ostatki), *(last Sat and Tue of the Carnival season, before Ash Wednesday)*. This is a time of parties before Lent.

Christmas decoration

PUBLIC HOLIDAYS

New Year's Day (1 Jan)
Easter Monday (Mar/Apr)
Labour Day (1 May)
Constitution Day (3 May)
Corpus Christi (Thu 8 weeks after Easter)
Assumption (15 Aug)
All Saints' Day (1 Nov)
Independence Day (11 Nov)
Christmas (25 & 26 Dec)

Sukiennice at night – view from the St Wojciech church ▷

CRACOW AREA BY AREA

WAWEL HILL

Wawel Hill was inhabited by the Vistulan (Wiślanie) people in ancient times. The settlement came to prominence during the reigns of Bolesław the Brave and Kazimierz the Restorer. The latter made Wawel the seat of his political power. In the late medieval period, from the 14th century onwards, the royal residence and a new cathedral were built. The Cathedral houses the relics of St Stanisław, patron saint of Poland. The last rulers of the Jagiellonian dynasty transformed the Gothic castle into one of the most magnificent Renaissance royal residences in Central Europe. They also endowed the Cathedral with important works of art and architecture. Although the capital of Poland was moved from Cracow to Warsaw at the end of the 16th century, royal coronations and funeral ceremonies continued to take place in Cracow. A series of events in the 17th and 18th centuries led to the dilapidation of the Castle. The Austrian army was garrisoned here from 1795 until the early 20th century. The Castle and Cathedral have both regained their former magnificence through an intensive restoration programme. Fortunately Wawel was saved from destruction in both World Wars.

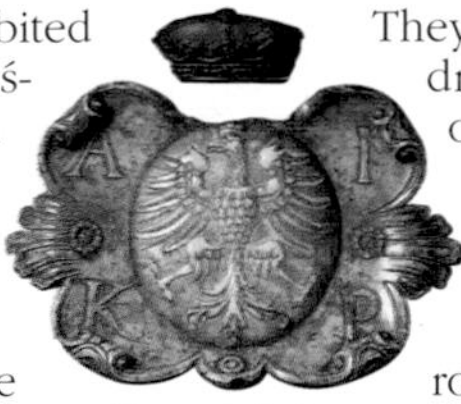

The eagle in the Zygmunt Chapel

SIGHTS AT A GLANCE

Churches

Cracow Cathedral pp64–9 ❸

Historic Sights, Buildings and Monuments

Archaeological Site ❼
Dragon's Lair ❽
Fortifications and Towers ❶
Statue of Tadeusz Kościuszko ❷

Museums

Cathedral Museum ❹
"Lost Wawel" Exhibition ❻
Wawel Royal Castle pp70–71

KEY

Street-by-Street map *pp60–61*

Fortifications

GETTING THERE

Bus routes 103, 128 and 502 pass along the Planty green belt and Straszewski Street. Get off there and walk. You can also use tram routes 8, 10, 18, 36, 38 to the Wawel, with the nearest stop by the Royal Hotel on Św Gertrudy Street.

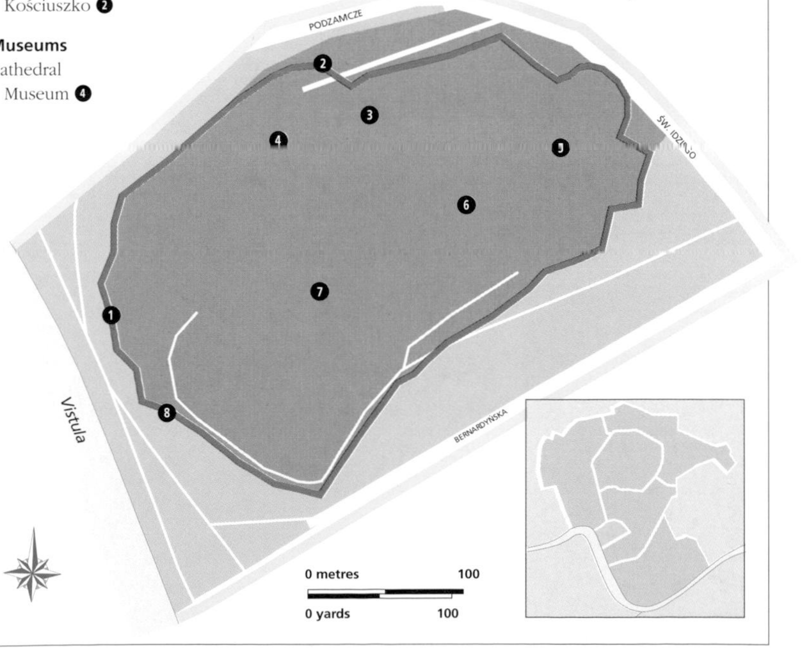

◁ **The arcaded courtyard of the Wawel Royal Castle on Wawel Hill**

Street-by-Street: Wawel Hill

The Wawel is exceptional because of its first-class collections and its unique atmosphere. To savour it unhindered by large crowds you should plan an early morning visit when the Cathedral and Castle courtyard are nearly deserted. Groups of tourists from every corner of the world gather here before noon, thereby enlivening the place. A trip to the Cathedral, where a variety of styles intermingle, as well as to the Royal Castle, is a must for visitors to Cracow.

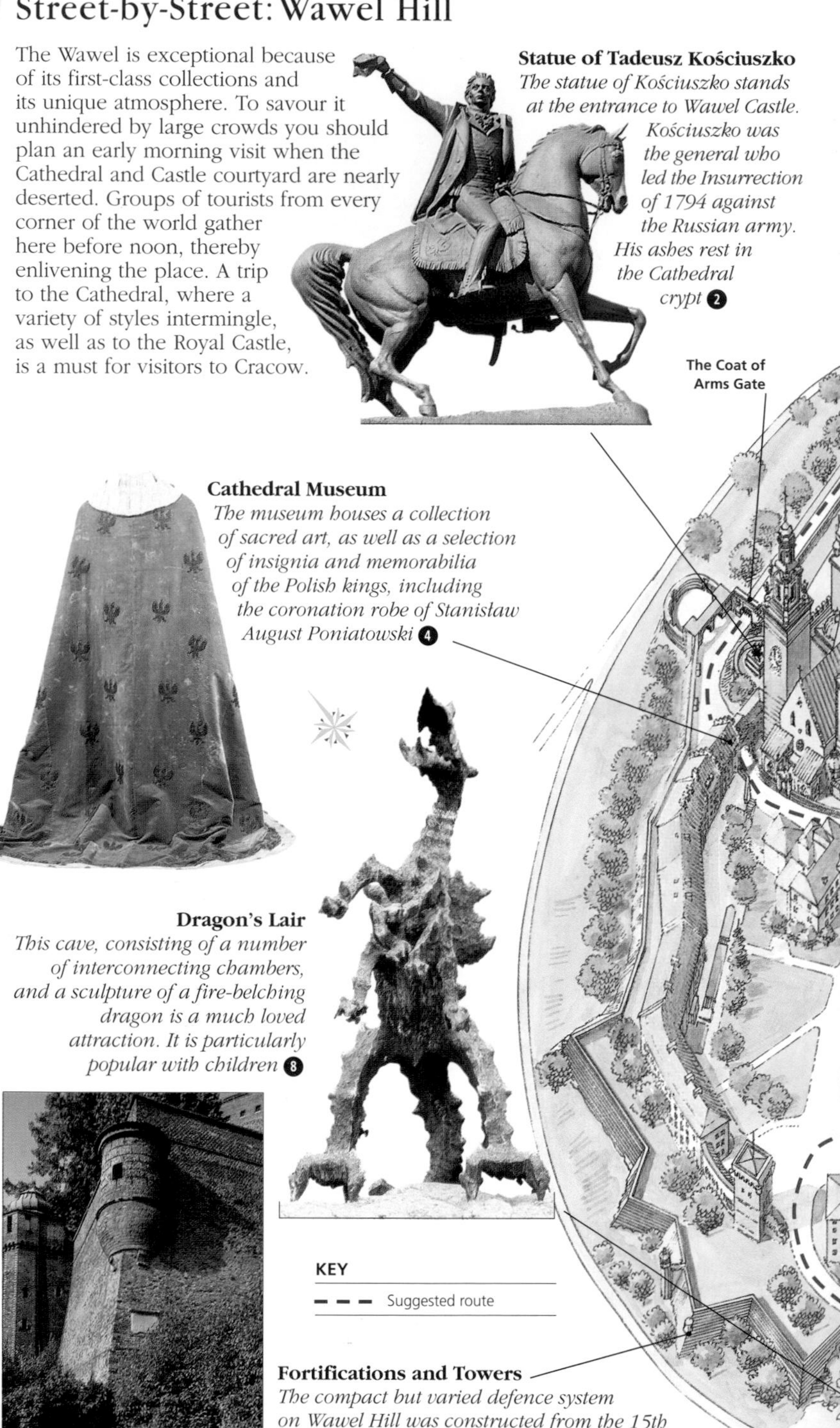

Statue of Tadeusz Kościuszko
The statue of Kościuszko stands at the entrance to Wawel Castle. Kościuszko was the general who led the Insurrection of 1794 against the Russian army. His ashes rest in the Cathedral crypt ❷

Cathedral Museum
The museum houses a collection of sacred art, as well as a selection of insignia and memorabilia of the Polish kings, including the coronation robe of Stanisław August Poniatowski ❹

Dragon's Lair
This cave, consisting of a number of interconnecting chambers, and a sculpture of a fire-belching dragon is a much loved attraction. It is particularly popular with children ❽

Fortifications and Towers
The compact but varied defence system on Wawel Hill was constructed from the 15th to the 19th centuries ❶

★ Wawel Royal Castle
A visit to the Castle includes the interior with its display of 16th-century tapestries, regalia, gold treasures and lavish Oriental objects ❺

LOCATOR MAP
See Street Finder maps 3, 5 & 6

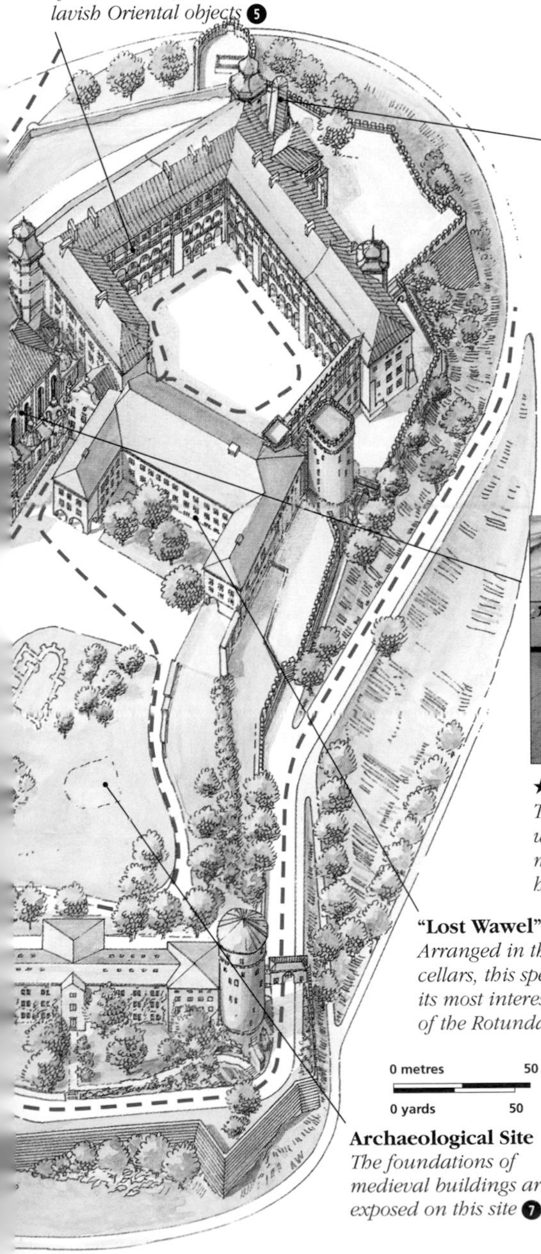

The "Hen's Claw" Wing (Kurza Stopka) is the most prominent remnant of the medieval castle. It was erected during the reign of Jadwiga and Władysław II Jagiełło.

★ Cracow Cathedral
The 19th-century sarcophagus of St Jadwiga, the Queen of Poland, is among many monuments associated with the history of the Church and Nation ❸

"Lost Wawel" Exhibition
Arranged in the former royal kitchen in the cellars, this special exhibition includes among its most interesting exhibits a reconstruction of the Rotunda of the Virgin Mary ❻

0 metres 50

0 yards 50

Archaeological Site
The foundations of medieval buildings are exposed on this site ❼

STAR SIGHTS

- ★ Cracow Cathedral
- ★ Wawel Royal Castle

Fortifications and Towers ❶

Wawel Hill. **Map** 3 C1 (5 C5). *103, 502.* *8, 10, 18, 36, 38.*

The fortifications surrounding Wawel Hill date from different periods. Three massive towers – the Thief's Tower (Złodziejska), Sandomierz and Senator's Towers (the latter also called Lubranka) are dominant features of the architectural silhouette of the Wawel. They date from the second half of the 15th and early 16th centuries, when the royal residence was rebuilt by the Jagiellonians. New, mainly earth fortifications designed by Jan Pleitner were erected under Władysław IV between 1644 and 1646 on the Castle's northern terrace. The southeast bastion and redan (fortification of two parapets) were constructed in the early 18th century for King August II. Later in the century star-shaped fortifications designed by Bakałowicz and Mehler were built on the side of the Vistula River. The Austrians expanded the system between 1849 and 1852. Two round towers, forming part of the Austrian additions, have survived. The Wawel Castle was thus transformed into a citadel surrounded by a complex defence system.

The Sandomierz Tower, one of the three Wawel defence towers

The Coat of Arms Gate and part of fortifications surrounding Wawel Hill

Statue of Tadeusz Kościuszko ❷

Wawel Hill. **Map** 3 C1 (5 C5). *103, 502.* *8, 10, 18, 36, 38.*

The statue of Tadeusz Kościuszko, general and main leader of the 1794 Uprising in Poland *(see p29)* and a participant in the American Revolution, was erected in 1921. It was designed by Leonard Marconi and completed by Antoni Popiel. The statue was destroyed by the Germans in 1940. The present reconstruction was donated in 1960. When approaching the Władysław bastion, where the statue stands, you can see a number of plaques mounted in the brick wall. These commemorate the donors who contributed to the restoration works carried out within the Castle during the inter-war years. Also of interest is the Coat of Arms Gate by Adolf Szyszko-Bohusz.

Cracow Cathedral ❸

See pp64–9.

Cathedral Museum ❹

Wawel 3. **Map** 3 C1 (5 C5). ***Tel** 012 422 51 55 ext. 396.* *103, 502.* *8, 10, 18, 36, 38.* *10am–3pm Tue–Sun.*

The Cathedral Museum was established in September 1978 by the then Archbishop Karol Wojtyła, the Metropolitan of Cracow. The display consists of objects from the Cathedral treasury. Among the exhibits are a sword, which was purposely broken in two places at the funeral of the last Jagiellonian king, Zygmunt August; the coronation robe of Stanisław August Poniatowski; the replica of the royal insignia found inside the royal coffins buried beneath the cathedral, and the stirrup of the Grand Vizier Kara Mustafa which was presented to the Cathedral by King Jan III Sobieski following his victory at the Battle of Vienna (1683). The outstanding collection of reliquaries, church vessels and vestments includes objects found in the tomb of Bishop Maur, as well as memorabilia of John Paul II.

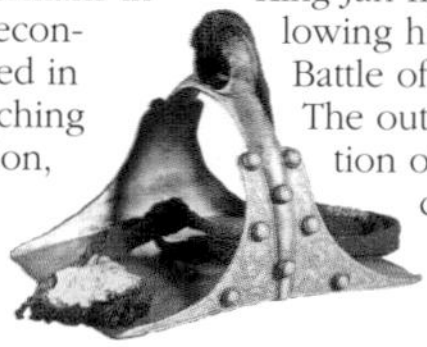

Stirrup that belonged to the Grand Vizier Kara Mustafa, Cathedral Museum

Wawel Royal Castle ❺

See pp70–71.

"Lost Wawel" Exhibition ❻

Wawel Hill 5. **Map** 3 C1 (5 D5). ***Tel** 012 422 16 97.* *103, 502.* *8, 10, 18, 36, 38.* *Apr–Oct: 9:30am–12 noon Mon, 9:30am–4pm Tue & Fri, 9:30am–3pm Wed, Thu & Sun, 11am–5pm Sat; Nov–Mar: 9:30am–3pm Mon, Wed–Sat, 10am–3pm Sun.* *public hols.* *Free Mon (Apr–Oct), Sun (Nov–Mar).* **www.**wawel.krakow.pl

This special exhibition, arranged in the basement of the former royal kitchen (now occupied by the administration office), will appeal to those interested in the medieval history of Wawel. There were possibly ten churches on Wawel Hill in the past. The Rotunda of the Virgin Mary (Sts Felix and Adauctus), unearthed in 1917 during excavations carried out by Adolf Szyszko-Bohusz, is of great interest. The excavations also brought to light the remnants of a man's body as well as some articles of jewellery nearby. It is believed that the circular rotunda formed part of the first palatium (the seat of the first ruler of Wawel), and was built sometime in the late 10th or early 11th century. Its plan resembles a quatrefoil, with strong evidence of Czech influences in the design of the structure. The rotunda was almost completety destroyed in the 19th century.

A virtual computer model of the Wawel architecture enables visitors to travel into the past to the early 10th century. The computer reconstruction of the medieval buildings shows the state of current research into the early history of Wawel. The models of the so-called Rotunda B, the Rotunda of the Virgin Mary and other buildings, including the palatium, the Church of St Gereon and the Cathedral, give a clear picture of the overall layout.

The Archaeological Site

Archaeological Site ❼

Wawel Hill. **Map** 3 C1 (5 C5). *103, 502.* *8, 10, 18, 36, 38.*

The archaeological site is an open area where foundations of medieval buildings can be seen. The buildings were numerous and once formed a small town. A vicarage in the Renaissance style was among them. All the buildings were demolished by the Austrians in 1803–04 and replaced by a drill ground. The lower parts of the walls of St Nicholas, the small Romanesque church rebuilt in the Gothic style during the reign of Kazimierz the Great, are of particular note. This church was an interesting example of a single nave church, supported on one central column. The plan of the small church of St George is also easy to discern.

Dragon's Lair ⓿

Wawel Hill. **Map** 3 C1 (5 C5). *103, 502.* *8, 10, 18, 36, 38.* *Apr–Oct: 10am–5pm daily.*

Within Wawel Hill there are a number of rock caves. The earliest records of these caves date from the 16th century and are thought to be concerned with crimes. A pub and a brothel were here in the 18th century. In the 19th century the Austrians sealed the entrance when constructing the fortification walls.

The Lair is open during the summer months only. Some 135 spiral steps lead down into the den, and there are 145 m (476 ft) of tunnels in total, of which only a part can be visited. The bronze statue of the Dragon, designed by Bronisław Chromy, which stands at the exit, was made in 1972.

According to an old legend the inhabitants of ancient Cracow were terrorized by a dragon until one day a brave shoemaker, Skuba by name, cheated the monster with a sheep stuffed with sulphur. The dragon swallowed the bait. When the fire heated its gut, the dragon drank so much water from the Vistula that its body burst. To reward the shoemaker King Krak gave him the hand of his daughter in marriage.

The metal monster belches fire and is always regarded as a major attraction by little visitors, both local and from further afield.

The Rotunda of the Virgin Mary at the "Lost Wawel" Exhibition

Cracow Cathedral ❸

The Eagle in Zygmunt Chapel

No other building is so strongly associated with the history of Cracow, and the whole nation, as the Cathedral. The existing building is the third to have been built on this site. The Cathedral was built by Władysław the Short to house the relics of St Stanisław, who was much venerated by the Poles. The basilica consists of a nave with single aisles, non-projecting transept, and a choir with ambulatory. There are also three towers. Many chapels adjoin the aisles. The chapels date from different periods and have been remodelled many times. The internal structure of the Gothic cathedral is now obscure because of later additions. Today the interior displays a variety of styles. Despite this eclecticism the layout of the interior is straightforward.

Baroque spire from the first half of the 18th century

Exterior of the Cathedral
Although dating from different periods, all the distinct parts of the Cathedral make a unique and picturesque ensemble.

Clock Tower
The top of the tallest tower is decorated with four statues of the patron saints of the Kingdom of Poland and the Cathedral: Wacław, Adalbert, Stanisław and Kazimierz (Casimir).

Entrance
The bones of an "ancient creature" hang above the entrance. According to legend the end of the world will come when they fall. The letter K on the door is the initial of Kazimierz the Great, during whose reign the Cathedral was completed.

Bell tower

STAR SIGHTS

★ Zygmunt Chapel

★ Zygmunt Tower

★ Zygmunt Tower
The Zygmunt bell in the tower, cast in 1520, is the largest in Poland. It weighs nearly 11 tons and is more than 2 m (6.5 ft) in diameter.

High Altar
The high altar was commissioned in 1649 by Piotr Gembicki, one of the most powerful bishops of 17th-century Cracow.

★ Zygmunt Chapel
This chapel is a mausoleum of the rulers of the Jagiellonian dynasty. Surmounted by a gilt dome, it is a Renaissance masterpiece.

Potocki Chapel
Remodelled in the 19th century, this chapel features The Crucifixion *by the 17th-century Bolognese artist Giovanni Francesco Barbieri, "Il Guercino".*

VISITORS' CHECKLIST

Wawel Hill 3. **Map** 3 C1 (5 C5). ***Tel*** *012 422 5155 ext 291.* *103, 502.* *8, 10, 18, 36, 38.* **Cathedral, Zygmunt Tower, Royal Tombs** *May–Sep: 9am–5pm Mon–Sat, 12:15–5pm Sun & hols; Oct–Apr: 9am–3pm Mon–Sat, 12:15–3pm Sun & hols.* *Easter, Sun in Advent, Christmas Day, 1 Jan, 1 Nov.*

TIMELINE

1020 Laying of the foundation stone of the Cathedral

1090–1142 Second (so-called Herman) Cathedral built

1320–64 Third Cathedral built

1519–33 Zygmunt Chapel built by Bartolomeo Berrecci

1521 The Zygmunt bell hung

1626–9 St Stanisław's Canopy erected

1664–76 Vaza Chapel built

1758–66 Bishop Załuski's Chapel built

1000 | 1250 | 1500 | 1750

Clock on the Clock Tower

Interior of the Cathedral

Bust of Bishop Piotr Gembicki from his monument

The Cathedral of Cracow is exceptional not only for the works of art which are housed here, but also because it has borne witness to many historic events such as coronations, royal weddings and funerals, as well as thanksgiving ceremonies. The Cathedral enjoys not only high sacred status but it also acquired symbolic importance during the occupation of Poland when it became a treasury of objects commemorating national glory. The Cathedral was chosen by the great Polish playwright Stanisław Wyspiański as a dramatic setting for his *Deliverance*. The Cathedral reflects the past and continues to exert much influence.

Poets' Crypt
Adam Mickiewicz and Juliusz Słowacki, the two foremost Polish poets, are buried here. The remains of Mickiewicz were laid here in 1890 and those of Słowacki in 1929 ❷

Zygmunt Chapel
The splendid double Monument of King Zygmunt the Old (top; by Santi Gucci, 1574–75) and his son, King Zygmunt August (below; by Bartolomeo Berrecci, 1530s) is the outstanding artistic feature of the Cathedral ❼

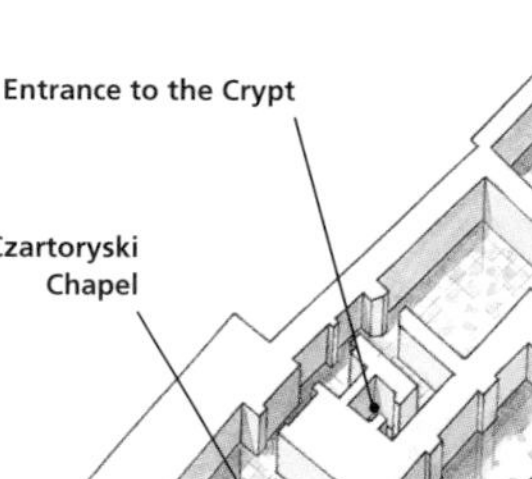

Sarcophagus of King Kazimierz Jagiellończyk
One of the most expressive works of Veit Stoss, this was made in 1492, the year of the king's death ❽

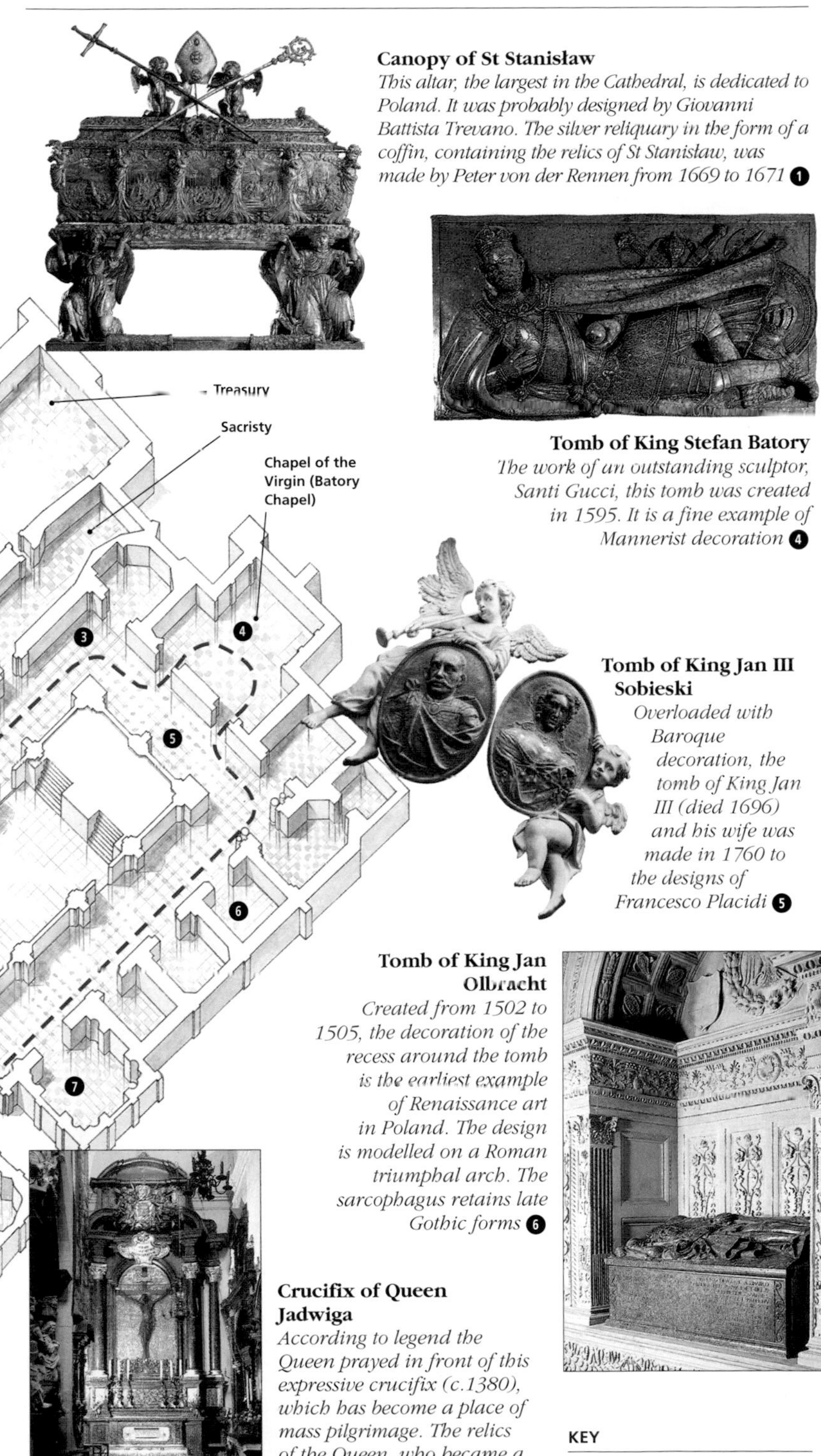

Canopy of St Stanisław

This altar, the largest in the Cathedral, is dedicated to Poland. It was probably designed by Giovanni Battista Trevano. The silver reliquary in the form of a coffin, containing the relics of St Stanisław, was made by Peter von der Rennen from 1669 to 1671 ❶

Tomb of King Stefan Batory

The work of an outstanding sculptor, Santi Gucci, this tomb was created in 1595. It is a fine example of Mannerist decoration ❹

Tomb of King Jan III Sobieski

Overloaded with Baroque decoration, the tomb of King Jan III (died 1696) and his wife was made in 1760 to the designs of Francesco Placidi ❺

Tomb of King Jan Olbracht

Created from 1502 to 1505, the decoration of the recess around the tomb is the earliest example of Renaissance art in Poland. The design is modelled on a Roman triumphal arch. The sarcophagus retains late Gothic forms ❻

Crucifix of Queen Jadwiga

According to legend the Queen prayed in front of this expressive crucifix (c.1380), which has become a place of mass pilgrimage. The relics of the Queen, who became a saint, rest in the altar ❸

KEY

– – – Suggested route

Exploring Cracow Cathedral

A Renaissance tondo by Giovanni Maria Mosca

Cracow Cathedral requires more than one visit to do justice to the magnificent building. Its interior with its variety of styles, from medieval to modern, is simply overwhelming. It is worth returning here for a careful visit to all the chapels in the aisles, and to the monuments and tombs of the kings and prominent people in the crypt. It is also possible to look at works in chronological order. The artistic backdrop adds to the spirituality of the Cathedral, which is above all else used for worship. To avoid crowds, the best time to visit is in the early morning or just before closing time.

CHAPELS

The chapel of the Holy Cross, erected on the initiative of King Kazimierz Jagiellończyk and his wife Elisabeth von Habsburg, has retained much of its medieval character. The cycle of old Russian wall paintings is one of the largest ensembles to have survived. It is of the Pskov School. Two triptychs of the Holy Trinity and the Virgin Mary of Sorrows both date from the second half of the 15th century. The most interesting furnishing is the tomb of Kazimierz made by Veit Stoss with Huber of Passau. The king is shown in majestic resplendence. It is also a dignifed image of death. The stained-glass windows were designed by Józef Mehoffer in the Art Nouveau style.

The Zygmunt Chapel (1519–33), designed by Bartolomeo Berrecci, is of exceptional beauty. The chapel is considered as one of the purest examples of the Italian Renaissance outside Italy. The chapel was modelled on the best Italian architectural and decorative works. The silver altar was made between 1531 and 1538 in Nuremberg by Melchior Baier to the designs of Peter Flötner. The royal tombs are equally interesting. The interior is peaceful and majestic and conveys the spirit of 16th-century humanism. Bishop Tomicki's Chapel is also Renaissance in style. Remodelled by Bartolomeo Berrecci from 1526 to 1535, the chapel played an important role as a model for mausolea for the nobility and gentry. The Chapel of the Virgin Mary (King Stefan Batory's Chapel) houses a 17th-century Baroque tabernacle with the Holy Eucharist. The tomb of Batory and the royal stalls were designed by Santi Gucci.

The altar in the Zygmunt Chapel

The Vaza Chapel, probably also designed by the same architect, exemplifies a 17th-century interior: monumental, heavy forms executed in black marble with large epitaphs. It acts as a reminder of the fragility and transcience of earthly life.

Among the chapels constructed in the 18th century, two are of particular interest. The Lipski Chapel (1743–7), designed by Francesco Placidi, displays light-catching and shadow effects. The decoration of Bishop Załuski's Chapel (1758–66) employs the allegory of the passage through the gate (note the enlarged entrance).

The *Crucifixion* by Guercino and the statue of the Risen Christ by Bertel Thorvaldsen are to be seen in the Chapel of Bishop Filip Padniewski. This Renaissance chapel was remodelled in the 19th century for the Potocki family. The statue of Włodzimierz Potocki in the Holy Trinity Chapel is also by Thorvaldsen.

Intricately carved stalls in the choir of the Cathedral

FURNISHINGS

As well as the canopy of St Stanisław, particularly noteworthy are the epitaphs of the bishops of Cracow placed on the pillars, and decorated with busts of the deceased. Marcin Szyszkowski, Piotr Gembicki, Jan Małachowski and Kazimierz Łubieński all rest here, providing eternal company for the relics of St Stanisław. The Baroque stalls in the choir were made around 1620; additions were made in the 19th century. The bas-relief epitaph of Cardinal Fryderyk Jagiellończyk shows superb craftsmanship. It was made after 1503 in the Vischer workshop in Nuremberg. The throne of Bishop Piotr Gembicki has splendid Baroque decoration. The organ loft, made around 1758 to the design of Francesco Placidi, is also of much interest.

SARCOPHAGI AND TOMBS

The cathedral is a resting place for Polish rulers, and all its medieval tombs follow a particular model. They show a figure laying in state on a massive sarcophagus, decorated with allegorical figures of the king's subjects lamenting the death of their sovereign. A dog, symbolizing fidelity, is usually placed at the king's feet, and the head of the ruler rests on a lion, the symbol of power. A stone canopy is suspended over the tomb. The tomb of Władysław the Short, dating from the mid-14th century is the earliest sarcophagus of this type. Kazimierz Jagiellończyk was the last to have such a monument erected.

Two tombs of much later date were inspired by this early type of sepulchre. The beautiful and majestic tomb of Queen Jadwiga is one of them. It was executed with great delicacy in white Carrara marble by Antoni Madeyski in 1902. The tomb is one of the most visited places of pilgrimage in the Cathedral. The other sarcophagus, also by Madeyski, was erected in 1906. It is a cenotaph (tomb without a corpse) commemorating King Władysław III Warneńczyk, who was killed in 1444 at the Battle of Varna against the Turks. His body was never found, giving rise to stories about his miraculous salvation.

The tomb of Władysław Jagiełło

ROYAL TOMBS

The Royal Tombs were placed in the crypt following the construction of the Zygmunt Chapel, which is a mausoleum. Zygmunt the Old and his sons are buried in the crypt under the chapel. Earlier rulers were buried in the Cathedral, except Bolesław the Brave, Bolesław the Bold, Przemysław II, Louis of Anjou, Władysław III Warneńczyk and Aleksander Jagiellończyk. A crypt was also constructed for the Vaza dynasty. Later rulers were buried beneath the Chapel of the Holy Cross and in St Leonard's crypt. In 1783 the last Polish king, Stanisław August Poniatowski, commissioned a grandiose sarcophagus for Jan III Sobieski. The elected kings Henri de Valois, August II of Saxony and Stanisław August Poniatowski do not rest in the Wawel. Two national heroes, Kościuszko and Prince Józef Poniatowski, were laid here during the Partitions of Poland. State funerals of Piłsudski and General Sikorski took place in the Cathedral in the 20th century.

The sarcophagi of the Vaza kings

Wawel Royal Castle ❺

Head in the Deputies' Hall

Little is known about the earliest Wawel residence. The Romanesque palatium was probably built by Kazimierz the Restorer; later Władysław the Short started to construct a new building but it was only completed by Kazimierz the Great. The present Renaissance castle was constructed in the first half of the 16th century. At the start of the 17th century the apartments in the north wing were remodelled in the early Baroque style. After the royal court moved from Cracow to Warsaw, the castle fell into ruin. Further devastation was caused by the occupying foreign powers. Early in the 20th century the castle was given back to Cracow, and restoration was begun.

CASTLE GUIDE

The Crown Treasury and Armoury, each with a separate entrance, are situated on the ground floor together with a number of state rooms. The remaining state rooms and other apartments are on the first and second floors. After leaving the Senators' Hall a visit to the "Orient in the Wawel Collections" exhibition on the first and second floors in the west wing is recommended.

Crown Treasury and Armoury
This 11th-century chalice belonged to the Abbots of Tyniec and is now in the Treasury. Adjacent to the Treasury is the Armoury with its rich collection.

The Castle Courtyard
A mix of architectural styles can be found at the castle. One of the highlights is the beautiful Renaissance-style courtyard, built in the 16th century.

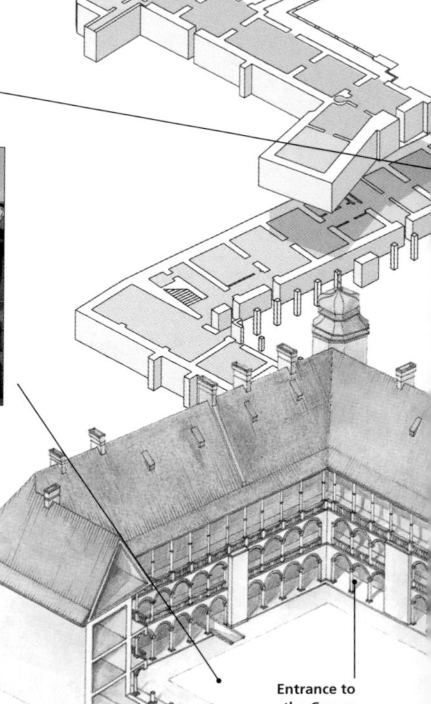

KEY

- Royal Apartments
- Treasury
- Armoury
- "Orient in the Wawel Collections" Exhibition
- Non-exhibition area

★ Birds Hall
This Baroque hall with a marble fireplace is the first of a suite of rooms decorated in the Vaza style.

VISITORS' CHECKLIST

Wawel Hill. **Map** 5 C1 (5 C5). ***Tel*** *012 422 16 97.* 103, 502. 8, 10, 18, 36, 38. *Nov–Mar: 9:30am–3pm Tue–Sat, 10am–3pm Sun; Apr–Oct: 9:30am–12 noon Mon, 9:30am–4pm Tue & Fri, 9:30am–3pm Wed, Thu & Sat, 10am–3pm Sun.* *1 Jan, Easter Sat & Sun, 1 & 11 Nov, 24–25 & 31 Dec.* *free Mon (Nov–Mar), Sun (Apr–Oct).*

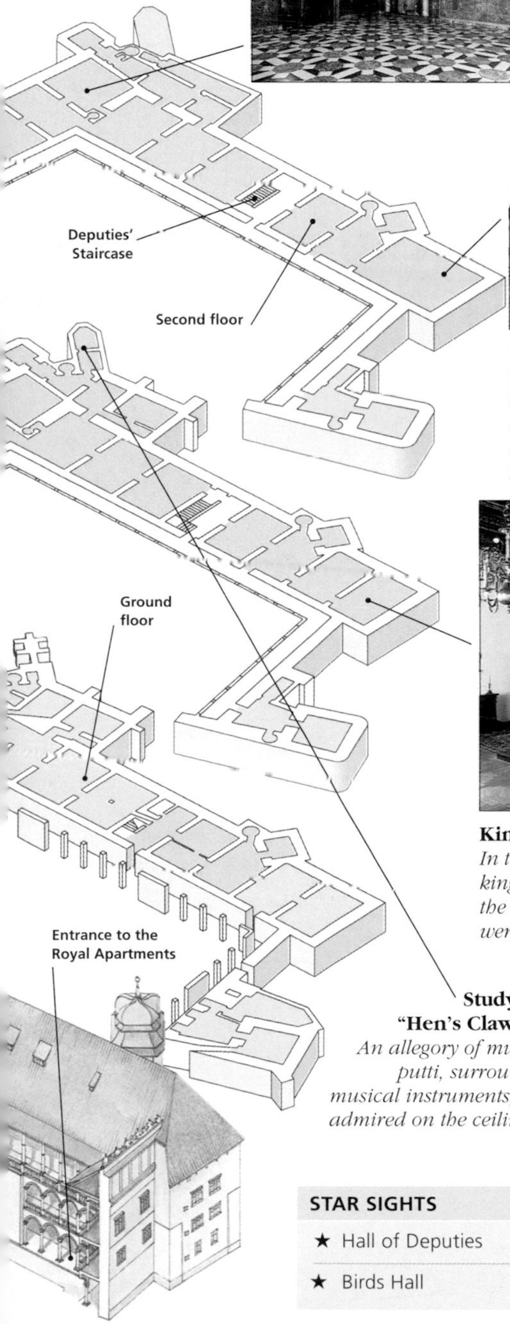

Deputies' Staircase

Second floor

★ Hall of Deputies
This hall used for debates by the lower house of Parliament (Sejm), *is decorated with a coffered ceiling containing realistically carved heads, as well as tapestries and a decorative frieze.*

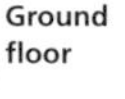

King's Bedroom
In the first half of the 16th century, the king's bedroom, the dining room and the apartments of the ladies-in-waiting were all situated on the first floor.

Entrance to the Royal Apartments

Study in the "Hen's Claw" Wing
An allegory of music and putti, surrounded by musical instruments, can be admired on the ceiling here.

STAR SIGHTS

★ Hall of Deputies

★ Birds Hall

Cracow Cathedral situated on Wawel Hill ▷

OKÓŁ AND STRADOM QUARTERS

Okół was probably the earliest settlement at the foot of Wawel. Timber-built houses and a palisade enclosure were already here in the 10th century. The settlement developed along the so-called Salt Route which led from Hungary to Greater Poland. The quarter became elitist as a result of its proximity to the Royal Castle and the Cathedral. High-ranking clergy resided here and many churches were built.

Heraldic emblem on the house at 32 Grodzka Street

The development of Stradom, situated between Okół and Cracow, was hidered by its location on peat marshes and the vicinity of the Wawel fortress. Splendid new churches and palaces were constructed here from the mid-17th century. Stradom developed rapidly at the end of the 19th century.

SIGHTS AT A GLANCE

Churches and Monasteries
Bernardine Church ⓳
Church of Saints Peter and Paul pp80–81 ❸
Church of St Andrew ❹
Church of St Giles ❼
Church of St Martin ❺
Church of the Bernardine Nuns ⓲
Church of the Missionaries ㉑
Franciscan Church pp86–7 ⓯

Museums and Galleries
Archaeological Museum ⓮
Archdiocesan Museum ❿
Cricoteka ⓭
Natural History Museum ㉒
Palace of Bishop Erazm Ciołek ⓫
St Vladimir's Foundation ⓬

Historic Parks
Dietl Plantations ㉓

Historic Monuments and Buildings
Collegium Iuridicum ❷
Częstochowa Seminary ⓴
Deanery ❾
Royal Arsenal ❻
Statue of Józef Dietl ⓱
Wielopolski Palace ⓰

Historic Streets
Grodzka Street ❶
Kanonicza Street ❽

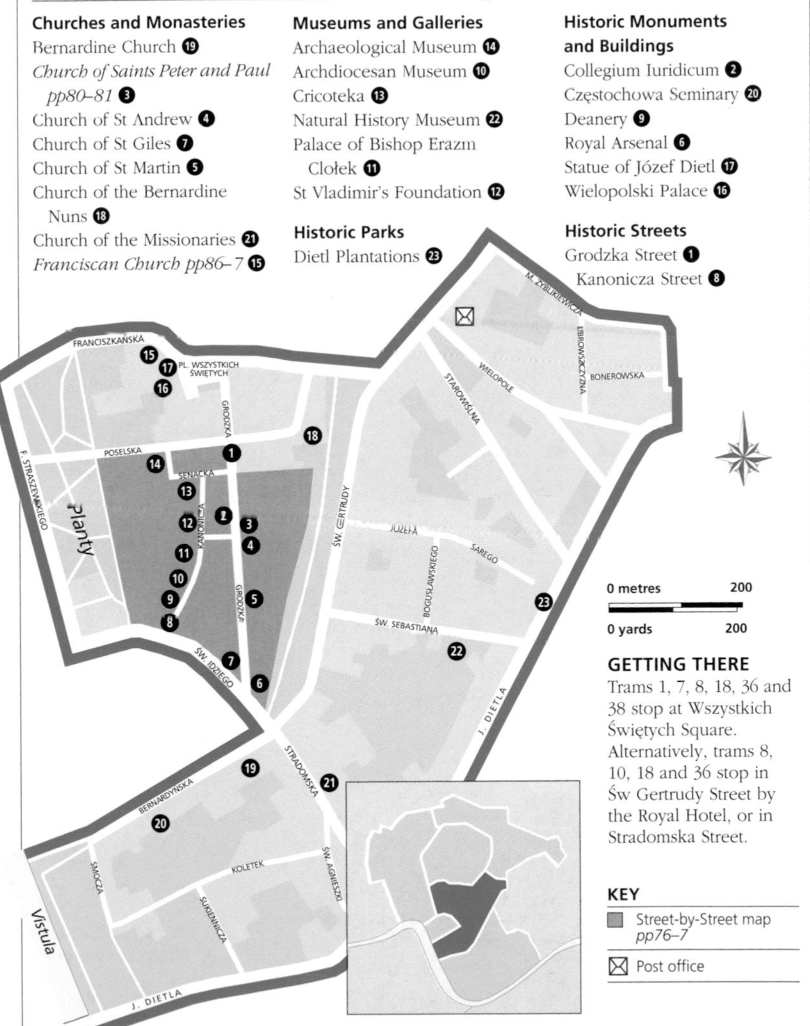

GETTING THERE

Trams 1, 7, 8, 18, 36 and 38 stop at Wszystkich Świętych Square. Alternatively, trams 8, 10, 18 and 36 stop in Św Gertrudy Street by the Royal Hotel, or in Stradomska Street.

KEY

Street-by-Street map *pp76–7*

⊠ Post office

◁ **Vault in the Franciscan Church**

Street-By-Street: Okół

The historic Okół district is more or less in line with the southern part of the medieval centre of Cracow. It is a picturesque area. Those who want a change from the regular plan of the Old Quarter will enjoy Okół's curving streets and dead-end mews, lined with some outstanding buildings. Fortunately the great fire of Cracow in 1850 did not damage the buildings in Okół, and much of the original architecture can still be seen here.

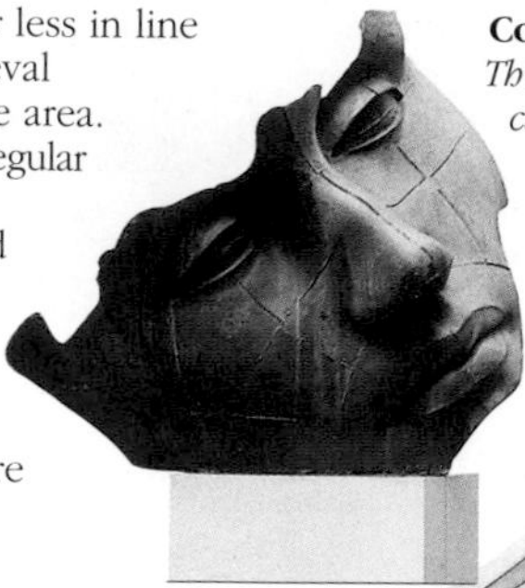

Collegium Iuridicum
This sculpture of classical beauty in the courtyard is by Polish-born Igor Mitoraj. It was presented to the Jagiellonian University by the artist, who now lives in Italy 2

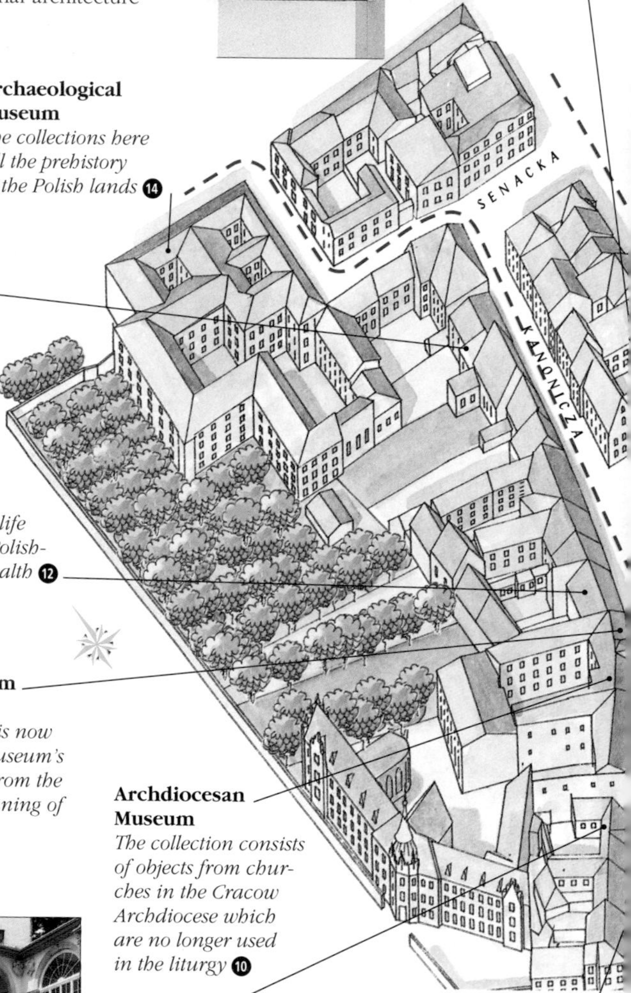

Archaeological Museum
The collections here tell the prehistory of the Polish lands 14

Cricoteka
The Cricot 2 Theatre and Museum are located in this Gothic house 13

SENACKA

KANONICZA

St Vladimir's Foundation
This building houses artifacts explaining the life of the Ruthenas in the Polish-Lithuanian Commonwealth 12

Palace of Bishop Erazm Ciołek
This beautiful building is now home to the National Museum's collection of Polish art from the Middle Ages to the beginning of the 19th century 11

Archdiocesan Museum
The collection consists of objects from churches in the Cracow Archdiocese which are no longer used in the liturgy 10

Deanery
The arcaded courtyard of this small house, formerly a canonry, gives the impression of a magnificent Renaissance residence 9

Kanonicza Street
This quiet street has retained much of the old royal character of Cracow 8

★ Church of Saints Peter and Paul

This early Baroque Jesuit church is a masterpiece of 17th-century Polish architecture. The façade, with its rich sculptural decoration, is remarkable ❸

LOCATOR MAP

See Street Finder maps 1, 3 & 6

Grodzka Street

The townhouses situated along one of the oldest streets in Cracow were once palaces ❶

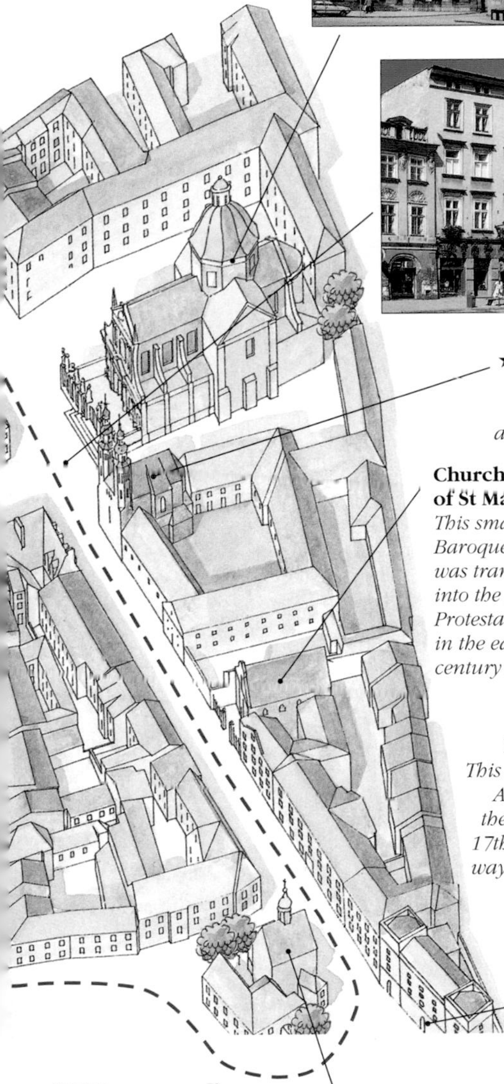

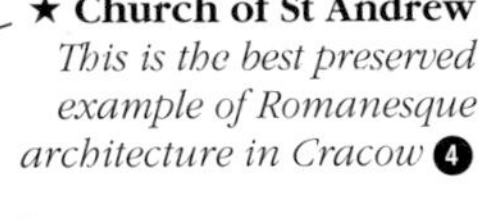

★ Church of St Andrew

This is the best preserved example of Romanesque architecture in Cracow ❹

Church of St Martin

This small early Baroque church was transformed into the Augsburg Protestant Church in the early 19th century ❺

Royal Arsenal

This entrance to the Arsenal is one of the most beautiful 17th-century doorways in Cracow ❻

Church of St Giles

This is a rather modest Gothic church dating from the first half of the 14th century ❼

0 metres 50

0 yards 50

KEY

– – – Suggested route

STAR SIGHTS

- ★ Church of Saints Peter and Paul
- ★ Church of St Andrew

Children wearing traditional clothing on Grodzka Street

Grodzka Street ❶

Ulica Grodzka

Map 1 C5 (6 D4). *1, 2, 8, 18.*

Grodzka is one of the oldest streets in Cracow. In the past it formed part of the important Salt Route from Hungary to Greater Poland. As part of the Royal Route it bore witness to coronation and funeral processions of Polish kings.

Grodzka Street was once lined with many palaces and a few churches. These palaces were rebuilt and converted into town houses. Grodzka is a lovely street full of character, owing to its irregular plan, varying width and diverse architecture.

Collegium Iuridicum ❷

Grodzka 53. **Map** 1 C5 (6 D4). ***Tel*** *012 633 63 77 ext. 2414.* *1, 2, 8, 18.* *10am–1pm Tue & Thu, 11am–2pm Sun.* **Natural History Museum (Muzeum Przyrodnicze UJ)** *10am–2pm Mon–Fri.* *summer hols.*

The Collegium Iuridicum of the Academy of Cracow was founded early in the 15th century through the bequest of Queen Jadwiga. The excavation work carried out at the site has confirmed that the building had replaced a large trade hall, probably built in the 14th century on the orders of Władysław the Short. The remnants of the hall have survived in the basement. The Collegium Iuridicum was rebuilt several times. The works were funded by Bishop Jan Rzeszowski, among others. The elaborate doorway decorated with the University's emblem

Two-tier arcaded courtyard of the Collegium Iuridicum

was made around 1680. The College was entirely rebuilt after a fire in 1719 and the two-tier arcaded courtyard added. The Institute of the History of Art and the Natural History Museum are both housed here, the latter being located in the basement. A collection of shells and butterflies is of interest.

In the summer months concerts and theatrical performances take place in courtyard, which features a sculpture by Igor Mitoraj.

Church of Saints Peter and Paul ❸

Kościół św. św. Piotra i Pawła

See pp80–81.

Church of St Andrew ❹

Kościół św. Andrzeja

Grodzka 56. **Map** 1 C5 (6 D4). ***Tel*** *012 422 16 12.* *1, 2, 8, 18.* *7:30am–5pm daily and during services.*

The Church of St Andrew in Okół is regarded as one of the finest examples of Romanesque architecture in Poland. It was built between 1079 and 1098 as a foundation of Sieciech, the powerful Palatine to Duke Władysław Herman. It was rebuilt around 1200. The towers and aisles were extended and a transept added. According to the chronicler Jan Długosz this was the only church in Cracow to resist the Tatar invasion of 1241. Around 1702 it was remodelled in the Baroque style to the designs of Baldassare Fontana, who also covered the internal walls and vaulting with stuccowork. Mural paintings by Karl Dankwart complete the decoration. Among furnishings worth noting are the pulpit, in the form of a boat, and the high altar with an imposing ebony tabernacle decorated with silver ornaments.

The treasury in the convent adjoining the church houses some priceless objects, such as a portable mosaic depicting the Virgin Mary from the end

Church of St Andrew with its two spires

of the 12th century, 14th-century marionettes used in Christmas nativity plays, and early medieval reliquaries.

Church of St Martin ❺

Kościół św. Marcina

Grodzka 58a. **Map** 6 D4. ***Tel*** *012 422 72 65. 8, 10, 18. 10am–1pm Mon–Sat and during services.*

The first church was probably built on this site in the 12th century. In 1612 the Discalced Carmelite Nuns were brought here. The old church was demolished and in 1637–40 the nuns commisioned a new, rather small church in the early Baroque style. After the convent was closed down, the church was taken over by the Protestant community. The interior was converted according to the needs of the Lutheran liturgy. The high altar features a 14th-century crucifix and *Christ Calming the Storm,* painted by Henryk Siemiradzki in 1882.

Royal Arsenal ❻

Arsenał Królewski

Grodzka 64. **Map** 6 D5. ***Tel*** *012 422 47 03. 8, 10, 18. to the public.*

In the first half of the 16th century Zygmunt the Old built an arsenal and a cannon foundry next to the city wall. They formed part of Cracow's fortifications. The present building was remodelled in 1927 by the architect Stanisław Filipkiewicz, who juxtaposed the Baroque structure of the arsenal with an austere extension thus achieving an interesting effect.

Church of St Giles ❼

Kościół św. Idziego

Św. Idziego 1. **Map** 6 D5. *8, 10, 18. during services only.*

According to historic evidence made popular by a song by Ewa Demarczyk (of the Piwnica pod Baranami Cabaret), this church was "built in 1082 by Władysław Herman and his wife Judith, after they bore a child through the intervention of St Giles". The present church was built in the early 14th century. In 1595 the Dominicans took over and soon remodelled it.

Among the furnishings, the stone stalls are particularly interesting. They were made in 1629 by reusing fragments of the Renaissance tomb of St Jacek (otherwise known as St Hyacinth) from the Dominican Church.

Kanonicza Street ❽

Ulica Kanonicza

Map 1 C5 (6 D4). *8, 10, 18, 36, 38.*

Kanonicza Street formed the last stretch of the Royal Route leading towards Wawel. From the 14th century onwards it was lined with the houses of Cracow's canons, who were given the use of these houses for life when they took up office in the Chapter of Cracow. Each successive inhabitant tended to modernize the house. As a result Gothic houses acquired arcaded Renaissance courtyards, Baroque doorways or Neo-Classical façades. The canons could afford to spend lavishly owing to their elite status within the church.

The great diversity of architectural styles which can be found within the narrow and winding little Kanonicza Street gives it a picturesque character.

Decorative bas-relief plaque of 1480 on the Długosz House, Kanonicza Street

Church of Saints Peter and Paul ❸

Emblem of the Jesuits

This church, modelled on the Jesuit Church of Il Gesù in Rome, is considered to be one of the most magnificent early Baroque churches in Central Europe. The history of its construction and the name of the architects involved are the subjects of an ongoing debate among architectural historians. The foundation stone was laid in 1596. The leading Jesuit architect, Giovanni de Rosis, contributed the design, and works were carried out by Giuseppe Brizio and Giovanni Maria Bernardoni. In 1605 the church neared its completion but, due to some structural problems, a number of walls had to be dismantled and rebuilt to an altered design. The court architect Giovanni Battista Trevano was put in charge of the second stage.

Cartouche with an Eagle
This exquisitely carved coat of arms belonged to the main founder of the church, King Zygmunt III Vaza.

Organ Gallery
The late Baroque organ gallery with a curved balustrade, designed by Kacper Bażanka, is in contrast with the austere and monumental architecture of the Church. It is located inside, just above the main entrance.

Statues of the Apostles
This railing was designed by Kacper Bażanka and is decorated with copies of statues originally carved by David Heel from 1715 to 1722.

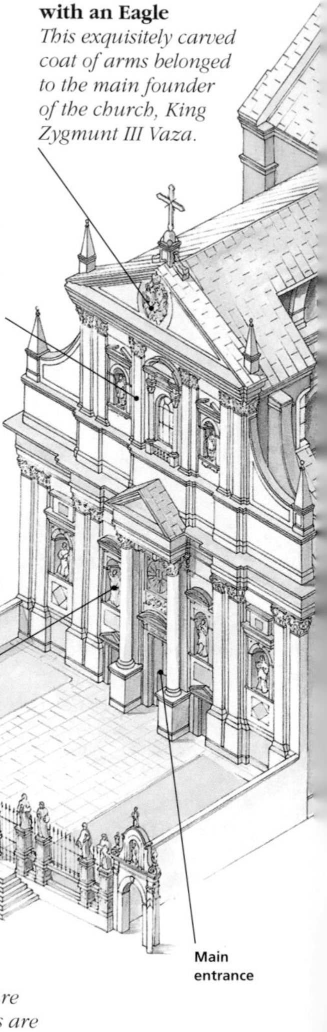

Statue of St Ignatius Loyola
The founder of the Society of Jesus is depicted in this late Baroque sculpture by David Heel. The adjoining statues are of Stanisław Kostka, Francis Xavier and Aloysius Gonzaga.

Main entrance

Stuccowork (1622–39)
The stuccowork above the high altar is by Giovanni Battista Falconi and includes scenes from the lives of Saints Peter and Paul, patrons of the church.

★ High Altar
Made in 1726–28 to Kacper Bażanka's design, the high altar was conceived to convey a call for unity between the Roman Catholic and Orthodox Churches.

★ Tomb of Bishop Andrzej Trzebicki
The monumental decoration of this tomb, created in 1695–96, commemorates the bishop with true Baroque ostentation.

Statue of Piotr Skarga
The author of Parliamentary Sermons *died in 1612 and was buried in the crypt beneath the high altar. This statue of Father Skarga was made by Oskar Sosnowski in 1869 and placed in the church in the early 20th century.*

VISITORS' CHECKLIST

Grodzka 38. **Map** 1 C5 (6 D4). ***Tel*** *012 422 65 73.* *1, 2, 8, 10, 18.* *9am–5pm Mon–Sat, 1pm–5pm Sun and during services.*

STAR SIGHTS

★ High Altar

★ Tomb of Bishop Andrzej Trzebicki

Massive portal of the medieval Deanery

Deanery 9

Dom Dziekański

Kanonicza 21. **Map** 1 C5 (6 D4). *1, 2, 8, 10, 18, 36, 38.*

This house is considered to be the most beautiful of all the canons' houses in Cracow. The medieval house was completely rebuilt in the 1580s, probably by the architect and sculptor Santi Gucci. The arcaded courtyard with its magnificent decoration, carved in stone, the impressive portal and the *sgraffiti* on the façade all date from this period. The statue of St Stanisław in the courtyard was added in the 18th century. In the 1960s this was home to the future Pope and then Suffragan Bishop of Cracow, Karol Wojtyła.

Archdiocesan Museum 10

Muzeum Archidiecezjalne

Kanonicza 19. **Map** 1 C5 (6 D4). ***Tel*** *012 421 89 63. 1, 2, 8, 18, 36, 38. 10am–4pm Tue–Fri, 10am–3pm Sat & Sun.*

This house is traditionally associated with the residence of St Stanisław while he was a canon in Cracow, hence the name, St Stanisław's House. It was actually built in the 14th century but entirely remodelled in the late 18th century. The Archdiocesan Museum is now housed here. It runs a programme of temporary exhibitions of sacred art based on loans from church treasuries in the Cracow Archdiocese. Interesting goldwork displays have taken place here.

Part of the Archdiocesan Museum is given over to the room of Karol Wojtyła, who became Pope John Paul II. The room has been faithfully reconstructed here as it stood originally in the adjoining Deanery, where he lived.

Palace of Bishop Erazm Ciołek 11

Pałac biskupa Erazma Ciołka

ul. Kanonicza 17. **Map** 1 C5 (6 D4). ***Tel*** *012 633 53 31. 8, 10, 18, 36, 38, 40. phone in advance.*

This museum was once home to the great diplomat and patron of the arts Bishop Erazm Ciołek (1474–1522). A magnificently distinguished residence, it has recently been extensively renovated and now houses the National Museum's large and notable collection of Polish Art. The house was built in a mix of Gothic and Renaissance styles, whilst the collection within ranges from the 13th to the 18th centuries. The latter includes such gems as large 15th-century tryptichs from Cracow guilds, exquisite Orthodox icons and encolpions, which reveal the ever-increasing influence and power of Western Europe in the 17th and 18th centuries.

St Vladimir's Foundation 12

Fundacja św. Włodzimierza

Kanonicza 15. **Map** 1 C5 (6 D4). ***Tel*** *012 421 99 96. 1, 2, 8, 10, 18, 36, 38. 10am–6pm Mon–Fri.*

St Vladimir's Foundation is based in a 14th-century house which displays fine Renaissance decoration. Icons from disused Orthodox

Karol Wojtyła's room in the Archdiocesan Museum

churches in the Beskidy, Bieszczady and Tomaszów Lubelski regions, dating mainly from the 17th and 18th centuries, are kept here.

The Greek Catholic Chapel is dedicated to the martyr saints Boris and Gleb and is decorated with paintings by Jerzy Nowosielski. This contemporary Cracow artist is influenced by Byzantine art but uses modern forms of expression.

The sanctuary features the miraculous icon of the Korczmin Madonna.

Cricoteka ⓭

Kanonicza 5. **Map** 1 C5 (6 D4). ***Tel*** *012 422 83 32.* *1, 2, 8, 18.* *10am–4pm Mon–Fri (Jul & Aug also Sat & Sun).*

The former canon's house at 5 Kanonicza Street has retained much of its Gothic form. In 1980 it became the home of the renowned avant-garde theatre Cricot 2. This theatre was founded in 1956 on the initiative of Tadeusz Kantor, the outstanding painter and stage designer. It became famous for performances which were permeated by a symbolic representation of man's existence. Performances relied on traditional theatrical forms while also borrowing from the "happenings" fashionable at the time. The most unusual sets added a surreal flavour. *The Dead Class*, *Wielopole, Wielopole* and *Let Artists Drop Dead* were among Cricot 2's most successful productions. After the death of Kantor in 1990 his actors continued his work. The house in Kanonicza Street is too small to have a stage, so performances take place in other venues. The Cricoteka housed here is a small museum and archive documenting the work of the theatre since its inception. Costumes, stage designs and props, photographs of the performances, as well as drawings and paintings by Kantor, are all here.

Archaeological Museum ⓮

Muzeum Archeologiczne

Poselska 3. **Map** 1 C5 (6 D4). ***Tel*** *012 422 71 00.* *103, 124, 502.* *8, 10, 18.* *Jul–Aug: 9am–2pm Mon, Wed & Fri, 2–6pm Tue & Thu, 10am–2pm Sun; Sep–Jun: 9am–2pm Sun–Wed & Fri, 2–6pm Thu.* *free on Sun.*

The museum is housed in the former Friary of the Discalced Carmelites, founded in 1606 and the oldest institution of its type in Poland. At the end of the 18th century the Austrian authorities took the building over and converted it into a prison. Mostly political prisoners were held here. In 1945 a group of imprisoned soldiers was rescued following heroic action by the Home Army (AK). After the prison closed down a museum was established here.

The Archeological Museum has its beginings in 1850, it was initially called the Museum of Antiquities.

The collection includes artifacts that tell the earliest history of the Lesser Poland region, but also Egyptian mummies. The statue of the idol Światowid, salvaged from the Zbrucz River, jewellery found in the tomb of a Scythian princess in Ryżanówka, gold objects from the tomb of a Hun from Jakuszowice and iron objects used as a form of payment *(see p21)* are the highlights of the collection.

Franciscan Church ⓯

Kościół Franciszkanów

See pp86–7.

Elaborate entrance to the Wielopolski Palace

Wielopolski Palace ⓰

Pałac Wielopolskich

Plac Wszystkich Świętych. **Map** 1 C5 (6 D3). ***Tel*** *012 616 12 07.* *1, 2, 7, 8, 18, 36, 38.* *by prior telephone arrangement only.*

The Wielopolski Palace was sold in the second half of the 19th century and transformed into a seat of municipal administration. Following remodelling work carried out from 1907–12 by architect Jan Rzymkowski, the building acquired a simplified modern form. A porch supported by pseudo-Romanesque columns covered by a timber roof was added to the wall facing Poselska Street. An Art Nouveau frieze featuring coats of arms of a number of cities can also be seen here. Inside the palace, the Debate Room and Portrait Hall are both worth visiting.

Archaeological Museum and garden

Statue of Józef Dietl ⑰

Pomnik Józefa Dietla

Pl. Wszystkich Świętych. **Map** 1 C5 (6 D3). *1, 2, 7, 8, 18, 36, 38.*

Józef Dietl (1804–78) was a medical professor who advocated treating the sick in spas. He was Rector of the Jagiellonian University, and became the first President (Mayor) of Cracow to be elected, in 1866, in the autonomous Galicia. He reformed the education system in Cracow, set up a project for the renovation of the city's heritage and was responsible for the restoration of the Cloth Hall.

The statue of Dietl was made between 1936 and 1938 by Xawery Dunikowski. The artist not only created the monumental figure but also took much trouble to find it a prominent location. Using a model he travelled all over Cracow and tried it out in various places before deciding upon the present location in All Saints Square. The result is stunning. The Statue of Dietl is regarded as one of the grandest and best located monuments in Poland.

Church of the Bernardine Nuns ⑱

Kościół Bernardynek

Poselska 21. **Map** 1 C5 (6 D4). ***Tel*** *012 422 22 46.* *1, 8, 18, 36, 38.* *9am–6:30pm daily and during services.*

A small convent of the Bernardine Nuns was established in Poselska Street in 1646. The Church of St Joseph was built here between 1694 and 1703 for the nuns. Though small and modest the church interior displays splendid furnishings which include altars and a pulpit from the workshop of Jerzy Hankis. The miraculous image of St Joseph and Child in the high altar was a gift from Jakub Zadzik, Bishop of Cracow, who possibly received it from Pope Urban VIII.

A small 17th-century statue of the child Jesus in the side altar is much venerated. It originally came from the Church of the Nuns of St Colette in Stradom and is therefore called the Koletański Christ.

Interior of the small Church of the Bernardine Nuns

Bernardine Church ⑲

Kościół Bernardynów

Bernardyńska 2. **Map** 3 C1 (6 D5). ***Tel*** *012 422 16 50.* *8, 10, 18, 36, 38.* *during services only.*

Giovanni da Capistrano, the reformer of the Franciscan Order, later canonized, arrived in Cracow in 1453. For the next year he preached repentance and the renouncement of wealth and the immoral way of life. He also incited the people against the Jews. Influenced by his sermons, a few Cracovians took up the habit of the Reformed Franciscans, then called the Observants but known as the Bernardines in Poland. In 1453 Cardinal Zbigniew Oleśnicki built in Stradom a small timber church for this new monastic community, and soon after began building a large brick church. It was completed by Jan Długosz after Oleśnicki's death.

In 1655, while preparing to defend Cracow against the Swedes, Stefan Czarniecki gave orders to set fire to the Bernardine Church, which was located at the foot of Wawel Hill, so that the invaders could not use the church for their own protection. The beautiful statue of the Virgin and Child with St Anne, from Veit Stoss's workshop, and remnants of Mannerist tombs (now on the porch wall) are the only furnishings to have survived.

The new Baroque Church of the Bernardines was built between 1659 and 1680. Krzysztof Mieroszewski is believed to have been the architect. The marble shrine of Blessed Simon of Lipnica was erected in 1662 and the high altar between 1758 and 1766.

The 17th-century Baroque Bernardine Church

Częstochowa Seminary 20

Seminarium Częstochowskie

Bernardyńska 3. **Map** 3 C1 (6 D5). ***Tel*** *012 422 47 03.* *8, 10, 18, 36, 38.* **Chapel** *by prior telephone arrangement only.*

In 1925 the Bishop of Częstochowa, Teodor Kubina, founded a seminary affiliated with the Faculty of Theology at the Jagiellonian University, for seminarists from his diocese. The monumental Modernist building was constructed between 1928 and 1930 to the designs of Zygmunt Gawlik and Franciszek Mączyński.

The façade is decorated with sculptures which were carved under the supervision of Xawery Dunikowski, one of the foremost Polish sculptors of the 20th century. The bas-relief at the top is particularly interesting. It shows Christ blessing the allegorical figure of Poland and the representatives of all social ranks, as well as the Virgin Mary accompanied by clergymen. The scene depicting a seminarist tempted by the devil, also on the façade, is worth noting.

Relief of a seminarist tempted by the devil, Częstochowa Seminary

Church of the Missionaries 21

Kościół Misjonarzy

Stradomska 4. **Map** 3 C1 (6 E5). ***Tel*** *012 422 88 77.* *103, 124.* *8, 10, 18, 36, 38.* *2–7pm daily and during services.*

The Missionaries were brought to Stradom in 1682 but built the Church of the Conversion of St Paul only in the years 1719 to 1728. The architect, Kacper Bażanka, was influenced in his design by two outstanding examples of Roman Baroque architecture. The interior of the Cracow church resembles that of Francesco Borromini's Church of the Magi at the Collegio di Propaganda Fide, and the exterior is close to Sant' Andrea al Quirinale designed by Gianlorenzo Bernini.

Baroque façade of the Church of the Missionaries

Some of the methods applied by Bażanka, such as the use of mirrors in the nave to direct reflected light onto the chapels, are characteristic of High Baroque. The church is regarded as one of the finest examples of 18th-century Baroque Polish architecture.

The same applies to the interior. Most altarpieces were painted by Tadeusz Kuntze and decorated with sculptures by Antoni Frączkiewicz.

Natural History Museum 22

Muzeum Przyrodnicze

Św. Sebastiana 9/11. **Map** 3 D1 (6 E5). ***Tel*** *012 422 59 59.* *8, 10, 18, 36, 38.* *9am–5pm Mon–Thu, 9am–6pm Fri–Sun.*

The core of the Natural History Museum was the collection of the Physiographic Commission of Cracow's Learned Society, established in 1865. It consisted mainly of stuffed birds and invertebrates. Today, the museum keeps numerous entomological specimens (insects) and pressed plants which can be found in Poland. A rhinoceros dating from the Pleistocene era, found in 1920 in Starunia, is a highlight of the collection.

Dietl Plantations 23

Planty Dietlowskie

Map 3 D1 (6 E5, F4). *128, 184.* *19, 22.*

The old river bed of the Vistula, from Stradom to Kazimierz, was filled in during the years 1878 to 1880 and transformed into a modern thoroughfare designed by Bolesław Malecki. It was a dual carriageway 1 km (0.6 mile) in length and 100 m (328 ft) wide, with a garden in the middle. The new scheme was named Planty Dietlowskie after Józef Dietl. This President of Cracow was first to advocate the filling in of the old Vistula bed which hindered the integration of Cracow with Kazimierz. Both sides of the avenue are lined with high tenement blocks and elegant public buildings, one of which is the PKO Bank built from 1922 to 1924.

Tree-lined avenue separating Dietl's dual carriageway

Franciscan Church ⓯

The Franciscans arrived in Cracow in 1237. The construction of the church was undertaken in 1255 as a foundation of Duke Bolesław the Chaste and his wife the Blessed Salomea. After the Swedish invasion, which caused much damage, the church was rebuilt in the Baroque style. The great fire of Cracow in 1850 damaged the church again. It was rebuilt partly in the Neo-Romanesque and partly in the Neo-Gothic style. The work of Stanisław Wyspiański on the interior decoration is of prime importance. Around 1900 this artist executed the Art Nouveau murals and designed a series of unusual stained-glass windows in expressive colours.

A 13th-century wall of the first church

Blessed Salomea
Stanisław Wyspiański's stained glass in the north window of the choir shows the foundress of the church who rejected the ducal coronet before taking the habit of a Poor Clare nun.

★ Mater Dolorosa
This late Gothic image by Master Jerzy, of Mary surrounded by angels holding instruments of Christ's Passion, is much venerated.

★ Murals
The polychrome decoration features flowers and conveys the Franciscan love of nature. This work illustrates the novel means of artistic expression employed by Wyspiański in sacred art.

Chapel of The Passion
The brothers of the Confraternity of The Passion have met in this chapel since the end of the 16th century to conduct their rituals (see p52). *Their liturgy is theatrical and evokes the spirit of Baroque devotion.*

Cloister
Portraits of Cracow's bishops were hung in the cloister of the Franciscan Friary from the 15th to the mid-20th centuries.

VISITORS' CHECKLIST

Wszystkich Świętych Sq.
Map 1 C5 (6 D3). ***Tel*** *012 422 53 76.* *1, 7, 8, 18, 36, 38.*
10am–4:30pm Mon–Sat, 1–4pm Sun and during services.

Portrait of Bishop Piotr Tomicki
This beautiful Renaissance portrait of Bishop Tomicki, painted before 1535 by Stanisław Samostrzelnik, is worth seeing in the cloister gallery.

Tomb of Giovanni Gemma (died 1608)
The monument to the Venetian physician to King Zygmunt III Vaza is one of the most interesting sepulchral sculptures of late Mannerism in Poland.

★ Wyspiański's Stained Glass *Let It Be*
This expressive image of God the Father emerging from the cosmic chaos was rendered using bold colours and sinuous, flowing Art Nouveau forms.

STAR SIGHTS

- ★ Mater Dolorosa
- ★ Murals
- ★ Wyspiański's Stained Glass *Let It Be*

OLD QUARTER

In 1257 Duke Bolesław the Chaste gave Cracow her charter. This law was of key importance to the city as it determined local government and trade privileges, thus stimulating the city's future development. The charter stipulated strict rules for this development: a large, centrally located square, surrounded by a regular grid of streets, was to become the city centre. The size of each plot determined the size of the houses. Although the architecture became ever more opulent, this urban scheme has survived almost intact. To this day the Old Quarter remains the heart of modern, fast developing Cracow. It is an area with a great concentration of important historic sights and other places for visitors to enjoy, including the restful Planty gardens.

Coat of arms of Cracow in St Mary's Church

SIGHTS AT A GLANCE

Churches

Church of St Anne pp108–9 15
Church of St John 24
Church of St Mark 21
Church of St Mary pp94–7 1
Church of the Holy Cross 33
Church of the Dominican Nuns 34
Church of the Reformed Franciscans 20
Dominican Church pp116–7 35
Piarist Church 26
St Adalbert's Church 9
St Barbara's Church 3

Historic Streets and Squares

Floriańska Street 31
Market Square pp98–101 4
St John Street 23
St Mary's Square 2

Historic Monuments and Buildings

Barbican 28
Collegium Nowodvorianum 14
Collegium Novum 11
Christopher Palace 5
Episcopal Palace 10
Jama Michalika Café 29
Old Theatre 16
Polish Academy of Skills 22
Słowacki Theatre 32
Statue of Copernicus 12
Statue of Adam Mickiewicz 8
St Florian's Gate and the the City Wall Remnants 27
Town Hall Tower 6

Museums and Galleries

"Bunker of Art" 18
Cloth Hall pp102–3 7
Collegium Maius pp106–7 13
Czartoryski Museum pp112–3 25
Matejko House 30
Palace of Art 17
Wyspiański Museum 19

KEY

Street-by-Street map *pp90–91*

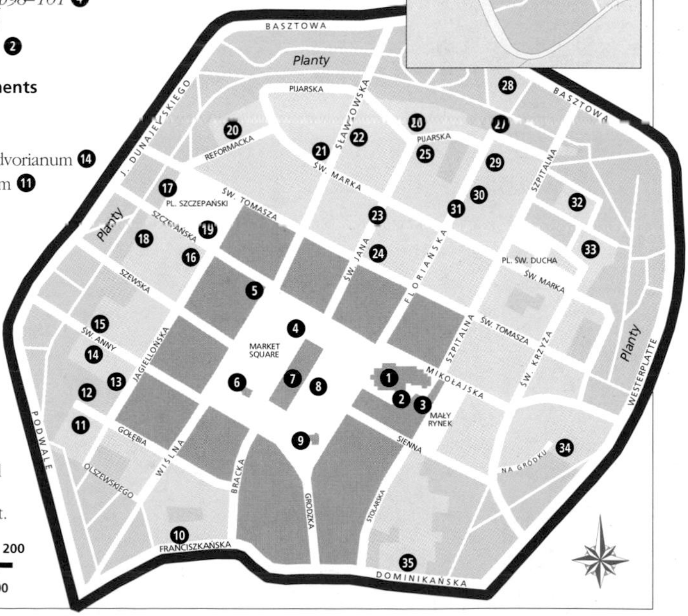

GETTING THERE

Tram and bus routes serve Podwale, Franciszkańska, Dominikańska, Westerplatte, Basztowa and Dunajewskiego streets, which all run along the Planty green belt.

◁ **Allegory of Poetry, a figure at the base of the Mickiewicz Statue**

Street-by-Street: Market Square

The Market Square (Rynek Główny) is located in the centre of Cracow's Old Quarter. Public, cultural and commercial activities have always concentrated around the Market Square. Museums and galleries of both old and modern art can be found here. Antiquarian shops selling works of art, bookshops and the best restaurants, cafés and bars are located in the houses around the square. Each summer nearly 30 street cafés open until the early hours. Flower stalls, street musicians, artists selling their works by the Cloth Hall and the general hustle and bustle made by the vendors of souvenirs and their clients all contribute to the lively atmospere of this place.

Market Square
This is the largest town square anywhere in Europe. The life of medieval Cracow was centred around the square ❹

★ Christopher Palace
The Museum of Cracow is housed in this palace ❺

★ Cloth Hall (Sukiennice)
Originally a market hall, the Sukiennice houses shops, cafés and the renowned Picture Gallery ❼

Town Hall Tower
The only remaining fragment of the Old Town Hall, the tower was remodelled after World War II ❻

STAR SIGHTS

- ★ Church of St Mary
- ★ Cloth Hall
- ★ Christopher Palace

★ Church of St Mary
The main parish church in Cracow is renowned for its Gothic high altar, one of the largest in the world, carved by Veit Stoss ❶

St Mary's Square
The parish cemetery was originally located on this site ❷

LOCATOR MAP
See Street Finder maps 1 & 6

St Barbara's Church
The architecture of the church is medieval. Its furnishings are mainly Rococo but also include this 15th-century Pietà ❸

"The Magical Cab", the poem by K. I. Gałczyński, was inspired by a horse-drawn cab similar to one which you can hire here for a sightseeing trip.

0 metres 50
0 yards 50

Statue of Adam Mickiewicz
This is a popular meeting point for Cracowians [illegible]

St Adalbert's Church
This is one of the oldest churches in Cracow. The picturesque structure is at the end of the vista formed by Grodzka Street ❾

KEY

– – – Suggested route

Church of St Mary ❶

Kościół Mariacki

See pp94–5.

St Mary's Square ❷

Plac Mariacki

Map 1 C4 (6 D2).

St Mary's Square was once a parish graveyard. It was relocated between 1796 and 1804. The statue of the Virgin Mary which was here originally is now in the Planty by Jagiellońska Street. The bas-relief attributed to Veit Stoss, which once decorated the Calvary Porch, has survived and is now in the National Museum. A copy can be seen on the wall at No.8 on the square. The prelate House and a Vicarage are among the houses in which original beamed ceilings and plasterwork have survived. St Barbara's Church is on the east side of the square, which also features a small water pump decorated with a figure of a student of medieval Cracow. It is a copy of a figure from the high altar in St Mary's *(see pp96–7)*.

A student of medieval Cracow, St Mary's Square

St Barbara's Church ❸

Kościół św. Barbary

Mały Rynek 8. **Map** 1 C4 (6 D2). ***Tel*** *012 428 15 00.* ◯ *during services.*

According to a legend St Barbara's Church was built using the bricks that were left over from the construction of the Church of St Mary. St Barbara's actually dates from 1394 to 1399, which coincides with one of the stages in the construction of St Mary's. Between 1415 and 1536 sermons were delivered in Polish in the former church, and in German in the latter. During this period the patricians of Cracow were mostly German and it was only much later that they became a minority among the Polish population. In 1586 the church was taken over by the Jesuits. Piotr Skarga preached here and Jakub Wujek, the translator of the Bible, is buried here. Added on the outside from 1488 to 1518 is a late Gothic chapel with a porch decorated with sculptures made by Veit Stoss' workshop. Furnishings date mostly from the 18th century but there is also an interesting early 15th-century Pietà in stone and a 15th-century crucifix on the high altar.

The Gothic porch with Christ in Gethsemane at St Barbara's

Market Square ❹

Rynek Główny

See pp98–101.

Christopher Palace ❺

Pałac Krzysztofory

Rynek Główny 35. **Map** 1 C4 (6 D2). **Museum of Cracow *Tel*** *012 619 23 00.* ◯ *May–Oct: 10am–5:30pm Wed–Sun; Nov–Apr: 9am–4pm Wed, Fri & Sat, 10am–5pm Thu. Closed 2nd Sat & Sun every month.* **www.**krakow.pl

This is one of the oldest and most beautiful palaces in Cracow, with a magnificent arcaded courtyard. It was remodelled in 1682 to 1685 by Jacopo Solari for Kazimierz Wodzicki, one of the richest noblemen in Lesser Poland.

The Palace is named after St Christopher, whose 14th-century statue decorates the building. It houses the Museum of Cracow, which is dedicated to the history and culture of the city. Old documents, maces, gold artifacts from local workshops, memorabilia and paintings are all on display. In the cellars there is a café and the art gallery of the Cracow Group (Grupa Krakowska), first established in 1930 and revived in 1957.

THE KHAN OF CRACOW

Every year, on the Thursday ending the Corpus Christi octave, a parade led by the Khan proceeds from the Convent of the Premonstratensian Nuns in Zwierzyniec to the Market Square. The event commemorates the victory over the Tatars in 1287. On his way, the Khan strikes some spectators with his mace, a sign which is thought to bring good luck, especially to girls. At the Market Square the Khan receives a symbolic tribute. The original costume of the Khan, designed in 1904 by Stanisław Wyspiański, is now in the Museum of Cracow.

The Khan of Cracow

Town Hall Tower 6

Wieża Ratuszowa

Rynek Główny 1. **Map** 1 C4 (6 D2). **Museum** ***Tel*** *012 619 23 00.* *May–Oct: 10:30am–6pm daily.*

Until the early 19th century there were several public buildings on Market Square: the Town Hall, the Small Weigh-House, the Large Weigh-House and a pillory. The 70-m (230-ft) high Town Hall Tower is, unfortunately, the only structure to have survived. The Gothic Town Hall itself was remodelled many times and finally demolished in 1846. The present dome is Baroque. The tower houses a branch of the Museum of Cracow dedicated to the history of local government and is a venue for the Ludowy Theatre.

Church of St Adalbert on Market Square

Cloth Hall 7

Sukiennice

See pp102–3.

Statue of Adam Mickiewicz 8

Pomnik Adama Mickiewicza

Rynek Główny. **Map** 1 C4 (6 D2).

The statue of the poet Adam Mickiewicz has occasioned, as often happens in Cracow, many scandals. Although the famous artist Jan Matejko had submitted a project, the competition was won by Teodor Rygier. After the statue was unveiled in 1895 it raised such criticism that the artist was forced to replace some of the figures.

The allegorical figures accompanying the poet represent the Motherland (a maiden facing Sienna Street), Education (an old man lecturing a boy), Poetry (a female figure playing a lute) and Patriotism or Courage (the soldier facing the Cloth Hall).

St Adalbert's Church 9

Kościół św. Wojciecha

Rynek Główny 3. **Map** 1 C4 (6 D2). **Museum of the History of the Market Square** (Muzeum Dziejów Rynku). *May–Sep: 9am–4pm Mon–Tue& Thu–Fri, 9am–1pm Wed, 1–5pm Sun.*

The small church of St Adalbert is one of the oldest in Cracow. A legend tells that St Adalbert preached here before leaving on his missionary journey to try to convert the Prussians in 997. The architecture of the church amalgamates several styles, from Romanesque and Gothic, through Renaissance and Baroque, to the modern interior design. This mixture reflects various stages in the development of the Market Square, an exhibition on which is located in the basement. The display includes a cross-section of the ground beneath the square, as well as medieval water pipes and other objects found during the excavations carried out after World War II, which have also revealed the remnants of the building dating from the time of St Adalbert.

Statue of Adam Mickiewicz in Market Square

Church of St Mary ❶
Kościół Mariacki

St Mary's, or the Church of the Assumption of the Virgin, was the main parish church of Cracow's burghers. It is a Gothic basilica composed of nave, aisles and side chapels. There are two towers. The north tower was extended in the early 15th century and in 1478 topped with a spire by Matthias Heringk. It was the city's watch-tower. Inside the church there are many outstanding works of art, among which the magnificent high altar by Veit Stoss *(see pp96–7)* should be mentioned. Other furnishings include the Baroque pulpit, marble altars decorated with paintings by the Italian artist Giovanni Battista Pittoni, and Renaissance tombs in the chapels.

South Bell Tower

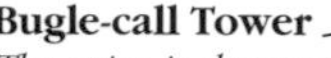

Bugle-call Tower
The spire is decorated with turrets and topped by a gilt crown. The famous bugle-call (hejnał) is played here at hourly intervals and broadcast at noon by the Polish radio.

The tracery of the Great West Window was designed by Jan Matejko and the stained glass is by Józef Mehoffer and Stanisław Wyspiański.

The Porch (1750-52)
The late-Baroque porch was designed by Francesco Placidi. Carved busts of the Apostles and saints by Karol Hukan were added to the door panels in 1929.

Main entrance

TIMELINE

- **1221–2** Building of the Romanesque church
- **End of the 13th century** Construction of the Gothic church begins
- **1355–65** New choir built
- **1392–7** Nave and aisles built
- **1477–89** High altar completed
- **1478** North tower receives a spire
- **1585** Choir stalls completed

1200 | 1300 | 1400 | 1500 | 1600

Detail of the main door

Choir Stalls
The stalls were made in 1585 but the biblical scenes in low relief which decorate the backs of the seats date from 1635.

VISITORS' CHECKLIST

Mariacki Sq 5. **Map** 1 C4 (6 D2).
11:30am–6pm Mon–Fri, 2–6pm Sun and during services.

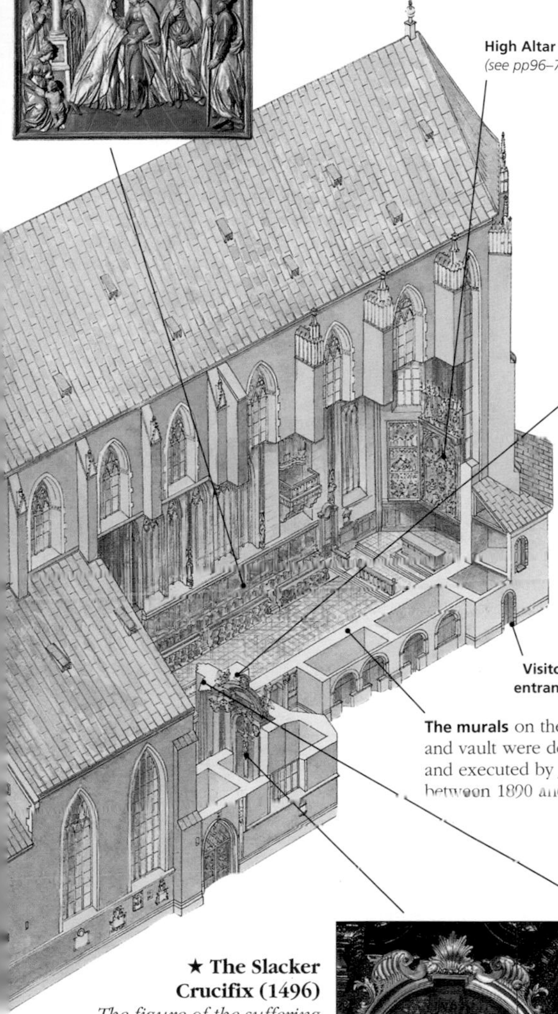

High Altar
(see pp96–7)

The Montelupi Tomb
This Mannerist tomb of one of the richest Cracow families was made around 1600 in the workshop of Santi Gucci.

Visitors entrance

The murals on the walls and vault were designed and executed by Jan Matejko between 1890 and 1892.

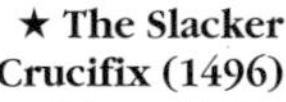

★ The Slacker Crucifix (1496)
The figure of the suffering Christ, carved in stone by Veit Stoss, is the most expressive sculpture ever made by the artist.

★ The Ciborium
This Renaissance ciborium (receptacle for containing the Eucharist) at the entrance to the choir was made around 1552 to the design by Giovanni Maria Mosca.

STAR SIGHTS

- ★ The Ciborium
- ★ The Slacker Crucifix

Exploring St Mary's: The High Altar

The high altar by Veit Stoss was made between 1477 and 1489. It is dedicated, like the church itself, to the Assumption of the Virgin Mary. The altar is a polyptych, some 11 m (36 ft) long and 12 m (39 ft) high. It was even higher originally. The iconography determined its composition. The shutters were closed throughout the liturgical year but opened during important church feasts. The treatment of the human figure is naturalistic, dynamic and dramatically expressive. The low reliefs and figures of saints are masterpieces of late-Gothic art.

The Lamentation
The design of this particular panel was influenced by Netherlandish painting.

The Meeting of St Anne and St Joachim

The middle shutters are opened every day at noon.

The Capture of Christ

The Birth of the Virgin

The Crucifixion

The Three Maries at the Sepulchre

The Descent into Hell

The Presentation of the Virgin in the Temple

The Entombment

The Risen Christ appearing to Mary Magdalene

The Presentation of Christ in the Temple
In this scene the artist tries to recreate the interior of the temple.

Christ Among the Doctors
This scene testifies to Stoss' masterly depiction of the diverse physiognomies.

VEIT STOSS (WIT STWOSZ)

Veit Stoss (1447–1533), one of the greatest wood-carvers of the late Gothic age, was born in Horb am Neckar in Germany. He lived in Cracow from 1477 to 1496, where he was exempted from paying taxes by the City Council. He created a number of sculptural works here.

The Assumption
Mary and Christ are raised to Heaven by eight angels.

The Coronation of the Virgin

St Adalbert

St Stanisław

The Annunciation

The Nativity

The Ascension

The Resurrection

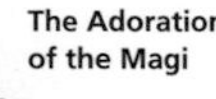

The Adoration of the Magi

Pentecost

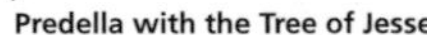

Predella with the Tree of Jesse

The Death of the Virgin
The figure of the youthful Mary is one of the greatest sculptures ever made in Poland.

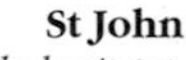

St John
Slightly hesitant, the saint is about to put a cape on the fainting Mary.

Market Square: North and West Sides ❹

The charter given to Cracow in 1257 determined the plan of the city. The square located in the middle of the medieval city has remained the centre of Cracow ever since. This square, some 200 m (656 ft) by 200 m (656 ft), is surrounded by a regular grid of streets, with three streets on each side. Only the off-the-grid location of the Church of St Mary, which pre-dates the charter, and Grodzka Street, with its funnel-like shape, vary the rigidity of the urban planning in this area. There were formerly many buildings in the square, but of those the Cloth Hall and the Town Hall Tower are the only ones to have survived. The square was a venue for many important events, including coronation ceremonies.

Deer House
This was once an inn. Johann Wolfgang von Goethe and Tsar Nicholas I both stayed here.

NORTH SIDE

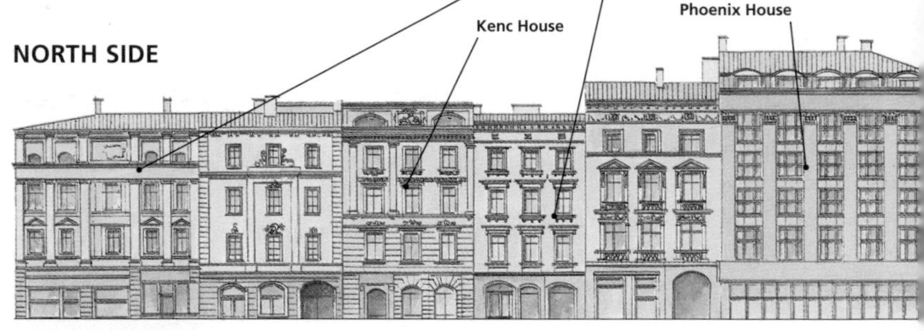

Palace of the Rams (Pałac Pod Baranami)
One of the most magnificent palaces owned by the Potocki family now houses a famous cabaret.

"PIWNICA POD BARANAMI" CABARET

The cabaret which is housed in the Palace of the Rams was established in 1956. Although it was originally intended to exist no longer than "five years, possibly even less", the cabaret has been active for more than 50 years and is one of Cracow's top attractions. Piotr Skrzynecki (1930–97) was the founder and heart and soul of the cabaret. Wiesław Dymny, Ewa Demarczyk, Marek Grechuta, Krystyna Zachwatowicz, Zygmunt Konieczny, Leszek Wójtowicz, Anna Szałapak, Grzegorz Turnau and Zbigniew Preisner were among the best-known contributors and performers. The cabaret is a lively place full of poetry and music, joy and laughter.

Piotr Skrzynecki

WEST SIDE

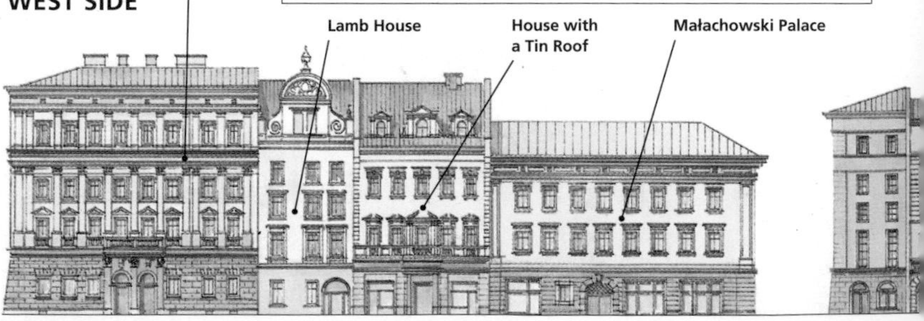

Betman House
This is also known as "Under the Beheaded" after a bas-relief which depicts the martyrdom of St John the Baptist.

LOCATOR MAP

Market Square: North and West sides

42 Market Square belonged to the Boner family and in the 19th century to the renowned collector Feliks Manggha Jasieński.

Margrave's House
A former mint and presently a bank, the façade of this house features a splendid Rococo portal.

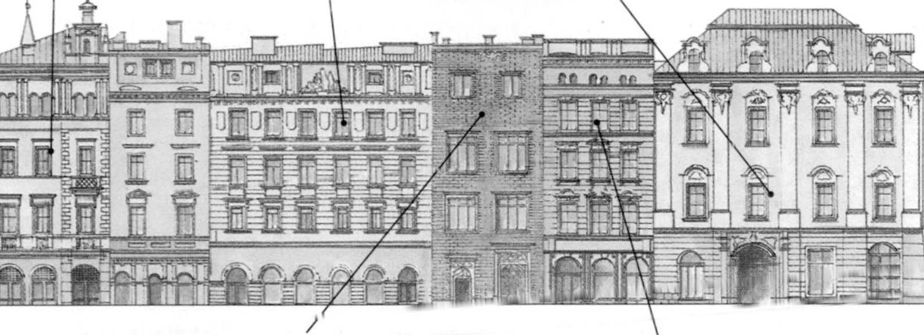

Red House

Eagle House (Dom Pod Orłem)
The basement of this fine Renaissance house formerly housed the Starmach Gallery of contemporary art.

House under Three Stars

Christopher Palace (Pałac Krzysztofory)
This palace houses the Museum of Cracow, among whose highlights is a gilded plaque, made in 1609, depicting St Eligius.

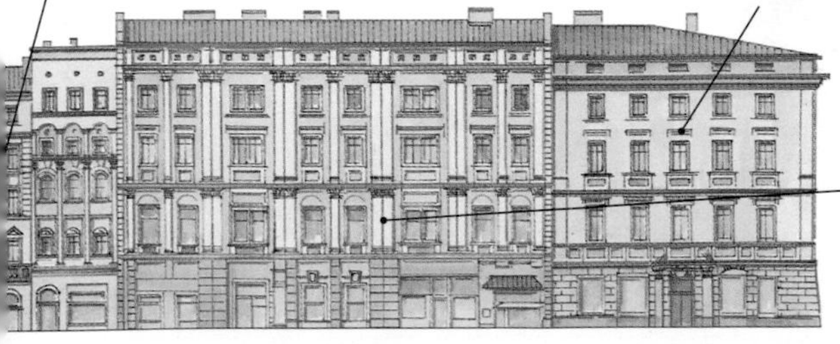

Spiš Palace (Pałac Spiski) is home to the exclusive Hawełka Restaurant.

Market Square: South and East Sides ❹

There are many stories about the Market Square. According to one of the legends Cracow's pigeons are the enchanted knights of Duke Henryk Probus, who agreed to their metamorphosis in exchange for gold that he needed to secure papal acceptance for his coronation. The knights were supposed to regain their human form after the coronation. But the duke lost the gold and his knights are still awaiting the promised transformation. The legend about the two brothers who built the St Mary's towers is more popular. When the older mason completed the taller tower he stabbed his younger brother to death in order to prevent him from surpassing his work but then, remorseful, killed himself.

Madonna House (Dom Pod Obrazem)
Formerly the palace of a wealthy burgher family called Cellari, its façade is decorated with the Madonna painted in 1718.

SOUTH SIDE

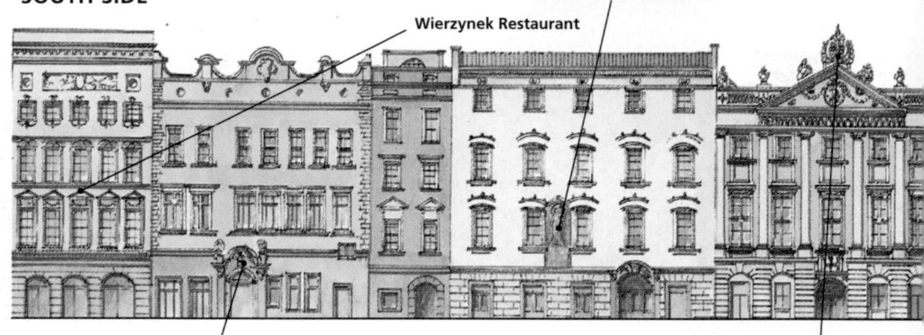

Wierzynek Restaurant

Hetman's House (Kamienica Hetmańska)
The Baroque portal leads to shops on the ground floor, in which Gothic vaults with carved keystones have survived.

Potocki Palace (Pałac Potockich)
Behind the Neo-Classical façade the original interiors and a small arcaded courtyard have survived.

4 Market Square
This is one of a few houses with Art Nouveau decoration. It was added during the remodelling carried out in 1907–8 by Ludwik Wojtyczka.

EAST SIDE

Grey House (Kamienica Szara)

Prince's House (Kamienica Książęca) *The famous sorcerer Master Twardowski is reputed to have lived here in the 16th century. The house is decorated with a statue of St Giovanni da Capistrano.*

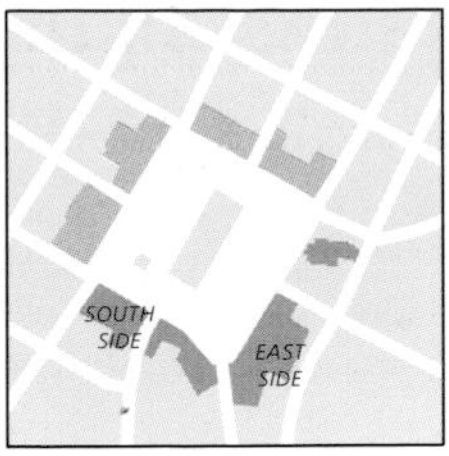

Lanckoroński House, also known as 'Under the Evangelists', features the remnants of an 18th-century chapel on the first floor.

The pharmacy 'Under the Gold Crown' was once housed here. Its emblem has survived above the entrance.

Kromer House (Kamienica Kromerowska)

Canary House (Kamienica Pod Kanarkiem)

LOCATOR MAP

Market Square: South and East sides

SOUTH SIDE

EAST SIDE

The Raven House (Kamienica Pod Krukiem) is a seat of the International Centre of Culture and Cracow's Cultural Club.

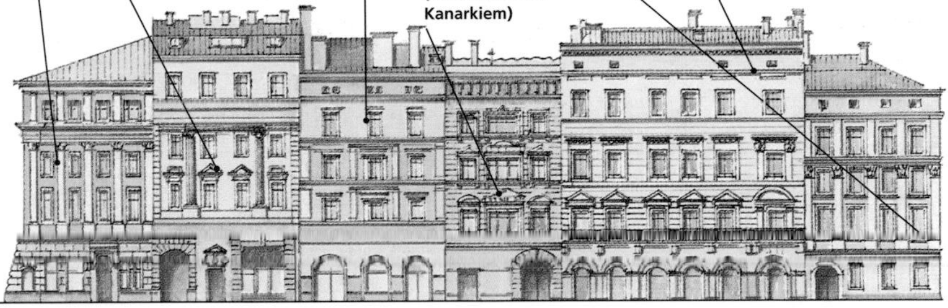

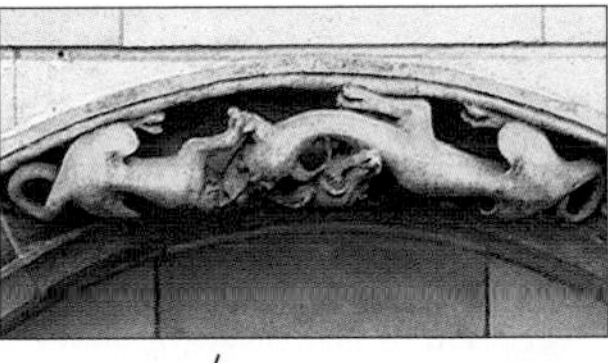

Lizards House (Kamienica Pod Jaszczurami) *Gothic vaults have survived in this house, in which a student club is located.*

Italian House (Dom Włoski) *The first Polish post office was housed here and coaches passed through this arch.*

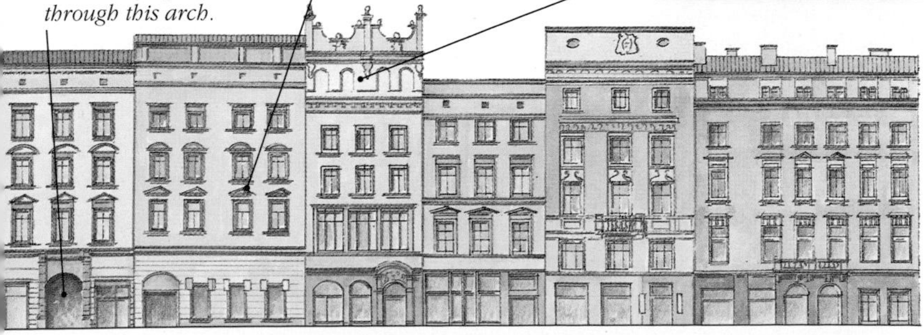

Boner House (Kamienica Bonerowska) *This is topped by a beautiful Mannerist parapet decorated with herms.*

The Cloth Hall (Sukiennice) ❼

A mask from the parapet

The Cloth Hall originated from a covered market. A stone structure protecting the stalls, with an internal passage, was probably here at the time of Kazimierz the Great. It was rebuilt to the design of Giovanni Maria Mosca following a fire in 1555, and remodelled entirely in 1875 by Tomasz Pryliński. The Gallery of 19th-century Polish Painting is housed here. The stalls sell a variety of souvenirs. The Noworolski Café, one of the best in Cracow, is a good place to relax after seeing the paintings.

***Folly* (1894) by Władysław Podkowiński**
This Modernist painting aroused much controversy. It began a Symbolist phase in Podkowiński's career.

***Four-in-hand* (1881) by Józef Chełmoński**
Paintings by Symbolists as well as Realists are exhibited alongside the Four-in-hand.

Roof with sunken rafters

Entrance to stalls

Arcades
The side arcades and oriels were added during the rebuilding in 1875. The arcades echo the medieval architecture of Venice.

The Renaissance parapet is not only decorative but also offers protection from fire.

★ ***Blue Hussars* by Piotr Michałowski**
A separate room is dedicated to the work of Michałowski, the foremost Polish Romantic artist who lived between 1800 and 1855.

VISITORS' CHECKLIST

Market Square 1/3. **Map** 1 C4 (6 D2). ***Tel*** *012 422 11 66.* *May–Oct: 10am–7pm Tue, Fri & Sat, 10am–3:30pm Wed, Thu & Sun; Nov–Apr: 10am–3:30pm Tue, Thu, Sat & Sun, 10am–6pm Wed & Fri.* *free Thu (May–Oct), Sun (Nov–Apr).*

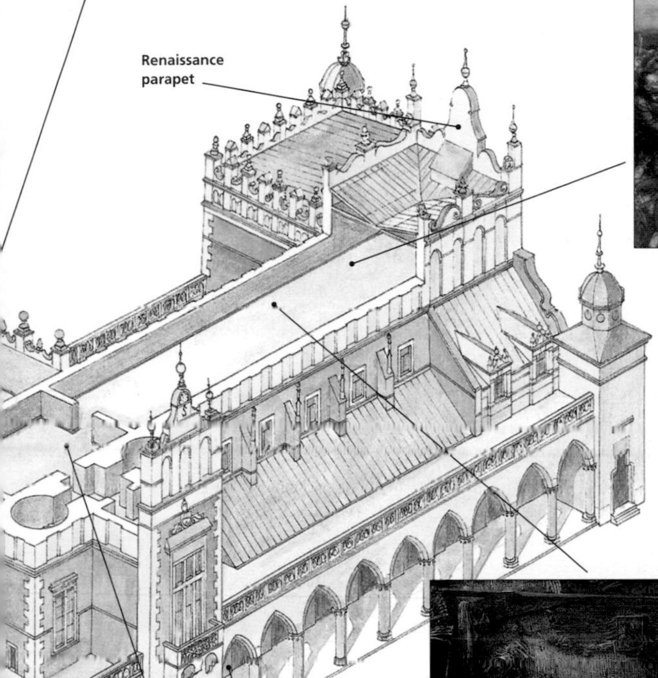

Renaissance parapet

★ ***Wernyhora* by Jan Matejko**
Jan Matejko and Henryk Siemiradzki were both exponents of 19th-century history painting which is displayed in the room dominated by Matejko's Prussian Homage.

Entrance to Gallery of Polish Painting

***The Death of Ellenai* by Jacek Malczewski**
Characteristic of the artist's early work, which was permeated by the memories of people who had been imprisoned in Siberia, this painting was inspired by a poem by Juliusz Słowacki.

***The Chocim Treaty* by Marcello Bacciarelli**
Late 18th- and early 19th-century Neo-Classical paintings are displayed in the same room.

STAR PAINTINGS

- ★ *Blue Hussars* by Piotr Michałowski
- ★ *Wernyhora* by Jan Matejko

JOHN PAUL II

Statue of John Paul II in the courtyard of the Episcopal Palace

Karol Wojtyła was born in 1920 in Wadowice *(see p158)*, but lived in Cracow for many years. He arrived here in 1938 to read Polish philology at the Jagiellonian University. The outbreak of World War II put a stop to his studies. During the war he worked for the Solvay Chemical Plant and was active in the underground Rhapsody Theatre. In 1942 he entered the underground theological Seminary. As a devout priest and artists' friend, he became very popular. Despite his election to the Apostolic See in 1978 his links with Cracow remained as close as ever. He continued to return here with his apostolic missions on many different occasions, until his death in 2005.

Episcopal Palace ⑩

Pałac Biskupi

Franciszkańska 3. **Map** 1 C5 (5 C3). ***Tel*** *012 429 74 14.* *1,2, 7, 8,18, 36, 38.* *to the public.*

First recorded in the 13th century, this is one of the oldest buildings in Cracow. It was damaged by fire and remodelled several times. Giovanni Maria Mosca contributed to the decoration. The present palace dates from the times of Bishop Piotr Tomicki (16th century) and Bishop Piotr Gembicki (17th century). A fire in 1850 caused extensive damage but the splendid furnishings have partly survived.

John Paul II lived here between 1964 and 1978. He was then the Archbishop of Cracow. A statue of him, made in 1980 by Ione Sensi Croci, is in the courtyard.

Collegium Novum ⑪

Gołębia 24. **Map** 1 B4 (5 C3). ***Tel*** *012 422 10 33.* *1, 2, 7, 8, 15, 18, 36, 38.*

The Collegium Novum replaced the Jerusalem College after it was destroyed by fire in the 19th century. The ruins were demolished between 1883 and 1887 and the new building constructed. Its official opening turned into a patriotic demonstration attended symbolically by delegations from all three parts of the partitioned Poland. According to the contemporary records the architect of the new building, Feliks Księżarski, intended to emulate the vernacular architecture, especially the crystal vaults and decoration of the Collegium Maius, but in fact he imitated German and Austrian models. The magnificent staircase is similar to the one in the Town Hall in Vienna. The College is the seat of the Rector of the Jagiellonian University. It also houses departmental offices, the bursary and the Great Hall where inauguration and graduation ceremonies take place. The Hall has a beamed and coffered ceiling and is decorated with portraits by Jan Matejko.

Statue of Copernicus ⑫

Pomnik Mikołaja Kopernika

Gołębia. **Map** 1 B4 (5 C3). *1, 2, 8, 15, 18, 36, 38.*

The statue of Nicolaus Copernicus was made in 1900 by Cyprian Godebski. The astronomer is represented as a young scholar holding an astrolabe. The statue was originally in the courtyard of the Collegium Maius, but was moved to the present location in front of the Witkowski College in 1953. The statue was intended to function as a fountain.

Collegium Maius ⑬

See pp106–7.

Collegium Nowodvorianum ⑭

Św. Anny 12. **Map** 1 B4 (5 C2). ***Tel*** *012 422 0411.* *4, 8, 14, 15, 18, 36, 38.* *124, 152, 192, 502.*

The Collegium Nowod–vorianum was founded by Bartłomiej Nowodworski, a Knight Hospitaller of St John, Secretary to the King and a warrior in the Battle of Lepanto. This foundation was a result of his bequest of 1617 to the Classes, one of the university colleges and the first secular secondary school in Cracow, established in 1586. The Collegium was

The Neo-Gothic building of the Collegium Novum

Arcaded courtyard of the Collegium Nowodvorianum

built between 1636 and 1643 by Jan Leitner. A beautiful courtyard with arcades and a grand stairway is one of the best preserved Baroque buildings in Cracow. The offices of the Collegium Medicum are housed here.

Church of St Anne ⓯

Kościół św. Anny

See pp108–9.

Old Theatre ⓰

Teatr Stary

Jagiellońska 1. **Map** 1 C4 (5 C2). ***Tel*** *012 422 40 40.* *2, 4, 7, 8, 13, 14, 15, 38.* *124, 152, 192, 502.* **Museum** *11am–1pm Tue–Sat and one hour prior to performances.*

The Old, or Modrzejewska Theatre is named after the great actress Helena Modrzejewska. The oldest theatre building in Poland, it has been in use continuously since 1798. It was remodelled in the Neo-Renaissance style between 1830 and 1843 by Tomasz Majewski and Karol Kremer. The next major rebuilding was undertaken from 1903 to 1905 by Franciszek Mączyński and Tadeusz Stryjeński. The reinforced concrete construction applied to the interior, and the exterior Art Nouveau decoration, both date from this time. The stucco frieze was made in 1906 by Józef Gardecki. The plaques on the Jagiellońska Street side commemorate the composer Władysław Żeleński, the director Konrad Swinarski and the actor Wiktor Sadecki.

The Old Theatre is regarded as one of the best in Poland. Many outstanding directors have worked here, including Zygmunt Hübner, Konrad Swinarski, Andrzej Wajda and Jerzy Jarocki.

There is a small theatre museum on the ground floor, and the Mask café, run by the actors, in the basement.

Palace of Art ⓱

Pałac Sztuki

Plac Szczepański 4. **Map** 1 C4 (5 C2). ***Tel*** *012 422 66 16.* *2, 4, 7, 8, 13, 14, 15, 38.* *124, 152, 192, 502.* *Nov–Apr: 8am–6pm daily; May–Oct: 8am–8pm daily.*

In 1854 the Friends of the Fine Arts Society was established in Cracow for the encouragement of Polish art. The Society embarked upon the organization of exhibitions by living artists, the acquisition of paintings and sculptures and the setting up of a comprehensive records office gathering documents of the history of Polish art in the 19th and early 20th centuries. The Art Nouveau building was designed by Franciszek Màczyński and modelled on the famous Secession Pavilion in Vienna. The finest Cracow artists worked on the decoration. Jacek Malczewski designed the frieze depicting the vicissitudes of fortune and the struggle of artistic genius. The sculptors Antoni Madeyski, Konstanty Laszczka and Teodor Rygier contributed busts of great Polish artists. A portico attached to the façade is topped with a statue of Apollo crowned with a sun halo. Exhibitions of 19th-century and contemporary art are held here.

Sculptural decoration on the Palace of Art

"Bunker of Art" ⓲

"Bunkier Sztuki"

Plac Szczepański 3a. **Map** 1 C4 (5 C2). ***Tel*** *012 423 12 43.* *2, 4, 7, 8, 13, 14, 15, 38.* *124, 152, 192, 502.* *11am–6pm Tue–Sun.*

This gloomy building in the Socialist Realist style of the 1960s, which replaced an Art Nouveau coffee house, is regarded as one of the ugliest in the city centre. However, in recent years it has become a venue for some of the most interesting exhibitions of contemporary art, by both Polish and foreign artists.

Collegium Maius ⓭

The Collegium Maius is the oldest building within the Academy of Cracow (now the Jagiellonian University). It was constructed in the 15th century by amalgamating a number of town houses. Lecture rooms and accommodation for professors were originally located here. In the 19th century the building housed the Jagiellonian Library. Between 1840 and 1870 the architects Karol Kremer, Feliks Księżarski and Hermann Bergman rebuilt the college in the Neo-Gothic style. After World War II the University Museum, established in 1867, was moved here.

★ Libraria
The Libraria was built in the 16th century as the College Library. Today it is a meeting place of the Senate and is decorated with portraits of rectors and professors of the University.

Oriel
This oriel window projecting from the Stuba Communis enlivens the austere exterior wall.

★ Stuba Communis
The Stuba Communis, or Common Room, served as the professors' refectory. The hall features a 14th-century statue of Kazimierz the Great and a 17th-century staircase made in Danzig.

University Treasury
The insignia of the rector, including a late 15th-century mace bequeathed by Bishop Zbigniew Oleśnicki and that of Queen Jadwiga from around 1405, are among the treasures.

Copernicus Room
The Room is dedicated to the great astronomer, who studied here between 1491 and 1495, thus rendering the Academy famous. The display features the so-called Jagiellonian armillary sphere made in 1510.

Cloister
The Gothic cloister, whose columns have a cut crystal-like decoration, is reminiscent of those in medieval Italian universities.

VISITORS' CHECKLIST

Jagiellońska 15. **Map** 1 B/C4 (5 C2). **Tel** 012 422 05 49. 124, 502. 2, 4, 7, 8, 13, 14, 15, 18, 38. 10am–3pm Mon–Fri (–6pm Thu May–Oct), 10am–2pm Sat.

A lavishly inlaid door was originally in the Senior Room of the old Town Hall.

Green Hall
A collection of national memorabilia, including the piano that Frédéric Chopin played, can be visited by prior arrangement.

Rector's Stairs

★ Great Hall
The Great Hall features stalls used by the Senate during the ceremonies at which honorary degrees are conferred.

Chapel
The former apartment of John of Kęty, the Professor of Theology who became the patron saint of the Jagiellonian University, has been converted into a chapel, which is on the ground floor.

STAR SIGHT

- ★ Great Hall
- ★ Libraria
- ★ Stuba Communis

Church of St Anne ⓯

St Anne

A professor of the Cracow Academy, John of Kęty (Jan Kanty) was already considered a saint at the time of his death in 1473, when he was buried in the Gothic Church of St Anne. Following his beatification, the Senate of the Academy commissioned Tylman van Gameren to build a new church. The construction began in 1689 under the supervision of Father Sebastian Piskorski. The Italian architect and sculptor Baldassare Fontana contributed the decoration and most of the furnishings, including the altars, between 1695 and 1703. He was assisted by the painters Carlo and Innocente Monti and Karl Dankwart. St Anne's, with its sumptuous interior, is considered to be a leading example of Baroque ecclesiastical architecture in Poland.

Nave
The architecture, sculpture and painting all contribute to the decoration of the nave and vault, and exemplify particularly well the wholeness of the Baroque design.

Procession Commemorating St John of Kęty, 1767
To mark the canonization of John of Kęty, a procession with his holy relics was held in Cracow. The saint's relics were carried into the Church of St Anne with great pomp and ceremony.

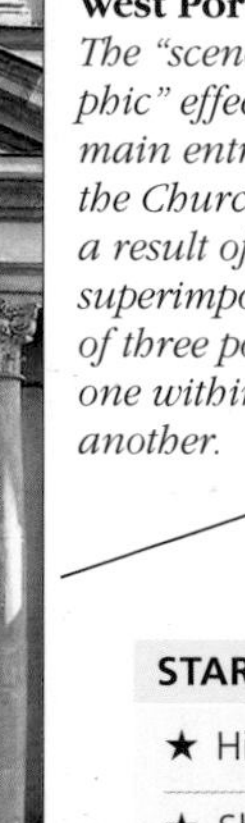

West Portal
The "scenographic" effect of the main entrance to the Church is a result of the superimposition of three portals, one within another.

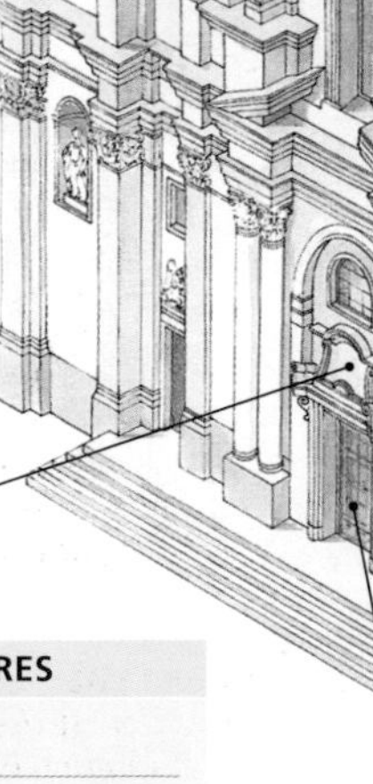

STAR FEATURES

★ High Altar

★ Shrine of St John of Kęty

Gloria Domini
The dome fresco by Carlo and Innocente Monti is an allegory of triumphant Catholicism, represented as the true Christian faith.

VISITORS' CHECKLIST

Św. Anny 11. **Map** 1 C4 (5 C2)
Tel *012 422 53 18.* 🚌 *124, 152, 192.* 🚋 *2, 4, 7, 8, 14, 15, 18, 36, 38.* ◯ *during services only.*

★ High Altar
The high altar is decorated with sculptures by Baldassare Fontana and the altarpiece, depicting the Virgin and Child with Anne, is by the painter to Jan III Sobieski, Jerzy Eleuter Siemiginowski.

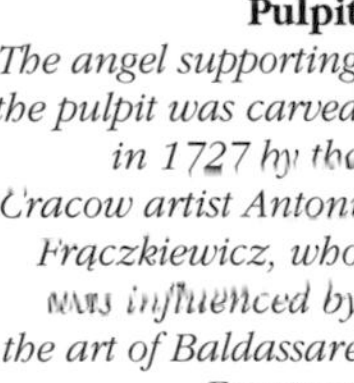

Pulpit
The angel supporting the pulpit was carved in 1727 by the Cracow artist Antoni Frączkiewicz, who was influenced by the art of Baldassare Fontana.

★ Shrine of St John of Kęty
The relics of the saint rest in a sarcophagus supported by four figures personifying the faculties of the Academy of Cracow: Theology, Philosophy, Law and Medicine.

Choir Stalls
The stalls are decorated with paintings by Szymon Czechowicz, a leading Polish painter of the 18th century.

Wyspiański Museum ⓳

Muzeum Stanisława Wyspiańskiego

ul. Szczepańska 11. **Map** 1 C4 (5 C2). ***Tel*** *012 422 70 21.* *124, 502.* *2, 4, 7, 8, 13, 14, 15, 38.* *10am–3:30pm Tue–Thu, Sat & Sun, 10am–6pm Fri.* *free Sun.* **www**.muzeum.krakow.pl

This museum, established in the 1980s as a branch of the National Museum, is devoted to the life and work of Stanisław Wyspiański, Cracow's foremost Art Nouveau artist (1869–1907). The multi-talented Wyspiański worked in many artforms, including writing plays, poetry, painting, cabinet making and architecture. The museum has recently moved into its current location, where the exhibits of particular interest include cartoons for stained glass and stage designs, as well as the model of Wawel Hill transformed into a Polish Acropolis *(see pp32–3).*

Helenka **by Stanisław Wyspiański**

Church of the Reformed Franciscans ⓴

Kościół Reformatów

Reformacka 4. **Map** 1 C4 (4 D1). ***Tel*** *012 422 06 23.* *124, 152, 192.* *2, 3, 4, 7, 8, 13, 14, 15, 19, 34, 38.* *during services only.*

The Church of the Reformed Franciscans was built between 1666 and 1672. The architecture and modest furnishings conform to the strict rule of the order. The altarpiece on the left that depicts St Kazimierz (Casimir) is an outstanding example of 17th-century work.

The specific microclimate within the crypt beneath the church causes the reposing corpses to undergo mummification. Those visitors seeking a shocking experience may request access.

Crucifix on the altar in the Church of St Mark

Church of St Mark ㉑

Kościół św. Marka

Św. Marka 10. **Map** 1 C4 (6 D1). ***Tel*** *012 422 21 78.* *124, 152, 192.* *3, 4, 5, 7, 13, 15, 19.* *during services only.*

The early Gothic church of the Monks of St Mark was founded in 1263 by Duke Bolesław the Chaste. It has been remodelled a number of times throughout its history and the interior acquired an early Baroque appearance in the first half of the 17th century. The high altar, with its lavish Mannerist ornamentation, was made in 1618 in the workshop of Baltazar Kuncz. On the left is the 17th-century tomb of Blessed Michał Giedroyć (died 1485).

Polish Academy of Skills ㉒

Gmach Polskiej Akademii Umiejętności

Sławkowska 17. **Map** 1 C4 (6 D1). ***Tel*** *012 424 02 00.* *124, 152, 192.* *3, 4, 5, 7, 15, 19.* *9am–4pm Mon–Fri.* **www**.pau.krakow.pl.

The building was constructed between 1857 and 1866 as the seat of the Academic Society of Cracow, which in 1872 became the Academy of Skills, the first academic body to bring together scholars from all three parts of partitioned Poland. It was designed by Filip Pokutyński in the Neo-Renaissance style. The exterior is decorated with portrait medallions of people in low relief who made important contributions to Polish academic and cultural life. Inside, a small meeting room features an impressive coffered ceiling. The rich print collection includes works by Albrecht Dürer and Rembrandt.

St John Street ㉓

Ulica św. Jana

Map 1 C4 (6 D2). *124, 152, 192.* *3, 4, 5, 7, 13, 15, 19, 34.*

This quiet street leading away from the Market Square, and closed off at its north end by

Portal to the House of the Cistercian Abbots of Jędrzejów, 20 St John Street

the façade of the Piarist Church, is lined with a selection of fine secular and ecclesiastic Baroque and Neo-Classical buildings.

The House of the Cistercian Abbots of Jędrzejów at No.20 is of particular interest. Remodelled in 1744 by Francesco Placidi, the house is decorated with a magnificent late Baroque portal featuring atlantes.

The Wodzicki Palace at No.11 was given a Neo-Classical façade by Ferdinand Nax after 1781. Around 1818 the Bernardine Friary was converted after a great deal of rebuilding.

St Florian's Gate at the end of Floriańska Street

Church of St John ㉔

Kościół św. Jana

Św. Jana 7. **Map** 1 C4 (6 D2). ***Tel*** *012 422 65 00.* *124, 152, 192.* *3, 4, 5, 7, 15, 19, 34.* *during services only.*

The chronicler Jan Długosz records that this church was founded in the 12th century. The Romanesque architecture has been lost through much remodelling. The Gothic buttresses still project from the exterior side walls, but the façade and the interior are Baroque. The high altar of 1730 is decorated with sculptures by Antoni Frączkiewicz and the 16th-century miraculous Madonna, the Refuge of Prisoners.

Czartoryski Museum ㉕

Muzeum Czartoryskich

See pp112–13.

Piarist Church ㉖

Kościół Pijarów

Pijarska 2. **Map** 1 C4 (6 D1). ***Tel*** *012 422 22 55.* *124, 152, 192.* *3, 4, 5, 7, 13, 15, 19, 34.* *during services only.*

This Baroque church was built between 1718 and 1728 probably to designs by Kacper Bażanka. The Rococo façade designed by Francesco Placidi was added in 1759 to 1761. Inside, the church is decorated with frescoes by a master of illusion, Franz Eckstein. The high altar painted on the wall is by the same artist, as is the fresco in the nave vault that glorifies the name of the Virgin Mary. The altars in the aisles feature 18th-century paintings by Szymon Czechowicz.

The crypt under the church is renowned for the decoration of Christ's Tomb, which usually alludes symbolically to patriotic themes, and is set up here every year during Holy Week. The crypt is also a venue for theatre performances and various exhibitions.

The Rococo façade of the 18th-century Piarist Church

St Florian's Gate and the City Wall Remnants ㉗

Brama Floriańska i Resztki Murów Miejskich

Map 2 D4 (6 E1). *124, 152, 192.* *3, 4, 5, 7, 13, 15, 19, 34.*

In 1285 Duke Leszek the Black gave Cracow the right to have the city surrounded by walls. These fortifications developed during the following centuries, finally consisting of inner and outer moated walls and 47 towers. Eight fortified gates lead into the city. With the introduction of artillery, the defence system became redundant. Disused, it fell into disrepair by the end of the 18th century. The walls were dismantled early in the 19th century and later replaced by the Planty gardens *(see pp166–67)*. St Florian's Gate, dating possibly from the end of the 13th century, and a small stretch of the adjoining walls have been saved, largely through the efforts of Professor Feliks Radwański. East of St Florian's Gate is the Haberdashers' Tower, and the towers of the Joiners and Carpenters are to the west.

Czartoryski Museum ㉕

At the core of the Czartoryski Museum is the collection assembled late in the 18th century by Princess Izabella Czartoryska. It was initially at Puławy, but partly moved to Paris following the 1830 November Uprising. In 1876 the collection was brought to Cracow, thanks to the efforts of Prince Władysław Czartoryski. It is located in three houses and the adjoining City Arsenal at St John Street. Works of art are displayed in period interiors which contribute to the museum's homely, intimate atmosphere.

Madonna and Child
By the Venetian Vincenzo Catena, this painting is a highlight of the Czartoryski's Italian collection.

Jesuit Saints
This fine bas-relief by the 17th-century Roman sculptor, Alessandro Algardi, depicts the Polish Jesuit, Stanisław Kostka, being admitted to the congregation of Jesuit saints.

GALLERY GUIDE
There is no gallery space on the ground floor. The first-floor display is dedicated to Polish history of the 14th-18th centuries as well as Western European decorative arts. The picture gallery is on the second floor.

Porcelain Figures
These two figures of a Polish nobleman and noblewoman were made in Meissen.

Entrance

Nautilus Cup
The museum collection is rich in decorative arts and includes this 17th-century drinking vessel made in Danzig (now Gdańsk) from a large shell.

★ *Lady with an Ermine* by Leonardo da Vinci
This late 15th-century work probably portrays Cecilia Gallerani.

VISITORS' CHECKLIST

Św. Jana 19. **Map** 1 C4 (6 D1). ***Tel*** *012 422 55 66.* *3, 4, 5, 7, 15, 19.* *124, 152, 192.* *May–Oct: 10am–4pm Tue & Thu, 10am–7pm Wed, Fri & Sat, 10am–3pm Sun; Nov–Apr: 10am–3:30pm Tue, Thu, Sat & Sun, 10am–6pm Wed & Fri.*

***Portrait of a Boy* by Caspar Netscher**
This sweet little portrait is one of several paintings in the collection by lesser Dutch artists of the 17th century.

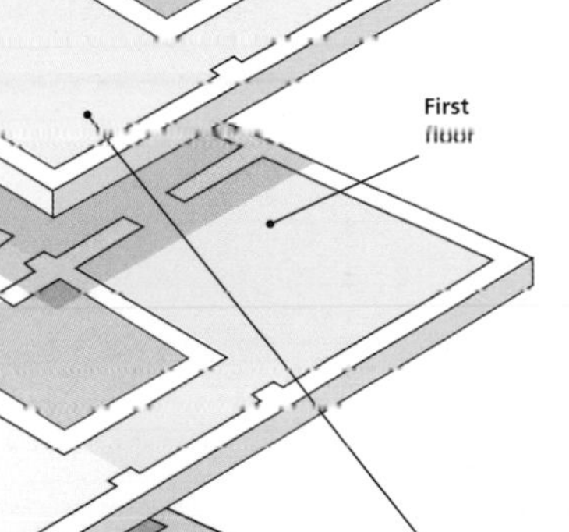

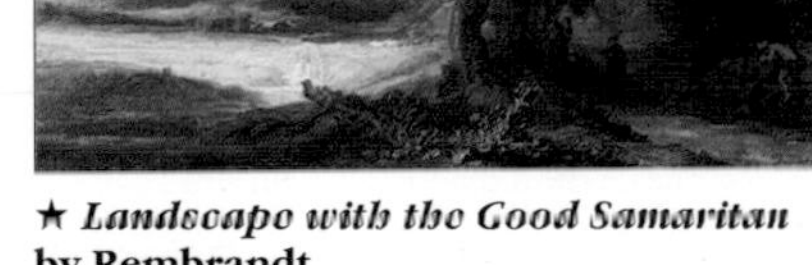

★ *Landscape with the Good Samaritan* by Rembrandt
One of the masterpieces in the collection of Western painting, Rembrandt's treatment of the natural world is breathtaking.

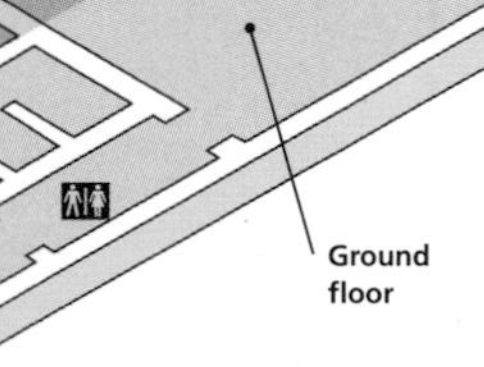

***Landscape* by Alessandro Magnasco**
This dramatic landscape is characteristic of Italian painting of the 18th century.

STAR PAINTINGS

- ★ Lady with an Ermine
- ★ Landscape with the Good Samaritan

KEY

- Non-exhibition space
- History of Poland 1300–1900
- Decorative Arts of Western Europe
- Picture Gallery

The impressive exterior of the Barbican

Barbican ㉘

Barbakan

Basztowa. **Map** 2 D3 (6 E1). *3, 4, 5, 7, 13, 15.* *124, 152, 192.*

The Barbican, a round bastion, was constructed in 1498–99 after King Jan Olbracht was defeated by the Turks in Bukowina, and further Turkish incursions were feared. It shows the changes that had been introduced to military architecture as a result of the rapid development of artillery. This relatively low structure projecting from the city walls with a considerable overhang enabled the defenders to fire with precision at the enemy from the loop-holes, positioned at different levels. The Barbican was originally surrounded by a moat and linked to St Florian's Gate by a corridor. It is the best preserved barbican in Europe.

Jama Michalika Café ㉙

Jama Michalika

Floriańska 45. **Map** 2 D4 (6 E1). ***Tel*** *012 422 15 61.* *3, 4, 5, 7, 13, 15, 34.* *124, 152, 192.* *noon–midnight daily.*

In 1895 Jan Michalik opened a patisserie near the Market Square. It became very popular with students of the Fine Arts School who called the place *jama* (grotto) for its lack of windows. Poets, writers and artists soon joined in and in 1905 established here the cabaret Zielony Balonik (The Green Balloon). The performances, based on texts by Tadeusz Boy-Żeleński, soon attracted a large audience. Satirical Christmas puppet shows, with marionettes by Ludwik Puget and Jan Szczepkowski, became particularly popular.

In 1910 Michalik extended and redecorated the premises to designs by Franciszek Mączyński. The main room received a glass ceiling. Karol Frycz designed the interior decoration, furniture and most of the stained glass in the Art Nouveau style.

The café is still an inviting place where customers can go back in time and enjoy the atmosphere of the fin de siècle, as well as see the enduring puppet show.

The interior of the Jama Michalika Café

Matejko House ㉚

Dom Matejki

Floriańska 41. **Map** 2 D4 (6 E1). ***Tel*** *012 422 59 26.* *3, 4, 5, 7, 13, 15, 34.* *124, 152, 192.* *10am–3:30pm Wed–Sun.*

The artist Jan Matejko was born here in 1838, and in 1873 returned to live with his family. He rebuilt the house and added a new façade designed by Tomasz Pryliński in the Neo-Baroque style. After Matejko died in 1893 the house was transformed into a museum and opened to the public five years later. The statue of a hussar on horseback, on the ground floor, was part of Leon Wyczółkowski's design for the Matejko Monument. The private rooms on the first floor have remained unchanged, whilst the second floor is used for a display of the artist's works, which include cartoons for the murals that are in the Church of St Mary. His studio on the third floor is full of props and curiosities he collected. Pieces of old armour and instruments of torture excavated on the site of the old Town Hall are of particular interest.

Floriańska Street ㉛

Ulica Floriańska

Map 1 C4, 2 D4 (6 D2, 6 E1, 2). *3, 5, 7, 13, 15, 19, 34.* *124, 152, 192.*

This street, leading from St Florian's Gate to the Market Square, formed part of the Royal Route which became fully established after the court moved from Cracow

Visitors in front of St Florian's Gate on Floriańska Street

to Warsaw. The Royal Route was often used by a sovereign arriving for a coronation, and again when his body was taken in procession for the funeral at Wawel. In the 19th century Floriańska was the busiest street in Cracow, with trams introduced in 1881. Medieval walls have survived in most houses, but the original architecture has been lost through later remodelling. More storeys and new eclectic façades were added to most buildings early in the 20th century, when Floriańska gained its present appearance.

Słowacki Theatre 32

Teatr im. Juliusza Słowackiego

Pl. Świętego Ducha 1. **Map** 2 D4 (6 E2). ***Tel*** *012 424 45 00.* *2, 4, 5, 7, 8, 13, 15, 19, 34.* *124, 152, 192.*

The proposal for a new theatre in Cracow, one which would replace the small and dilapidated Old Theatre, was put forward in 1872. Jan Zawiejski submitted the design and was put in charge of the works which were to be financed entirely through donations. The foundation stone was laid in 1891, and the theatre opened in 1893. Zawiejski designed an opulent building in which vernacular elements, such as the parapet inspired by the Cloth Hall, and foreign influences were blended into an eclectic whole. Allegorical sculptures decorate the exterior of the theatre.

The opulent interior features a grand staircase decorated with stuccowork by Alfred Putz. The four-tiered auditorium can seat up to 900 people. The stage curtain, one of the major attractions, was painted by Henryk Siemiradzki. It depicts Apollo striking an accord between Beauty and Love, surrounded by muses as well as other allegorical figures which represent Art drawing inspiration from man's fate.

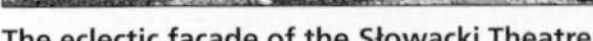

The eclectic façade of the Słowacki Theatre

Church of the Holy Cross 33

Kościół św. Krzyża

Świętego Krzyża 23. **Map** 2 D4 (6 E3). *2, 4, 5, 7, 8, 15.* *124, 152, 192.* *during services only.*

The Gothic church of the Order of the Holy Cross was built in two stages. The construction of the choir began immediately after 1300. The main nave and tower date from the first half of the 14th century. The interior is extremely well preserved and the nave impresses with its intricate pattern of vaulting ribs, supported on a single, round pillar. Among its furnishings, the Gothic font made in 1423 by Jan Freudenthal and the late Renaissance triptych in the Węgrzyn Chapel (next to the porch) are of particular interest. There are also various Baroque altars and stalls, as well as a number of memorial plaques of famous sculptors, active at the end of the 19th century, which are worth seeing.

The Church of the Holy Cross

Church of the Dominican Nuns 34

Kościół Dominikanek

Mikołajska 21. **Map** 2 D4 (6 E3). ***Tel*** *012 422 79 25.* *2, 3, 7, 8, 10, 13, 19, 34.* *during services only.*

The church, dedicated to the Virgin Mary, Queen of Snow, was founded in 1632–34 by Anna Lubomirska. Prior to the church, a fortified manor of Albert, Cracow's *wójt* (chief officer), was on this site in the 14th century. As a result of Albert's revolt against King Władysław the Short, a new building for the local government was erected. The latter was converted in the 1620s into a convent for the Dominican nuns. The church contains a miraculous 17th-century icon of the Virgin.

Dominican Church 35

Kościół Dominikanów

See pp116–17.

Dominican Church 35

Angel in the Chapel of the Virgin Mary of the Rosary

The Dominicans began the construction of a new church in 1250. It contained the shrine of St Jacek, a place of mass pilgrimage. Opulent mausolea, modelled on the Zygmunt Chapel at Wawel, were added in the 17th century by noble families, and in the 18th century the church was furnished with late Baroque altars. The fire of Cracow in 1850 destroyed the church almost completely. It was rebuilt by 1872 and today is an important evangelical centre which attracts masses of the faithful.

Cloister
The Gothic cloister was a burial place of burghers whose memorial plaques and tombs can still be seen here.

Crowstep gable

★ Zbaraski Chapel
The fine decoration of the chapel, built in 1627 to 1633 by the Castelli artists, is in sharp contrast with the monumental forms of the altar and tombs in black marble.

The Lubomirski Chapel displays lovely paintings and sculptures.

Tomb of General Jan Skrzynecki (died 1860)
This beautiful monument carved by Władysław Oleszczyński commemorates the hero of the November Uprising of 1830.

★ Shrine of St Jacek
The Renaissance Chapel of St Jacek was rebuilt around 1700 by Baldassare Fontana, who also designed this magnificent monument. The chapel is decorated with paintings by Tommaso Dolabella.

VISITORS' CHECKLIST

Stolarska 12. **Map** 1 C5 (6 D3). ***Tel*** *012 423 16 13.* *103, 502.* *1, 3, 7, 8, 10, 13, 18, 19, 36, 38.* *6am–8pm daily.*

The memorial plaque of Filippo Buonacorsi (Callimachus) (died 1496) honours the great humanist at the Polish royal court *(see p45)*.

Chapel of the Virgin Mary of the Rosary
In 1621 the icon of the Virgin of the Rosary was carried in a procession in order to secure, through prayers, victory over the Turks at Chocim.

The Myszkowski Chapel
This was built between 1603 and 1614 by masters from Santi Gucci's circle, using marble from the Świętokrzyskie (Holy Cross) Mountains. Portrait busts of the Myszkowskis form part of the splendid decoration of the dome.

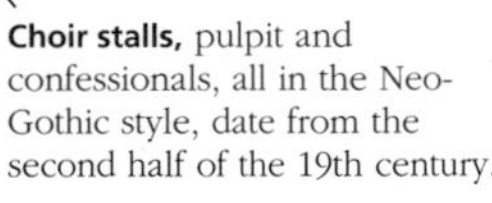

Choir stalls, pulpit and confessionals, all in the Neo-Gothic style, date from the second half of the 19th century.

Tomb of Prospero Provano
The monument of this salt magnate (died 1584) is one of the finest Polish sculptural works of circa 1600. It is located next to the Myszkowski Chapel.

STAR SIGHTS

★ Zbaraski Chapel

★ Shrine of St Jacek

KAZIMIERZ QUARTER

The town of Kazimierz near Cracow was founded in 1335 by Kazimierz (Casimir) the Great. With its own Town Hall and a defence wall, Kazimierz competed with the capital in position and wealth. The king built two large churches, St Catherine's and Corpus Christi, and planned to establish a university here. After King Jan Olbracht had moved the Jewish population here from Cracow in the late 15th century, the separate nature of Kazimierz became more pronounced. The town was soon to become a leading centre of Jewish culture. Although Kazimierz was integrated administratively into Cracow in 1791, the distinctive character of this quarter is still evident. With narrow streets lined with low buildings, it seems to belong to a different world. It bears witness to centuries of peaceful co-existence of two peoples, Jewish and Polish. Magnificent sacred architecture of both religions can be seen as further confirmation of this symbiosis.

A sepulchral matzeva

SIGHTS AT A GLANCE

Churches

Church of the Order of St John of God ⓫
Church of St Catherine ⓬
Corpus Christi Church ❽
Paulite Church "On the Rock" ⓭

Synagogues

Isaak's Synagogue ❷
High Synagogue ❸
Old Synagogue ❹
Remu'h Synagogue ❺
Tempel Synagogue ❶

Historic Buildings

Hospital of the Order of St John of God ❿
Kazimierz Town Hall ❾

Historic Cemeteries

New Jewish Cemetery ❼
Remu'h Cemetery ❻

GETTING THERE

Trams 3, 9, 11 and 13 stop at Starowiślna Street in the Jewish Quarter. Trams 8 and 10, which stop at Krakowska Street, are best for the major churches.

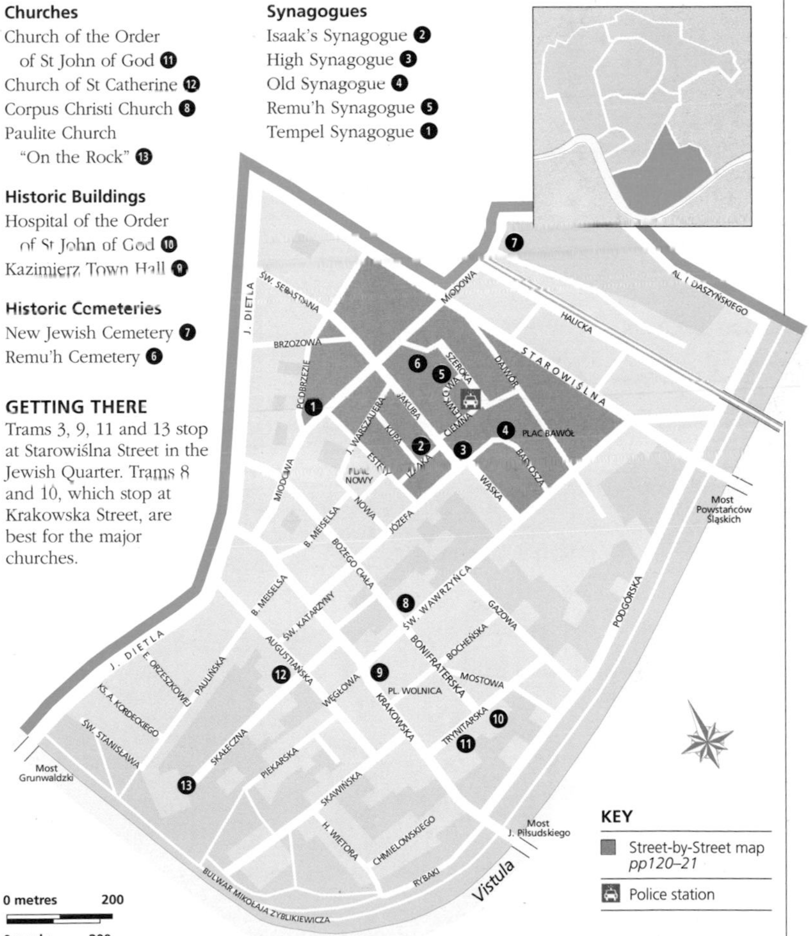

KEY

Street-by-Street map *pp120–21*

Police station

0 metres 200

0 yards 200

◁ **Bimah (pulpit) in the Old Synagogue**

Street-by-Street: Szeroka Street Area

The Jewish quarter was located in the east part of Kazimierz and concentrated first around Szeroka Street, then Libusza Square, which was later known as New Square. As well as the Jews displaced here in the late 15th century from Cracow, Czech and German refugees also came to live in Kazimierz. The Jewish community had its own jurisdiction and culture, and was never totally assimilated with the Poles. Many synagogues, baths, schools and cemeteries were established in Kazimierz, which became an active centre of Judaic culture and learning. The Nazis annihilated this unique world. Recently, however, a number of art galleries and restaurants have been opened here, which evoke the past.

Tempel Synagogue
The decoration of this synagogue, built in the Neo-Renaissance style, was influenced by Moorish art ❶

MIODOWA
JAKUBA
MIODOWA
KUPA

0 metres 50
0 yards 50

KEY

- - - Suggested route

JEWISH TOMBS

The signs carved on tombs convey symbolic meanings. The grave of a rabbi is indicated by hands joined in prayer. Basins and jugs for the ritual ablution of hands can be found on graves of the Levites. Three interlaced snakes feature on the grave of a physician, and a crown of knowledge on that of a learned man. A lion or a six-pointed star of David signifies a descendant of Judah.

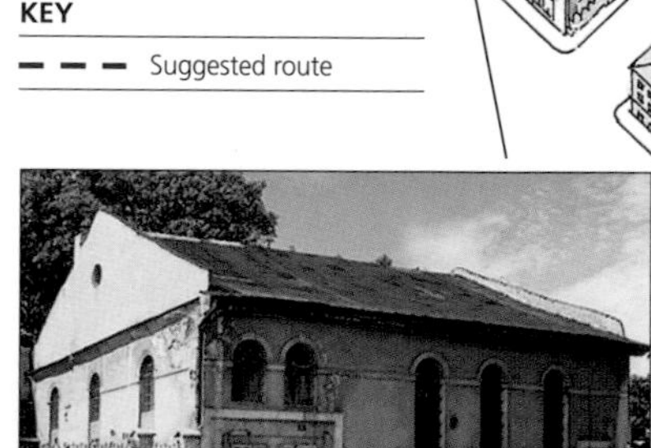

The Kupa Synagogue was built in the 17th century, financed by the Kahal of Kazimierz. It was remodelled many times and was also used for non-religious purposes. It is now disused and neglected.

★ Remu'h Cemetery
The Wailing Wall commemorates the tragic fate of the Jews from Cracow during World War II ❻

LOCATOR MAP
See Street Finder map 4

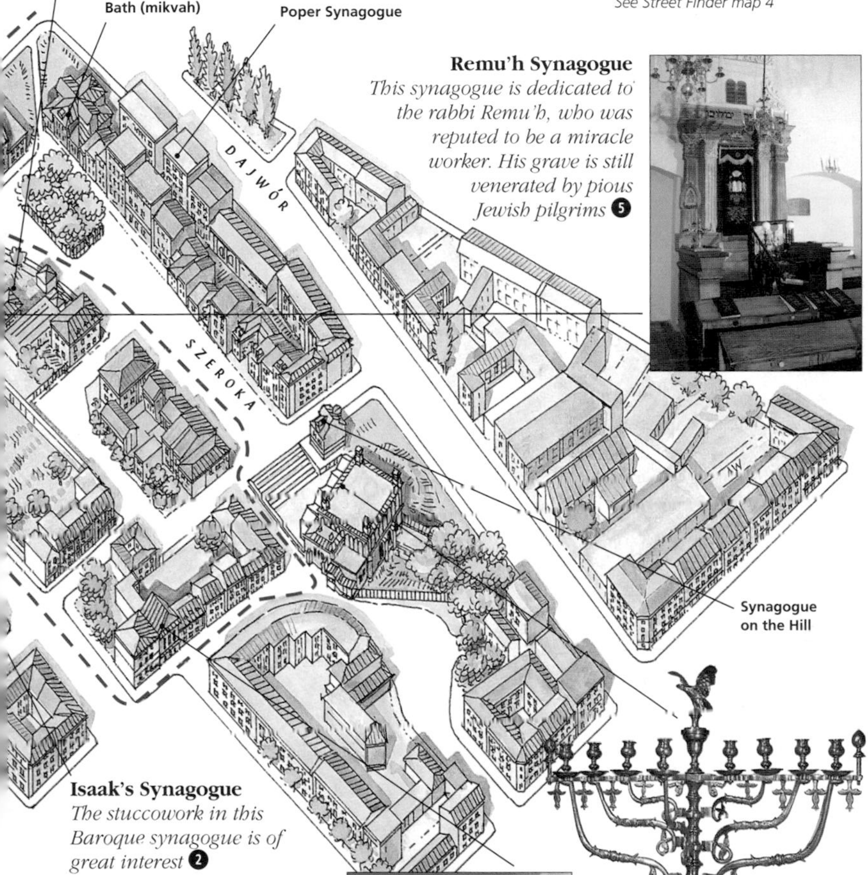

Bath (mikvah)

Poper Synagogue

DAJWÓR

SZEROKA

Remu'h Synagogue
This synagogue is dedicated to the rabbi Remu'h, who was reputed to be a miracle worker. His grave is still venerated by pious Jewish pilgrims ❺

Synagogue on the Hill

Isaak's Synagogue
The stuccowork in this Baroque synagogue is of great interest ❷

High Synagogue
With its late Gothic architecture and Renaissance decoration, this is one of Cracow's most picturesque synagogues ❸

★ Old Synagogue
This menorah is among the treasures in Poland's oldest synagogue. The building was destroyed by the Nazis, and later painstakingly restored ❹

STAR SIGHTS

- ★ Old Synagogue
- ★ Remu'h Cemetery

Tempel Synagogue ❶

Synagoga Tempel

Miodowa 24. **Map** 4 D1 (6 F5). *3, 9, 11, 13, 32, 34. 103. 10am–4pm Mon–Fri.*

The most recent of all the synagogues in Kazimierz, the Tempel, also known as the Progressive Synagogue, was built in the Neo-Renaissance style between 1860 and 1862. It is used by non-Orthodox Jews. Inside note the stained glass and period decoration.

Façade of Isaak's Synagogue

Isaak's Synagogue ❷

Bożnica Izaaka

Kupa 18. **Map** 4 D1. ***Tel*** *012 430 55 77. 3, 8, 9, 11, 13. 103. 9am–7pm Sun–Fri. public hols.*

This synagogue was built between 1638 and 1644 as a foundation of Izaak Jakubowicz, an elder of the Jewish community. Inside, the plaster work by Giovanni Battista Falconi has survived in a large nave with a barrel vault. The Jewish Education Centre is housed here.

High Synagogue ❸

Bożnica Wysoka

Józefa 38. **Map** 4 D1. *3, 8, 9, 10, 11, 13.*

This synagogue dates from 1556 to 1563. It is a picturesque structure supported by buttresses. A Renaissance portal is worth noting. Only a few furnishings have survived, including a money box and the remains of an altar. The Studio for the Restoration of Monuments is located here.

Old Synagogue ❹

Synagoga Stara

Szeroka 24. **Map** 4 D1. *3, 9, 11, 13, 32, 34.* **Jewish Museum**. ***Tel*** *012 422 09 62. Apr–Oct: 10am–5pm Tue–Sun, 10am–2pm Mon; Nov–Apr: 10am–2pm Mon, 9am–4pm Wed, Thu, Sat & Sun, 10am–5pm Fri. first Sat & Sun of each month. free Mon.*

The Old Synagogue was used in the past as a temple and was also a seat of the Kahal and other offices of the Jewish community. Religious and social life was concentrated here. The synagogue houses the Jewish Museum, which is dedicated to the history and culture of Cracow's Jews.

The brick building goes back to the mid-15th or beginning of the 16th century. Its present appearance is the result of a remodelling in 1557–70. The parapet, and Gothic interior with ribbed vaulting supported by slender columns, all date from then.

The hall used for prayer is almost bare, in accordance with the rule of the Jewish religion. The bimah, an elevated platform with an iron balustrade used for readings from the Torah, is the only piece of furnishing.

The east wall features the aron hakodesh, an ornamental shrine for the Torah Scrolls.

Entrance to the Remu'h Synagogue and Cemetery

Remu'h Synagogue ❺

Bożnica Remuh

Szeroka 40. **Map** 4 D1. ***Tel*** *012 421 29 87. 3, 9, 11, 13, 32, 34. 9am–4pm Mon–Fri.*

One of the two still active synagogues, the Remu'h temple is used by Orthodox Jews. It was founded by Israel Isserles Auerbach around 1553 and named after his son, the great author, philosopher and reputed miracle worker, Rabbi Moses Remu'h.

Inside, the bimah and an ornamental aron hakodesh are worth noting.

Remu'h Cemetery ❻

Cmentarz Remuh

Szeroka 40. **Map** 4 D1. *3, 9, 11, 13, 32, 34. 9am–4pm Mon–Fri.*

The Remu'h Cemetery, established in 1533, is one of the very few Jewish

Hall of Prayers in the Old Synagogue

cemeteries in the whole of Europe with so many tombs, both gravestones (matzeva) and sarcophagi. Their rich floral and animal decoration is of particular interest.

The cemetery was almost entirely destroyed during World War II. However, the tomb of Remu'h, which still attracts pilgrims from all over the world, was spared from Nazi destruction. Over 700 tombs have been excavated since World War II. They were probably buried during the Swedish invasion in the early 18th century. The Wailing Wall by the entrance was made using fragments of tombstones destroyed during the war.

New Jewish Cemetery ❼

Nowy Cmentarz Żydowski

Miodowa 55. **Map** 4 E1. *3, 9, 11, 13, 32, 34.*

Established in the early 19th century, this cemetery is a burial place of the great Jews of Cracow of the 19th and 20th centuries. All Kazimierz's rabbis and many of the great benefactors of Cracow rest here. They include Józef Oettinger and Józef Rosenblatt (professors of the Jagiellonian University), Józef Sare (the city President), and Maurycy Gotlieb (one of the foremost Polish artists of the 19th century).

Corpus Christi Church ❽

Kościół Bożego Ciała

Bożego Ciała 25. **Map** 4 D2. *8, 10.* *9am–noon and 1:30–7pm Mon–Sat and during services.*

Corpus Christi Church was built on marshland where, according to legend, a monstrance (religious container) with the Eucharist stolen from the Collegiate Church of All Saints had been found. A mysterious light shining in the darkness indicated the site where the profaned monstrance had been abandoned. The construction of the church, founded by King Kazimierz the Great, began in 1340 and was completed in the early 15th century. As a parish church it was bestowed by local burghers with sumptuous furnishings, most of which have survived.

In 1634 to 1637 the high altar was decorated with a painting of *The Nativity* by Tommaso Dolabella, court artist to Zygmunt III Vaza. The large stalls for monks, matching the altar, were made in 1632. An opulent 17th-century stone altarpiece with the relics of Blessed Stanisław Kazimierczyk is located in the north aisle.

The altar of Christ the Redeemer, decorated with sculptures by Anton Gegenbaur, is also worth noting. A slab in the north aisle indicates the burial place of the architect Bartolomeo Berecci, who was assassinated in 1537.

Image of the Madonna in the Church of Corpus Christi

Town Hall in Kazimierz, housing the Ethnographical Museum

Kazimierz Town Hall ❾

Ratusz kazimierski

Pl. Wolnica 1. **Map** 4 D2. ***Tel*** *012 430 60 23.* *502.* *3, 8, 10, 36, 38, 40.* **Ethnographical Museum** *10am–6pm Mon, 10am–3pm Wed–Sun.*

The Town Hall was the seat of local government until 1791. The oldest parts of the building date back to 1414, the year of its foundation. After much remodelling, the north section of the Town Hall, including a crenellated parapet, was finally completed in 1620. The south section was added in 1875 to 1877 by Filip Pokutyński.

The Ethnographic Museum was established here in 1947. Its rich collection includes costumes from Lesser Poland and Silesia, traditional Cracovian Christmas cribs, folk art and musical instruments.

Hospital of the Order of St John of God ❿

Szpital Bonifratrów

Trynitarska 11. **Map** 4 D6. ***Tel*** *012 430 55 10.* *502.* *8, 10, 36, 38, 40.*

This monumental building was constructed between 1897 and 1906 to commemorate the 50th anniversary of Emperor Franz Joseph's reign. Designed by Teodor Talowski in the late Modernist style, the façade, with its central bay projection decorated with the Crucifix and bust of St John of God, is of particular interest.

Cracow's Jewish Community

Before it was all but annihilated in the Holocaust, Cracow had one of the most vibrant, wealthy and prominent Jewish communities in Europe. An important trading post between Prussia, Prague and Vienna, Jews have lived here since the 14th century. In 1938 the Jewish population was over 60,000, one quarter of the total population. However, anti-semitic protests date back to 1369 and in 1495 Jews were expelled from Cracow to Kazimierz *(see p119)*. In 1948, the post-Holocaust Jewish population was 5,900 and by 1978, a mere 600.

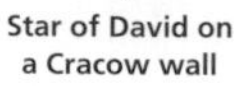

Star of David on a Cracow wall

King Kazimierz the Great *founded the city that took his name in 1335. Originally a separate town, it became a leading centre of Jewish culture.*

Rabbi Moses ben Isserles *(1525–1572) was one of the greatest rabbis of the 16th-century, and lived and taught in Kazimierz. He is revered by Jews for his learned additions to the Shulkhan Arukh (the code for everyday life). He was also a keen historian, astronomer, geometrician and philosopher.*

GOTTLIEB'S *DAY OF ATONEMENT*

This famous painting by Maurycy Gottlieb, a Polish Jew, was executed in 1878. It portrays the artist (the figure in the middle resting on his arm) attending synagogue on the holiest day of the Jewish year, Yom Kippur (the Day of Atonement). Beset with woes, the painter's pose reflects the conflict that faced Polish Jewry as a whole in the late 19th-century: whether they were in the first place Jews or Poles.

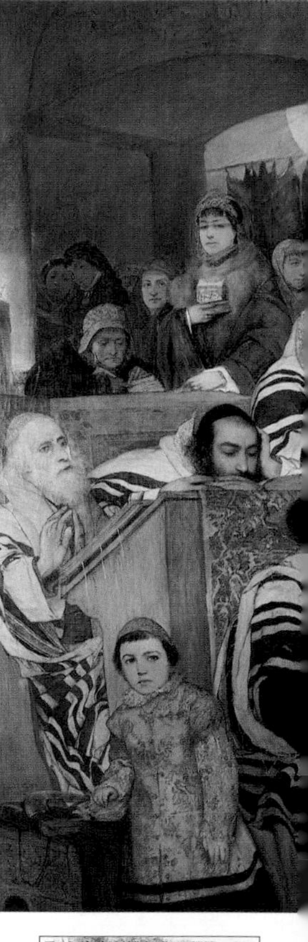

Jewish diversity in Cracow *is shown in these three professional portraits from the late 1870s: on the left is an Orthodox Jew and the two on the right are Hassidic Jews. Cracow was long considered to be one of the primary centres of Jewish debate, as all parts of the religious and political spectrum were represented in the city's wide-ranging Jewish population.*

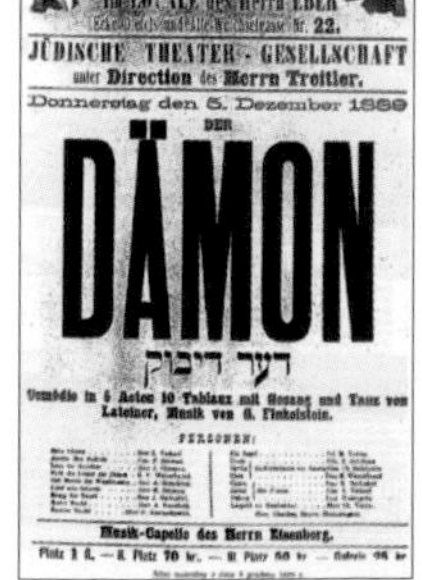

Jewish theatre *was a crucial part of Jewish life in Cracow until the late 1930s. Besides entertainment, it also provided one of the last bastions of the Yiddish language.*

The Nazis ordered *large numbers of Jews to move from Kazimierz and enter the Ghetto; often, homes were swapped with Polish families going the other way. The Cracow Jewish Ghetto was centred on Bohaterow Getta Square on the south side of the river.*

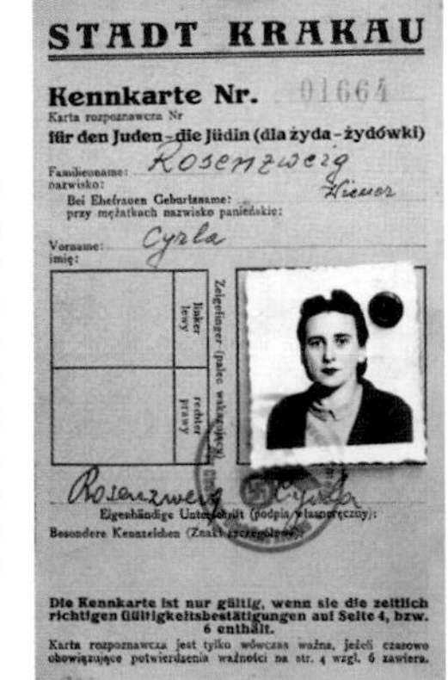

STADT KRAKAU

Kennkarte Nr. 01664
Karta rozpoznawcza Nr
für den Juden - die Jüdin (dla żyda - żydówki)

Familienname: / nazwisko: Rosenzweig
Bei Ehefrauen Geburtsname: / przy mężatkach nazwisko panieńskie: Wiener
Vorname: / imię: Cyrla

Zeigefinger (palec wskazujący): linker / lewy; rechter / prawy

Eigenhändige Unterschrift (podpis własnoręczny): Rosenzweig Cyrla
Besondere Kennzeichen (Znaki szczególne):

Die Kennkarte ist nur gültig, wenn sie die zeitlich richtigen Gültigkeitsbestätigungen auf Seite 4, bzw. 6 enthält.
Karta rozpoznawcza jest tylko wówczas ważna, jeżeli czasowo obowiązujące potwierdzenia ważności na str. 4 wzgl. 6 zawiera.

Identity documents *were issued even before the creation of the Cracow Ghetto in 1941. All Poles had to carry a card that clearly stated their ethnic provenance in order to limit the civil rights and entitlements of the holder. The card shown here belonged to Cyrla Rosenzweig, a Polish Jew who was rescued from the Holocaust by Oskar Schindler.*

Modern-day Jewish Cracow *has become a thriving centre of Jewish tradition and culture since the reintroduction of democracy to Poland in 1989. The growing population is estimated to be well over 5,000. While some are former residents who have returned to their birthplace, many are young descendants of those who died in the Ghetto and at Auschwitz. Many have found success as entrepreneurs, opening hotels and kosher restaurants.*

SCHINDLER'S CRACOW

Oskar Schindler (1908-1978), made famous by the Steven Spielberg film *Schindler's List*, was a German businessman who saved over 1,000 Jews from the gas chambers during World War II, by employing them at his factories. The original Schindler factory is at Ul. Lipowa 4, and is currently undergoing transformation into a museum. Schindler lived at Straszewskiego 7, in the upstairs flat.

Oskar Schindler with Holocaust survivors in Tel-Aviv

Church of the Order of St John of God, detail of the façade

Church of the Order of St John of God ⓫

Kościół Bonifratrów

Krakowska 48. **Map** *4 D2.* ***Tel*** *012 430 61 22. 502. 8, 10, 36, 38, 40. during services only.*

This interesting Baroque church was built between 1741 and 1758 to designs by Francesco Placidi. A rather small structure is hidden behind a monumental, wavy façade inspired by the best designs of the leading Roman Baroque architect, Francesco Borromini. The façade, intended to be viewed at an angle, closes the vista formed by Krakowska Street. Inside, the excellent *trompe-l'oeil* painting of the vault was made by Josef Piltz of Moravia in 1757–58. It depicts St John of Matha buying slaves from the heathens. The side altars, with their architectural forms painted directly on the walls, are unusual. They are decorated with Rococo paintings, among which the effigy of St Cajetan is worth noting.

Church of St Catherine ⓬

Kościół św. Katarzyny

Augustiańska 7. **Map** *4 D2.* ***Tel*** *012 430 62 42. 128, 184, 502. 8, 10, 18, 19, 22. during services only.*

According to the chronicler Jan Długosz, the Church of St Catherine was built by King Kazimierz the Great as a penance for murdering Father Marcin Baryczka in 1349. Baryczka delivered a document issued by bishops excommunicating the king. The king repaid the messenger with the order to have Baryczka drowned in the Vistula. However, the construction of the church possibly began in 1343 and continued until the early 16th century. Regarded as one of the most beautiful Gothic churches in Cracow, its furnishings were lost in the 19th century when it was briefly transformed into a warehouse. The Baroque high altar, decorated with the *Mystical Marriage of St Catherine* by Andrea Venesta, 1634, has survived. Worth visiting is the Gothic cloister which dates from the time of Kazimierz the Great. It features late Gothic murals and large 17th-century paintings. Two chapels adjoin the cloister: one houses the miraculous *Madonna of Consolation* and the other the relics of Blessed Isaiah Boner.

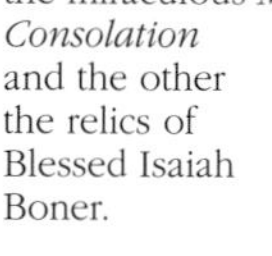

Fresco in the cloister in the Church of St Catherine

Paulite Church "On the Rock" ⓭

Kościół Paulinów Na Skałce

Skałeczna 15. **Map** *3 C2.* ***Tel*** *012 421 74 18. 128, 184, 502. 8, 10, 18, 19, 22. 9am–4pm Mon–Sat and during services.* **The Crypt** *9am–noon and 1:30pm–3pm Mon–Sat.*

A small church of St Michael "On the Rock" was recorded already in the 11th century. This was the site where Bishop Stanisław of Szczepanów, later canonized, was murdered *(see pp22–3)*.

In the 14th century this small Romanesque church was replaced by a large Gothic church founded by Kazimierz the Great. Four hundred years later it was in danger of collapsing. It was, therefore, rebuilt in the late Baroque style, between 1733 and 1742. The design by Anton Gerhard Müntzer was modified by Antonio Solari. The uniform furnishings all date from the 1740s. A small font by the church is decorated with a statue of St Stanisław, made in 1731. The tormentors of the saint, who are said to have quartered his body, threw his cut-off finger into the font. The water is reputed to have healing properties ever since.

Paulite Church and Monastery "On the Rock"

The Crypt in the Church "On the Rock"

Pantheon in the Church "On the Rock"

Jan Długosz, the great Polish historian of the Middle Ages, was buried in the crypt beneath the Church "On the Rock" in 1480. In 1876 it was decided to transform the crypt into a national pantheon for the burial of those who had made important contributions to Polish culture. The architect Teofil Żebrawski remodelled the crypt, transforming it into a gallery with a separate chapel housing the altar. Recesses, three on each side, were designed to house the sarcophagi. The stained-glass window above the altar depicts the Madonna of Częstochowa, theQueen of Poland. Coats of arms of provinces of the Polish-Lithuanian Commonwealth were painted on the vault.

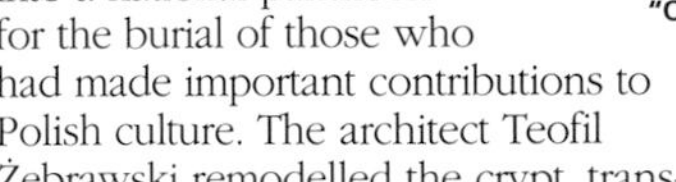

Sarcophagus of Adam Asnyk (1838–97)
This foremost Polish poet of 19th-century Positivism rests in a sarcophagus made by Karol Knaus and Jan Tombiński.

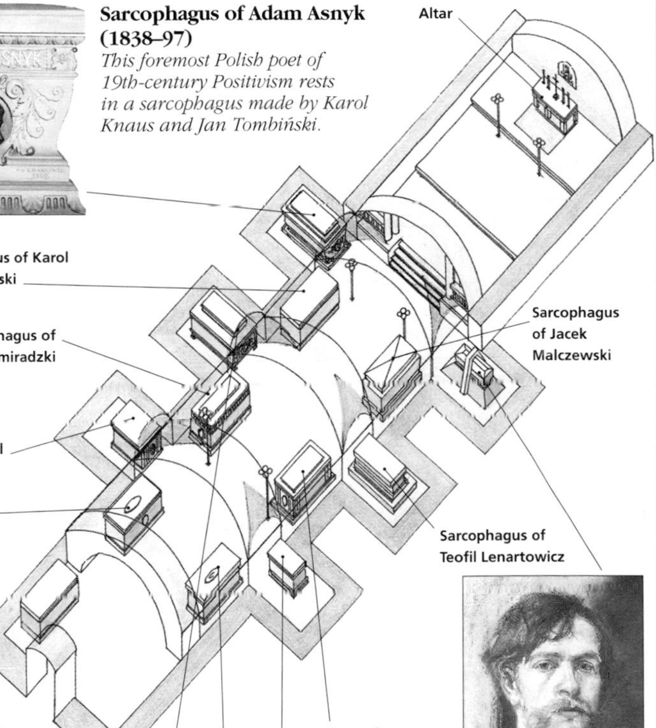

Altar

Sarcophagus of Karol Szymanowski

Sarcophagus of Henryk Siemiradzki

Sarcophagus of Wincenty Pol

Sarcophagus of Tadeusz Banachiewicz

Sarcophagus of Jacek Malczewski

Sarcophagus of Teofil Lenartowicz

Entrance

Sarcophagus of Józef I. Kraszewski

Sarcophagus of Jan Długosz

Sarcophagus of Ludwik Solski

Sarcophagus of Lucjan Siemieński (1807–77)
The sarcophagus of this popular writer and critic was designed by Karol Knaus. The portrait medallion is by Jan Tombiński.

Stanisław Wyspiański (1869–1907)
The monumental sarcophagus of Wyspiański was designed by Jan Rzymkowski.

GRUNWA

WESOŁA, KLEPARZ AND BISKUPIE

A number of settlements developed around Cracow over the centuries. They were linked culturally and economically with Cracow but were independently administered. As there were no specific boundaries between them and land ownership often changed, the settlements north and east of the city walls developed to constitute a complex urban mosaic, and included Przedmieście Mikołajskie, the royal town of Kleparz, and the privately owned Wesoła, Lubicz and Biskupie. They all looked like small towns. Imposing churches and a few palaces were surrounded by irregularly scattered residential timber buildings. Merchants and craftsmen who were active here avoided paying taxes to the Town Hall, thus contributing to the economic decline of Cracow. As a result, in 1791 the City Council decided to incorporate these quarters into Cracow. This part of the city saw the greatest surge in building activity during the great development of Cracow in the second half of the 19th century.

Statue of St Florian, St Florian's Church

SIGHTS AT A GLANCE

Historic Monuments and Buildings
Academy of Fine Arts 12
Astronomical Observatory 6
Cracow Main Railway Station 8
Globe House 15
Grunwald Monument 10
National Bank of Poland 11
Polish State Railways Headquarters 13
Society of Physicians 2

Churches and Monasteries
Church of the Discalced Carmelite Nuns 5
Church of the Immaculate Conception of the Virgin Mary 4
Church of the Nuns of the Visitation 16
Church of St Nicholas 1
Church of St Vincent de Paul 14
Jesuit Church pp134–5 3
St Florian's Church 9

Historic Parks
Jagiellonian University Botanical Gardens 7

GETTING THERE
Tram routes 3, 4, 5, 7, 10, 15, 19 and bus routes 124 and 502 all serve Basztowa Street. Tram routes 2, 3, 7, 10 and 19 serve Westerplatte Street.

KEY
- Street-by-Street map *pp130–31*
- Street-by-Street map *pp136–7*
- Coach station
- Bus depot
- Post office
- Tourist information

◁ **Grunwald Monument**

Street-by-Street: Along Kopernika Street

Wesoła Quarter, originally a small settlement by the Romanesque Church of St Nicholas, developed along the old route to Mogiła, which is today Kopernika Street (ulica Mikołaja Kopernika). Its skyline was dominated by churches, monasteries and suburban residences of the nobility, set in well-kept gardens. In the 19th century a number of university buildings, mostly hospitals belonging to the Medical School, were built here. Some of these buildings display interesting architectural forms.

★ Jesuit Church
This is one of the most interesting examples of modern ecclesiastical architecture ❸

★ Society of Physicians
The metal balusters were designed by Stanisław Wyspiański in the Art Nouveau style, featuring sinuous floral ornaments ❷

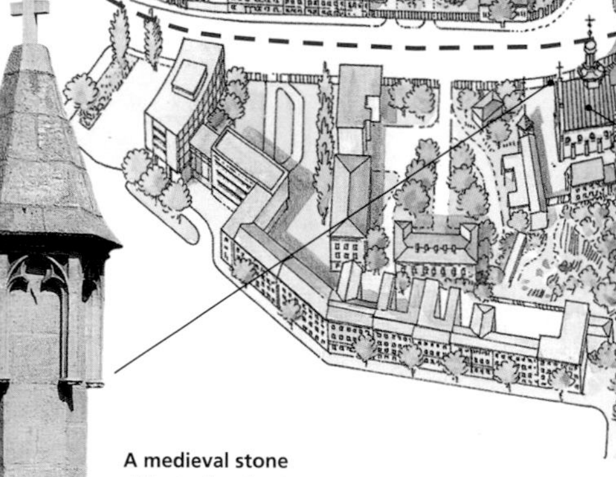

A medieval stone pillar to the dead by the Church of St Nicholas is unique. It was originally located in the courtyard of St Valentine's Hospital in Kleparz.

Church of St Nicholas
For centuries this church was a landmark of the settlement which developed along the Cracow-Mogiła route ❶

Kopernika Street lined densely with trees, is one of the most beautiful streets in Cracow.

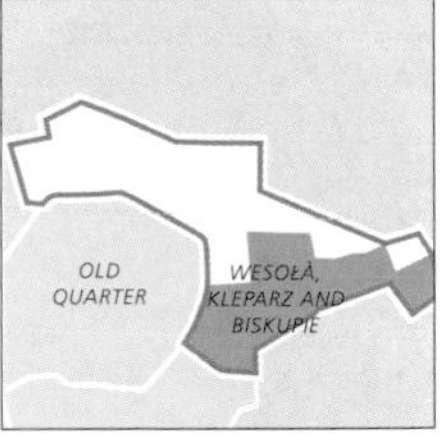

LOCATOR MAP

See Street Finder maps 1 and 3

Church of the Discalced Carmelite Nuns
The Baroque façade, one of the most beautiful in Cracow, is worth seeing ❺

Astronomical Observatory
Belonging to the Jagiellonian University, with its elegant architecture and location next to the Botanical Gardens, this observatory looks more like a Neo-Classical villa than a university building ❻

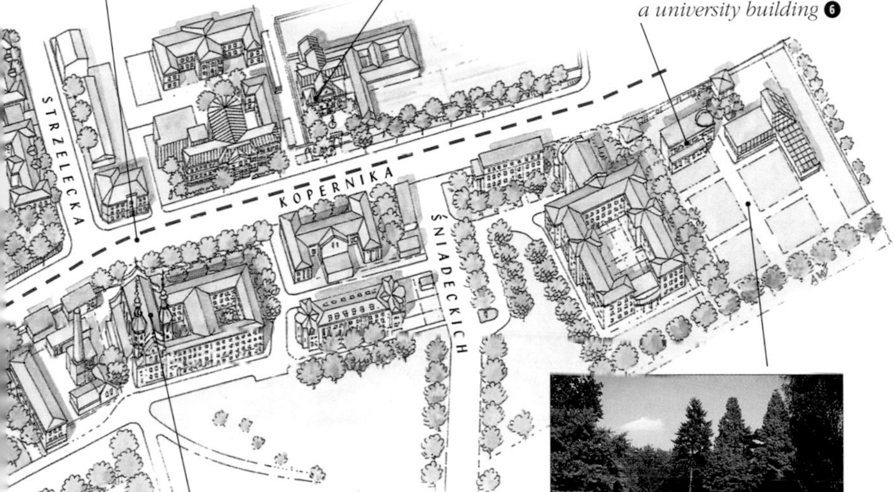

Jagiellonian University Botanical Gardens
Exotic and local flora make the gardens a favourite place for days out ❼

Church of the Immaculate Conception of the Virgin Mary
The entrance to the Baroque interior is through this monumental portal ❹

0 metres 50

0 yards 50

KEY

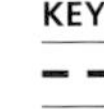

Suggested route

STAR SIGHTS

★ Society of Physicians

★ Jesuit Church

Madonna and Child with Saints Adalbert and Stanisław

Church of St Nicholas ❶

Kościół św. Mikołaja

Kopernika 9. **Map** 2 D4 (6 F3). ***Tel*** *012 431 22 77.* *2, 3, 10, 11, 13, 14, 15, 19, 32, 40.* *during services only.*

Recorded in the first half of the 13th century, this is one of the oldest churches in Cracow. The remnants of the Romanesque church and a Gothic portal have survived in the chancel. The present church is the result of a Baroque remodelling undertaken between 1677 and 1682. Furnishings were commissioned by the Academy of Cracow, whose patronage over this collegiate foundation goes back to 1465. A coat of arms of the Academy (a shield with crossed maces) decorates the backs of the stalls. The high altar was probably designed by Francesco Placidi. It features an effigy of St Nicholas and architectural decoration forming coulisses. The church also houses a late Gothic triptych, depicting the Coronation of the Virgin, and a Renaissance Madonna and Child with Saints Adalbert and Stanisław, patron saints of Poland. A bronze font, dating from 1536, is worth noting.

It is also of interest that Feliks Dzierżyński, who was to become the founder of the *Cheka* (Bolshevik secret police) and a Bolshevik revolutionary, was married in this church in 1910.

Society of Physicians ❷

Gmach Towarzystwa Lekarskiego

Radziwiłłowska 4. **Map** 2 D4 (6 F2). ***Tel*** *012 422 75 47.* *2, 3, 7, 10, 11, 13, 14, 15, 19, 32, 40.* *10am–3pm daily.*

This building was constructed in 1904 to designs by the architects Władysław Kaczmarski and Józef Sowiński. A rather modest Neo-Classical exterior is in contrast to the sumptuous interior decoration designed by Stanisław Wyspiański. This multi-talented artist created here complex decoration in which, typically for the Art Nouveau movement, the arts and crafts complement each other. Wyspiański chose colour schemes for the walls and designed the exquisite stained glass showing *Apollo, The Solar System*, as well as the metal balusters and furniture.

***Apollo, The Solar System*, a stained-glass window by S. Wyspiański in the Society of Physicians building**

Jesuit Church ❸

Kościół Jezuitów

See pp132–3.

The Baroque Church of the Immaculate Conception

Church of the Immaculate Conception of the Virgin Mary ❹

Kościół Niepokalanego Poczęcia NMP

Kopernika 19. **Map** 2 E4. *2, 3, 10, 11, 13, 14, 15, 19, 32, 40.* *8am–4pm daily and during services.*

This church, also known as the Church of St Lazarus, was used in the past by novices of the order of the Discalced Carmelites. The rigidity of the Baroque architecture of this church, built between 1634 and 1680, reflects the strict building regulations of the Carmelite order. Large and complex, the high altar dominates the small interior. Modelled on the high altar in the Carmelite Church of Santa Maria della Scala in Rome, it was made in 1681 of black marble from the Dębnik quarry, which was owned by the Carmelites.

Church of the Discalced Carmelite Nuns ❺

Kościół Karmelitanek Bosych

Kopernika 44. **Map** 2 E4. ***Tel*** *012 421 41 18.* *124, 128.* *4, 5, 9, 10, 11, 14, 15, 32, 40.* *during services only.*

A large convent was built in the neighbourhood of the friary of the same order between 1720 and 1732. The church is small and has a Greek cross groundplan. The interior with its many columns is impressive. The sumptuous façade has elegant decoration in the late Baroque style.

The architect of the church is unknown. Karol Antoni Bay of Warsaw and Kacper Bażanka are considered likely to have designed it. Due to the strict rule of the order, the church is open to the public only during services. The painting on the high altar depicts Saint Theresa of Avila, to whom the church is dedicated.

Portal in the Church of the Discalced Carmelite Nuns

Astronomical Observatory ❻

Obserwatorium Astronomiczne UJ

Kopernika 27. **Map** 2 F4. ***Tel*** *012 425 14 57.* 🚌 *124, 128, 184, 502.* 🚋 *4, 5, 9, 10, 15, 19, 34, 40.* ● *to the public.*

The establishment of the Observatory in Wesoła was directly linked to the reform of the Academy of Cracow carried out in the 1770s by Hugo Kołłątaj, a task he was given by the Commission for National Education. As a result, experimental sciences gained a more prominent role in the curriculum. The suburban Jesuit residence, taken over by the Commission after the abolition of the order, was rebuilt to house the Observatory. Stanisław Zawadzki, the architect to King Stanisław Augustus, redesigned the building in an austere Neo-Classical style. He decorated the façade with astronomical signs.

The building is now occupied by the Jagiellonian Botanical Institute. A modern astronomical observatory is located in the former Skała fortress in Bielany.

Jagiellonian University Botanical Gardens ❼

Ogród botaniczny UJ

Kopernika 27a. **Map** 2 F4. ***Tel*** *012 421 26 20.* 🚌 *124, 184, 502.* 🚋 *4, 5, 9, 10, 15, 19, 34, 40.* ○ *May–Oct: 9am–7pm daily.* **Greenhouses** ○ *10am–1pm Sat–Thu.* **Museum of Botanical Gardens** ○ *10am–2pm Wed & Fri, 11am–3pm Sat.* ♿

Next to the Observatory, the Botanical Gardens of the Jagiellonian University are located on the former grounds and lodge of the Czartoryski family. The gardens were established in 1780 by Jan Jaśkiewicz and designed by the Viennese gardener Franz Kaiser. A 500-year-old oak tree in the depths of the garden, as well as exotic and native plants, are particularly worth seeing. Also of interest are late-Gothic pillars, originally from the Collegium Maius, used here as plinths supporting plant pots.

Two of the gardens' palm houses are interesting examples of 19th-century architectural structures. They are complemented by a third, 20th-century palm house designed by Stanisław Juszczyk and built in 1964 to mark the 6th centenary of the Jagiellonian University. Busts of celebrated botanists decorate the gardens.

Flowers in the Botanical Gardens

Cracow Main Railway Station ❽

Dworzec Główny PKP

Pl. Kolejowy 1. **Map** 2 D3 (6 F1). 🚌 🚋 *Served by most bus and tram routes.*

A railway link was established in 1847 between Cracow and Silesia. It was known as the Northern, or Franz Joseph Railway. Between 1844 and 1847 a new station was built north of the city. It was designed by Piotr Rosenbaum, an architect from Breslau, and was considered to be one of the most elegant stations in Europe. It was later rebuilt. In 1898 Teodor Talowski constructed a viaduct next to the station, in the Romanesque Revival style. Work is currently being carried out on the platforms.

Cracow's Main Railway Station

Jesuit Church ❸

This monumental church was built between 1909 and 1921 to designs by the architect Franciszek Mączyński. He applied a number of historic styles which he modified and combined in new ways. What he created is one of the most interesting ecclesiastical buildings of the first quarter of the 20th century in Poland. Leading artists worked on the interior. Karol Hukan carved sculptures for the altars, while Jan Bukowski painted murals of striking beauty and designed unusual confessionals. The mosaic above the high altar is by Piotr Stachiewicz, and the south portal facing Kopernika Street was designed by Xawery Dunikowski. A small statue of Mączyński on the exterior of the east wall is also by Dunikowski.

★ South Portal
The main entrance to the church is through this monumental portal. Note the exquisite ornaments and figures which are both regarded as outstanding examples of Polish sculpture of the early 20th century.

Mosaic in the Porch
Made of mosaic pieces in vivid colours and set against a shiny background, the figures of Mary and Child have an almost unreal, mystical appearance.

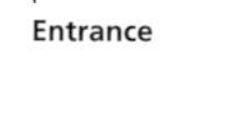

Murals Decorating the Nave Vaulting
These murals contribute to the rich and monumental character of the interior. They were painted by Jan Bukowski, who also executed decoration in other churches in Cracow, including St Mary's and the Bernardine Nuns' church, as well as the Loretto Chapel by the Capuchin Church.

★ Altar of St Joseph
Altars in the aisles were made by the sculptor Karol Hukan. Of particular interest is the altar of St Joseph, made in 1922 to 1923. It features this figurative group, which is rich in dynamic and wavy forms.

VISITORS' CHECKLIST

Kopernika 26. **Map** 2E4. ***Tel*** *012 629 33 00.* *2, 3, 4, 5, 10, 13, 14, 15, 19, 34, 40.* *9:30am–noon daily and during services.*

Confessional
The confessionals were designed by Jan Bukowski, Professor of the Industrial School of Art, in the style of the Baroque Revival and are freely decorated with ornaments.

Mosaic above the high altar

High Altar
The design of the high altar, featuring a half-dome supported by a free-standing colonnade, was influenced by Italian Renaissance architecture. The statues above the altar portray Christ and Jesuit saints.

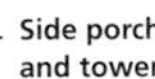

Side porch and tower

Statue of Franciszek Mączyński
The Jesuit Church was Mączyński's most important design. His statue, outside the east wall, is by Xawery Dunikowski.

STAR FEATURES

- ★ South Portal
- ★ Altar of St Joseph

Street-by-Street: Matejko Square

Kleparz, an independent settlement north of Cracow, was granted a municipal charter in 1366. It was incorporated into Cracow in 1791. After the introduction of the railway, Kleparz developed rapidly around the railway station. In the heart of the quarter, the empty space in front of the Barbican was transformed into an elegant square welcoming visitors to Cracow, arriving here by rail or approaching the city from the north, via Warszawska Street.

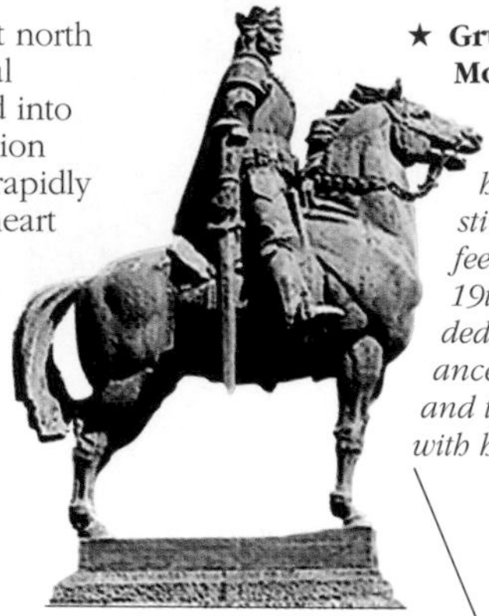

★ Grunwald Monument
The making of this monument helped to stimulate patriotic feelings in the late 19th century. It is dedicated "to the ancestors' glory and to the brethren with hope" ⑩

Academy of Fine Arts
The Academy houses a collection of works by its leading professors and students, including a Self-Portrait *by Jacek Malczewski* ⑫

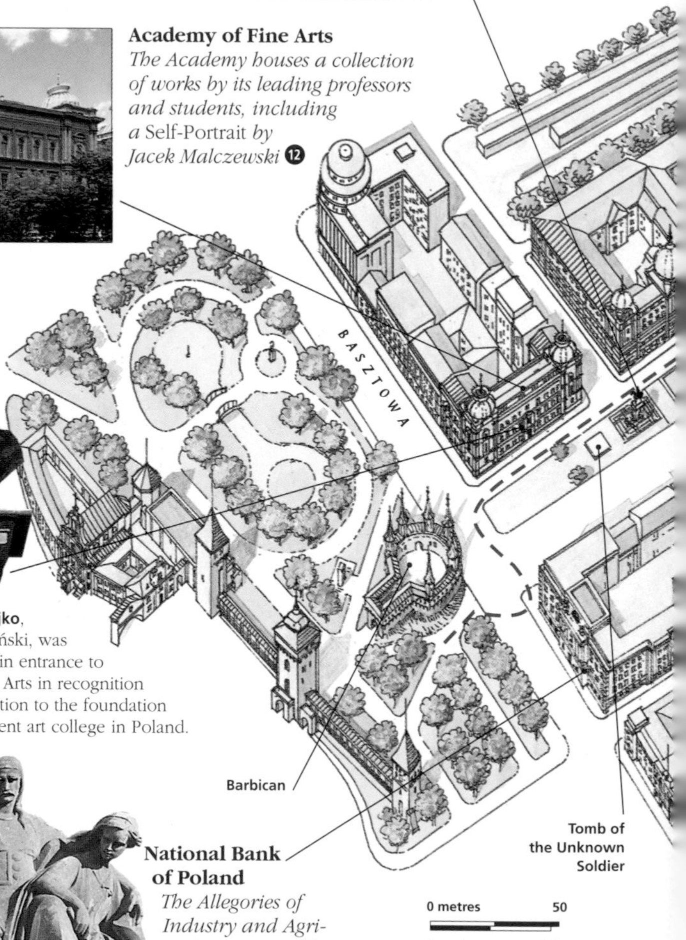

BASZTOWA

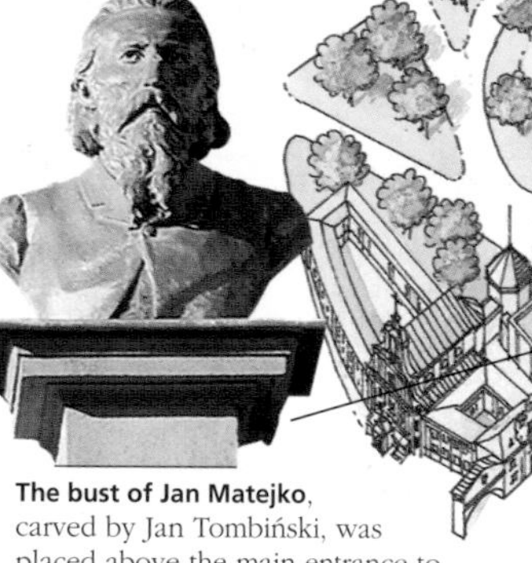

The bust of Jan Matejko, carved by Jan Tombiński, was placed above the main entrance to the Academy of Fine Arts in recognition of Matejko's contribution to the foundation of this first independent art college in Poland.

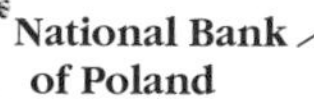

Barbican

National Bank of Poland
The Allegories of Industry and Agriculture, carved by Karol Hukan, decorate the façade of this bank ⑪

Tomb of the Unknown Soldier

0 metres 50

0 yards 50

KEY

– – – Suggested route

Church of St Vincent de Paul
This church was built from 1875 to 1887 to designs by Filip Pokutyński. The façade was inspired by Italian medieval architecture ⓮

LOCATOR MAP
See Street Finder maps 1 and 3

The Church of the Sisters of Charity was built by Filip Pokutyński from 1869 to 1871.

★ St Florian's Church
In days gone by life in Kleparz centred around this collegiate church. The effigy of St Florian by Jan Tricius decorates the high altar ❾

Polish State Railways Headquarters
This was the most opulent building erected in Cracow at the end of the 19th century ⓭

Elegant town houses at Matejko Square show a range of different architectural styles of the early 20th century.

STAR SIGHTS

- ★ St Florian's Church
- ★ Grunwald Monument

The Baroque altar of St John of Kęty in St Florian's Church

St Florian's Church ❾

Kościół św. Floriana

Warszawska 1. **Map** 2 D3. ***Tel*** *012 422 48 42.* 🚌 *105, 129, 130, 154, 179.* ◯ *during services only.*

In 1184 Duke Kazimierz the Just received the relics of St Florian from Pope Lucius III and decided to deposit them in Cracow. The horses which drew the carriage carrying the relics of the martyr stopped suddenly in Kleparz, before reaching the city's gate, and refused to move forward. This was interpreted as a miraculous sign indicating where the relics should be placed. The church was, therefore, built on this spot between 1185 and 1212. After the capital was transferred to Warsaw, the church came to prominence as it was used to receive the deceased royalty brought from Warsaw for burial at Wawel. The funeral processions started here.

The church was damaged by frequent invasions and no trace of the medieval architecture has remained. The present interior and its decoration date from 1677 to 1684. The high altar with an effigy of St Florian, painted by Jan Tricius in the late 17th century, as well as an incomplete late-Gothic altar of St John the Baptist are of interest. The exterior was entirely remodelled by Franciszek Mączyński in the early 20th century.

Grunwald Monument ❿

Pomnik Grunwaldzki

Pl. Matejki. **Map** 2 D3 (6 E1). 🚌 *105, 129, 130, 154, 179.* 🚋 *3, 4, 5, 7, 12, 13, 15, 19.*

The monument, featuring King Władysław Jagiełło on horseback, was raised to mark the 500th anniversary of the 1410 victory at Grunwald (Tannenberg in German) over the Teutonic Knights. It was commissioned by the statesman, composer and pianist, Ignacy Jan Paderewski, from the sculptor Antoni Wiwulski.

The monument was inspired by grandiose German monuments of the second half of the 19th century. It was generally well received but some critics mocked the theatrical treatment of the figures. Some even suggested that the only lifelike figure was that of the dead Grand Master Ulrich von Jungingen. The monument was destroyed by the Nazis in 1939 and only reconstructed in 1975 by the sculptor Marian Konieczny.

National Bank of Poland ⓫

Basztowa 20. **Map** 2 D3 (6 E1). ***Tel*** *012 618 58 00.* 🚌 *124, 152, 502.* 🚋 *3, 4, 5, 7, 13, 14, 15, 19, 34.* ◯ *7am–5pm Mon–Fri.*

The bank, built between 1921 and 1925 by the architects Teodor Hoffman and Kazimierz Wyczyński, exemplifies the Neo-Classical style which became popular during the inter-war years. Neo-Classicism was then applied to important public buildings housing administrative and financial institutions, and was in sharp contrast to the Functionalism favoured in left-wing circles. The exterior sculptural decoration is by Karol Hukan and Stanisław Popławski. Inside, the domed banking hall is worth a visit.

The Academy of Fine Arts in Renaissance Revival style

Academy of Fine Arts ⓬

Pl. Matejki 13. **Map** 2 D3 (6 E1). ***Tel*** *012 299 20 14.* 🚌 *105, 129, 130, 154, 179.* 🚋 *3, 4, 5, 7, 13, 15, 19.* **Museum** *by appointment only.*

The school of Fine Arts in Cracow gained independent status in 1873 through the efforts of the artist Jan Matejko. Three years later the school was allocated a plot in Kleparz by the city's authorities. The building was constructed in 1879 to 1880 to designs by Maciej Moraczewski. The

The imposing building of the National Bank of Poland

architect adopted the Renaissance Revival style for this building, in accordance with the spirit of 19th-century Historicism which favoured such forms for school architecture. On the first floor is a studio where Matejko painted his *Kościuszko at Racławice* and *The Vows of King Jan Kazimierz*.

In 1900 the school gained university status, becoming the Academy of Fine Arts. Some of the best Polish artists were among its students. The building in Kleparz is currently the seat of the Academy's governing body and houses the faculties of painting, printmaking and sculpture.

Polish State Railways Headquarters ⓭

Pl. Matejki 12. **Map** 2 D3 (6 E1). *124, 502.* *3, 4, 7, 13, 15, 19.* *to the public.*

This imposing building was constructed in 1888 by an unknown Viennese architect who combined the forms of both Romanesque and Baroque Revival into an eclectic whole. It is possibly the only building in Cracow to have been directly influenced by the 19th-century monumental architecture of its Austrian neighbour, Vienna.

Church of St Vincent de Paul ⓮

Kościół św. Wincentego de Paul

Św. Filipa 19. **Map** 2 D3. ***Tel*** *012 422 56 40.* *124, 502.* *3, 4, 5, 7, 13, 15, 19.* *during services only.*

The present church was built between 1875 and 1877 and replaced the medieval Church of Saints Philip and James which had been dismantled by the Austrian authorities in 1801. The architect, Filip Pokutyński, was inspired by Italian late-Romanesque architecture. Although modest in design, the church differs from other

The interior of St Vincent de Paul

19th-century ecclesiastical architecture in Cracow because of its clear, compact and monumental forms.

The side altar features a miraculous icon depicting Christ Crucified. This much venerated image was brought after World War II from Milatyn near L'viv.

Globe House ⓯

Dom pod Globusem

Długa 1. **Map** 1 C3. ***Tel*** *012 422 54 23.* *124, 502.* *3, 4, 5, 7, 12, 13, 15, 19, 34.* **Mehoffer Hall** *by appointment only.*

This house was built in 1904 to 1906 for the Chamber of Commerce and Industry. It was designed by the architects Franciszek Mączyński and Tadeusz Stryjeński. The building is considered to be one of the best examples of the Art Nouveau style in Polish architecture. It is an interesting asymmetrical structure dominated by a pyramidal tower topped by a globe. The interior decoration, including murals in the great hall, is

The Globe House, a prime example of Art Nouveau architecture, topped by a pyramidal tower and globe

mainly the work of Józef Mehoffer. Stained-glass windows above the stairs depict allegorical subjects such as the progress of mankind through industry and commerce, thus reflecting the function of the building. The many cast-iron decorations are also of interest. Today, the building houses the publishers Wydawnictwo Literackie.

The façade of the Church of the Nuns of the Visitation

Church of the Nuns of the Visitation ⓰

Kościół Wizytek

Krowoderska 16. **Map** 1 C3. ***Tel*** *012 632 16 28.* *3, 5, 7, 19, 34.* *during services only.*

The convent was founded by Bishop Jan Małachowski as a votive offering after he was miraculously saved from drowning in the Vistula. The church is an interesting example of Cracow's Baroque ecclesiastical architecture. It was built from 1686 to 1695 by Giovanni Solari.

The façade is richly decorated with sculptures and ornaments. Some lavish decoration is also characteristic of the interior which, although small, is very elegant. The unusual high altar was made in 1695 by the sculptor Jerzy Golonka. The plasterwork is by Jan Liskowicz. The 18th-century murals decorating the vault have been much altered.

PIASEK AND NOWY ŚWIAT

Piasek, known as Garbary until the 19th century, is located west of the Old Quarter. Its development was hindered in the past by frequent invasions and lack of fortifications. A number of settlements with independent jurisdictions were located between Garbary and Wawel. They included Groble, Smoleńsko, Wielkorządowa, Wygoda, Retoryka and Rybaki, as well as Nowy Świat which remained under Cracow's jurisdiction. All these settlements were integrated by the Austrian authorities. By the end of the 19th century Piasek (Sand) and Nowy Świat (New World) began to flourish; wealthy residents moved in, drawn by the pleasant and quiet atmosphere away from the noisy town centre. As a result, some of the best residential architecture can be found here. It is mostly eclectic in style, dating from the start of the 20th century.

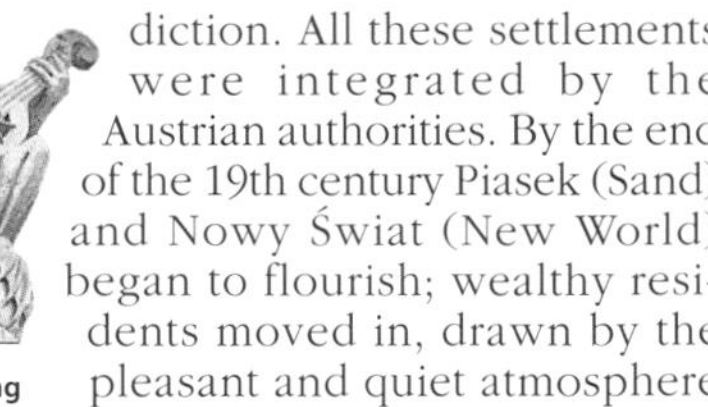

A singing frog

SIGHTS AT A GLANCE

Historic Monuments and Buildings
Academy of Mines and Metallurgy, Main Building 18
Ekielski House 7
Former Museum of Industry and Technology 2
House of the Singing Frog 6
Jagiellonian Library 17
Philharmonic Hall 1
School of Industry 16
"Sokół" Gymnastics Society 8
Spider House 21
Wyspiański Monument 14

Museums and Galleries
Hutten-Czapski Palace 10
Mehoffer Museum 12
National Museum, Main Building pp148–9 15

Churches
Capuchin Church 11
Carmelite Church 22
Church of the Felician Nuns 3
Church of the Merciful God 4
Church of the Sisters of the Sacred Heart of Jesus 9

Historic Streets
Avenue of Three Poets 19
Karmelicka Street 20
Retoryka Street 5

Open Space
Błonia Fields 13

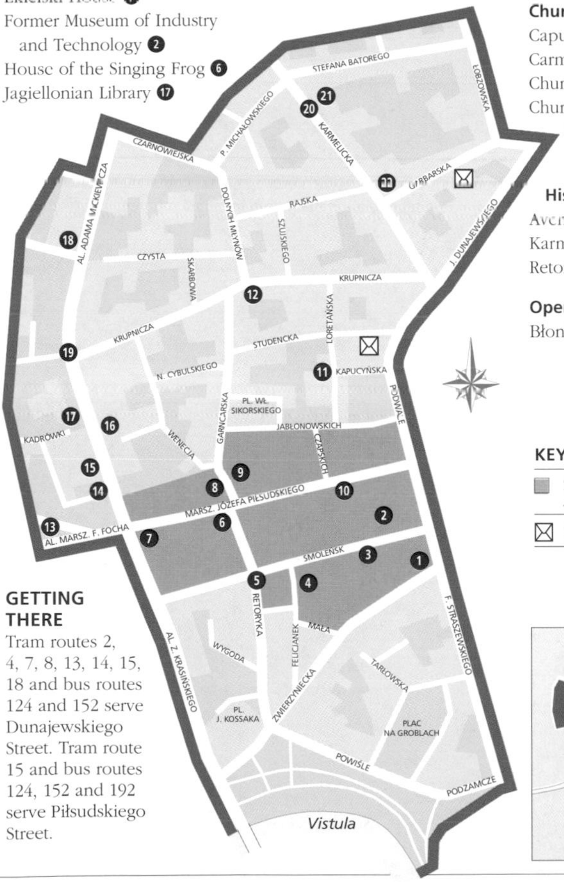

0 metres 200
0 yards 200

KEY
Street-by-Street map *See pp142–3*
Post office

GETTING THERE
Tram routes 2, 4, 7, 8, 13, 14, 15, 18 and bus routes 124 and 152 serve Dunajewskiego Street. Tram route 15 and bus routes 124, 152 and 192 serve Piłsudskiego Street.

◁ **An ivy-covered house on Łobzowska Street, typical of the north part of Piasek**

Street-by-Street: Piłsudski Street

Piłsudski (formerly Wolska) Street formed part of the route connecting Cracow with Wola Justowska. This route was first recorded in the 16th century. After Nowy Świat and the neighbouring jurisdictions were incorporated into Cracow, it became one of the main avenues in this part of town. The vista formed by the street is closed by the vast Błonia Fields with Kościuszko Mound in the distance, behind which Piłsudski Mound can also be seen. Elegant residential and public architecture developed here by the end of the 19th century. Some of the buildings show Polish architecture at its best.

Church of the Sisters of the Sacred Heart of Jesus
The square in front of this church was once a flood plain of the Rudawa river which was filled in prior to the construction of the convent buildings 9

"Sokół" Gymnastics Society
Looking at this beautiful mosaic frieze, one does not expect a building that houses an ordinary sports hall 8

★ Ekielski House
This unusual house was built by the architect Władysław Ekielski as his own home 7

House of the Singing Frog
This house was designed by Teodor Talowski and is decorated with some exquisite, though somewhat overdone, sculptures of fantastic creatures 6

★ Retoryka Street
The houses designed by Teodor Talowski have a unique "antiquarian" look and contribute to the picturesque character of the street 5

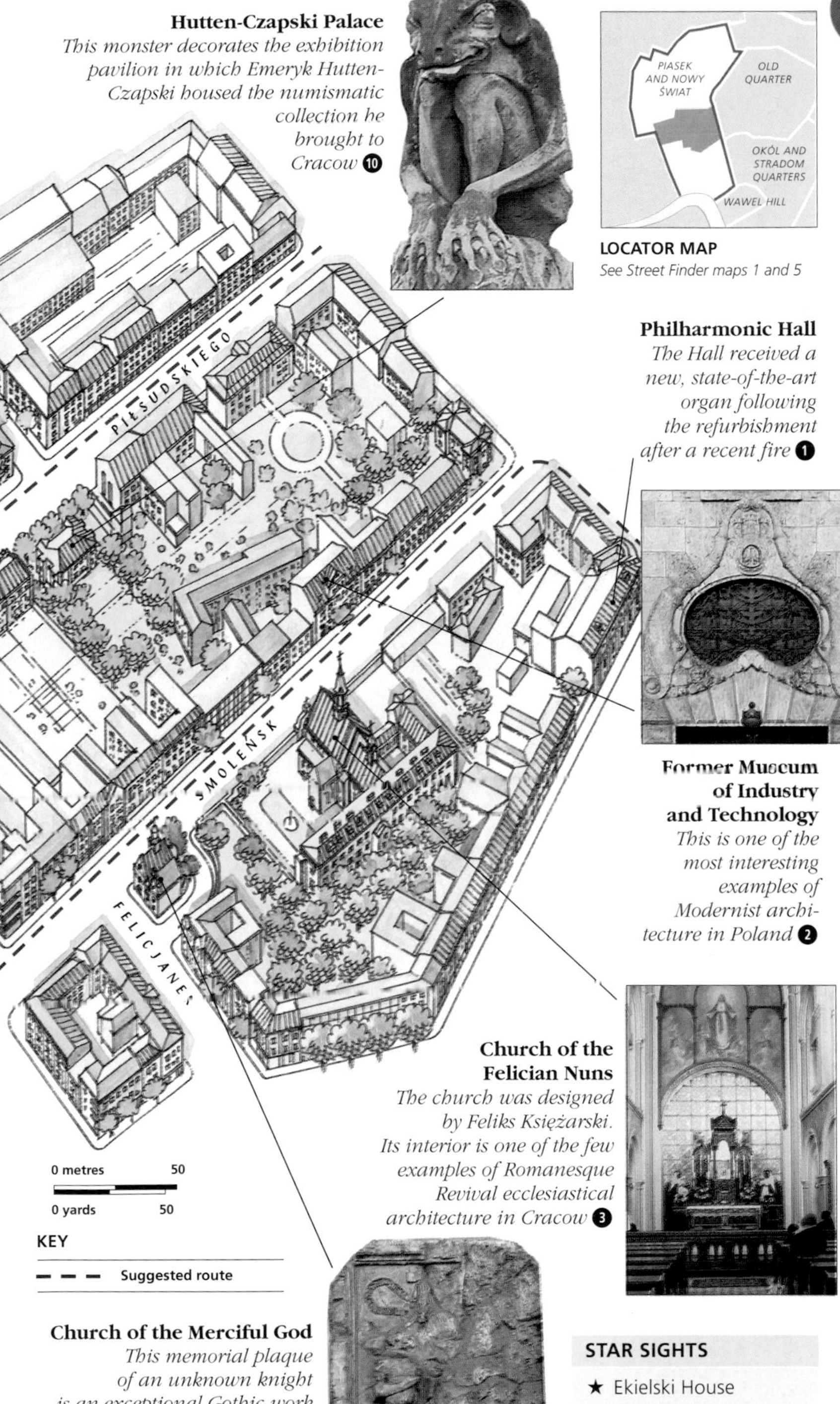

Hutten-Czapski Palace
This monster decorates the exhibition pavilion in which Emeryk Hutten-Czapski housed the numismatic collection he brought to Cracow ⑩

LOCATOR MAP
See Street Finder maps 1 and 5

Philharmonic Hall
The Hall received a new, state-of-the-art organ following the refurbishment after a recent fire ❶

Former Museum of Industry and Technology
This is one of the most interesting examples of Modernist architecture in Poland ❷

Church of the Felician Nuns
The church was designed by Feliks Księżarski. Its interior is one of the few examples of Romanesque Revival ecclesiastical architecture in Cracow ❸

0 metres 50

0 yards 50

KEY

– – – Suggested route

Church of the Merciful God
This memorial plaque of an unknown knight is an exceptional Gothic work surrounded by 19th-century architecture ❹

STAR SIGHTS

★ Ekielski House

★ Retoryka Street

The exterior of the Neo-Classical Philharmonic Hall

Philharmonic Hall ❶

Filharmonia

Zwierzyniecka 1. **Map** 1 B5 (5 C3). ***Tel*** *012 422 94 77. 124. 1, 2, 7, 8, 18, 36, 38.*

The Society of Friends of Music which was active in Cracow between 1817 and 1884 was regarded as the first philharmonic organization in occupied Poland. The Szymanowski State Philharmonia was established in Cracow in 1945. Walery Bierdiajew, Andrzej Panufnik and Krzysztof Penderecki were among the principal conductors. The orchestra and choir are complemented by the renowned chamber orchestra, Capella Cracoviensis. The Hall is housed in the former Catholic Cultural Institution. It was built between 1928 and 1930 by Pokutyński and Filipkiewicz in the Neo-Classical style which was popular with Polish architects around 1930.

Former Museum of Industry and Technology ❷

Gmach dawnego Muzeum Techniczno-Przemysłowego

Smoleńsk 9. **Map** 1 B5 (5 B3). *124. 1, 2, 7, 8, 18, 36, 38.*

This museum was established in 1868 by Andrzej Baraniecki who presented the city with his library and large collection of decorative arts. The museum ran courses in fine art, as well as a school of painting for women, and workshops on crafts. Collaboration with other institutions at the forefront of modern design was established. The museum published a number of titles, including journals such as *Przegląd Techniczny* (Technical Revue) and *Architekt* (The Architect). It also played an important role in the development of Polish applied art.

The museum was initially housed in the west wing of the Franciscan friary. The new building was constructed in 1908–14 to designs by Tadeusz Stryjeński. Józef Czajkowski designed the elegant façade, which is rich in geometrical forms. The structure of the building, which uses reinforced concrete, was novel at the time and the layout of the rooms was unusual. It is a leading example of Modernist architecture in Poland. The Museum of Industry and Technology was closed down in 1952. Today the Faculty of Industrial Design of the Academy of Fine Arts is housed here.

Façade detail, former Museum of Industry and Technology

Church of the Felician Nuns ❸

Kościół Felicjanek

Smoleńsk 4/6. **Map** 1 B5 (5 B3). ***Tel*** *012 422 00 39. 124. 1, 2, 8, 18. 8:30am–6pm daily and during services.*

The church of the Felician Nuns is one of the largest churches built in Cracow in the 19th century. This basilica in the Romanesque Revival style was built between 1882 and 1884 to designs by Feliks Księżarski, but modified by Sebastian Jaworzyński. The monumental and austere forms are striking, but softened inside through lavish decoration of the altars. The church houses relics of Blessed Maria Angela Truszkowska, the foundress of the Order, who died in 1899.

Altar of Blessed Maria Angela, Church of the Felician Nuns

Church of the Merciful God ❹

Kościół Miłosierdzia Bożego

Bożego Miłosierdzia 1. **Map** 1 B5 (5 B3). *1, 2, 7, 8, 15, 18, 36, 38. during services only.*

In 1555 Jan Żukowski established in Nowy Świat a home for the destitute and a small church. The church was consecrated in 1665. Located outside the city wall, both buildings were badly damaged during a number of invasions. The church has survived. On the outside wall facing Smoleńsk Street, remnants of a Gothic sepulchre, with a kneeling figure of a knight, can be seen.

Among the rather modest Baroque furnishings, the one of most interest is the image of the *Misericordia Domini* (The Suffering Christ and Sorrowful Mary) of 1650, hanging in the chancel.

Adjacent to the church is a presbytery, built in the eclectic style in 1905 to 1906 by Jan Zubrzycki.

Retoryka Street ❺

Ulica Retoryka

Map 1 B5 (5 B3, 4). *15, 18.*

The name of this street comes from the Retoryka jurisdiction, which was established in this area by the Ossolińskis in the first half of the 18th century. In the late 19th century the construction of boulevards began along the Rudawa river, which ran here. They were lined with houses whose architecture was marked by imaginative forms and unusual decoration. In 1910 the river was enclosed in a tunnel beneath street level. The houses designed by Teodor Talowski are most interesting. He used pseudo-antiquarian, intentionally-damaged motifs such as mosaics and plaques bearing popular Latin inscriptions for the external decoration. The plaque on his own house reads *festina lente* (hasten slowly) and that on the Ass House, *faber est suae quisque fortunae* (one works one's own destiny).

The houses in Retoryka Street, designed by Talowski and other leading architects active in Cracow around 1900, are interesting examples of Polish architecture at the dawn of the modern age.

House of the Singing Frog ❻

Dom Pod Śpiewającą żabą

Retoryka 1. **Map** 1 B5 (5 B3). *15, 18.*

The corner house at No. 1 Retoryka Street is considered to be the most interesting of Talowski's

House of the Singing Frog

designs. It was built in 1889 to 1890. The unusual structure consists of a number of segments varying in height and decoration. It was intended to be viewed at an angle from the adjacent street corner. The name of the house is a joke which refers to both the function and location of the building: it used to house a music school whose singing students were often accompanied by croaking frogs in the nearby Rudawa river.

Ekielski House ❼

Dom W. Ekielskiego

Piłsudskiego 40. **Map** 1 A5 (5 A3). *103, 114, 124, 152, 173, 179, 192.* *15, 18.*

This was the house of Władysław Ekielski, one of the foremost architects active in Cracow around 1900. He built this eclectic house for himself in 1899, borrowing from medieval and Renaissance architecture. The historic forms received a novel treatment. Fanciful and asymmetrical, the finished building is closer to an imaginary castle than a tenement house. Some features, such as the open loggia and the towers enclosing stairs, are characteristic of a suburban villa.

"Sokół" Gymnastics Society ❽

Gmach Towarzystwa Gimnastycznego „Sokół"

Piłsudskiego 27. **Map** 1 B5 (5 A3). ***Tel*** *012 421 73 97.* *15, 18.* *to the public.*

The "Sokół" Gymnastics Society was established in Lwów (L'viv) in 1867. The Society promoted physical fitness and ran a programme of lectures and self-educational courses. It also organized celebrations commemorating important events throughout Polish history.

The Society's sports hall is a simple brick building. It was constructed in 1889 to designs by Karol Knaus. In 1894 Teodor Talowski extended the eastern part of the building and embellished the whole exterior with decoration inspired by Romanesque and Gothic art. The original building was also decorated with a *sgraffito* frieze in which its designer, Antoni Tuch, depicted the Society's goals: physical fitness, spiritual self-development and the virtues of good citizenship. Important sporting events continue to take place in this hall.

The "Sokół" Gymnastics Society

Church of the Sisters of the Sacred Heart of Jesus ❾

Kościół Sercanek

Garncarska 26. **Map** 1 B5 (5 B3). ***Tel*** *012 421 86 68.* 15, 18. *during services only.*

The Convent of the Sisters of the Sacred Heart of Jesus was built between 1895 and 1900 to designs by Władysław Kaczmarski and Sławomir Odrzywolski. The architects designed the building along Garncarska Street so as to close one side of a square located here. They adjusted the façade of the church and the adjoining buildings of the convent to fit the slight bend in the street. This explains the irregularity of the plan.

The church is eclectic in style. The exterior walls show bare brickwork, ornamented in the Romanesque Revival style, as well as with pseudo-Renaissance *sgraffiti* and Neo-Classical sculptures by Jan Tombiński. Furnishings display Neo-Romanesque forms.

Detail from Church of the Sisters of the Sacred Heart of Jesus

Hutten-Czapski Palace ❿

Pałac Hutten-Czapskich

Piłsudskiego 12. **Map** 1 B5 (5 B3). ***Tel*** *012 422 27 33.* 15, 18. *Access to the collection for professional researchers only.*

This small palace in the Renaissance Revival style was built in 1884 by the architect Antoni Siedek for Hubert Krasiński. A few years later the property was purchased by Emeryk Hutten-Czapski who moved from the Vilnius area, bringing with him an exquisite numismatic collection. A pavilion, purpose-built to house this collection, was added in 1896. It was designed by Tadeusz Stryjeński and Zygmunt Hendel. The inscription decorating the pavilion reads *Monumentis Patriae naufragio ereptis* (To the national heritage salvaged from destruction). In 1903 the Czapskis bequeathed the palace and collection to the city of Cracow.

The Hutten-Czapski Palace in the Renaissance Revival style

Today the palace is the seat of the directors of the National Museum and houses the Museum's special holdings. A collection of salvaged architectural fragments can be found outside.

Capuchin Church ⓫

Kościół Kapucynów

Loretańska 11. **Map** 1 B4 (5 B2). ***Tel*** *012 422 48 03.* *124, 152, 192, 502.* *2, 4, 7, 8, 13, 14, 15, 18, 38.* *9:30am–4:30pm and 5–7pm daily as well as during services.*

The Capuchin friars arrived in Cracow in 1695. They began constructing the church and friary a year later. The work was supervised at first by Carlo Ceroni, who was later succeeded by Martino Pellegrini. The architecture and furnishings, the latter dating from 1775, reflect the strict rule of the Order which espouses extreme poverty. Hence the simplicity and functionalism of the architecture and the modest composition of the altars made of painted timber and lacking decoration. The altars, however, feature good paintings. They include *The Annunciation* by Pietro Dandini, *St Erasmus and St Cajetan*, two 18th-century effigies by Łukasz Orłowski, and *St Francis of Assisi* by Szymon Czechowicz. A number of sepulchres are of interest. A wooden crucifix in front of the church indicates the tomb of the Confederates of Bar who fell in a rebellion against the Russians in 1768.

Between 1712 and 1719 an external Loreto Chapel was built to a design by Kacper Bażanka; this is linked to the church through a cloister. The chapel houses a Neo-Classical altar with a miraculous statue of the Madonna of Loreto and a beautiful tabernacle. The latter was also designed by Bażanka. An animated Christmas crib is erected here every year, featuring historic Polish characters.

The interior of the Loreto Chapel by the Capuchin Church

Mehoffer Museum ⓬
Muzeum Józefa Mehoffera

Krupnicza 26. **Map** 1 B4 (5 B2). ***Tel*** *012 421 11 43.* *103, 114, 144, 164, 169, 173, 179.* *8, 13, 15, 18.* *10am–3:30pm Wed, Thu, Sat & Sun, 10am–6pm Fri.* *free Sun.*

Stanisław Wyspiański was born in this house in 1869. In 1930 it was bought by Józef Mehoffer (1869–1946), one of the foremost Modernist artists in Poland. He was also a painter, stage and interior designer. In 1968 the house was acquired by the National Museum and the Mehoffer Museum was established. The interiors have been preserved in the tasteful way they were arranged by the artist himself. Many of his works, including paintings, stained glass, cartoons for stained glass and murals, are on display.

***Portrait of Mrs Mehoffer* by Józef Mehoffer**

Błonia Fields ⓭

Map 1 A5. *100, 103, 114, 164, 173, 179.* *15, 18.*

The Błonia Fields formed part of the grounds owned by the Convent of Premonstratensian (Norbertine) Nuns in Zwierzyniec and were originally used as pastures. In 1366 the nuns made a rather bad deal with the city's authorities and exchanged Błonia for a house in Floriańska Street. The house proved to be unprofitable and was eventually destroyed by fire. This gave rise to a joke about the nuns who had exchanged pastures for a bonfire. For centuries the nuns tried in vain to regain the land. The Błonia Fields remain the property of the City of Cracow.

Błonia were used in the past as a venue for mass religious and national celebrations. The first football match in Cracow took place here in 1894. Pope John Paul II said a Holy Mass here on two occasions. Today it is a wildlife sanctuary in the centre of Cracow and a popular place for recreation. It should, however, be avoided on days when football matches between Wisła and Cracovia take place.

Wyspiański Monument ⓮
Pomnik S. Wyspiańskiego

Map 1 A5 (5 A3). *103, 114, 164, 173, 179.*

The monument was unveiled in 1982 to mark the 75th anniversary of the death of the great artist and playwright of the so-called Young Poland movement (Polish Modernism). The sculptor, Marian Konieczny, depicted Stanisław Wyspiański surrounded by the characters from two of his plays, *The Wedding* and *November Night*. The monument was badly received and prompted unfavourable interpretations. Its location, right behind the parking place in front of the National Museum, proved to be particularly unfortunate as the figures seem to emerge from behind parked cars. The agitated gestures of the figures have even been interpreted as an expression of their astonishment at the fast rate of automobile development.

Wyspiański Monument

National Museum, Main Building ⓯

See pp148–9.

School of Industry ⓰
Szkoła Przemysłowa

Krupnicza 44. **Map** 1 A4 (5 A2). ***Tel*** *012 422 32 20.* *103, 114, 164, 169, 173, 179.* *to the public.*

In 1834 the Institute of Technology was established in Cracow, and funded by the bequest of the architect Szczepan Humbert. It was later transformed into the State School of Industry. In 1912 the school moved to a new building designed by Sławomir Odrzywolski. This irregular brick structure, decorated with Art Nouveau ornaments, resembles an imaginary castle.

National Museum, Main Building ⓯

Jacek Malczewski by W. Szymanowski

The modern building of the National Museum was designed by Czesław Boratyński, Edward Kreisler and Bolesław Schmidt in 1934 but the building was not completed until 1989. Permanent galleries display Polish painting and sculpture of the 20th century, decorative arts and arms and other mementos of the Polish Army. Temporary shows are also organized here. The art collection is one of the largest in Poland and includes works by leading Modernist artists, as well as some outstanding works from the period between the two World Wars. Post-1945 art, however, predominates.

Execution *(1949)*
The art of Andrzej Wróblewski, who died prematurely, is a personal analysis of the tragic war years.

Emballage *(1975)*
This work by Tadeusz Kantor is an artistic interpretation of Jan Matejko's great history piece depicting The Prussian Homage.

The Uniform of Józef Piłsudski
"The uniform of the grey rifleman" reminds one of the tragic but nevertheless victorious history of the Polish Legions between 1914 and 1917.

Baton
This gilded "buzdygan" baton belonged to Grand Hetman Stanisław Jabłonowski, who fought in the Battle of Vienna in 1683.

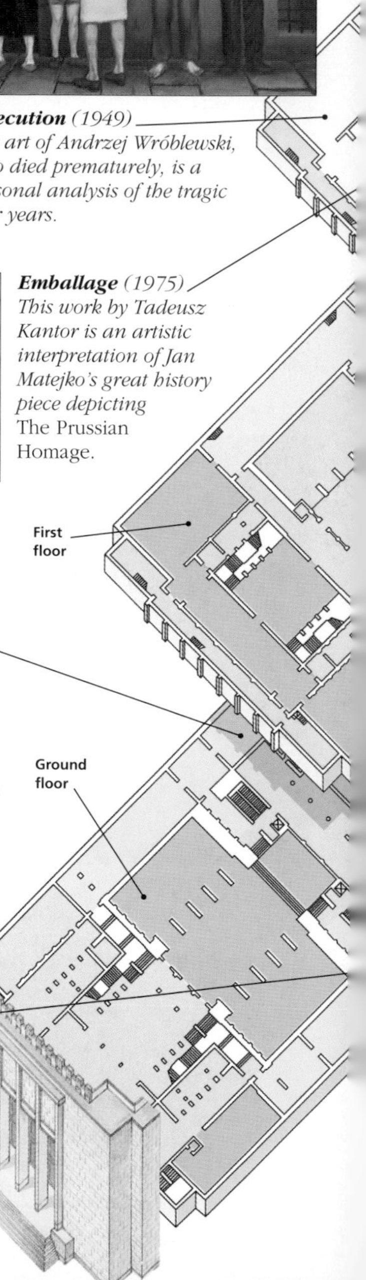

First floor

Ground floor

Main entrance

KEY

- Temporary exhibitions
- Arms and Colours in Poland
- Gallery of Polish Art of the 20th c.
- Gallery of Decorative Arts
- Non-exhibition space

Self-Portrait with Masks
This self-portrait by Wojciech Weiss (1875–1950) dates from the early years when the artist remained under the influence of Symbolism.

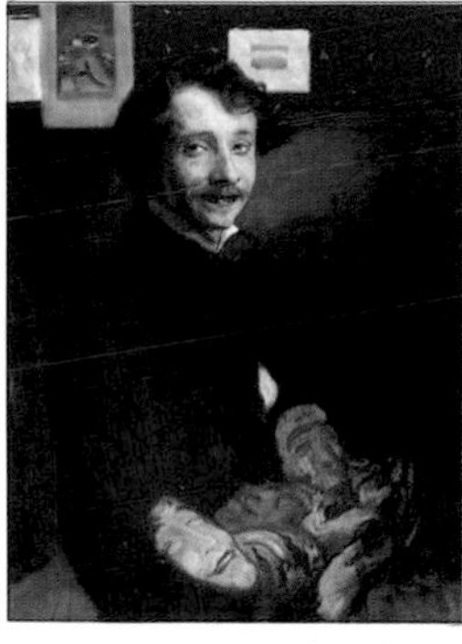

Second floor

VISITORS' CHECKLIST

Al. 3 Maja 1. **Map** 1 A3, 4 (5 A3). ***Tel*** *012 633 53 31.* *103, 109, 114, 124, 134, 144, 152, 164, 169, 173, 179, 192, 194, 409* *15, 18.* *10am–4pm Tue & Thu, 10am–7pm Wed, Fri & Sat, 10am–3pm Sun.* *free Thu.*

★ A Design for Mickiewicz's Statue in Vilnius
This monumental statue by the Cubist artist Zbigniew Pronaszko (1885–1958) was never executed and exists only as a model.

GALLERY GUIDE
Temporary displays and the exhibition "Arms and Colours in Poland" are located on the ground floor. The display on the first floor is dedicated to decorative arts and temporary exhibitions. The Gallery of Polish Art of the 20th Century is housed on the second floor.

★ *Polonia*, a Cartoon for Stained Glass
Stanisław Wyspiański's cartoons for stained-glass windows in the Cathedral symbolically depict visions of the past but also relate to modern issues.

Nike of the Legions
This is one of Jacek Malczewski's symbolic tours de force. *Nike, the goddess of victory, is sitting by the body of a legionary whose face resembles Józef Piłsudski.*

STAR EXHIBITS

★ *Polonia*, a Cartoon for Stained Glass

★ A Design for Mickiewicz's Statue

Jagiellonian Library ⓱

Biblioteka Jagiellońska

Al. Mickiewicza 22. **Map** 1 A4 (5 A2). ***Tel*** *012 633 63 77.* *15, 18.* *103, 114, 144, 164, 169, 173, 179, 194.* *8am–8pm Mon–Fri, 8am–3pm Sat.*

For many centuries the Library of the Jagiellonian University was housed in the Collegium Maius *(see pp106–7)*. The new building was constructed between 1931 and 1939 to designs by Wacław Krzyżanowski. It has impressive modern forms and a spacious and functional interior. It is not only the success of the design but also the high quality of craftsmanship and the use of luxurious materials that make this building an outstanding example of Cracow's architecture in the interwar years.

During the 1990s work was undertaken on a new wing of the Library, designed by Romuald Loegler. This was completed in 2001, when the University celebrated the 6th centenary of its re-establishment. The new wing matches the forms of the old building and is one of the most interesting examples of architecture of the 1990s.

The Library's holdings include 25,000 priceless manuscripts and 100,000 rare books and prints.

An illuminated page in the Behem Codex, Jagiellonian Library

Academy of Mines and Metallurgy, Main Building ⓲

Al. Mickiewicza 30. **Map** 1 A3, 4 (5 A1). ***Tel*** *012 617 33 33.* *103, 114, 144, 164, 169, 173, 179, 194.* *7:30am–8pm daily.*

The Academy of Mines was established in Cracow in 1919. In 1922 the Faculty of Metallurgy was added. After 1945 the Academy was transformed into a large and well-equipped technological university. It has its own nuclear reactor and modern acoustic laboratory. The enormous main building, with 110,000 sq m (1,183,600 sq ft) of floor space, was built between 1923 and 1935. It was designed by Sławomir Odrzywolski and Wacław Krzyżanowski in a Neo-Classical style that is particularly prominent in the façade and portico. The statues of miners and steel workers in front of the building are by Jan Raszka.

Statues in front of the Academy of Mines and Metallurgy

In German-occupied Poland the building became the seat of the Governor-General. A museum housed in Building C-1 is dedicated to the history of the Academy.

Avenue of Three Poets ⓳

Aleje Trzech Wieszczów

Map 1 A3, 1 A4, 1 B2, 1 C2. *103 114, 129, 139, 144, 164, 173, 179.*

In the mid-19th century an earthen embankment was constructed along what is today this avenue, and in 1887 to 1888 a railway line was laid for trains connecting Cracow to Płaszów. East of the embankment, new streets were laid out and new houses constructed in the eclectic and Art Nouveau styles. When in 1910 the borders of Cracow were extended, the railway and the embankment were dismantled. Their site was replaced by a wide avenue comprising a dual carriageway with a belt of greenery in the middle. Each of the sections of the avenue was named after a Romantic poet, namely Krasiński, Mickiewicz and Słowacki. The intention was to transform the avenue into Cracow's Champs Elysées.

A view looking down Karmelicka Street

Karmelicka Street 20

Ulica Karmelicka

Map 1 B3, 4 (B5, C1). *114, 124, 152, 159, 164, 169, 179.* *4, 8, 13, 14, 38.*

Karmelicka Street formed part of the old route connecting Cracow to Czarna Wieś and Łobzów. Formerly known as Czarna, Karmelicka was always the main street in the Garbary quarter. The Carmelite Church and, at No. 12, the Town Hall of Garbary were built here. Initially the street was divided into two parts: the wider part stretched from the Cobblers' Gate to a small bridge, beyond which the street narrowed considerably. This explains why the Carmelite friary building projects into the present-day street.

By the end of the 19th century Karmelicka became one of the most elegant streets in Cracow. Splendid houses were built to designs by Maksymilian Nitsch, Teodor Talowski and Filip Pokutyński. The writers Stanisław Przybyszewski and Tadeusz Boy-Żeleński were among the celebrated residents.

Spider House 21

Dom pod Pająkiem

Karmelicka 35. **Map** 1 B3 (5 C1). *4, 8, 13, 14, 38.* *to the public.*

This house was built in 1889 by Teodor Talowski, one of the leading architects in Cracow in the late 19th century. His intention was to give this irregular structure "an ancient appearance" by adding a "Gothic" round corner tower and a high gable in the style of Netherlandish Mannerism. By using different architectural styles of the past he wanted to pretend that the house had been rebuilt many times. He inserted, for example, a parapet modelled on the Renaissance Cloth Hall into the crenellated "Gothic" frieze. The decoration is rich in inventive detail.

Carmelite Church 22

Kościół Karmelitów

Karmelicka 19. **Map** 1 B3 (5 C1). ***Tel*** *012 632 67 52.* *144, 152, 159, 164, 169, 192.* *4, 8, 13, 14.* *9:30am–4:30pm and 5–7pm daily and during services.*

According to a legend, Duke Władysław Herman cured his skin disease by rubbing sand on the infected areas. He took the sand from a site miraculously indicated by the Virgin Mary. This site was therefore named Piasek (sand), and a votive church founded by the duke was built in 1087. Thus was born the legend of the Madonna of the Sand.

The church was actually founded by Queen Jadwiga in 1395. It was almost entirely destroyed during the Swedish invasion in the 17th century and its remnants were incorporated into the new Baroque church which was consecrated in 1679. The magnificent high altar, made in 1698 to 1699, and lavishly decorated with acanthus leaves, is worth noting. The splendid stalls and the balcony with the organ, both by Jan Hankis, are also of interest. An icon of the Madonna of the Sand, painted directly on the wall, is much venerated.

The Calvary Chapel in the side wall of the Carmelite Church

QUEEN JADWIGA (HEDWIG)

Queen Jadwiga (c. 1374–99) was famous for her piety and charity. She contributed to the development of the Academy of Cracow. Venerated since the Middle Ages, she was finally canonized in 1997. A touching legend links Jadwiga to the Carmelite Church. It tells the story of a mason employed at the construction of the church who lamented to Jadwiga about his poverty and lack of money to buy medicine for his wife. The Queen removed a gold brooch from her shoe and offered it to the man. The imprint of her foot can still be seen today.

The imprint of Queen Jadwiga's foot

FURTHER AFIELD

Lesser Poland is the most densely populated and richest region of the former Polish-Lithuanian Commonwealth. Until the 17th century the local nobility held the highest offices and played an important political role at the royal court of Cracow, influencing matters of state. The nobles spent their time carrying out official duties in the capital as well as staying in their country estates, where they built castles, churches and monasteries. They introduced the art and culture of Cracow to the rest of Lesser Poland. In the centuries that followed, Cracow continued to dictate the local fashion and was a centre of artists for the whole province. Cracow's strong influence over neighbouring regions contributed to their unique artistic climate, in which the elitist merged with the vernacular, often with surprising effects. To appreciate the long tradition of Cracow's links with the area, visitors should certainly consider excursions out of town. They are ideal for those who are interested in historic/traditional architecture and places of historical interest, as well as those who like to relax in beautiful natural surroundings.

A font holding holy water in Kalwaria Zebrzydowska

SIGHTS AT A GLANCE

Auschwitz (Oświęcim) 12
Branice 3
Grodzisko 8
Kalwaria Zebrzydowska 13
Mogiła 2
Niepołomice 4
Nowa Huta 1
Ojców 7
Pieskowa Skała 9
Staniątki 5
Tyniec 10
Wadowice 11
Wieliczka 6

KEY

- City Centre
- Greater Cracow
- Railway station
- Balice Airport
- Motorway
- Major road
- Minor road

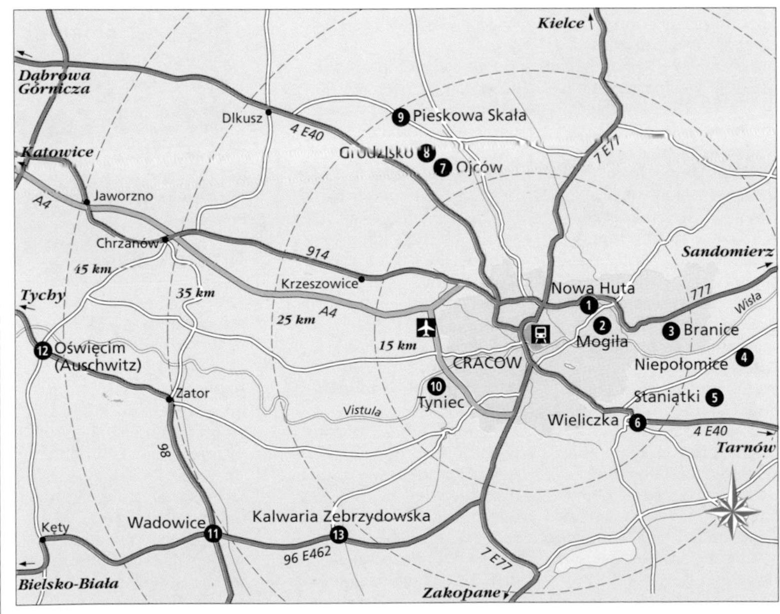

The Socialist Realist architecture of Nowa Huta

Nowa Huta ❶

117, 132, 138, 139, 142, 148, 149, 163, 174. 4, 15, 17, 21, 22.

The Communist authorities in Cracow suffered a humiliating and crushing defeat in the 1946 referendum. This they blamed upon an inappropriate social balance within the class-based society. In order to "rearrange" this balance, a programme of quick industrialization of the Cracow region was undertaken to increase the working-class population. In 1948 a contract was signed between Poland and the Soviet Union for a new giant steelworks, named after Lenin. The construction of a new town named Nowa Huta (New Steelworks) began in 1949. It was designed by Tadeusz Ptaszycki in the Socialist Realist style. This Socialist Realism, a style imported directly from the Soviet Union, was influenced by classical and Renaissance architecture.

The housing estate, Centre, built between 1949 and 1955, is an interesting example of urban planning. Cheap concrete blocks predominated in the architecture that was developed after 1956. In this "model Communist town" there was no room for churches. But, despite official intentions, the people of Nowa Huta demanded, and from the 1950s even struggled for a church. The construction of churches on the estates of Nowa Huta began in the 1970s. Among these, the well-known Ark of God *(see p37)* is an outstanding piece of modern sacred Polish architecture. During the period of Martial Law (1981–1983) the workers residing in Nowa Huta clearly demonstrated that they were not the best allies of the Communists. The town became notorious for riots, which were suppressed by the ZOMO stormtroopers.

The Lenin Steelworks have been renamed Sendzimir.

Mogiła ❷

7 km (4 miles) east of Cracow. *123, 153, 163.* *15.* **Cistercian Church** *Klasztorna 226.* ***Tel*** *012 644 23 31.* *6am–7pm daily.*

Mogiła village developed around the Cistercian Abbey, a religious centre of great importance in the past. The Cistercians were brought to Poland in 1222, or 1225, by Iwo Odrowąż, the Bishop of Cracow. They settled by the Dłubnia river, a tributary of the Vistula. The new monastery was named *Clara Tumba* (Bright Tomb, Jasna Mogiła, in Polish) because of the proximity of a prehistoric mound and the reputed burial place of the legendary princess Wanda. The church was consecrated in 1266.

This Romanesque church followed the strict building regulations of the Cistercian order. The chancel ended with a flat perpendicular wall; pairs of chapels which have a square ground-plan were added to the transept. In 1447 the church was destroyed by fire. Gothic forms were introduced during its rebuilding. A wooden crucifix has miraculously survived. Stanisław Samostrzelnik decorated the interior with murals in the first half of the 16th century. These Renaissance paintings are complemented by 18th-century furnishings. The Baroque façade was added by Franz Moser as late as 1779 to 1780. Other wall paintings in the church were made by Jan Bukowski in the early 20th century.

The Gothic cloister built in the time of Kazimierz the Great is the most beautiful part of the Abbey. It leads to the Chapter House, which features murals painted in the 19th century by Michał Stachowicz. These illustrate scenes from the life of Wanda. Not far from the abbey is the Church of St Bartholomew. Built in 1466, it is one of the oldest timber churches in Poland.

The Renaissance Old Manor in Branice

Branice ❸

12 km (7.5 miles) east from Cracow. **Manor** Branice 131. *Temporarily closed to the public.*

Branice is situated not far from Niepołomice and is worth visiting for its two manors which exemplify the small-scale residential architecture of the gentry of Lesser Poland. The Old Manor, later converted into a store, was built around 1603 for the Castellan of Żarnów, Jan Branicki, by an architect from the circle of Santi Gucci.

The exterior of the manor is decorated with *sgraffiti* and topped with a parapet. The doors and fireplace inside are lavishly decorated with imaginative Mannerist ornaments carved in stone.

The New Manor was built in the early 19th century. Its high hipped roof, and the entrance marked by a small portico supported by columns, make this building characteristic of Polish architecture of this type. Both manors are set in a picturesquely landscaped park, laid out in the 19th century.

Next to Branice is the village of Ruszcza with the Church of St George. The church was built around 1420 by the Royal Master of the Pantry, Wierzbięta of Branice. His Gothic memorial plaque and the Baroque high altar are both of interest.

Niepołomice ❹

24 km (15 miles) southeast of Cracow. *minibus from Cracow's Main Railway Station.* *from Cracow's Main Railway Station.* **Church** *7am–6pm daily.* **Castle** ***Tel*** *012 281 11 17.* *10am–5pm Mon–Fri, 10am–4pm Sat & Sun.*

The royal grounds in Niepołomice, situated on the outskirts of a vast woodland, were much favoured by Polish kings. They came here to rest and hunt, and developed magnificent buildings in the town they owned. The Gothic church in Niepołomice was founded by King Kazimierz the Great between 1350 and 1358. Like other sacred buildings founded by this sovereign, this church had two aisles separated by pillars.

It was later rebuilt in the Baroque style. Fragments of the rich stone decoration from the interior of the medieval church have survived and are displayed in the Old Sacristy. Outstanding Gothic paintings made between 1370 and 1375 by an Italian master, commissioned by Princess Elźbieta (daughter of Władysław the Short), are also in the Old Sacristy.

Next to the church are two mausolea of noble families, both in the form of chapels covered by domes. Built in 1596, the Branicki Chapel is the earlier of the two. It features an ornamental tomb made by the Italian architect and sculptor Santi Gucci in the Mannerist style. In the Chapel of the Lubomirski family, built in 1640, wall paintings depicting scenes from the life of St Carlo Borromeo are of interest. Late-Baroque altars were added in the 18th century.

The hunting lodge in Niepołomice was originally built by Kazimierz the Great. It was transformed by Zygmunt August into a magnificent residence. The new castle was constructed between 1550 and 1571. Its regular plan and the central, square courtyard differ from other royal Renaissance houses in Poland. In 1637 massive stone arcades were added to the courtyard. Part of the castle is used to house the Museum of Hunting.

The dense forest (Puszcza Niepołomicka), a favourite hunting ground of Polish kings, stretches right behind the town. Brown bears, bison, lynx, wildcat and deer are known to have inhabited it. The forest is not so magnificent as it used to be, though wild areas have been preserved, including the bison sanctuary in the Proszowo forest.

Façade of the palace in Niepołomice, a residence of Polish kings

Belfry by the Church of the Benedictine Nuns in Staniątki

Staniątki ❺

24 km (15 miles) southeast of Cracow. *from Cracow's Main Railway Station and Cracow-Płaszów.* **Church** *during services only.*

The Convent and Church of the Benedictine Nuns in Staniątki is not far from Niepołomice. The convent was founded in 1228 by Klemens of Ruszcza, Castellan of Cracow. The Church of St Mary and St Adalbert, dating from the same period, is Poland's oldest hall-church (a type of church in which the aisles and nave are of the same height).

The church is a brick structure. Its rather modest decoration is carved in stone. The interior was refurbished completely in the 18th century. The lavishly decorated organ gallery, added in 1705, and wall paintings executed in 1760 by the Rococo artist Andrzej Radwański of Cracow, are of great interest.

Wieliczka ❻

12 km (7.5 miles) southeast of Cracow. *Luxbus coaches from Cracow's Main Railway Station.* *from Cracow's Main Railway Station and Cracow-Płaszów.* **Salt Mines** Daniłowicza 10. ***Tel*** *012 278 73 02.* *Apr–Oct: 7:30am–7:30pm daily; Nov–Mar: 8am–4pm daily.* *1 Jan, Easter, 1 Nov, 24–25 & 31 Dec.*

Wieliczka developed and was granted a municipal charter in 1290 due to her rich deposits of salt. Salt was probably excavated here as early as the 11th century. The Latin name for Wieliczka was *Magnum Sal* (Great Salt) and indicated the importance of this mine in comparison to a smaller one in nearby Bochnia. According to a legend, the salt in Wieliczka constituted the dowry of St Kinga (Cunegunda) when she marrried Duke Bolesław the Chaste. The salt dowry was supposedly transposed magically from Hungary to Cracow for the wedding.

The salt in Wieliczka was regarded for centuries as a major natural asset of the Kingdom of Poland. An enormous network of underground galleries and chambers was created here over the centuries. Salt was also used as a building material in the carving of underground chapels and altars in front of which the miners prayed for God's providence and protection against accidents.

The Wieliczka Salt Mine Museum is housed inside the mine. The exhibits on display illustrate the old mining methods and tools. A unique underground sanatorium is also housed here.

The small chapel overhanging the mountain river in Ojców

Ojców ❼

24 km (15 miles) northwest of Cracow. *from Cracow's Main Coach Station.* **Ojców National Park Museum** ***Tel*** *012 389 20 40.* *Apr–Oct: 9am–4:30pm daily; Nov–Mar: 8am–3pm Tue–Fri.* **Castle Tower** *May–Sep: 9am–4pm Mon–Sat; Oct–Apr: 10am–3pm Mon–Sat.*

The valley of the Prądnik river is the most beautiful part of the local uplands. The river eroded a deep gorge through the limestone. The steep cliffs are overgrown with trees through which rock formations – some of which resemble pulpits, organs and needles – can be seen.

Kazimierz the Great had a number of hill-top castles built in the area to guard the western border of his Kingdom. These castles were called eagles' nests. In 1956 part of the Prądnik valley was transformed into the Ojców National Park.

Among the natural formations of particular interest is a cave, which is said to have provided protection to King Władysław the Short while he was in hiding from the Czech King Venceslaus. Kazimierz the Great, the son of Władysław the Short, built in Ojców one of the most important fortresses in Poland, of which only remnants have survived.

Following the discovery of the healing properties of the local springs in the mid-19th century, the village at the foot of the castle was transformed into a spa, and therapy clinics were set up. Newly-built hotels imitated the architecture of luxurious foreign resorts. The Łokietek Hotel was regarded as the most sumptuous of all the buildings. It now houses the museum of the Ojców National Park. During the Partition era, the Tsarist authorities refused to give planning permission for a church. So only a small timber chapel was built in 1901 to 1902 overhanging the Prądnik river.

Grodzisko ❽

28 km (17 miles) northwest of Cracow. *from Cracow's Main Railway Station.* **Church** *9–10am Sun.*

Grodzisko is situated not far from Ojców, on the opposite bank of the Prądnik river. The Convent of the Poor Clares was established here in 1262. Blessed Salomea, the sister of Duke Bolesław the Chaste, was the first Mother Superior. The nuns moved to Cracow in 1320 and the convent buildings fell into ruin. The cult of the Blessed Salomea developed over time, and in 1677 Canon Sebastian Piskorski transformed Grodzisko into a sanctuary devoted to this pious nun. He designed a complex hermitage consisting of a church and a number of chapels enclosed within a wall. This is a charming place with surprising Baroque ideas, some of which were borrowed from Bernini, the leading architect of Roman Baroque. The elephant bearing an obelisk, for example, was modelled on his art.

The Chapel of St Kinga in Wieliczka salt mine

A room in the Pieskowa Skała Castle

Pieskowa Skała 9

35 km (22 miles) northwest of Cracow. *from Cracow's Main Coach Station.* **Castle Tel** *012 389 60 04. 10am–3:30pm Tue–Fri, 10am–5:30pm Sat, Sun (3:30pm Nov–May). free Wed.*

The castle in Pieskowa Skała was built by King Kazimierz the Great in the 14th century as an important part of the defence system on the Cracow-Częstochowa Uplands. It became private property in 1377.

Between 1542 and 1544, extensive enlargement of the castle was undertaken by Stanisław Szafraniec and his wife, Anna Dębińska. The commission was probably given to the Italian architect Nicolo da Castiglione. The rock on which the castle was built determined the scale of its enlargement. Despite limited space, the architecture of the castle developed around a trapezium-shaped inner courtyard and included arcades, modelled on Wawel Castle, as well as a suite of rooms on the second floor with decorative ceilings. An external open gallery offering a view over the Prądnik valley was an interesting addition. A Gothic tower, later remodelled and covered with a Baroque dome, is a picturesque feature of Pieskowa Skała Castle's irregular structure.

The castle houses a museum affiliated to the Royal Castle at Wawel, which is dedicated to the history of Polish interiors from medieval times to the 19th century. Some lavish pieces of furniture, tapestries and other decorative objects, as well as paintings and sculptures, are on display. Of particular interest are paintings by 19th-century English artists.

Tyniec 10

10 km (6 miles) west of Cracow. *112.* **Benedictine Abbey** Benedyktyńska 37. ***Tel*** *012 267 59 77. 7:30am–6:30pm daily.*

The Benedictine Abbey at Tyniec is situated on a high rocky escarpment by the Vistula, west of Wawel. The monks were brought to Cracow in 1044, probably by King Kazimierz the Restorer. A Romanesque basilica was built here soon after. Only parts of the walls and a few architectural fragments of this basilica have survived. The new church and monastery were built in the 15th century. The church was remodelled in the early 17th century in the Baroque style, and magnificent stalls were added to the chancel. Large altars in black marble were made in the 18th century, possibly to designs by Francesco Placidi.

In the 12th and 13th centuries, during the period when Poland was fragmented into principalities, Tyniec was transformed into a fortress and played an important role during the struggles for the crown of the suzerain province of Cracow. By the end of the 16th century the fortifications were extended. A number of gates linked through an angled corridor were introduced as part of a defence system modelled on Wawel. Tyniec was a strategic site and as a result often came under attack from the enemy.

Today, the Benedictine Abbey is a picturesque sight.

Benedictine Abbey in Tyniec on the Vistula

The Church of the Presentation of the Virgin Mary in Wadowice

Wadowice ⑪

40 km (25 miles) southwest of Cracow. from Cracow's Main Coach Station. **Family House of John Paul II** ***Tel*** *033 326 62.* *May–Sep: 9am–1pm and 2–6pm daily; Oct–Apr: 9am–noon and 2–6pm daily.*

Wadowice was first recorded in 1327, but the town came to international attention in 1978 when Karol Wojtyła, born here on 18 May 1920, was elected Pope. Almost immediately the town became a place of mass pilgrimage and the local sites associated with the Pope include the Baroque Church of the Presentation of the Virgin Mary in Market Square, where he was baptised, and his family home, which now houses a museum dedicated to the pontiff.

Another site associated with John Paul II is the monumental votive Church of St Peter the Arch-shepherd which was built on the outskirts of Wadowice in thanksgiving for the Pope's survival of an assassination attempt on 13 May 1981. Designed by Ewa Węcławowicz-Gyurkovich and Jacek Gyurkovich, the walls of its nave seem to give way under the power of light, symbolizing the triumph of good over evil.

The town has had a chequered history, especially in the last century. Whilst under German occupation during World War II, it was renamed Frauenstadt and the entire Jewish population was either executed or sent to nearby Auschwitz *(see below)*.

More recently, Wadowice has been growing as a tourist centre, replacing the local industries which collapsed in the newly democratic economy of the 1990s.

Auschwitz (Oświęcim) ⑫

See pp160–63.

Kalwaria Zebrzydowska ⑬

30 km (19 miles) sw of Cracow. *from Main Coach Station or Cracow-Dębniki.* *from Cracow's Main Railway Station or Cracow-Płaszów.* **Bernardine Church** *6am–7pm daily.*

Calavaries, or Ways of the Cross, were introduced in the 16th century and were built throughout Europe to commemorate the Passion and Death of Christ. The landscaping of Calvary grounds had to imitate the topography of Jerusalem. They consisted of structures commemorating the "tragedy of Salvation" and imitations of holy sites connected to the Virgin Mary.

Poland's first Calvary was built by Mikołaj Zebrzydowski from 1600 onwards. He located the chapels representing the Stations of the Cross along Christ's route to Golgotha on the Żary Hill near his residence in Zebrzydowice.

Mystery plays enacting Christ's Passion are staged in Kalwaria during Holy Week. The "funeral of the Virgin" takes place on the feast of the Assumption. Crowds of pilgrims arrive to venerate the miraculous icon of the Mother of God, whose cult in the Bernardine Church goes back to the 17th century. Kalwaria is one of the main religious centres in Lesser Poland. It is also a place where the architectural heritage of Cracow's environs is seen at its best.

The Baroque façade of the early 17th-century Bernardine Church in Kalwaria Zebrzydowska

Kalwaria Zebrzydowska

The most interesting chapels in the Kalwaria Zebrzydowska are those designed by Paulus Baudarth, a Flemish architect and goldsmith. He was commissioned to design many chapels, and avoiding repetition must have been a difficult task. He applied many different ground-plans, including a Greek cross, a circle and even a triangle. In some chapels he resorted to truly Baroque ideas, and based the plans on the shape of a heart or rose.

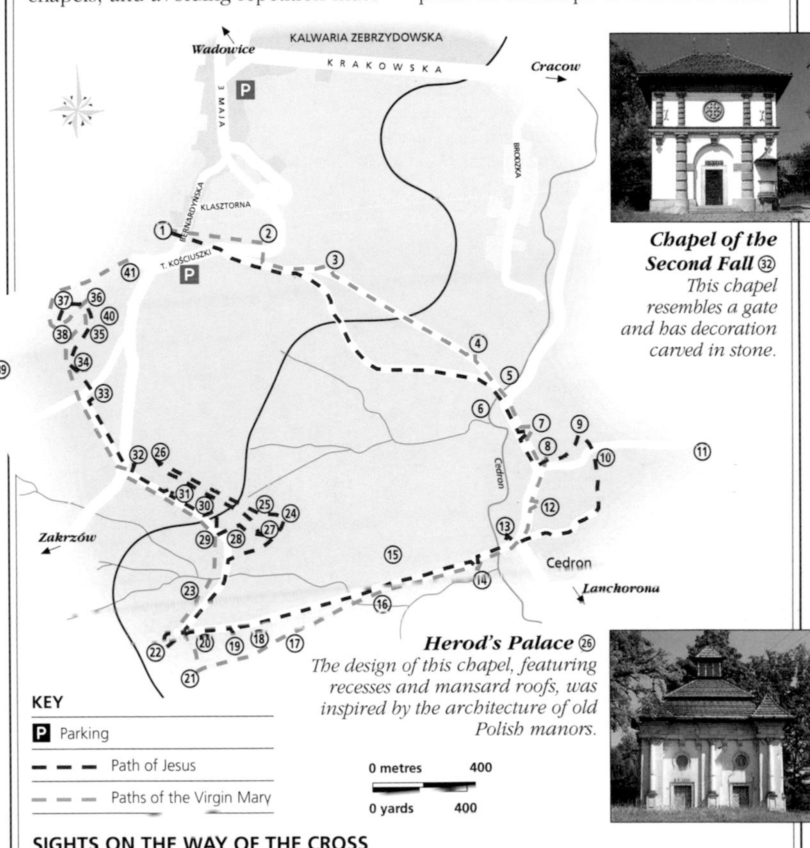

Chapel of the Second Fall (32)
This chapel resembles a gate and has decoration carved in stone.

Herod's Palace (26)
The design of this chapel, featuring recesses and mansard roofs, was inspired by the architecture of old Polish manors.

SIGHTS ON THE WAY OF THE CROSS

St Raphael's Chapel (1)
Chapel of the Throne (2)
Chapel of the Joyful Patriarchs (3)
Chapel of the Triumphant Apostles (4)
Chapel of St John Nepomuk (5)
Bridge of Angels (6)
Chapel of Farewell (7)
Church of the Sepulchre of the Virgin Mary (8)
Gethsemane (9)
Chapel of the Arrest of Christ (10)
Church of the Ascension (11)
Jewish Chapel (12)
Bridge over the Cedron (13)
East Gate (14)
Bethsaida (15)
Apostles' Chapel (16)
Chapel of the Veneration of the Soul of the Virgin (17)
Angels' Chapel (18)
House of Annas (19)
The Cenacle (20)
House of Mary (21)
House of Caiaphas (22)
Chapel of the Fainting Virgin (23)
Pilate's Town Hall (24)
The Holy Steps (25)
Herod's Palace (26)
Chapel of the Taking up of the Cross (27)
Chapel of the First Fall (28)
Chapel of the Heart of Mary (29)
Chapel of Simon of Cyrene (30)
St Veronica's Chapel (31)
Chapel of the Second Fall (32)
Chapel of the Sorrowful Women (33)
Chapel of the Third Fall (34)
Chapel of the Stripping of Christ (35)
Church of the Crucifixion (36)
Chapel of the Anointment (37)
Chapel of the Holy Sepulchre (38)
Hermitage of St Mary Magdalene (39)
Hermitage of St Helen (40)
Chapel of the Madonna of Sorrows (41)

Auschwitz I ⓬

SS watch tower

For most people, Auschwitz represents the ultimate horror of the Holocaust. The Nazis began the first mass transportation of European Jews to Auschwitz in 1942 and it soon became the centre of extermination. Over the next three years, more than one and a half million people, a quarter of those who died in the Holocaust, were killed at Auschwitz and the neighbouring Birkenau camp *(see pp162–3)*, also known as Auschwitz II. Today, the grounds and buildings of both camps are open to visitors, as a museum and a poignant memorial. Auschwitz is now a UNESCO World Heritage site.

Exhibitions
The daily horrors of life in the camp are today displayed in some of the barracks.

THE CAMP

Auschwitz I opened in 1940 on the site of former Polish army barracks. Originally built to incarcerate Polish political prisoners, further buildings were added in the spring of 1941 as the number of prisoners dramatically increased. Camp administration was also based at Auschwitz I.

Gas Chambers and Crematoria
The entire Auschwitz complex had seven gas chambers and five crematoria. Four of the gas chambers were in Birkenau but the first was at Auschwitz, operating from 1941.

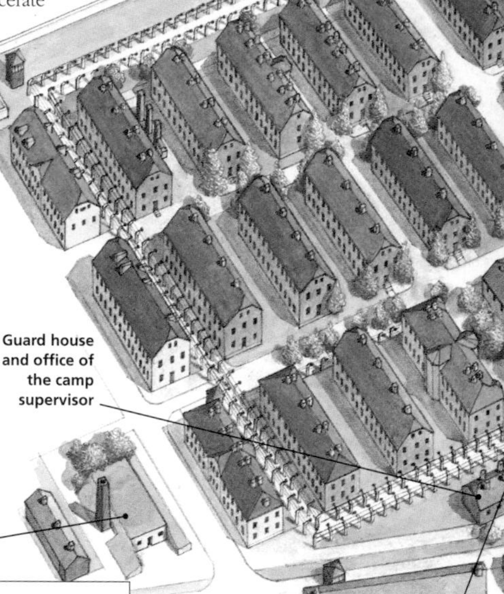

SS Guard house and office of the camp supervisor

THE TWO CAMPS

Though part of the same camp complex, Auschwitz and Birkenau are in fact 3 km (2 miles) apart. The small Polish town of Oświęcim was commandeered by the Nazis and renamed Auschwitz. Birkenau was opened in March 1942 in the village of Brzezinka, where the residents were evicted to make way for the camp. There were an additional 47 sub-camps in the surrounding area.

Aerial view of the complex taken by the Allies in 1944. The yellow dotted line marks Birkenau; the blue shows Auschwitz I.

"Arbeit Macht Frei" entrance
The words above the infamous entrance to Auschwitz translate as "Work makes you free". This was certainly not the case for the prisoners transported here, who were often worked to death.

The "Wall of Death"
This is a reconstruction of the wall near Block 11 used for the summary executions carried out by a firing squad. Usually covered in flowers, it now serves as a place of remembrance.

VISITORS' CHECKLIST

Oświęcim. **Road map** D5.
to Oświęcim, then
24, 25, 26, 27, 28, 29.
www.auschwitz.org.pl
Dec–Feb: 8am–3pm; Mar–Nov: 8am–4pm; Apr & Oct: 8am–5pm; May & Sep: 8am–6pm; Jun–Aug: 8am–7pm.
1 Jan, Easter Day, 25 Dec.
Call to arrange, fee applies.
Shuttle bus to Birkenau runs hourly; leaving from the Information Centre.

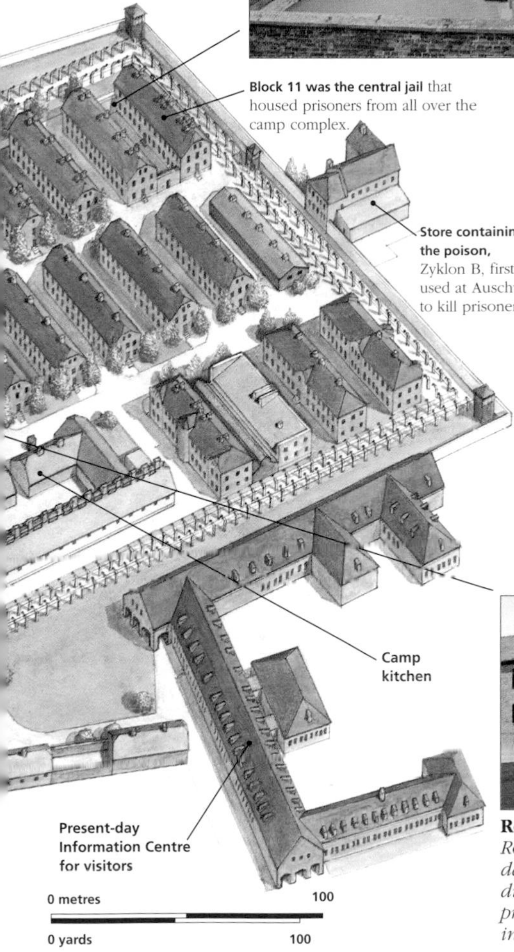

Block 11 was the central jail that housed prisoners from all over the camp complex.

Store containing the poison, Zyklon B, first used at Auschwitz to kill prisoners.

Maksymilian Kolbe
The camp jail, in Block 11, was used for those who broke camp rules. Few emerged alive. Father Kolbe (see p35) *died here after sacrificing his life for another inmate's.*

Camp kitchen

Roll Call Square
Roll call took place up to three times a day and could last for hours. Eventually, due to the increasing numbers of prisoners, roll call was taken in front of individual barracks.

Present-day Information Centre for visitors

0 metres 100

0 yards 100

TIMELINE

1939 1 Sep, Hitler invades Poland.

1940 First deportation of German Jews into Nazi-occupied Poland.

1941 Hitler reported to have ordered the "Final Solution".

1942 First section of Birkenau camp completed

1944 As the Soviet Army closes on Auschwitz, the SS begin destroying all evidence of the camp.

1945 27 Jan, Soviet soldiers liberate the few remaining prisoners at Auschwitz.

1939	1940	1941	1942	1943	1944	1945

1940 Oświęcim chosen as the site of the Nazis' new concentration camp.

1941 Himmler makes first visit to Auschwitz and orders its expansion.

1941 First gas chamber goes into operation.

1942 Beginning of mass deportation to Auschwitz.

1943 Four gas chambers built for mass murder.

1945 18 Jan, 56,000 prisoners evacuated on "Death March".

1945 7 May, Germany surrenders to the Allies.

Auschwitz II–Birkenau

Birkenau was primarily a place of execution. Most of Auschwitz's machinery of murder was housed here. In its four gas chambers, over one million people were killed, 98% of whom were Jewish. Victims included Poles, Russian prisoners of war, gypsies and Czech, Yugoslav, French, Austrian and German citizens. Birkenau was also an enormous concentration camp, housing 90,000 slave labourers by mid-1944 and providing labour for many of the factories and farms of southwestern, Nazi-occupied Poland. The gas chambers were quickly destroyed by the Nazis shortly before the Soviet Army liberated the camp in January 1945.

Hell's Gate
In 1944 the numbers arriving began to increase dramatically. A rail line was extended into the camp. The entrance gate through which the trains passed was known as "Hell's Gate".

Visiting Birkenau
There is little left of the camp today; its main purpose is for remembrance. Most visitors come to pay their respects at the Monument to the Victims of the Camp, on the site of the gas chambers.

Gas chamber and crematorium

The Unloading Ramp
This was possibly the most terrifying part of the camp. It was here that SS officers separated the men from the women and children, and the SS doctors declared who was fit for work. Those declared unfit were taken immediately to their death.

Towers and barbed wire isolated the camps from the outside world.

Women's Barracks
The conditions of the living quarters at the camps were terrible. With little or no sanitation, poor nutrition and no medical care, diseases such as typhus and cholera spread rapidly. This image shows the women's barracks at Birkenau shortly after liberation.

Kanada
"Kanada" was the nickname of the barracks where property stolen from prisoners was stored. It was the preferred place to work at Auschwitz II-Birkenau as it offered opportunities for inmates to pilfer items to barter for food or medicine later.

The Sauna
New arrivals selected for work were deloused and disinfected in this building, which became known as the "sauna". Periodic disinfections of existing prisoners were also carried out here.

The Ash Pond
Tons of ash – the remains of hundreds of thousands of Auschwitz victims – were dumped in ponds and troughs dug around the outskirts of the camp.

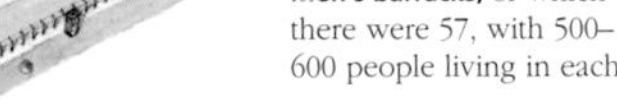

THE CAMP

Birkenau was the largest concentration camp in Nazi-occupied Europe. In 1944 the camp had more than 90,000 prisoners, the majority of whom were exterminated. From the unloading ramp to the gas chambers, the crematoria to the ash dumping grounds, the whole process of murder was carried out systematically and on an enormous scale. This reconstruction shows the camp at its peak in 1944, when as many as 5,000 people were killed every day.

THE LIBERATION OF THE CAMPS

With the war all but lost, in mid-January 1945 the Nazi authorities gave the order for all the camps to be destroyed. Such was the speed of the collapse of the German army, however, that only part of Birkenau was destroyed. Between 17–21 January more than 56,000 inmates were evacuated by the Nazis and forced to march west; many died en route. When the Soviet army entered the camps on 27 January 1945, they found just 7,000 survivors.

Survivors of Auschwitz II-Birkenau, filmed by Soviet troops

THREE GUIDED WALKS

Cracow is an ideal place for walks. The Old Quarter has become a pedestrian precinct with a large concentration of historic monuments, all within a short walking distance of each other. Suggestions for three walks, each with its own unique character, are included here. The first walk is along the Planty park which was laid out on the site of the medieval wall that surrounded the Old Quarter and Okół. It will give you an idea of the extent of the medieval city and provide an opportunity to enjoy this quiet park in the middle of a densely built city. Many statues decorate this park, commemorating those who had links with Cracow.

Cast-iron fixture, Camaldolese Monastery

The two other walks will lead you away from the busy city centre to suburban Cracow, which has retained much of an idyllic countryside character. Zwierzyniec is rich in heritage and offers beautiful views over Cracow owing to its high location on hills. Las Wolski (Wolski Wood) is an extensive woodland where you can enjoy nature at her best or visit first-class historic buildings situated on its peripheries. Among the finest buildings are the Villa of Decius, famous for its arcaded loggia and today a seat of the European Academy, and the complex of the Camaldolese Monastery. Bear in mind that women are only allowed into the monastery on a few festive days. Children will cer-tainly enjoy a visit to the Zoo in the middle of Wolski Wood.

Greater Cracow is quite large but every district is well served by buses and trams which run from early morning till late at night. An average journey by bus or tram lasts no more than a quarter of an hour. In recent years new restaurants, bars and cafés have opened around Cracow. Tourists can visit historic buildings, relax in the open, and enjoy nature and a good meal at the same time.

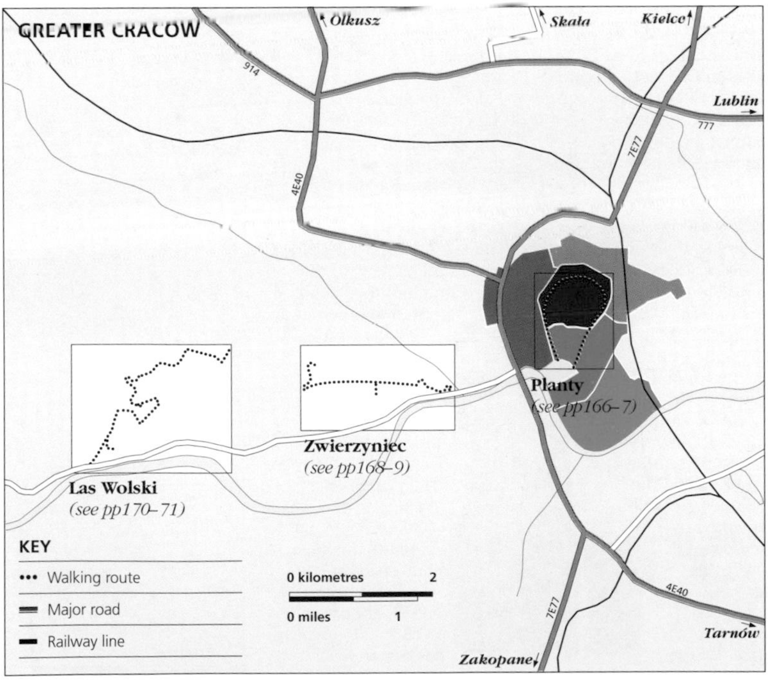

GREATER CRACOW

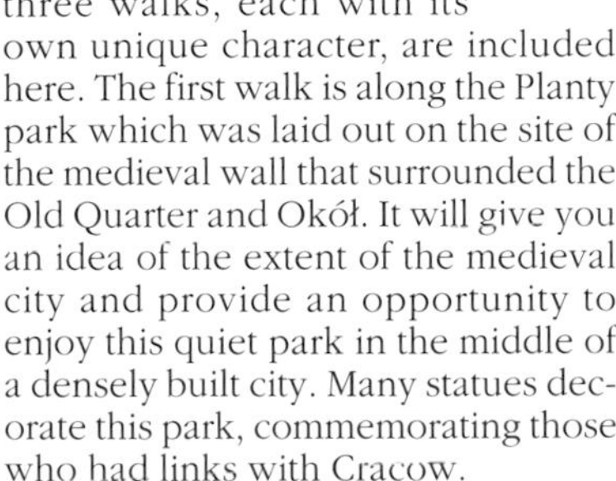

◁ The park by the Villa of Decius

A Two-Hour Walk around Planty

The Planty green belt in Cracow has replaced the city's medieval fortifications, built between the late 13th and 15th centuries. They were demolished early in the 19th century and the small stretch of wall by Floriańska Street is the only fragment to have survived. The gardens of Planty were landscaped to include a network of radiating lanes and beautiful vistas. In the second half of the 19th century the well-kept Planty became a popular venue for socializing. In 1988 a programme of regeneration began: the original appearance of Planty is being recreated through such additions as period fencing, benches and street lamps.

One of many fountains in the Planty gardens

Wawel to the University

The walk begins by the Coat of Arms Gate at Wawel. Walk downhill and cross the street to enter the so-called Wawel gardens. The Gothic Revival Seminary building will be on your right, and a sculpture depicting *Owls* can be seen on your left ①.

Continue down the park some 40 m (130 ft) towards a little square decorated with a statue of the renowned translator of French literature into Polish, Tadeusz Boy-Żeleński, carved by Edward Krzak ②. Turn right and after some 50 m (165 ft) you will reach the wall enclosing the gardens of the Archaeological Museum *(see p83)*. Mounted in the wall are small plaques, overrun with greenery, commemorating the contributions made by the honorary Committee for the Renovation of Cracow's Monuments.

Carry straight on and cross Poselska Street. Those interested in archaeology may turn right to visit the museum. On the other side of the street is a plinth indicating the site of one of many medieval towers which formed part of the defence wall. The outline of the wall is marked by sandstones which you can see positioned along the lanes. Take a sharp left turn and walk down 20 m (65 ft) to a little square where, hidden behind trees, is a statue made in 1884 of Grażyna and Litawor ③, two characters from a poem by Adam Mickiewicz.

From this statue, take a right turn to return to the main lane. You will notice the buildings of the Franciscan Church *(see pp86–7)* and the Episcopal Palace *(see p104)*. Go straight ahead and cross Franciszkańska Street to enter the University Gardens. Walk down the main lane along the wall of the Episcopal Palace, passing by the end of Wiślna Street. Some 150 m (492 ft) further down, by Jagiellońska Street, is an 18th-century statue of the Virgin Mary of Grace ④, which originally was in the graveyard of Church of the St Mary. After another 40 m (130 ft), you may choose to rest, looking at the Kościuszko Mound which can be seen through Piłsudski Street in the distance. Then carry on, passing by the façade of the Collegium Novum, the main university building. An oak planted in 1918, known as the Oak of Liberty, can be seen in front of the college. A red-brick paved pattern

Owls **(1964) by Bronisław Chromy ①**

Planty in autumn, with visitors strolling along a path

in the square imitates the curves of Copernicus's astrolabe. The statue of the astronomer ⑤ *(see p104)*, surrounded by trees, is to the left of Collegium Novum and in front of the Witkowski College. Further down, you will pass by the Collegium Nowodvorianum *(see pp104–5)* and after some 50 m (165 ft) cross St Anne's Street. The university Collegiate Church of St Anne *(see pp108–9)* will be on your right.

Palace of Art to the Barbican

Continue some 100 m (330 ft) and cross Szewska Street. The "Bunker of Art" *(see p105)* will be on your right. A little further down, some 20 m (65 ft) after crossing Szczepańska Street, continue to walk down the Planty's main lane. You will pass a little square where you will see the Palace of Art *(see p105)* on the right, while on your left will be a most beautiful statue of Artur Grottger ⑥ made in 1901 by Wacław Szymanowski. Cross St Thomas's Street (ulica św. Tomasza) and after some 300 m (985 ft) turn left. In this "corner" of the Planty is the statue of Lilla Veneda ⑦, the leading character in a play by Juliusz Słowacki. Walk some 200 m (655 ft) down one of the lanes which run along Basztowa Street. The next monument you will notice is that of Queen Jadwiga and King Władysław Jagiełło ⑧. It was raised to commemorate the fifth centenary of the union between Poland and Lithuania in 1386. After crossing Sławkowska Street, you will find on your left a large pond where in summer swans can be seen. You can cross a little bridge over the pond and this will lead you to a statue of the Harpist ⑨. Continue down the main lane. Pass by the remains of the defence wall with St Florian's Gate *(see p111)* to finally reach the Barbican *(see p114)*.

Cracow's Main Railway Station to Stradom

Walk some 300 m (985 ft) through the so-called Station Gardens. The major attractions here are the Słowacki Theatre *(see p115)* and the Church of the Holy Cross *(see p115)*. Continue to the subway entrance by which the Straszewski Obelisk ⑩ is located. Florian Straszewski was the man who laid out Planty. Behind the Church of the Holy Cross is a statue of the playwright Michał Bałucki ⑪. Walk another 300 m (985 ft) cross Mikołajska Street to enter the "Na gródku" Gardens. The Church of the Dominican Nuns *(see p115)* will be on your right. Continue down the lane and cross Sienna Street. The Dominican Church *(see pp116–7)* will be on your right. You will pass by an unusual statue of Colonel Narcyz Wiatr-Zawojny ⑫, who was shot dead in 1946 by the secret police (UB). The statue was made in 1992 by Bronisław Chromy. Stroll another 500 m (0.3 mile) down to enter the so-called Stradom Gardens and the end of the walk.

Statue of Lilla Veneda by Alfred Daun ⑦

KEY

••• Suggested route

TIPS FOR WALKERS

Starting point: *At the foot of Wawel, by Kanonicza Street.*
Length: *approx. 5 km (3 miles).*
Getting there: *Bus Nos. 103, 124 and 502; the nearest stop is by Straszewskiego Street.*
Stopping-off points: *Café at the "Bunker of Art" near the Collegium Novum. There are benches near the Barbican and throughout the park.*

A One-Hour Walk around Zwierzyniec

In the 12th century Zwierzyniec was a small village, founded as the endowment to the Premonstratensian nuns, whose convent was located by the Rudawa river, a tributary of the Vistula. Polish sovereigns used to take a rest in the royal gardens located in this village. Henri de Valois is reputed to have organized orgies here to the outrage of his subjects. The richest Cracovians followed in the kings' footsteps by establishing their country residences in Zwierzyniec. Despite being incorporated into Cracow in the early 20th century, Zwierzyniec has managed to retain its original village character.

Zwierzyniecki Cemetery ⑤

Altar in St Margaret's Chapel ②

Salwator

After arriving at the tram depot, walk to the Church of the Premonstratensian Nuns ①. The church was founded in the second half of the 12th century but its appearance today is a result of a remodelling undertaken between 1595 and 1638. The Neo-Classical decoration of the choir is most interesting. It was created between 1775 and 1779 to designs by Sebastian Sierakowski. The convent building next to the church is one of the largest in Poland. It is worth visiting for its courtyard. After leaving the church, go up the steep Św. Bronisławy Street. The Chapel of St Margaret ②, built in 1690, will be on your left. Those who died of the plague were buried by the chapel. The Church of the Holy Redeemer ③ is further up. According to Polish chroniclers, it was built

0 metres 300

0 yards 300

KEY

···· Suggested route

Viewpoint

Tram stop

Bus stop

Tourist information

The Kościuszko Mound and Zwierzyniec seen from Wawel

immediately after Poland had accepted Christianity in 966, by Duke Mieszko I. The duke presented the church with a miraculous crucifix. Evidence shows, however, that the church was actually constructed later and consecrated in 1148. Despite extensive remodelling, the church has retained much of its Romanesque character. An interesting painting of 1605 by Kasper Kurch depicts a most unusual scene of the crucified Christ shaking off his shoe in order to pass it to a poor fiddler playing under the Cross. A 17th-century pulpit has also survived by the church, as well as a number of interesting tombs from the first half of the 19th century.

A residential estate ④ established in the early 20th century is located near the church. Its Art Nouveau architecture is worth seeing.

Zwierzyniecki Cemetery

Walk down Anczyc Street and turn right into Aleja Jerzego Waszyngtona (Washington Avenue). The small Zwierzyniecki Cemetery ⑤ consecrated in 1865 is located on the outskirts of the Salwator estate. A chapel, built in 1888 to 1889 in the Neo-Gothic style, can be seen in the middle of the cemetery. Sebastian Jaworzyński was the architect. A great number of tombs of those who made important contributions to Polish culture can be found here.

Chapel of the St Bronisława at the foot of the Kościuszko Mound ⑥

Kościuszko's Mound

The tree-lined Aleja Jerzego Waszyngtona will lead you to the Kościuszko Mound on the Sikornik Hill. At its foot, the Chapel of St Bronisława ⑥ marks the site of the hermitage of the eponymous nun. The chapel was built between 1856 and 1861 by Feliks Księżarski in the Neo-Gothic style. The Kościuszko Mound ⑦ was erected between 1820 and 1823 to commemorate the leader of the insurrection of 1794. This monument to the hero in the struggle for Polish independence was inspired by the mounds of two mythical Polish rulers, Krak and Wanda, which are located in the environs of Cracow. The construction of the mound became a patriotic endeavour and the monument itself a destination for national pilgrimages arriving in Cracow. Fortifications ⑧ at the foot of the Kościuszko Mound were constructed after 1850 by the Austrians as part of a project which aimed to transform Cracow into a massive fortress. The fortress is currently used as a hotel and houses the popular RMF FM radio station. A bus stop, which serves the city centre, is situated by the entrance to the hotel.

Church and Convent of the Premonstratensian Nuns at Salwator ①

TIPS FOR WALKERS

***Starting point**: The Salwator tram depot.*

***Length:** 2.5 km (1.6 miles).*

***Getting there:** The walk starts from the tram depot in Salwator. You can get there by tram Nos. 1, 2 and 36. Return by bus No. 100 which stops at the foot of the Kościuszko Mound.*

***Stopping-off points**: Benches to relax can be found in Aleja Jerzego Waszyngtona. There is a café and restaurant in the Hotel "Pod Kopcem".*

A Walk in Las Wolski

Las Wolski (the Wolski Wood) is the largest green area in Cracow. It has partly retained its original character as a forest, while the remaining ground is maintained as a park. Paths and lanes wind up and down this hilly terrain, leading to many wild spots of surprising beauty created either artificially or naturally. The lovely architecture of the Camaldolese Monastery and Decius Villa, both on the outskirts of the park, are worth exploring. The walk route described below includes sights in the Wolski Wood and the surrounding neighbourhood.

Entrance to the Camaldolese Monastery ①

Srebrna Góra (Silver Mount)

The walk begins at the bus stop at the intersection of Aleja Wędrowników (Wędrowników Avenue) and Księcia Józefa Street. Walk some 500 m (0.3 mile) down Aleja Wędrowników then turn right into Aleja Konarowa (Konarowa Avenue). Climb up the Silver Mount to visit the Camaldolese Monastery ①. The monastery of this strict Reformed Benedictine order was built between 1605 and 1642 by two outstanding architects, Valentin of Säbisch and Andrea Spezza, among others. The stone-clad façade of the church is particularly impressive. The austerity of the interior is in striking contrast with the lavishness of the decoration of the chapels, which feature stuccowork by Giovanni Falconi. The so-called Royal Chapel, dating from 1633 to 1636, is very beautiful. The stairs on either side of the high altar lead down to the crypt which houses a catacomb. This subterranean gallery has recesses excavated in the sides for tombs of the deceased monks. Next to the catacomb is the *ossuarium,* a common grave containing bones removed from the recesses in the catacomb. The hermitages are closed to visitors but can be seen from the ossuary chapel. Women are allowed into the church on a few festive days only.

The Wolski Wood, a favourite place for walks ②

The park by the Decius Villa

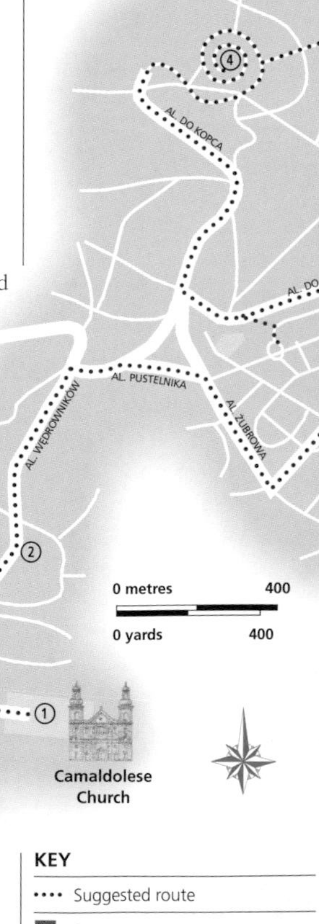

Wolski Wood (Las Wolski)

Leave the monastery by Aleja Konarowa (Konarowa Avenue), the same route by which you arrived, then turn right into Wędrowników Avenue which is the main lane of Wolski Wood ②. This wood was transformed into a public park in 1917 through the efforts of Juliusz Leo, the President of the City of Cracow. Turn right again into a path which leads to Aleja Żubrowa (Bison Avenue). After a few minutes' walk the entrance to the Zoo ③ will be in front of you.

The Zoo was established in 1929. It differs from other zoological gardens owing to its location in the middle of a forest. Leave the Zoo via Al Do Kopca (Towards the Mound Avenue) which will take you to the Marshal Piłsudski Mound ④ on top of Sowiniec Mount. The mound was constructed between 1934 and 1936 as a monument commemorating the Poles who fell during the long struggle for independence from the three powers which partitioned Poland between 1772 and 1918. The mound is called "a Tomb of Tombs" and contains ashes from many battlefields. Walk down the mound and continue along Aleja Panieńskich Skał (Virgin Rocks Avenue) toward the Sanctuary of the Virgin Rocks ⑤ where you will find picturesque limestone formations. According to a legend, this was the place where the Premonstratensian nuns of Zwierzyniec took refuge and hid from the Tatars. A 16th-century timber church ⑥ at the end of the avenue was moved here from Komorowice.

Wola Justowska

Continue walking along Aleja Panieńskich Skał and turn right at the T-junction into Aleja Kasztanowa (Chestnut Avenue). Wola Justowska, a fashionable district of Cracow, begins here. Carry on until you see the Decius Villa (Willa Decjusza) ⑦. Justus Decius was Secretary to King Zygmunt the Old. In 1530 he transformed a late-Gothic manor, dating from the 15th century, into a Renaissance residence. The villa was extended in the first half of the 17th century and a loggia added, offering a view over the area. The Villa houses the European Academy, which is dedicated to the study of European cultural heritage. A nearby bus stop serves the city centre.

A statue of the Virgin in Panieńskie Skały ⑤

A suburban residence known as the Villa of Decius ⑦

TIPS FOR WALKERS

Starting point: *The bus stop at the intersection of Księcia Józefa Street with Wędrowników Street.*
Getting there: *Bus routes 109, 209, 229, 239, 249, 259 and 269 will take you to Srebrna Góra. Take bus 134 by the entrance to the Zoo or bus routes 102, 134, 152 and 192 from Wola Justowska to return to the centre.*
Stopping-off points: *There are benches to relax throughout the Wolski Wood. Restaurants are at the foot of Srebrna Góra and near the Zoo and café in the Villa of Decius.*
Note: *Women are only permitted into the Camaldolese Church on 7 Feb, 25 Mar, Easter Sun, Whit Sun; Whit Mon, Corpus Christi; 19 Jun, Sun after 19 Jun, 15 Aug, 8 Sep, 8 Dec and 25 Dec.*

TRAVELLERS' NEEDS

WHERE TO STAY

Cracow is home to some of Poland's best hotels. Besides the big international names, such as Radisson SAS and Sheraton, visitors will also find many independent hotels famous for their architecture, for traditions extending back to the 19th century, and for their *fin-de-siècle* atmosphere. The best of these have managed to recapture the magnificence that was lost during the period of Communist rule. Many of the hotels in the older parts of the city have been renovated since 1989, while new hotels have sprung up on the city's fringes and around the river. Visitors can still expect to pay a premium for an Old Quarter location, but the new competition helps keep prices in check. From all the hotels in Cracow, this section highlights some of the best; they have been categorized according to location and price on pages 178–81.

The Hotel Pollera *(see p179)*

WHERE TO LOOK

Most of Cracow's hotels can still be found in the Old Quarter, which is surrounded by the Planty, or within close proximity. Cracow is not a sprawling metropolis so even the distant hotels should be no more than a 15–20 minutes, tram or bus ride from the centre of the town. It takes longer to come in from Nowa Huta, whose hotels were built for workers. They now tend to accommodate traders from across Poland's eastern borders, who come to trade at the local markets. Tourists travelling by car may find overnight accommodation in hotels, motels, bed and breakfast in private homes and farms located in particularly attractive areas round Cracow. Myślenice, for example, is located 27 km (17 miles) south of Cracow on the main route to Zakopane. It is beautifully located on the hills of the middle Beskidy, within the Raba river valley. Some 24 km (15 miles) north of Cracow is Ojców, an old summer resort, lying at the heart of the Jurassic Ojców National Park. Close by lies the castle of Pieskowa Skała, a gem of Polish Renaissance architecture *(see p157)*.

Tourists on a limited budget may want to use student halls of residence, campsites or youth hostels *(see p176)*. Rooms and flats are available for rent from private landlords; many are for longer-term lets of several months, though some are available for short-term stays. On the other hand there are no problems in renting accommodation in private homes in the pleasant villages around Cracow. Orbis *(see p177)* has lists of ecology-conscious farms, which offer accommodation and attractions such as horse-riding and locally-grown food.

MAKING A RESERVATION

Early booking is advisable with most of Cracow's hotels, especially during high summer when it can be a challenge to find good-quality accommodation. The tourist season does, in fact, last all year round, but with fewer visitors in autumn and winter. However, there is a constant flow of international conferences, meetings and festivals. Finding a hotel on arrival may prove to be difficult at any time.

FACILITIES

In most rooms there is a toilet and bathroom (often just with a shower, not a bath), a radio and satellite television. The more expensive hotels' rooms may have a mini-bar, 24-hour room service and laundry service, while some have facilities such as computers, Internet access and fax machines. Tourist information is sometimes available at the

A room in the Alef Hotel, formerly known as the Ariel *(see p180)*

◁ **Feeding pigeons in the Market Square**

reception desk as well as the ability to book tickets for various events.

Check-out time is generally noon, but luggage can usually be left with reception. Hotel personnel frequently speak both English and German.

DISCOUNTS

Some of the best hotels reduce their prices in the autumn-winter season. It is always worth asking for a discount, and you stand a good chance of getting one if you are planning a longer stay. It may also be worth trying an Internet agent, such as Stay Poland (www.staypoland.com), who can often offer discounts. The cheapest options are student halls of residence (which become hotels in summer), campsites and youth hostels.

The Royal Hotel *(see p178)*

HIDDEN EXTRAS

In accordance with Polish law, in every hotel the prices quoted or displayed have to include tax and service. In most establishments, they also include breakfast, but this is not always the case so it is best to check. Telephone calls from hotel rooms are never included (even in the best hotels) and are far more expensive than elsewhere. An alternative in town are the numerous card-operated public telephones. Phonecards for these are available from newsagents and tobacco kiosks as well as post offices, where you will also find public telephones. Telephone booths situated on the street have their own number and some are specially adapted for wheelchair users.

The reception area in the Novotel Centrum Hotel *(see p181)*

Alongside these hidden extra costs, however, Polish hospitality almost always extends to providing hotel guests with a free supply of mineral water. Regardless of the standard of hotel, a fresh bottle of sparkling water is usually left in your room every day. As a rule, if it is not in the mini-bar it is free.

When it comes to tipping at hotels and other restaurants it is usual to offer 10 per cent. You may, however, choose to give less depending upon the service you have received. It is also worth being aware that saying "thank you" when paying a bill is automatically taken to mean "keep the change". Tips are not offered to hotel staff, except at the most exclusive places. There are not many single-bed hotel rooms available for solo travellers, so negotiate a discount when offered a double room for single use.

TRAVELLING WITH CHILDREN

Children are welcome everywhere in Poland. Most hotels offer additional beds for children, and usually no extra charge is made for this when the child is under the age of seven or eight. However, when making a reservation it is always advisable to check. In hotel restaurants there should be no problem in ordering children's portions and most places have high chairs. Only the very best hotels offer baby-sitting facilities as part of their service. Alternatively, you can call the Topolina Agency, 31 Friedleina Street, tel. 012 633 06 62. It is open daily from 11am to 3pm. Outside these hours contact 050 309 12 19. The agency works with British travel agents and their babysitters speak English.

Entrance to the Grand Hotel *(see p179)*

ROOMS AND FLATS TO LET

If you intend to rent a flat or room it is worth approaching an agent specializing in this type of letting. They have lists of private rooms and flats for rent. In Cracow, the majority of the agents deal only with longer-term lets. It is quite a different matter, however, out in the country resorts around Cracow. Here, lettings are an additional source of income for landlords during the summer. Lists are available from travel agents and local suburban councils.

DISABLED TRAVELLERS

With Poland now a member of the European Union (EU), all hotels have had to fall in line with EU legislation. This means that any new hotels must include a certain number of rooms for disabled travellers, while all existing hotels must adapt their rooms and common areas to the needs of disabled guests within a strict timeline. The latter part of this legislation has not been strictly enforced, however, and many hotels in Cracow, especially those in the Old Quarter which have no space for new elevators, remain devoid of any facilities for the disabled. As a rule, the newer the hotel the more likely you are to find suitable access. In the hotel listings on the following pages we have highlighted those which already offer disabled-friendly accommodation.

YOUTH HOSTELS

Youth hostels are not what they used to be: while still offering cheap, dormitory-style accommodation with communal washroom facilities, the days when they were opened only to young backpackers are over. Today, most hostels welcome travellers of all ages, and even families, with open arms. That said, many retain strict rules, and some still close their doors for the night at 10 or 11pm, and do not allow access to the dormitories between mid-morning and early evening. An increasing number are becoming more relaxed about this, however; Nathan's Hostel – one of the ones where the young and young-at-heart mix freely – is just such. Discounts are available to students (on presentation of an International Student Card) and holders of an International Youth Hostel Federation card. One hostel that is still predominantly occupied by student travellers is that on Kościuszki Street.

CAMPING

Although most campsites are located on the outskirts of Cracow, travelling into the centre does not take very long so they can provide a good base from which to explore the city. They are usually open from the beginning of May until the end of September.

On the Krakowianka campsite there is a budget, single-storey hotel offering shared rooms for three people as well as public showers. During the summer months there is also an open-air swimming pool for the use of the campers. The Smok campsite, also open during the tourist season, has a particularly pleasant location and the reputation of being very clean.

Entrance to the Polski Hotel (White Eagle Hotel) ***(see p179)***

Dom Polonii (Polonia House) in Market Square ***(see p179)***

DIRECTORY

ACCOMMODATION INFORMATION

Tourist Information and Accommodation Centre (Centrum Informacji Turystycznej)
Pawia 8. **Map** 2 D4 (6 F1).
Tel *012 422 60 91.*
www.jordan.pl
it@jordan.pl

Almatur
Rynek Główny 27.
Map 1 C4 (6 D2).
Tel *012 422 46 68.*

Gromada
Pl. Szczepański 8.
Map 1 C4 (5 C1).
Tel *012 422 72 13, 012 422 37 45.*

Holiday Hotels
Rostafińskiego 2.
Tel *012 637 24 16.*

Juventur
Sławkowska 1.
Map 1 C4 (6 D2).
Tel *012 422 24 37.*

Malopolska Tourist Information
Rynek Główny 1/3.
Map 1 C4 (6 D2).
Tel *012 421 77 06.*

Orbis
Rynek Główny 41.
Map 1 C4 (6 D2).
Tel *012 619 24 62, 012 619 24 63.*
ul. Kremerowska 5.
Map 1 B3.
Tel *012 422 46 32, 012 421 99 79.*
www.orbis.krakow.pl

Point Travel Agency
Przy Rondzie 2.
Map 2 F3.
Tel *012 421 84 33, 012 411 36 09.*
www.point.travel.pl
point@point.travel.pl

Polish Tourist Promotion Agency (Polska Agencja Promocji Turystycznej)
Pl. Wszystkich Świętych 8.
Map 1 C5 (6 D3).

PTTK
Westerplatte 5.
Map 2 D4 (6 F2).
Tel *012 422 26 76.*

Waweltur
Pawia 8.
Map 1 D4 (6 F1).
Tel *012 422 19 21.*
www.waweltur.com.pl
waweltur@wp.pl

TOURIST HOSTELS

Ekspres
Wrocławska 91.
Tel *012 633 88 62.*

Marina Hotel
Myślenice, Stoneczna 13
Tel *012 272 32 31.*

Wagabunda
Oś. Złotej Jesieni 15c.
Tel *012 643 02 22.*

LETTING AND ESTATE AGENTS

Note: Leases are available from these agents for several months only.

Dom
Kazimierza Wielkiego 32.
Tel *012 634 20 41.*

Grodzkie Estate Agency (Grodzkie Biuro Nieruchomości)
Starowiślna 1/6.
Map 2 D5 (6 E3).
Tel *012 422 32 21.*
www.gbn.com.pl
biuro@gbn.com.pl

GUEST ROOMS

Eurokrak
Cicha 8.
Tel *012 638 32 10.*

Accommodation Hall (U Witka)
Zielonki Gliniki 4.
Tel *012 285 06 43.*
Modlniczka 129.
Tel *012 285 12 61.*

Ośrodek ZHP (Polish Scouts Centre)
Korzkiew.
Tel *012 419 42 32.*

Rekliniec
Myślenice, Leśna 2a.
Tel *012 272 39 89.*

YOUTH HOSTELS

Oleandry 4.
Map 1 A4.
Tel *012 633 88 22.*

Kościuszki 88.
Tel *012 422 19 51.*

Szablowskiego 1.
Tel *012 637 24 41.*

Wrocławska 91.
Tel *012 633 88 62.*

STUDENT HALLS OF RESIDENCE

AWF
Al. Jana Pawła II 82.

Bydgoska
Bydgoska 19a.
Tel *012 637 44 34.*

Nawojka
Reymonta 11.
Tel *012 633 58 77.*

Olimp
Rostafińskiego 9.
Tel *012 637 22 11.*

Piast
Piastowska 47.
Tel *012 637 21 76.*

Strawberry Youth Hostel
Racławicka 9.
Map 1 A1.
Tel *012 294 53 63.*
Jul–Aug.
ul. Urzędnicza 68.
Tel *012 633 27 77.*

Żaczek
Al. 3 Maja 5.
Map 1 A5.
Tel *012 633 54 77.*
www.zaczek.bratniak.krakow.pl

CAMPING

Cracow Automobile Club Camp Site (Automobilklub Krakowski Pole biwakowe)
Pcim Lipiny
Tel *012 274 80 42.*
30 Apr–3 Sep.
Pcim Madoń
Tel *012 274 81 10.*
30 Apr–3 Sep.

Clepardia
Mackiewicza 11.
Tel *012 415 96 72.*

Expans-Krak
Mackiewicza 14.

Kemping Ogrodowy
Al. Kasztanowa 49.
Tel *012 425 23 12.*

Korona
Gaj Myślenicka 32.
Tel *012 270 13 18.*

Krakowianka
Żywiecka Boczna 2.
Tel *012 266 41 91.*

Prima
Myślenice, Parkowa 1f.
Tel *012 272 26 46.*

Smok
Kamedulska 18.
Tel *012 421 02 55.*

Choosing a Hotel

The hotels in this guide have been selected across a wide range of price categories for the excellence of their facilities, location or character. The hotels are listed in their price categories within each particular area, starting with the central areas and continuing with hotels outside the centre. For restaurant listings, see pp188–93.

PRICE CATEGORIES
Based on a standard double room, including breakfast, service and tax.
zł under 300
zł zł 301–400
zł zł zł 401–500
zł zł zł zł 501–600
zł zł zł zł zł over 600

OKÓŁ AND STRADOM QUARTERS

Royal — zł

ul. św. Gertrudy 26-29 **Tel** *012 421 35 00* **Fax** *012 421 58 57* **Rooms** *120* **Map** *6 D5*

There are two sections to this elegant hotel (one-star and two-star), both of which offer relatively basic amenities, but all the rooms have televisions and full en-suite facilities. The Royal is housed in a gem of a 19th-century Art Nouveau building and the setting, opposite a lovely Cracow park, is as grand as they come. **www.royal.com.pl**

Awiw — zł zł

ul. Dietla 91 **Tel** *012 433 90 00* **Fax** *012 433 90 01* **Rooms** *15* **Map** *6 E5*

Not exactly the quietest location – direct onto a busy Cracow street – but everything else about this converted town-house recommends the place. Restaurant, car hire and tourist services are available, and pets are allowed. An excellent buffet breakfast is included in the price, which makes a stay here great value. **www.awiw.pl**

Monopol — zł zł

ul. św. Gertrudy 6 **Tel** *012 422 76 66* **Fax** *012 269 15 60* **Rooms** *75* **Map** *6 E4*

The RT hotel chain have three establishments in and around Cracow, and the Monopol is the best of them. While a recent refit has given it a modern edge, the Monopol still retains a presence on Planty Park in keeping with the other buildings around it. Car parking and a good restaurant add to its attractions. **www.rthotels.com.pl**

Rezydent — zł zł zł

ul. Grodzka 9 **Tel** *012 429 54 95* **Fax** *012 429 55 76* **Rooms** *59* **Map** *6 D3*

Behind its medieval façade, the Rezydent's rooms and suites offer good value to those looking for a bit more than the standard three-star hotel. Owned by the RT chain, all the rooms have satellite television and one has been specially adapted for disabled guests. The restaurant is good and pets are welcome. **www.rthotels.com.pl**

Wawel — zł zł zł

ul. Poselska 22 **Tel** *012 424 13 00* **Fax** *012 424 13 33* **Rooms** *40* **Map** *6 D3*

There are few hotels in Cracow that mix the ancient and the modern better than the Wawel. Set in an elegant 19th-century building, the rooms are large, individually furnished and offer every convenience. The hotel has a wellness centre, offering water treatments for many ailments, and a simple jacuzzi for tired legs. **www.hotelwawel.pl**

Pugetów — zł zł zł zł

ul. Starowiślna 15a **Tel** *012 432 49 50* **Fax** *012 429 61 13* **Rooms** *7* **Map** *6 E4*

If money is no object, then this place takes some beating. Set in a particularly lovely house, this is an art hotel with original oil-paintings lining the walls. Rooms are enormous and individually furnished, but there are not many of them so it is advisable to book well in advance. **www.donimirski.com/hotel_pugetow**

Senacki — zł zł zł zł

ul. Grodzka 51 **Tel** *012 422 76 86* **Fax** *012 422 79 34* **Rooms** *20* **Map** *6 D4*

Set in a beautifully renovated historic building, the rooms here are on the small side but offer good value. All have en-suite bathrooms and are elegantly decorated with plenty of little extras. The windows overlooking Grodzka Street give a breathtaking view of the Church of Saints Peter and Paul (*see pp80–81*). **www.senacki.krakow.pl**

Copernicus — zł zł zł zł zł

ul. Kanonicza 16 **Tel** *012 424 34 00* **Fax** *012 424 34 05* **Rooms** *29* **Map** *6 D4*

Everything about the Copernicus stands for high quality and elegance, from the delightful entrance to the period-furnished rooms – all have high ceilings and deep brown, traditional wooden flooring. There is a popular piano bar downstairs and a good restaurant too. **www.hotel.com.pl**

Holiday Inn — zł zł zł zł zł

ul. Wielopole 4 **Tel** *012 619 00 00* **Fax** *012 619 00 05* **Rooms** *154* **Map** *6 F3*

Holiday Inn may not be the first name that springs to mind when luxury is mentioned but here, at the Cracow franchise, everything is the very best you can imagine. From the great location to the exemplary service, the tasteful decor and the large rooms, this is one of the best in the chain, anywhere in the world. **www.hik.krakow.pl**

Key to Symbols *see back cover flap*

OLD QUARTER

Trecius — zł

ul. Św.Tomasza 18 ***Tel*** *012 421 25 21* ***Fax*** *012 426 87 30* ***Rooms*** *6* ***Map*** *6 E2*

There are just six rooms in this oft-renovated 13th-century house, but each is decorated in a fabulous way. They all have showers (but not baths) and there is satellite television in each room too. While prices are low for the location, note that breakfast is not included and smoking is not allowed in any of the rooms. **www.trecius.krakow.pl**

Dom Polonii — złzł

Rynek Główny 14 ***Tel*** *012 428 04 60* ***Fax*** *012 422 43 55* ***Rooms*** *3* ***Map*** *6 D2*

Located on the third floor of a classic town house, this hotel may be the smallest in Cracow (it has just three double rooms), but the rooms themselves are enormous. With high, vaulted ceilings and a friendly member of staff always on hand to help out, the low prices make reservations here essential. **www.wspolnota-polska.krakow.pl**

Pollera — złzł

ul. Szpitalna 30 ***Tel*** *012 422 10 44* ***Fax*** *012 422 13 89* ***Rooms*** *42* ***Map*** *6 E2*

An Art Nouveau classic in the heart of the Old Quarter. The Pollera was founded in 1834 by Kasper Poller and has welcomed guests with style and grace ever since. During World War II the Germans fell in love with the place and forbade anyone else (except staff) from entering. Today, all are welcome once again. **www.pollera.com.pl**

Polski Hotel "Pod Białym Orłem" — złzłzł

Pijarska 17 ***Tel*** *012 442 11 44* ***Rooms*** *54* ***Map*** *1 C4*

This hotel is ideally located next to St Florian's Gate and opposite the remnants of the city's wall. It was much neglected during the communist regime, but has seen a revival in recent years and is now considered a good value option for those looking for traditional Old Quarter accommodation. **www.podorlem.com.pl**

Wentzl — złzłzł

Rynek Główny 19 ***Tel*** *012 430 26 64* ***Fax*** *012 430 26 65* ***Rooms*** *12* ***Map*** *6 D3*

If what is required is an exclusive address on Market Square, then the Wentzl, named after the eponymous restaurant on the first floor *(see p191)* offers it. Every one of its refined rooms possesses an outstanding view as well as all the usual facilities, including free Internet access. Utterly recommended. **www.wentzl.pl**

Elektor — złzłzłzłzł

ul. Szpitalna 28 ***Tel*** *012 423 23 17* ***Fax*** *012 423 23 27* ***Rooms*** *21* ***Map*** *6 E2*

Prince and Princess Takamodo of Japan, King Harald V of Norway and Princess Maha Chakri Sirindhorn of Thailand have all stayed here recently. Widely regarded as the city's best, nothing is beyond the staff of the Elektor, who fall over themselves to help all their guests, royalty or otherwise. **www.hotelelektor.com.pl**

Grand — złzłzłzłzł

ul. Sławkowska 5/7 ***Tel*** *012 421 72 55* ***Fax*** *012 421 83 60* ***Rooms*** *62* ***Map*** *6 D2*

For almost 150 years the Grand has been welcoming guests through its doors and every one of them has admired the stucco exterior. Recently renovated, today it offers the full range of modern facilities without losing any of its old charm. Most of the pieces of furniture in the rooms double as historic treasures. **www.grand.pl**

Gródek — złzłzłzłzł

ul. Na Gródku 4 ***Tel*** *012 431 90 30* ***Fax*** *012 431 90 40* ***Rooms*** *23* ***Map*** *6 E3*

Adjoining a Dominican convent, the Gródek is in one of the quietest parts of the Old Quarter. Rooms vary in design and decor, but are invariably elegant, with large windows, high ceilings and every facility you could expect, not to mention some of the fluffiest pillows in Cracow. Well worth the price. **www.donimirski.com**

KAZIMIERZ QUARTER

Abel — zł

ul. Józefa 30 ***Tel*** *012 411 87 36* ***Fax*** *012 411 87 36* ***Rooms*** *14* ***Map*** *4 D1*

While the rooms at this adorably eclectic hotel are not exactly large, what they lack in size they more than make up for in character. Each is individually furnished and comes with en-suite bathroom (sometimes just with a shower) and television. Not all are air-conditioned, however. **www.hotelabel.pl**

Eden — zł

ul. Ciemna 15 ***Tel*** *012 430 65 65* ***Fax*** *012 430 67 67* ***Rooms*** *27* ***Map*** *4 D1*

More of a multi-faceted kosher experience than a hotel, the Eden is home to a salt grotto (for meditation), a mikvah (for ritual Jewish bathing) and a kosher restaurant. The rooms are simply furnished, large and comfortable. All rooms are non-smoking, have en-suite bathrooms and televisions but some lack air conditioning. **www.hoteleden.pl**

Kazimierz Ⓩ

ul. Miodowa 16 ***Tel*** *012 421 66 29* ***Fax*** *012 421 66 29* ***Rooms*** *35* ***Map*** *4 D1*

Modern, but nevertheless impressive, stained-glass windows, most depicting the Kazimierz of long ago, dominate this hotel. The rooms are not quite luxurious but meet the standards of most travellers, with en-suite facilities and air conditioning. Pets are welcome. **www.hk.com.pl**

Alef ⓏⓏ

ul. Szeroka 17 ***Tel*** *012 421 38 70* ***Fax*** *012 421 38 70* ***Rooms*** *4* ***Map*** *4 E1*

This popular hotel, featured in the film *Schindler's List*, has enormous beds, each a wooden antique with a painted base depicting scenes from a bygone Kazimierz. A great buffet breakfast is included, but air conditioning and televisions are not. The legendary Alef restaurant *(see p192)* is in the basement. **www.alef.pl**

Regent ⓏⓏ

ul. Bożego Ciała 19 ***Tel*** *012 430 62 34* ***Fax*** *012 430 59 77* ***Rooms*** *39* ***Map*** *4 D2*

Located in the heart of Kazimierz, the Regent is a stylish hotel housed inside a wonderful 19th-century building. Most (but not all) of the rooms are generously sized, and all come with televisions, en-suite bathrooms and Internet connections. One has been adapted for use by disabled guests. **www.rthotels.com.pl**

Secesja ⓏⓏⓏ

ul. Paulińska 24 ***Tel*** *012 430 74 64* ***Fax*** *012 430 74 05* ***Rooms*** *26* ***Map*** *3 C2*

The Hotel Secesja (or Secession) is, in fact, a modern hotel which has made a few gestures towards Art Nouveau. Rooms are bright and comfortable, and all have large en-suite bathrooms. The public areas are a real feature, the lobby in particular, which evokes a real sense of old-fashioned good living. **www.hotelsecesja.krakow.pl**

WESOŁA, KLEPARZ & BISKUPIE

Europejski ⓏⓏ

ul. Lubicz 5 ***Tel*** *012 423 25 10* ***Fax*** *012 423 25 29* ***Rooms*** *49* ***Map*** *2 D4 (6 F1)*

This hotel has been in the same family since it first opened more than 120 years ago. The current director is the great-grandson of the original owner, who designed and built the place. Recently renovated, the rooms are well appointed, if a little small, with bathrooms that are modern (but also small). **www.he.pl**

Jordan ⓏⓏ

ul. Długa 9 ***Tel*** *012 430 02 92* ***Fax*** *012 422 82 26* ***Rooms*** *19* ***Map*** *1 C3*

Here you will find simple, but reasonably priced rooms, in a decent location. The Jordan is situated above a travel agent of the same name, which offers sightseeing tours and other tourist services. Parking is limited, so it is advisable to reserve a place in advance. **www.jordan.pl**

Polonia ⓏⓏ

ul. Basztowa 25 ***Tel*** *012 422 12 33* ***Fax*** *012 422 16 21* ***Rooms*** *62* ***Map*** *2 D4 (6 F1)*

One of the most outstanding buildings in Cracow: the balconies are works of art, every one an Art Nouveau gem. This hotel has been welcoming guests since 1917, and while the luxury has somewhat faded, it remains a grand and well-priced place to stay. Rooms are spacious, while the amenities can be a bit basic. **www.hotel-polonia.com.pl**

Atrium ⓏⓏⓏ

ul. Krzywa 7 ***Tel*** *012 430 02 03* ***Fax*** *012 430 01 96* ***Rooms*** *52* ***Map*** *1 C3*

Modern and a little lacking in character, the hotel Atrium nevertheless offers good-value accommodation in a central location. Rooms are large and well furnished, and a number have been adapted for use by disabled guests. There are non-smoking rooms too. Most of the bathrooms have showers rather than baths. **www.hotelatrium.com.pl**

Batory ⓏⓏⓏ

ul. Sołtyka 19 ***Tel*** *012 294 30 30* ***Fax*** *012 294 30 33* ***Rooms*** *29* ***Map*** *2 E5*

Not the most attractive hotel in Cracow, but all doubts fade once you enter the bright lobby and are greeted by the friendly staff. The well-sized rooms are all decorated in loud colours, come with televisions, en-suite bathrooms (some just with shower), safes and Internet connections. **www.hotelbatory.pl**

PIASEK AND NOWY ŚWIAT

Logos ⓏⓏⓏ

ul. Szujskiego 5 ***Tel*** *012 632 33 33* ***Fax*** *012 632 42 10* ***Rooms*** *49* ***Map*** *1 V4*

A not altogether welcoming hotel from the outside, the Logos is another of those three-stars that improves once the threshold has been crossed. Rooms are quite large, well equipped and have great bathrooms. Staff are among the friendliest in Cracow. The hotel's wellness centre has a sauna and offers massages too. **www.hotel-logos.pl**

Fortuna

ul. Czapskich 5 ***Tel*** *012 422 31 43* ***Fax*** *012 411 08 06* ***Rooms*** *25* ***Map*** *1 B5 (5 C4)*

A newly renovated, historic hotel where the service always comes with a smile. Set in a charming building, the Fortuna's rooms are larger than is usually found in this type of building, as are the bathrooms. There is guarded parking, though reservations are needed for the handful of places on offer. **www.hotel-fortuna.com.pl**

Maltanski

ul. Straszewskiego 14 ***Tel*** *012 431 00 10* ***Fax*** *012 431 06 15* ***Rooms*** *16* ***Map*** *1 B5 (5 C4)*

This boutique hotel, which dates from the 1830s, drips with luxury from the moment the visitor passes through the Neo-Classical lobby and chats with the friendly staff at the oak reception desk. Upstairs the rooms are sublimely understated, yet contain every luxury imaginable. **www.donimirski.com**

Radisson SAS

ul. Straszewskiego 17 ***Tel*** *012 618 88 88* ***Fax*** *012 618 88 89* ***Rooms*** *196* ***Map*** *5 B4*

The opening of a Radisson hotel in Cracow was a major event. Despite being a new building, the sleek, elegant exterior complements the older buildings nearby, while inside the rooms are enormous and luxurious. There is an excellent restaurant and a fully-equipped fitness centre. Expensive, but worth every penny. **www.radissonsas.com**

Sheraton

ul. Powiśle 7 ***Tel*** *012 662 10 00* ***Fax*** *012 662 11 00* ***Rooms*** *232* ***Map*** *5 B4*

The hotel atrium is a modern wonder, all glass and marble, colonnades and fountains. Of the rooms, visitors can expect only the best standards with the biggest bathrooms in Cracow to boot. Outstanding restaurants and entertainment make this a refuge that some do not ever want to leave. **www.sheraton.com/krakow**

FURTHER AFIELD

Ruczaj

ul. Ruczaj 44 ***Tel*** *012 269 10 00* ***Fax*** *012 269 20 30* ***Rooms*** *44*

The Ruczaj is a good attempt at recreating a Teutonic castle in a leafy suburb around 4 km (2.5 miles) from central Cracow. Rooms are blessed with huge windows and enormous beds, but suffer for their rather small bathrooms. Nevertheless, prices are highly competitive. **www.ruczajhotel.com.pl**

Teresita

ul. Schweitzera 3 ***Tel*** *012 657 57 04* ***Fax*** *012 657 57 04* ***Rooms*** *40*

Somewhat ugly and yellow, the Teresita describes itself as being *cyganski* (gypsy) in design. Kitsch and loud colours dominate. All said, however, the rooms are comfortable, if basic, and all contain televisions and full Internet access. Some distance from the city centre, the Teresita does offer excellent value for money. **www.teresita.pl**

Art Hotel Niebieski

ul. Flisacka 3 ***Tel*** *012 431 27 11* ***Fax*** *012 431 18 28* ***Rooms*** *13*

If getting away from it all in style is important, the Art Hotel Niebieski is ideal. The building is a fine example of Art Nouveau, set on the banks of the river, a short drive west of the city. Rooms are generously sized with lots of character and all the usual mod cons. Reservations are a must. **www.niebieski.com.pl**

Chopin

ul. Przy Rondzie 2 ***Tel*** *012 299 00 00* ***Fax*** *012 299 00 01* ***Rooms*** *219* ***Map*** *2 F4*

A 20-minute walk east away from the centre brings you to the Chopin. Housed in a rather utilitarian building, the rooms are decent in size and all have bathrooms, televisions and Internet access. Here you will find good value for money in somewhat nondescript surroundings. There is also a small fitness centre. **www.chopinhotel.com**

Ibis

Przy Rondzie 2 ***Tel*** *012 421 81 88* ***Rooms*** *219* ***Map*** *2 F3*

Just a ten-minute journey by tram from the city centre, this tourist-class hotel offers exceptional value for money, though it is situated rather close to a busy road. The restaurant forms part of the open-space lounge and reception area and the rooms meet the typical standards of the Ibis chain. **www.ibishotel.com**

Novotel Centrum

ul. T. Kościuszki 5 ***Tel*** *012 299 29 00* ***Fax*** *012 299 29 99* ***Rooms*** *198* ***Map*** *5 A5*

What this establishment lacks in location (it is a long taxi ride from the city centre), it makes up for in every other regard. Possessing a swimming pool is a real bonus, though there is more to the Novotel than that: bright, breezy rooms for a start, outstanding service and a generous buffet breakfast. **www.orbis.pl**

Sympozjum

ul. Kobierzyńska 47 ***Tel*** *012 261 86 00* ***Fax*** *012 261 87 99* ***Rooms*** *80* ***Map*** *3 A5*

As the name might suggest, this hotel is popular with conferences and businessmen, though tourists are more than welcome. It offers great rooms and outstanding bathrooms, as well as excellent public areas, including a health club, good dining and a lively lobby bar. Children and pets are welcome. **www.hotel.sympozjum.com.pl**

RESTAURANTS, CAFÉS AND BARS

Cracow has always been known as a good place for eating out. Even during the Communist era, when restaurants were uninviting places with very little on offer, visitors from other parts of the country were surprised to find in Cracow a multitude of busy cafés serving tea in fine china, espresso coffee, fresh crisp rolls and eggs *à la Viennoise* for breakfast. The traditional politeness of waiters was even more surprising. After the collapse of Communist Poland the best was yet to come. Hundreds of new places opened in the 1990s. A number of restaurants have been returned to their former owners, who spare no effort in reviving old traditions. Places serving Middle Eastern, Chinese, Vietnamese, Indian, Korean, French, Greek, Mexican and Italian food can all be found in Cracow.

Ice cream of many flavours

SOMETHING FOR EVERYONE

Visitors to Cracow who are short of time and travelling on a budget may choose to eat in a canteen or fast-food bar where they can have a three–course meal for only 20 zł. It is often a good traditional Polish meal. Such places, however, close early (usually late afternoon or early evening, or when the food has been sold out).

A *pretzel,* known in Cracow as a bagel, from a street vendor can often do for a snack. It is a local speciality, traditionally coated with salt crystals or poppy seeds, and recently also with sesame seeds. Boiled corn on the cob and broad beans are offered by street vendors throughout the year and in late autumn roasted chestnuts as well.

Fast food is also available from well-known chains such as McDonald's, Kentucky Fried Chicken and Pizza Hut, but this is less varied and more expensive. Hamburgers in Polish bars are less expensive than the international brands. In some places you will find street vendors selling grilled sausages. The best sausages are sold near the Market Hall in Grzegórzecka Street, where they are available until 3 o'clock in the morning.

The Wentzl Restaurant ***(see p191)***

"Pod Aniołami" Restaurant ***(see p189)***

Those who enjoy good food in a pleasant atmosphere will not be disappointed in Cracow. Most of Cracow's restaurants have a nice location and are housed in period interiors or medieval cellars, all painstakingly restored and furnished tastefully. Evenings and weekends tend to be particularly busy and it often happens that there are more customers than tables. Booking a table in advance is, therefore, advisable.

EATING AT NIGHT

The majority of restaurants in Cracow close around midnight but if you happen to be hungry early in the morning there are alternatives to buying food in one of the shops which are open round the clock. The Greek restaurant Dionisos in Dominikański Square is open

24 hours. A bar in Kramy Dominikańskie (Dominican Stalls) in Stolarska Street is also open round the clock, serving burgers and chips.

The main Railway Station (Dworzec Główny PKP), with its bars and restaurants, is another place open 24 hours. They are unusual for Polish station bars because of their pristine cleanliness and the good food on offer.

The Endzior Bar in Nowy Square in Kazimierz district opens at 5am. You will enjoy their fantastic spare ribs served with cabbage, pea soup and *schnitzels*, in the company of their usual customers – coal merchants, stall-holders, street traders and porters.

It is worth noting that most restaurants remain open until the last customer leaves, so you may stay as long as you place orders.

PRICES AND TIPS

The price of food in Cracow's restaurants is below the national average for restaurants in cities. While some critics say that the relatively low prices reflect the stinginess of the Cracovians, market research suggests that this is a result of wages which are lower than in Warsaw and other parts of Poland. Certainly 100 zł per person will suffice for a three-course meal without alcohol in all but the most expensive places. Naturally, if you do wish to drink alcohol with your food, this will add a substantial amount to your bill. All alcohol, especially imported wines and spirits, is subject to excise duty and taxed heavily. Not to mention the mark-up added by the restaurant.

One of the period rooms at the Noworolski Café *(see p194)*

Chimera Restaurant *(see p190)*

Credit cards are becoming ever more popular and should be readily accepted by all the larger restaurants and those located on the main tourist trails. Signs on windows or doors indicate which cards are accepted by the establishment.

All over Poland a customary tip amounts to ten per cent of the bill, but in Cracow if you give less no one will feel offended.

Chef in the Wierzynek *(see p192)*

VEGETARIAN FOOD

Polish culinary customs have changed enormously since the borders opened up with the fall of Communism. Mass tourism abroad has brought Poles into contact with the cuisines of many foreign countries and new trends in the eating habits of the West. Easy access to foodstuffs that were previously unavailable has also contributed to these changes. For most people, meat still plays a central role in their diet, but vegetables and fruit are becoming ever more popular. The majority of restaurants in Cracow serve some vegetarian dishes. Traditional local dishes, such as *pierogi* (dumplings) filled with sauerkraut, wild mushrooms, cheese or fruit, as well as all kinds of pancakes, omelettes and *knedle* (potato dumplings), are very popular. A choice of many colourful and tasty salads is available in all restaurants. Beetroot, carrots, cabbage, cauliflower, celeriac and leeks are old favourites. Broccoli, aubergines, celery, endives and courgettes have recently been introduced to Polish cuisine. Vegetarian food is available not only from most ethnic restaurants but also from salad bars, which are very popular and also serve freshly pressed fruit and vegetable juices. In some restaurants you can make your own choice of salad ingredients.

The well-stocked bar at the modern Demel Hotel *(see p194)*

The Flavours of Cracow

Polish cuisine, like that of many central European countries, makes heavy use of meat, especially pork, which is often served quite plainly with potatoes or rice and cabbage. However, because of the long Baltic coastline in the north of the country, fish is also likely to feature on many menus. Carp, trout and herring are particular favourites. Around Cracow, in the south, the local forests yield a bounty of quality game, with duck being very popular. The legacy of former rule by Austria is also evident in the south, especially in some of the sophisticated cakes and pastries.

Pickled herring

Barbecuing meat at a street celebration on Palm Sunday

MEAT

Pork *(wieprzowina)* is the most popular meat by far in Poland. It usually comes as a steak *(kotlet schabowy)* or on the bone *(golonka wieprzowa)* and also appears in soups, sausages and as hams. Polish hams are generally cured and have a rich, sweet flavour. Ham is mainly served cold as an appetizer with cheese and pickles, though it may also be eaten for breakfast. Poland also produces high quality veal *(cielęcina)*, which is often dished up with a rich mushroom sauce *(cielęcina po staropolsku)* or with cabbage and raisins.

POULTRY AND GAME

Chicken *(kurczaka)* is a staple food in Poland and drumsticks *(podudzie)* are especially popular. Chicken livers *(wątróbka)*, served with a fruit sauce, are considered a delicacy.

A wide variety of game roams the forests of southern Poland. Pheasant *(bażant)*, duck *(kaczka)*, goose *(gęś)*, venison *(comber)*, rabbit *(królik)* and hare *(zając)* are found on many local menus. Availability varies with the season; autumn is the best time to enjoy game.

Wiejska (garlic and herb sausage)

Panòwka (pork frankfurters)

Gruba krakowska (smoked garlic sausage)

Chicken kabonos (air-cured sausage with caraway seeds)

Podwawelsk (smoked sausage)

Smoked pork loin

Zagorska (smooth textured, smoked sausage)

Selection of typical Polish sausages and cured meat

LOCAL DISHES AND SPECIALITIES

Many classic Polish dishes are offered at restaurants all over the country, but fish also features prominently on northern menus, while those of the the south offer a range of game. The most varied and cosmopolitan cuisine is found in large cities, such as Warsaw and Cracow, where top chefs run the kitchens of some of the grand hotels. The national dish, *bigos*, comes from eastern Poland. It is hearty and warming for the long, bleak winters found there, as is another dish from this chilly region, *pierogi* (pasta dumplings, stuffed with meat, cheese or fruit). Both are influenced by the food of neighbouring Russia. Polish cakes and desserts also tend to be heavy and rich, although most originate in the warmer south, once ruled by Austria.

Green cabbage

Bigos *Chunks of meat and sausage are simmered with sauerkraut, cabbage, onion, potatoes, herbs and spices.*

A colourful display of locally grown vegetables at a city market stall

FISH

Fish features strongly on menus in northern Poland, where herring *(śledź)* is a central part of the diet. It comes pickled, in oil, with onions, with soured cream – in fact, with just about everything. *Rolmops po kaszubsku* (marinated herring wrapped around pickled onion, then spiked with cloves and dipped in soured cream) are widely enjoyed. Other popular fish are freshwater trout *(pstrąg)* – served simply grilled with boiled potatoes; carp *(karpia)* – often accompanied by horseradish sauce; and salmon *(łosoś)*. A treat in early summer is smoked salmon served with spears of fresh asparagus *(łosoś wędzony ze szparagami)*, which is then in season.

VEGETABLES

Poland produces many fine quality vegetables. The hardy cabbage *(kapusta)* remains the country's top vegetable. It is used in so many ways, including raw in salads and simply boiled to partner meat or fish. Cabbage soup *(kapusniak)* and sauerkraut are on every menu. Potatoes are also a staple. They come boiled, baked and mashed, though rarely roasted. Peppers are popular too, often served stuffed with rice and minced meat or pickled in summer salads. Root vegetables such as carrots, parsnips, swede (rutabaga), turnips and beetroot make their way into a range of dishes. Mushrooms grow wild all over Poland and come both cooked and pickled as a tasty addition to many meals.

Polish pretzels on sale in a Cracow bread shop

SNACKS

Sausages A wide range of smoked and unsmoked varieties are on offer at the profusion of street stalls and snack bars that can be found on most city streets.

Precles (pretzels) Another favourite street snack, these are popular, freshly baked, at train and bus stations first thing in the morning.

Zapiekanki Often referred to as Polish-style pizzas, these are tasty, open-top baguettes, spread with cheese and tomato, then toasted and served piping hot. They are also a common item on street-stall menus.

Smalec This snack consists of fried lard, liberally sprinkled with sea salt, and eaten with chunks of crusty bread. It can be found as a bar snack in most pubs and makes a good accompaniment to beer.

Pierogi *These ravioli-style dumplings may be stuffed with meat, sauerkraut, mushrooms, cheese or fruit.*

Barszcz *This beetroot soup, flavoured with lemon and garlic, may be served clear or with beans or potatoes.*

Poppy seed roll *A rich yeasted dough is wrapped around a sweet poppy-seed filling and baked until lightly golden.*

What to Drink in Cracow

In Cracow, as indeed anywhere in Poland, you may try many different brands of exquisite vodkas, both clear and flavoured. Beer is becoming ever more popular and its production is growing rapidly. There are many bars in Cracow that offer a large selection of beers, especially beers brewed in Poland. Poland does not produce quality wines but shops and restaurants offer a large selection of brands imported from all over the world, especially from throughout Europe and the New World.

Cracovia, one of the best Polish clear vodkas

VODKA

Vodka distilled from potatoes or grain is a Polish speciality. Such brands as clear *Wódka Wyborowa* and dry but flavoured *Żubrówka* are both world-famous. The variety of vodka brands produced in Poland may be bewildering. Clear *Cracovia*, which has been produced in Cracow for some years, is very popular. *Starka* is definitely the oldest brand among quality vodkas. For centuries *starka* was made from unrectified grain spirit, which was aged for at least six years in reused oak wine-casks. The casks used to be buried for ageing, but this is no longer the case. Cracow *Starka* was once regarded as the "queen" of all *starkas*, but has lost this status. Polish distilleries have been decentralized, but have retained the recipes imposed during Communist rule. Above all the lack of an *appellation contrôlée* has resulted in the fact that, if you buy a *Starka krakowska* (Cracow starka), be prepared to accept that it may have been produced elsewhere. (Another example is the renowned Goldwasser liqueur which was unique to Gdańsk but is now produced in Poznań.) *Starka bankietowa* is aged for longer and is definitely one of the best. It is sold in crystal-glass bottles and is a luxurious drink difficult to find elsewhere.

Starka krakowska vodka

***Dzięgielówka*, a dry vodka flavoured with angelica root**

Good kosher plum vodka is distilled in Poland. *Śliwowica łącka* is the best and most famous of all plum vodkas. Paradoxically, it is produced illegally owing to the lack of proper regulations. It is home-made in the small village of Łącko in the mountain region, some 70 km (43 miles) south of Cracow. Śliwowica Łącka is not available from off-licences (liquor stores) but is offered in many households in Cracow.

A vodka glass

Amaretto liqueur

Plum Łąck brandy

Passover Plum vodka

Senator vodka

Krakus vodka

Harnaś vodka

Żywiec Beer Label
Many brands of beer are produced by the Żywiec Brewery, but bottles with the couple dressed in traditional Cracow costumes sell best.

Light Brackie Beer from Żywiec

Krakus Beer from Żywiec

Beer from the Okocim Brewery

BEER

Polish breweries have developed rapidly in recent years. The production of quality beer has grown and been modernized. Figures show that Poles are drinking more and more beer and less strong alcohol.

Pre-1939 advertisement of the Okocim Brewery

Beers from Okocim and Żywiec are traditionally the most popular in Cracow. Cracovians are conservative and still very aware that both breweries were established in Galicia. The Okocim brewery was founded by the Goetz family who were raised to the rank of hereditary barons by Emperor Franz Joseph. The Żywiec brewery was set up and owned, until World War II, by the Habsburg Archdukes. The grim paradox was that this Żywiec branch of the Habsburgs, who took up Polish citizenship after World War I, had their brewery confiscated by the Nazis after they refused to sign the *Volkslist*. After World War II the Communists nationalized Żywiec as a former German property. Heineken, the Dutch brewer, acquired a majority holding in the enterprise a few years ago, and the brewery is now one of the most technologically advanced in Europe.

WINE

Although vineyards were cultivated in the Cracow area quite successfully, they disappeared in the 15th century. Large quantities of quality wine were produced until World War II in the Zaleszczyki region on the then Romanian border. Today only a few vineyards can be found near Zielona Góra in the far west of the country, which means that Poland's wine production is negligible. Any visitor to Cracow wishing to drink wine will find a large selection of imported wines both in shops and restaurants.

Wine comes from many countries, including France, Italy, Spain and Austria, as well as California, Australia, Chile and New Zealand. Hungarian wine, however, is to be recommended in Cracow. This is not only because of its budget price. For centuries Cracow was a place where Tokay wines were stored for ageing, in barrels housed in large cellars beneath Market Square, before being exported all over the world.

NON-ALCOHOLIC DRINKS

Mineral water, sparkling and still, is the most popular non-alcoholic drink. Many brands of mineral water come from the springs in the mountain foothills or highlands not far from Cracow. Fruit juices are also popular. Apple and blackcurrant juices are Polish specialities.

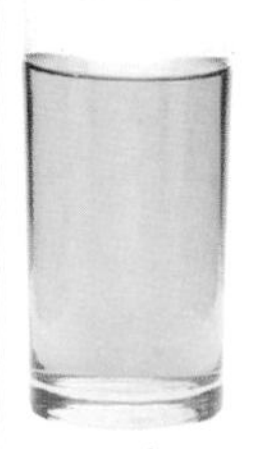

Apple juice

Blackcurrant juice

Choosing a Restaurant

The restaurants in this listing have been selected for their good food, ambiance and value for money. They are grouped according to the area into which they fall, then according to their price category. For more on Polish cuisine found in Cracow, see pp184–5. For hotel listings see pp178–81.

PRICE CATEGORIES
Based on the cost of a three-course meal for one, with a half bottle of house wine, and including tax and service

zł under 40
złzł 41–60
złzłzł 61–90
złzłzłzł over 90

WAWEL HILL

Na Wawelu — złzłzł

Wzgórze Wawelskie 9 ***Tel*** *012 421 19 15* ***Map*** *3 C1*

A Cracow stalwart located up on Wawel Hill. As one of the very few restaurants in the vicinity, it could be a tourist trap but with its good cuisine and reasonable prices, it manages successfully to avoid this. The menu features Polish favourites, though there are plenty of international dishes as well.

OKÓŁ AND STRADOM QUARTERS

Akropolis — zł

ul. Grodzka 9 ***Tel*** *012 421 77 25* ***Map*** *1 C5*

Good Greek food can be eaten here, though it can, at times, be a little rough and ready. The Akropolis is a good lunchtime choice, and there is plenty on the menu for vegetarians to choose from. You need to order your food at the counter before sitting down.

La Strada — zł

ul. Stradomska 13 ***Tel*** *012 431 12 72* ***Map*** *3 C1*

Standard Italian *trattoria* food in an above-average setting. The decor is convincing and the food is passably Italian, with healthy portions. Their home-baked *focaccia* bread is excellent, and the pizzas are really rather good too. The reasonable prices make a meal here light on your pocket.

Taco Mexicano — zł

ul. Poselska 20 ***Tel*** *012 421 54 41* ***Map*** *1 C5*

Tex-Mex treats for the homesick Americans who throng to this place at lunchtime. Most leave full if a little underwhelmed; for while the service is great, prices good and the portions large, the food is not really authentic Tex-Mex, with almost everything on the menu having a slightly Polish feel to it.

CK Dezerter — złzł

ul. Bracka 6 ***Tel*** *012 422 79 31* ***Map*** *1 C5*

Charming Polish restaurant serving large helpings of meaty dishes. The sour soups are terrific, while cabbage has never tasted as good as in the *kaputsa* (cabbage and sauerkraut) served here. The decor is enjoyably cluttered, and prices are very reasonable. Service can be very slow, so be prepared to be patient.

Il Calzone — złzł

ul. Starowiślna 15a ***Tel*** *012 429 51 41* ***Map*** *2 D5*

High-quality Italian restaurant that would get top marks were it not for the pizzas that clutter the menu. Il Calzone specialises in grilled meats in subtle sauces, rather than pasta or pizzas, and in this category nearly every dish is excellent. Prices can be a little high for those items that have to be imported, so watch what you are ordering.

Orient Ekspres — złzł

ul. Stolarska 13 ***Tel*** *012 422 66 72* ***Map*** *1 C5 (6 D3)*

As the name may suggest, the Orient Ekspres aims to recreate the look and feel of luxury train journeys of the past, and in many regards it succeeds. It is doubtful if the passengers on the real Orient Express ever ate sitting next to suitcases, but never mind. The menu is eclectic, with good fish options and a number of forest mushroom dishes.

Balaton — złzłzł

ul. Grodzka 37 ***Tel*** *012 422 04 69* ***Map*** *1 C5 (6 D4)*

Hungarian cuisine served in a less than salubrious setting, but redeemed by the delicious food. Try the Hungarian national dish, goulash, or spicy Hungarian sausages. Paprika is used in almost everything on the menu, but most of the patrons appear to like it that way. Reservations are often needed as Balaton fills up early most evenings.

Key to Symbols *see back cover flap*

Copernicus

ul. Kanonicza 16 ***Tel*** *012 424 34 21* ***Map*** *1 C5 (6 D3)*

Cracow's restaurants are not, in general, known for their excellent service; however the staff at the Copernicus have clearly had the benefit of good training. Everything runs well, from kitchen to table, and a daring menu of game-dominated dishes warrants the relatively high prices charged for most of them. Excellent wine list.

Pod Aniołami

Grodzka 35 ***Tel*** *012 421 39 99* ***Map*** *1 C5 (6 D4)*

This restaurant is housed in very old, painstakingly restored cellars which were used by medieval alchemists. Polish cuisine is served here, and it is that from the Podhale region which dominates the menu. Try the grilled smoked ewe's cheese (*oszczypek od Mulicòw*), bread rolls (*kikiełki*) and *żurek* (a fermented, sour soup).

Senacka

ul. Grodzka 51 ***Tel*** *012 421 11 61* ***Map*** *1 C5 (6 D4)*

In a sublime setting that blends the modern with the historic, Senacka, which is attached to a hotel *(see p178)*, is a great place to try any number of Cracow's special game dishes. A fine wine list, helpful staff and a real sense of culinary excellence make for a memorable dining experience. Expensive, but worth every penny.

Pugetów

ul. Starowiślna 15a ***Tel*** *012 432 49 50* ***Map*** *2 D5 (6 E3)*

One of Cracow's best restaurants, this establishment is located in the hotel Pugetów *(see p178)*. Here every diner is made to feel special, even before the food arrives. The menu is international with a Polish twist (or vice versa), and game makes a number of excellent entries. The wine list is outstanding.

Smak Ukraiński

ul. Kanonicza 15 ***Tel*** *012 421 92 94 ext.25* ***Map*** *1 C5 (6 D4)*

Though overpriced and overrated, the Smak Ukraiński still brings in the crowds because of the lively atmosphere that never fails to materialize, indeed it is advisable to make a reservation owing to its popularity. There is a good selection of wines from the former Soviet Union, including sparkling wine from the famed Cricova vineyards.

OLD QUARTER

Green Way

ul. Mikołajska 14 ***Tel*** *012 431 10 27* ***Map*** *6 D1*

Relatively expensive vegetarian fast food bar with some tables at the back where diners can enjoy their meat-free snacks. The Green Way is part of a Poland-wide chain and the food can be a little unadventurous at times; but with vegetarian options so thin on the ground in this city, you may need to wait for a table at lunchtime.

Gruzińskie Chaczapuvi

ul. Floriańska 26 ***Tel*** *050 954 28 00* ***Map*** *6 E2*

Fast food-style burgers and salads, as well as Polish favourites, in a cheap and cheerful setting. Great for quick lunches, the location of this eatery could not be better, right on the tourist strip that is Floriańska. Surprisingly for a fast-food outlet, there is a very good choice for vegetarians.

Pierogarnia

ul. Sławkowska 32 ***Tel*** *012 422 74 95* ***Map*** *6 D1*

No visitor to Cracow should leave the city without tasting *pierogi* *(see pp184–5)*, and the Pierogarnia is about the best place in town to try them. Fillings are innumerable, and these tasty treats can be eaten as a snack or as part of a larger meal. The restaurant also serves other Polish food, though not to try the *pierogi* is considered a sin.

Aqua e Vino

ul. Wiślna 5/10 ***Tel*** *012 421 25 67* ***Map*** *6 D1*

Outrageously trendy, where only the coolest fashionistas will feel at home, this relatively new Italian is the home of some superb food. It takes a clever chef to take standard Italian cuisine to a new level, yet the chef at Aqua e Vino has pulled it off. The prices are reasonable, if you avoid the expensive imported wines. Dress well.

CK Browar

ul. Podwale 6-7 ***Tel*** *012 429 25 05* ***Map*** *6 D1*

In a cellar deep under the Old Quarter this famous Polish restaurant is an excellent place to enjoy local favourites such as sour soups, sausages, *bigos*, cabbage and beer. While the food is good, it is the beer that really brings the customers in. It is outstanding and brewed on the premises.

Del Papa

ul. św. Tomasza 6 ***Tel*** *012 421 83 43* ***Map*** *6 D2*

From the moment you walk through the elegant black door, you know that quality is not going to be a problem here. A small but perfectly formed Italian restaurant, Del Papa's authentic menu includes everything from salmon and orange salad to grilled prawns in garlic. Take the table by the window for great views of the passing masses.

El Paso

ul. św. Krzyża 13 ***Tel*** *012 421 32 96* — ***Map*** *5 C3* — zł zł

A good place for Tex-Mex food, though the usual Cracow problem of the food not being spicy enough remains. The burritos are tasty and come in a variety of flavours, including a vegetarian option. The cocktails are fine, and prices are reasonable. El Paso is popular, so reservations are a good idea especially at weekends.

La Bodega

ul. Sławkowska 12 ***Tel*** *012 425 49 81* — ***Map*** *6 E2* — zł zł

Cracow's best tapas bar, where the food is not just seen as something that merely gets in the way of the wine. A wide variety of tapas are served and, though not cheap, by ordering with care you can eat well for a reasonable price. The wine list is what really brings people here, however: outstanding, with something for every pocket.

Sukiennice

Rynek Główny 1/3 ***Tel*** *012 422 24 68* — ***Map*** *6 D2* — zł zł

One of the trendiest venues on Market Square. During the summer the terrace, set under the colonnades of a fantastic building, is packed as live bands perform impromptu sets to delighted diners. If the weather is poor, head inside where elegant tables, smooth lighting and simple fusion dishes make this a romantic place for a light meal.

Amadeus

ul. Mikołajska 20 ***Tel*** *012 429 60 70* — ***Map*** *6 E2* — zł zł zł

Situated in the hotel of the same name, international and Polish dishes take pride of place on the adventurous menu. The establishment's signature dish – crayfish soup made to a traditional Polish recipe – is well worth trying. The service is outstanding, and the wine list exemplary.

Chimera

Św. Anny 3 ***Tel*** *012 423 21 78* — ***Map*** *6 E2* — zł zł zł

This restaurant was built as an extension to an existing salad bar, which is one of the best places in Cracow for fresh fruit, salad and vegetables. Popular amongst students in particular, it even serves baked potatoes cooked in the fireplace during the winter. If you prefer something more hearty, the restaurant serves traditional Polish cuisine.

Cherubino

ul. św. Tomasza 15 ***Tel*** *012 429 40 07* — ***Map*** *6 D2* — zł zł zł

Poland has a real fondness for Italy, and Cracow in particular has a knack of recreating super Italian *trattorias*. This is one such, where real Tuscan food is prepared by experts. A couple of sour soups have slipped onto the menu, but that only adds to the eclectic nature of the place. The decor is wonderfully scatty, including a horse-drawn carriage.

Chłopskie Jadło

ul. św. Jana 3 ***Tel*** *012 429 51 57* — ***Map*** *6 D2* — zł zł zł

This one is definitely not for vegetarians as the chef takes a very meat-centred approach to cooking. Polish classics dominate the menu, with plenty of meats in heavy sauces. The menu is very reasonably priced making it a good place for a hearty dinner after a day exploring Kazimierz.

Czwarta Pora Roku

Rynek Główny 15 ***Tel*** *012 424 96 00* — ***Map*** *6 D2* — zł zł zł

Cracow is famous for its cellar restaurants and this one, underneath Market Square, is perhaps the best. With a wide and varied menu, it avoids the meat-fest so often found elsewhere. The restaurant is famous for its Cracow Salad: crunchy green lettuce with sausage, parmesan, tomatoes, onion slices, sprinkled with garlic and vinaigrette dressing.

Da Pietro

Rynek Główny 17 ***Tel*** *012 422 32 79* — ***Map*** *6 D2* — zł zł zł

While unquestionably expensive, the attention to detail at this lively Italian restaurant makes a visit here definitely worth the cost. The menu is not especially inventive, but there is a wide selection of genuine Italian dishes which are all made with high-quality, imported ingredients. Da Pietro has a great location on Market Square too.

Grill 15/16

Rynek Główny 16 ***Tel*** *012 424 96 00* — ***Map*** *6 D2* — zł zł zł

Salads, grilled meats and well-mixed cocktails, Grill 15/16 serves these in the jungle-like surroundings of a leafy garden behind Market Square. During the summer it offers live jazz almost every evening, which brings in a sophisticated crowd. Tables are hard to come by after 7pm so make a reservation.

Hawełka

Rynek Główny 34 ***Tel*** *012 422 06 31* — ***Map*** *6 D2* — zł zł zł

For fine Polish cuisine in a historic setting, it is difficult to do better than this restaurant, which has been serving the rich and famous since 1876. Polish classics abound *(see pp184–5)* from humble but tasty *pierogi* to *bigos* and roasted duck. The wine list is one of the best in the city (with prices to match).

Ipanema

ul. św. Tomasza 28 ***Tel*** *012 422 53 23* — ***Map*** *6 D2* — zł zł zł

A taste of the exotic comes to Cracow in the shape of this South American bar and grill. The restaurant claims to import all of its beef from Argentina, while many of the soups have Brazilian origins: try the *creme de milho*, a sweet, creamy corn soup, or the strangely enticing *sopa de abacate* (avocado soup).

Key to Price Guide *see p188* **Key to Symbols** *see back cover flap*

Metropolitan

(zł)(zł)(zł)

ul. Sławkowska 3 ***Tel*** *012 421 98 03* ***Map*** *6 D1*

It is difficult to categorize this Cracow legend, which serves dishes from as many countries as you can think of. What is surprising is that almost everything on the extensive menu is always available, and always brilliantly cooked. Prices are high, but value for money is guaranteed, and there is also a great wine and cocktail list to choose from.

Miód i Wino

(zł)(zł)(zł)

ul. Sławkowska 32 ***Tel*** *012 422 74 95* ***Map*** *6 D1*

Traditional Polish food in a traditional setting, operated by the same people as the more upmarket Hawełka *(see p190)*. This place is all serving wenches and long wooden tables, flagons of beer and meat, cabbage and onions. The overall experience is superb, however, and large groups will have an especially good time here.

Pod Różą

(zł)(zł)(zł)

ul. Floriańska 14 ***Tel*** *012 424 33 81* ***Map*** *6 E2*

Under a glass-covered atrium at the Pod Różą hotel, this outstanding restaurant is a favourite with visiting dignitaries and local high-flyers. The menu is a combination of traditional ingredients (with an emphasis on game) and modern invention and flavours. The wine list is equally well chosen.

Poezja Smaku

(zł)(zł)(zł)

ul. Jagiellońska 5 ***Tel*** *012 292 80 20* ***Map*** *5 C2*

Another cellar restaurant, but one where the lighting is perfect and the waiters serve you with style and finesse in freshly pressed, liveried uniforms. The chef is a master at creating all sorts of modern takes on Polish classic dishes. There is also a good wine list to choose from.

Pod Krzyżykiem

(zł)(zł)(zł)

Rynek Główny 39 ***Tel*** *012 433 70 10* ***Map*** *6 D2*

Since 1580 the Pod Krzyzykiem (literally "under a small cross") has been serving huge portions of good local dishes to visitors. In recent times the chefs here have been taking Polish cuisine to new heights of creativity. The crowds who spend warm summer evenings on the large terrace appear not to mind the relatively high prices.

Redolfi

V (zł)(zł)(zł)

Rynek Główny 38 ***Tel*** *012 423 05 79* ***Map*** *6 D2*

Another good Market Square venue, especially for vegetarians who can choose from a fine selection of salads (though note that some contain meat: ask for a non-meat version and the house usually obliges). The rest of the menu is dominated by exuberant fusion cuisine, which at times tends to combine too many disparate flavours.

Rooster

(zł)(zł)(zł)

ul. Szczepańska 4 ***Tel*** *012 411 36 72* ***Map*** *5 C2*

Excellent American diner-style restaurant. There is a host of grilled meat, pasta dishes and burgers (Cracow's best) to choose from, and while prices are a little on the high side the friendliness of the staff is legendary. The barman makes a great Tom Collins and most of the other cocktails are not far behind.

Szara

(zł)(zł)(zł)

Rynek Główny 6 ***Tel*** *012 421 66 69* ***Map*** *6 D2*

An important-looking restaurant with vaulted ceilings, crisp linen and a grand menu featuring the likes of butter-fried Zanderfillet and chicken 'yakitori'. You'll find hugely mixed reports about this place, ranging from "never again" to "unmissable". Arrive on the right night and you are in for a treat.

U Szkota

V (zł)(zł)(zł)

ul. Mikołajska 4 ***Tel*** *012 422 15 70* ***Map*** *6 E2*

An enormous cellar restaurant devoted to Scotland. The waiters wear genuine kilts and sporrans, while bagpipes and gentle watercolours featuring horses and the Scottish Highlands adorn the stone-clad walls. The food is, to all intents and purposes, Polish and prices are high. Eating here is a surprisingly enjoyable experience.

Wentzl

(zł)(zł)(zł)

Rynek Główny 19 ***Tel*** *012 429 57 12* ***Map*** *6 D2*

John Wentzl, a local merchant, opened a restaurant here in 1792. Today it is one of the best eateries in Cracow where the high ceilings, polished oak-floors and outstanding service complement the Central European menu. Czech, Slovak and Hungarian dishes dominate, while the wine list features grapes from Europe, Chile and South Africa.

Chiński Pałac

V (zł)(zł)(zł)(zł)

ul. Mikołajska 5 ***Tel*** *012 421 68 41* ***Map*** *6 E2*

If it is Chinese food that you are after, then this is the only restaurant in Cracow worth visiting. That does not make it all that good, however, but most of the dishes do have a Chinese style to them. Prices are high, though, and do not always represent good value for money. The service is patchy and the decor can be overbearing.

Cyrano de Bergerac

V (zł)(zł)(zł)(zł)

ul. Sławkowska 26 ***Tel*** *012 411 72 88* ***Map*** *6 D1*

If prices here are high, then the diners who reserve tables weeks in advance don't appear to mind. Simply put, this is a world-class French restaurant set in two elegant rooms, with a quiet patio used in summer. The food is exquisite, all cooked under the auspices of masterchef Pierre Gallard. Try the *garbure soupe béarnaise*, made with goose.

Farina

ul. Św. Marka 16 **Tel** *012 422 16 80* **Map** *6 D1*

A simple, uncluttered atmosphere of bare, highly polished wooden floors and whitewashed walls helps to focus the diner's attention on the excellent menu. A sound mix of Polish and Italian dishes brings in a mixed crowd of locals and visitors. You definitely have to reserve a table if you wish to eat in the evening.

Leonardo

ul. Szpitalna 20-22 **Tel** *012 429 68 50* **Map** *6 E2*

There are never any more that 15 items on the Italian menu at Leonardo, and that includes the puddings. Here everything is simple, expensive and exquisite. From luxurious mushroom ravioli with rosemary sauce to the tiger prawns in garlic butter, all of the dishes are mouthwatering. The wine list complements the food very well.

Sioux Steakhouse

Rynek Główny 22 **Tel** *012 421 34 62* **Map** *6 D2*

At this Wild West-themed restaurant complete with wagon wheels and cacti at every turn, the staff dress somewhat unconvincingly as Native Americans and serve American delights such as steaks, burgers and wings. The terrace is packed every summer evening, even though prices are quite high for the quality of the food.

Tetmajerowska

Rynek Główny 34 **Tel** *012 422 06 31* **Map** *6 D2*

One of three restaurants operated by the Hawełka outfit, this is their flagship: a quite sensational, modern Polish establishment where only the best is on offer. From the elegant decor to the sublime service, everything is done to make dining here wonderful. An outstanding wine list too.

Wierzynek

Rynek Główny 15 **Tel** *012 424 96 00* **Map** *6 D2*

This place was reputedly the venue for a vast banquet hosted in 1364 by a Cracow burgher, Mikołaj Wierzynek, for five European sovereigns. As such it claims to be the oldest resaurant in Cracow, though the present establishment dates from 1945. Today, it is a fine eatery serving traditional Polish food at high prices to local VIPs.

KAZIMIERZ QUARTER

Fabryka Pizzy

ul. Józefa 34 **Tel** *012 433 80 80* **Map** *4 D2*

Great pizzas cooked just how you like them, all with gimmicky names, and popular with the city's students. Now firmly established as part of the Kazimierz tourist trail, Fabryka Pizzy is becoming a popular lunch-time stop for locals too. It is quite small, so making a reservation is a good idea on weekday evenings.

Alef

ul. Szeroka 17 **Tel** *012 421 38 70* **Map** *4 E1*

This non-kosher Jewish restaurant is situated in a delightful house in Kazimierz. On the same street, at No.6, is the restaurant's other outlet. The *gefilte fisch* (stuffed carp) and vine leaves stuffed with goose liver fried with almonds and raisins are not to be missed. In the evenings there is ethnic music, including gypsy and Russian folk songs.

Arka Noego

ul. Szeroka 2 **Tel** *012 429 15 28* **Map** *4 E1*

The name means Noah's Ark and Arka Noego provides a real shelter from the tourist trail outside. The menu includes both kosher and non-kosher dishes, while the drinks list includes kosher beers and wines, some imported from France and very good indeed. Prices are low and the whole place represents excellent value for money.

Klezmer Hois

ul. Szeroka 6 **Tel** *012 411 12 45* **Map** *4 E1*

While this restaurant is bold enough to admit that it has no rabbinical certificate of supervision (the *kashrut*), it does keep strict standards and all the dishes are kosher. You can enjoy sabbath soup, shubaha herring and Sephardic salads alongside meaty treats such as stuffed goose necks. Great value.

Pepe Rosso

ul. Kupa 15 **Tel** *012 431 08 75* **Map** *4 E1*

With Italian restaurants two-a-penny in Cracow, it is nice to come across an exceptional place like this. Everything at Pepe Rosso is authentic Italian and of the highest quality – even the olive oil is outstanding. Prices are reasonable considering what is on offer and there is plenty to choose from for vegetarians.

Kuchnia i Wino

ul. Józefa 13 **Map** *4 D2*

With a good range of vegetarian options, this international restaurant offers a welcome break from the many faux-Jewish restaurants that have cropped up in the Kazimierz area. The food here is inventive, modern and comes in good portions at great prices. A super venue for lunch.

Key to Price Guide *see p188* **Key to Symbols** *see back cover flap*

Szeroka
V zł zł zł

ul. Szeroka 1 ***Tel*** *012 421 21 17* ***Map*** *4 E1*

The only restaurant in Cracow certified by the rabbi as fulfilling all kosher requirements, Szeroka's minced herrings, roast duck and Passover Slivovitz (plum vodka) are not to be missed. A kosher fast-food bar is housed on the ground floor, which is particularly popular with tourists from Israel.

PIASEK AND NOWY ŚWIAT

Solfeż
V zł zł zł

ul. Straszewskiego 17 ***Tel*** *012 618 88 88* ***Map*** *1 C5 (5 C4)*

The Radisson Hotel's flagship restaurant is everything you would expect from this chain. Service is smart and efficient, the food inventive and tasty, and the surroundings elegant. Any doubts about eating in a hotel restaurant should be put to one side because this place is really worth a visit.

Someplace Else
V zł zł zł

ul. Powiśle 7 ***Tel*** *012 662 10 00* ***Map*** *5 B4*

Tex-Mex food served at the Sheraton Hotel at very non-Sheraton prices. The television screens bring in expatriates when there is a big football match on, while many locals also frequent the place as the food really is authentic. The *burritos* and *fajitas* are the best in the city. Great cocktails too and the portions are enormous.

Dong Yang
V zł zł zł zł

ul. Straszewskiego 16 ***Tel*** *012 422 48 93* ***Map*** *1 C5 (5 C4)*

Good Korean food does not come cheap in these parts and, though prices here are astronomical, that does not appear to put off the many returning diners who swear by the place. This is the most authentic Asian restaurant in Cracow. Be careful to note how much things cost though.

The Olive
V zł zł zł zł

ul. Powiśle 7 ***Tel*** *012 662 10 00* ***Map*** *3 B1 (5 B4)*

As expensive as any restaurant in Cracow, the Sheraton Hotel's showpiece is an award-winning establishment famed for its refined Mediterranean cuisine. There is a good selection of seafood and fish dishes and the wine list is perfect. A glass roof makes dining here in winter a particularly pleasurable experience.

FURTHER AFIELD

Kawaleria
zł zł zł

ul. Gołębia 4 ***Tel*** *012 430 24 32* ***Map*** *5 C3*

Close to Planty Park, Kawaleria serves classic Polish dishes in a cluttered but enchanting setting. On the menu are such local favourites as *bigos* and *pierogi*, as well as plenty of game and a couple of fish dishes. Prices are reasonable, though ordering any of the imported wines can make the bill unexpectedly high.

Villa Decius
zł zł zł

ul. 28 Lipca 17a ***Tel*** *012 425 33 90*

A luxurious restaurant housed in the beautiful Renaissance Villa Decius. The villa belonged originally to Justus Decius, an Italian courtier to Zygmunt the Old, and was painstakingly restored in the 1990s. The menu features international, French and Polish cuisine, served to the sound of music from the Renaissance played live most evenings.

Jarema
V zł zł zł zł

pl. Matejki 5 ***Tel*** *012 429 36 69* ***Map*** *2 D3 (6 E1)*

The Jarema prides itself in reminding diners of the days when Poland had an empire. As such you will find dishes from Lithuania, Ukraine and even Russia. For a restaurant of this type, there is an excellent range of vegetarian options and, with its large tables, it is a great choice for groups.

Mesa Kapitana Cooka
zł zł zł zł

ul. Zamoyskiego 52 ***Tel*** *012 656 08 93* ***Map*** *4 D4*

One of very few good seafood and fish restaurants in Poland, let alone Cracow. The garlic pancakes with bran and salmon are delicious, while in summer tables are set up outdoors in a lovely garden. The menu is excellent and tempting, all at fairly reasonable prices considering the quality on offer.

U Ziyada
V zł zł zł zł

ul. Jodłowa 13 ***Tel*** *012 429 71 05*

Perched on the top of high white cliffs above the Vistula River, the views from this restaurant-cum-café, which extend over the river, Tyniec Abbey and Bielany Monastery, are breathtaking. Run by a Kurd, the menu offers one of the few opportunities in Poland to try outstanding Kurdish cuisine. Polish dishes are available too.

Cafés and Bars

Cracow's cafés are an important part of everyday life and often institutions in their own right. It would be unthinkable to deny a Cracovian his or her daily 15 minutes or so spent chatting with a friend or reading a newspaper in a café. The majority of cafés have regular customers, who come year in, year out to their chosen place, every day except at weekends.

CAFÉS

Situated in the very heart of the city, the **Noworolski** is one of the longest established cafés. It is housed in the Cloth Hall, with its entrance facing the Mickiewicz Monument. It dates back to the end of the 19th century. The interior, modelled on Viennese cafés, has preserved its original appearance. A visit to the **Jama Michalika** *(see p114)*, renowned for the Zielony Balonik (Green Balloon) Cabaret, is a must. However, the Art Nouveau rooms offer a feast for the eye rather than the palate. They are now often deserted, possibly because of a total ban on smoking (smoke would damage the historic interior).

The **Pożegnanie z Afryką** (Out of Africa) is the best place for lovers of good coffee. The coffee served here will satisfy even the most demanding customer. Situated in St Thomas Street (Św. Tomasza), it is a coffee bar and shop. A variety of brands are available here, which can be prepared in small espresso machines. The smell is so fantastic that even a connoisseur will not be able to resist the temptation. There are many outlets of Pożegnanie z Afryką in other cities throughout Poland but the company started in Cracow and has its headquarters here.

The **Café Larousse** is a tiny place, ideal for a romantic date. The walls of this lovely café are all papered with pages taken from 19th-century editions of the well-known French dictionary. If you want to travel back in time and see how a patisserie looked in the early 19th century, then **Redolfi** in Market Square is the place to visit, to see the original period furnishing. This café was established by a Swiss man, Lorenzo Paganino Cortesi, in 1823, but the name Redolfi refers to its second owner, also a Swiss. Lunch is also served here.

The **Maska** is a favourite haunt with celebrities, especially from the theatre and film circles. It is housed in the cellars of the Stary (Old) Theatre and is decorated in Art Deco style. The Maska was co-founded some years ago by the well-known actor, Tadeusz Huk. The film and theatre director Andrzej Wajda is one of those who have a permanent reservation here. Take a break from eyeing the stars to sample the delicious roast garlic and a drink called "Teraz Polska" (Poland Now). This famous cocktail imitates the colours of the Polish flag.

Delicious canapés served on bread from the highlands and tea with home-made raspberry syrup are just two specialities of the **Café Camelot**. The walls here are decorated with pictures by the celebrated Polish naive artist Nikifor. The **Dym** (Smoke) is next door, serving delicious Pischinger cake as well as beer and spirits.

STREET CAFÉS

Most of the eating establishments in Market Square open street bars and cafés in the spring and summer. The square is thus transformed into a huge open-air café for thousands of customers.

The **Bambus** (Bamboo) Café, situated in front of the Palace of the Rams, is very popular during the day. The street café set up by the **Black Gallery** is very busy at night, sometimes till the early hours. An enormous parachute will protect you from rain, and the house drink Kamikaze, a deceptive mixture of Blue Curacao, vodka and lemon juice, may well help you not to notice any change in the weather.

If you decide to eat at one of the outdoor restaurant tables, expect a lunch rather than a full dinner menu. Dishes served outside are less elaborate. Bear in mind that the journey from the kitchen to the table is a long one and makes serving an exotic *flambé* lobster, for example, almost impossible.

All sorts of street buskers roam and play in and around the street cafés. They request gratuities but you are not obliged to give any. It is worth listening to the Gypsy band, with a partially paralysed fiddler in a wheelchair, who plays his violin holding it like a double-bass.

BARS

A number of new bars have opened in Cracow in recent years. They are often called pubs as in England. They are housed in cellars and are open till late. Live music is played in many. The **Free Pub** and **Roentgen** are open longest. They are both very popular with young people (but generally not teenagers) and artists. The Roentgen has a dental chair, in which you can sit and drink. Young people like to meet in the **Pod Papugami** (Parrots) where there is a disco.

The **Pod Złotą Pipą** is popular with more conservative customers. The place is nostalgically decorated in the Austro-Hungarian style and features many portraits of His Imperial Majesty Franz Joseph and the Empress Sissi. White sausage with cabbage and peas is served here, and to accompany this you may order authentic Czech Budweiser on draught.

The **Klub Kulturalny** (Culture Club) has recently become very fashionable. The large cellars have a mosaic floor, which leads some to believe, after a few drinks, they are in Ravenna.

DIRECTORY

Albo Tak
Mały Rynek 4.
Map 2 D4 (6 E3).
Tel *012 421 11 05.*

Arka Noego
Szeroka 2. **Map** 4 E1.
Tel *012 429 15 28.*

Arlekin
Rynek Główny 24.
Map 1 C4 (6 D2).
Tel *012 430 24 57.*

Bambus Café
Rynek Główny 27.
Map 1 C4 (6 D2).
Tel *012 421 97 25.*

Black Gallery
Mikołajska 24.
Map 2 D4 (6 E2).
Tel *012 423 00 30.*

Bosto
Floriańska 33.
Map 2 D4 (6 E2).
Tel *012 421 16 93.*

Durzliwy Poniedziałek
Grodzka 4.
Map 1 C5 (6 D3).
Tel *012 292 23 62.*

Café Cabaret
Jabłonowskich 6.
Map 1 B4 (5 B4).
Tel *0802 90 21.*

Café Camelot
Św. Tomasza 17.
Map 1 C4 (6 D2).
Tel *012 421 01 23.*

Café Larousse
Św. Tomasza 22.
Map 1 C4 (6 E2).

Café Molier
Szewska 4.
Map 1 C4 (5 C2).
Tel *012 292 64 00.*

Café Numero
Rynek Główny 6.
Map 1 C4 (6 D2).
Tel *012 421 13 05.*

Casa de la Pizza
Mały Rynek 2.
Map 1 C4 (6 E3).
Tel *012 421 64 98.*

Dandy Café
Św. Tomasza 19.
Map 1 C4 (6 D2).
Tel *012 421 73 91.*

Deja vu
Rynek Główny 9.
Map 1 C4 (6 D2).

Dym
Św. Tomasza 13.
Map 1 C4 (6 D2).
Tel *012 429 66 61.*

Free Pub
Sławkowska 4.
Map 1 C4 (6 D2).
Tel *0802 90 82.*

George
Lea 5a.
Map 1 A3.

Hamlet
Miodowa 9.
Map 4 D1 (6 F5).
Tel *012 422 12 11.*

Jama Michalika
Floriańska 45.
Map 2 D4 (6 E2).
Tel *012 422 15 61.*

Jazz Rock Café
Sławkowska 12.
Map 1 C4 (6 E1).
Tel *012 422 19 00.*

John Bull
Mikołajska 2.
Map 2 D4 (6 E2).
Tel *012 423 11 68.*

Kapsuła
Rynek Główny 6.
Map 1 C4 (6 D2).

Kawiarnia Noworolski
Rynek Główny 1, Cloth Hall.
Map 1 C4 (6 D2).
Tel *012 422 47 71.*

Klub Kulturalny
Szewska 25.
Map 1 C4 (5 C2).
Tel *012 429 67 39.*

Krzysztofory
Szczepańska 2.
Map 1 C4 (6 D2).

Lamus
Karmelicka 54.
Map 1 B3.
Tel *012 633 37 24.*

Le Fumoir
Sławkowska 26.
Map 1 C4 (6 D2).
Tel *012 411 72 88.*

Manggha
Starowiślna 10.
Map 2 D5 (6 E3).

Maska
Jagiellońska 1.
Map 1 C4 (5 C2).
Tel *012 429 60 44.*

Milano
Praska 18.
Tel *012 266 64 83.*

Piwnica pod Ogródkiem
Jagiellońska 6.
Map 1 C4 (5 C2).
Tel *012 292 07 63.*

Pod Białym Orłem
Rynek Główny 45.
Map 1 C4 (6 D2).
Tel *012 421 57 97.*

Pod Chochołami
Plac św. Ducha 1.
Map 2 D4 (6 E2).
Tel *012 421 15 51.*

Pod Papugami
Św. Jana 18.
Map 1 C4 (6 D2).
Tel *012 422 82 99.*

Pod Złotą Pipą
Floriańska 30.
Map 2 D4 (6 E2).
Tel *012 421 94 66.*

Poezja Smaku
Jagiellońska 5.
Map 1 C4 (6 D2).
Tel *012 292 80 20.*

Pożegnanie z Afryką
Św. Tomasza 21.
Map 1 C4 (6 E2).
Tel *012 421 23 39.*

Prohibicja
Grodzka 51.
Map 1 C5 (6 D4).
Tel *012 422 86 41.*

Ratuszowa
Rynek Główny 1.
Map 1 C4 (6 D2).
Tel *012 421 13 26.*

Redolfi
Rynek Główny 38.
Map 1 C4 (6 D2).
Tel *012 423 05 79.*

Roentgen
Plac Szczepański 3.
Map 1 C4 (5 C2).
Tel *012 431 11 77.*

Santos
Grodzka 65.
Map 3 C1 (6 D5).
Tel *012 423 14 87.*

Stare Mury
Pijarska 21.
Map 2 D4 (6 E1).
Tel *012 421 38 98.*

Strawberry
Św. Tomasza 1.
Map 1 C4 (6 D2).

U Literatów
Kanonicza 7.
Map 1 C5 (6 D4).
Tel *012 421 86 66.*

U Louisa
Rynek Główny 13.
Map 1 C4 (6 D3).
Tel *012 617 02 22.*

Vis-a-vis
Rynek Główny 29.
Map 1 C4 (6 D2).
Tel *012 422 69 61.*

Windsor
Rynek Główny 25.
Map 1 C4 (6 D2).
Tel *012 421 98 94.*

Zdarzenie
Plac Mariacki 7.
Map 1 C4 (6 D2).
Tel *012 421 84 86.*

SHOPS AND MARKETS

Cracow has always been a favourable place for merchants. Recent reforms have stimulated trade. Unlike in other Polish cities, most of the prewar buildings in Cracow have remained in private hands. After 1989 the number of new shops opening surged. House owners opened shops themselves or let premises out. A profusion of shop-signs appeared on façades, inner courtyards and basements. Quality soon took over and big Western names also began to appear. Today one can hardly tell the difference between a Cracow shop and its Viennese or Parisian counterpart. The area around Market Square is especially good for shopping. It offers a variety of elegant shops, little traffic and many cafés. Markets and street stalls offer a different kind of shopping and a lively atmosphere. There is something for everyone.

A wooden statue of Christ

SHOPPING HOURS

In Poland, unlike in many other Western European countries, there is no law regulating the hours of trade. Each shop owner decides for themselves when to open and close their shop, and this is regarded as a necessary part of a free-market economy. Grocers open in Cracow at 6 or 7 o'clock in the morning and close at 7pm at the earliest. Many remain open until 10pm or longer, and a dozen or so shops are open 24 hours. Other types of shops are generally open between 10am and 7pm on weekdays, but on Saturdays close at 2 or 3pm. All shops within the Planty green belt tend to trade on Sundays for similar periods to those on Saturdays. All shops are customarily open on the Sunday preceding Christmas and Easter Day. Supermarkets are at their busiest on Friday afternoon and evening. The great number of tourist shops in the centre attract customers all the time regardless of the day of the week but Saturdays are possibly the busiest.

Pictures for sale, displayed on the wall near St Florian's Gate

HOW TO PAY

Cash is the most popular form of payment throughout Poland. The situation is different in major cities, where most of the shops in the city centre do accept major credit cards, as indicated by stickers displayed in their windows. Supermarkets and department stores also accept credit cards as well as cheques, but the latter must be issued by a Polish bank. All the prices displayed are inclusive of VAT.

A collectors' fair in Market Square

DEPARTMENT STORES AND SHOPPING CENTRES

Jubilat, built in the mid-1970s, is the largest department store in Cracow. The food department is on the ground floor, and on the other floors you will find household goods, furniture and electrical appliances, clothes, shoes and cosmetics, as well as toys and books. The "Galeria Centrum", another departament store, is located by Market Square. The large Krakchemia shopping centre was built after 1989. It houses two enormous halls. Food, shoes, clothes, cosmetics and kitchenwares are sold in one of them and items for the home and garden in the other. Just out of town, but well served by a bus route, is the Nico store. It sells Italian clothes and shoes.

The Mozart Shopping Centre was established recently next to the Billa supermarket. Mozart has many small fashion and shoe boutiques, as well as chemists (drug stores) served by an escalator.

The large Herbewo store is housed in a building which dates from the inter-war years. Its name originates from the then famous manufacturer of the most popular cigarette holders and other products.

Dolls in regional costumes sold in the Cloth Hall

Jewellery shop on Floriańska Street

MARKETS AND FAIRS

Cracow's markets are never called bazaars as in other Polish towns. Here the term bazaar has a pejorative connotation. In Cracow one goes to the 'square' to buy fruit and vegetables, cheese, meat, fish or other produce from the stall-holders.

The Old Kleparz market is the nearest to the city centre. The New Kleparz market sells not only food but also flowers and clothes, while every Tuesday and Friday you will find stalls selling brooms, clay pots and wickerware. The market in Grzegórzecka Street by the Market Hall is the biggest and full of stalls selling meat, fruit and vegetables. On Sundays you have the added attraction of book and antique stalls.

The unique atmosphere of the New Market in Kazimierz was used to good effect in the filming of *Days and Nights (Noce i dnie)*, a Polish film after a well-known novel by Maria Dąbrowska of the same title. The late 19th-century round butchers stalls, which are centrally located, are still in use. These stalls are surrounded by vegetable and fruit stands. On Sundays this place becomes an extensive flea market, where among other things you can buy famous Harris tweed jackets from Scotland and woollen coats and Tyrolean tunics from Austria. The Tomex Market in Nowa Huta is dominated by sellers from the former Soviet Union. The so-called Tandeta Market sells mostly clothes. Although *tandeta* means rubbish in Polish, this term is used in Cracow to mean an ordinary clothes market and has no derogatory meaning.

SALES

Seasonal sales are now quite common in a number of larger shops but, in terms of the selection of goods on offer and prices, are not as attractive as those in other Western European countries. Goods are no longer reduced because they are imperfect or no longer in fashion, as used to be the case, but because of promotions, end of season sales or the arrival of new collections.

A flower stall in Market Square

Shopping in Cracow

If you are a Western visitor you can expect to be able to find everything in Cracow you can buy at home. It is no longer necessary to bring items of everyday use. On the other hand you should not expect luxury Western merchandise, such as perfumes, alcohol, designer clothes and shoes and other branded items, to be cheaper in Poland. You may, however, find bargains in shops and galleries selling handicrafts, silver jewellery, contemporary paintings and prints, as well as leather goods, bric-à-brac and coffee-table books.

BOOK AND RECORD SHOPS

There are many excellent bookshops in Cracow. Some of them, like the **Księgarnia Hetmańska** situated in the Hetmański Arcade in Market Place, are open till very late. This often surprises visitors but is typical of Cracow, where the way of life is still heavily influenced by artists, professors and students.

The **Empik** (formerly the Odeon) in Market Square is a mega-bookstore occupying several storeys, selling different types of publications, as well as records, CDs and stationery. There is another branch of Empik, selling the same sorts of products, on Bora Komorowskiego.

For visitors with more literary tastes, the prestigious **Znak** bookshop in Sławkowska Street has a large selection of foreign titles. Academic books and fiction can be bought at the **Ossolineum** and Elefant bookshops. The **Księgarnia Muzyczna** in Market Square specializes in music books, scores and recordings. The shop of the **Polskie Wydawnictwo Muzyczne** (Polish Music Publishers) has a similar assortment with an emphasis on classical music. Among many shops in the centre selling CDs and cassettes, the one in Poselska Street offers a particularly good selection of jazz and classical recordings. It also has a useful sale-or-return section. The music shop found in Mikołajska Street specializes in jazz.

ANTIQUES

Cracow is possibily the best place in Poland for antiques because the city was saved from destruction during World War II and Cracovians did not have to migrate. Foreigners are advised that exporting pre-1945 antiques from Poland is illegal without special permission, which is very difficult to obtain *(see p212)*. As far as valuable works of art are concerned, as well as those which form part of the cultural heritage, such as paintings, furniture, jewellery, old prints, rare books and maps, this law is rigorously observed, but less so in the case of objects of lesser value and bric-à-brac, which are plentiful in Cracow.

Antique dealers are mainly located in the area around the Planty gardens. Occasional antique markets take place in Market Square. Every Sunday, sellers of collectors' items and second-hand books put up their stalls by the Market Hall in Grzegórzecka Street. They are worth visiting.

FOLK ART

The annual folk Art Fair in Market Square takes place in September. Dozens of stalls are set up, selling sculpture, earthenware, woven rugs and wood carvings made in various parts of Poland.

The stalls in the **Cloth Hall** offer a large selection of crafts and are a must for the tourist. You will find here colourful, embroidered traditional costumes of the Cracow and Podhale regions, as well as walking sticks from the highlands, with an axe-like handle (a favourite souvenir with children); chess sets and jewellery boxes, devotional statues and Jewish objects all carved in wood; paper cut-outs, painted Easter eggs and much more.

CRAFTS AND CONTEMPORARY ART

The stands in the Cloth Hall also sell silver jewellery, amber *objets d'art*, leather items and fabrics for the home. Shopping in this Renaissance hall has the added bonus of sustaining a trading tradition that goes back to the 16th century. The old and charming **Kramy Dominikańskie** (Dominican Stalls) also specialize in crafts. The **Galeria Osobliwości** (Gallery of Curiosities) in Sławkowska Street sells rare and unusual objects. The **Calik** Gallery is famous for Christmas decorations and attracts customers from all over the world.

Cracow is a good centre for Polish contemporary art, which is enjoying an ever greater demand. Works by contemporary artists can be found in the **Starmach Gallery, Zderzak, Space Gallery, Galeria Mariana Gołogórskiego, Dominik Rostworowski Gallery, Stawski Gallery, Kocioł Artystyczny** and many others. The open-air gallery by St Florian's Gate is the place for lovers of images of sunsets and sunrises, galloping horses or large-scale nudes. This kind of painting is displayed on the city wall throughout the year. Fans of satirical drawings by **Andrzej Mleczko** will find a visit to his gallery in St John's Street (Św. Jana) a must.

CLOTHES AND SHOES

Jeans can be found in abundance in almost any clothes shop and those who prefer the well-known brands can go to the shops of **Levi Strauss, Mustang, Diesel, Wrangler** or Lee. There are also shops that sell the leading brands of sports shoes: **Adidas, Reebok** and **Nike**. Benetton and the **House of Carli Gry** have fashion selections for the young. Designer menswear is available from **Pierre Cardin**. Polish brands, such as **Vistula**, offer less expensive suits for men, and **Wólczanka** specializes in shirts.

Paradise offers a good selection of clothes and shoes from both leading foreign brands and designers as well as Polish names.

The **Zebra** and **Olivier** chain of shops are best for Italian shoes and the **Nico** store is great for Italian fashion for the whole family – men, women and children.

FOOD SHOPS

There are no supermarkets in the centre of Cracow. The Delikatesy general grocery store next to the Hawełka Restaurant is the largest in Market Square. Its selection of alcoholic drinks is particularly good. Apart from a number of small shops close to Market Square there are several self-service ones, such as **Dominik**.

The large supermarkets such as **Géant, Hypernova, Krakchemia, Tesco** and **Billa** are located away from the centre and cater for shoppers who come by car. There are supermarkets on most of the housing estates, catering for local needs.

Most Cracovians purchase their fruit and vegetables from local stalls and markets. The Old Kleparz market is the closest to the city centre being only a few minutes' walk away. The selection of coffee brands available from the charming **Pożegnanie z Afryką** (Out of Africa) is hard to beat. Julius Meinl's famous Viennese coffee is only available from the Meinl supermarket in the Azory (Azores) housing estate. The little and delightfully decorated **Pod Aniołami** (Angels) shop sells exquisite cold meats prepared according to old Polish recipes, *bundz* and *oszczypek* cheese from the highlands, as well as country-style bread baked in log-fired ovens. Wines are also sold here but the largest selection from around the world can be found in the off-licence (liquor store) In Vino Veritas, as well as in the drinks department at the **Billa** supermarket. Those who favour strong spirits may choose the **Polmos** shop, where they can not only buy but also sample drinks at the bar.

Lovers of chocolate will be welcomed in the **Wawel** shop in Market Square, selling goods from the local sweet factory, Zakłady Przemysłu Cukierniczego. Many patisseries throughout Cracow offer a wonderful selection of cakes and pastries. The best doughnuts can be bought at Michałek and nougat at Cichowski. The shop in the Cracovia Hotel is famous for *kremówki*, a delicious puff-pastry cake filled with custard. Note that what is known as *kremówka* in Cracow, in Warsaw is called *napoleonka*.

Other language differences between Mazovia and Lesser Poland include the names given to fruits of the forest. Blueberries are called *borówki* in Cracow and Galicia, and *czarne jagody* in the Warsaw region. All berries, including the non-edible varieties, are called *jagody* in Cracow; *brusznice* is the name given to small red berries, which are called *borówki* in Warsaw, but in both regions *żurawiny* is the name for cranberries.

There are further differences in bread terminology which will probably confuse first-time visitors to the city. A long white loaf of bread called *weka* in Cracow is known as Wrocław bread in Warsaw.

COSMETICS

All chemists (drug stores) and supermarkets sell basic cosmetic goods, but expensive international brands are best purchased from specialist shops where expert advice is also available. **Guerlain** and Yves Rocher have their own outlets and beauty clinics.

Well-known foreign brands of perfumes, such as Gucci, Biagotti, Trussardi, Bulgari, Carolina Herrera and Burberrys are available from the large **INA Center** shop. Another place to find a good selection of brands is in hotel shops.

PHARMACIES

The majority of drugs are available from Polish chemists on prescription only. Prescriptions issued by overseas doctors are generally accepted without any problem. Non-prescription drugs and medicines are readily available throughout the city. In the centre there are many chemists in the following streets, among others: **Szczepańska, Grodzka** or **Dunajewskiego**. If you need some medication after normal opening hours, then go to one of the chemists that are open 24 hours; their addresses are displayed in all the chemists' shop windows. A 24-hour telephone service (012 94 39) will provide you with general medical information, including the location of the nearest hospital with an accident and emergency unit.

FLORISTS

Cracow would not be Cracow without the flower stalls by the Mickiewicz statue in Market Square. On the day of the great poet's birthday, these street vendors have made it a tradition to lay flowers at the base of the statue in tribute. They also regularly make a gift of flowers to visiting foreign VIPs. On warm summer days you can buy flowers till late into the evening. There are many flower stalls to be found in New Kleparz market. Of the specialist florist shops, Niezapominajka (Forget-me-not) is particularly well known. Alternatively, you can buy bunches of flowers in one of the many 24-hour shops and at petrol stations.

DIRECTORY

DEPARTMENT STORES

Billa
Mackiewicza 17.

Galeria Centrum
Św. Anny 2.
Map 1 C4 (5 C2).
Tel *012 422 98 22.*

Géant
Bora Komorowskiego 37.
Tel *012 617 06 00.*

Jubilat
Al. Krasińskiego 1–3.
Map 1 B5 (5 B4).
Tel *012 422 80 40.*

Krakchemia
Pilotów 6.

Tesco
Wielicka 259.

BOOKSHOPS

Columbus. Multi-language Bookshop
Grodzka 60.
Map 1C5 (6 D4).
Tel *012 431 20 98.*

Empik
Sienna 2.
Map 1 C4 (6 D2).
Tel *012 429 45 77.*

EGIS Bookshop
Plac Matejki 5.
Tel *012 422 16 44.*

Kossakówka Bookshop and Gallery
Pl. Kossaka 4.
Map 1 B5 (5 B4).

Księgarnia Muzyczna Kurant
Rynek Główny 36.
Map 1 C4 (6 D2).
Tel *012 422 98 59.*

Ossolineum
Św. Marka 12.
Map 2 D4 (6 E2).
Tel *012 422 58 44.*

Polskie Wydawnictwo Muzyczne (Polish Music Publishers)
Al. Krasińskiego 11a.
Map 1 B5 (5 A4).
Tel *012 422 70 44 ext. 113.*

Znak
Sławkowska 1.
Map 1 C4 (6 D2).
Tel *012 422 45 48.*

RARE AND SECOND-HAND BOOKS

Antykwariat AB
Rynek Główny 43.
Map 1 C4 (6 D2).
Tel *012 421 69 03.*

Antykwariat księgarski
Stolarska 8/10.
Map 1 C5 (6 D3).
Tel *012 422 62 88.*

Bibliofil
Szpitalna 19.
Map 2 D4 (6 E2).
Tel *012 422 18 61.*

Krakowski Antykwariat Naukowy
Św. Tomasza 8.
Map 1 C4 (6 D2).
Tel *012 421 21 43.*

Rara Avis
Szpitalna 7.
Map 2 D4 (6 E2).
Tel *012 422 03 90.*

ANTIQUES

Antique
Św. Tomasza 19.
Map 1 C4 (6 D2).
Tel *012 421 79 44.*

Connaisseur
Rynek Główny 11.
Map 1 C4 (6 D2).
Tel *012 421 02 34.*

Desa
Floriańska 13.
Map 1 C4 (6 D2).
Tel *012 422 27 06.*

Desa
Mikołajska 10.
Map 2 D4 (6 E2).
Tel *012 422 49 33.*

Galeria Hetmańska
Rynek Główny 43.
Map 1 C4 (6 D2).
Tel *012 421 33 74.*

Sopocki Dom Aukcyiny
Rynek Główny 45.
Map 1 C4 (6 D2).
Tel *012 429 12 17.*

FOLK ART

Cloth Hall
Rynek Główny 1/3.
Map 1 C4 (6 D2).

CRAFTS AND CONTEMPORARY ART

Autorska Galeria Andrzeja Mleczki (Mleczko Gallery)
Św. Jana 14.
Map 1 C4 (6 D2).
Tel *012 421 71 04.*

Bunkier Sztuki
Pl. Szczepański 3A.
Map 1 C4 (5 C2).
Tel *012 422 40 21.*

Calik
Rynek Główny 7.
Map 1 C4 (6 D2).
Tel *012 421 77 60.*

Dominik Rostworowski Gallery
Św. Jana 20.
Map 1 C4 (6 D2).
Tel *012 423 21 51.*

Galeria Mariana Gołogórskiego
Grodzka 29.
Map 1 C5 (6 D4).
Tel *012 421 44 19.*

Galeria Osobliwości
Sławkowska 16.
Map 1 C4 (6 D1).
Tel *012 429 19 84.*

Galeria Związku Polskich Artystów Plastyków (Gallery of the Association of Polish Artists)
Rynek Główny 1–3.
Map 1 C4 (6 D2).
Tel *012 430 24 55.*

Kocioł Artystyczny
Mikołajska 6.
Map 2 D4 (6 E2).
Tel *012 292 00 29.*

Krakowska Szkoła Malarstwa
Sławkowska 14.
Map 1 C4 (6 D1).

Kramy Dominikańskie
Stolarska 8/10.
Map 1 C5 (6 D3).
Tel *012 422 19 08.*

Pryzmat
Łobzowska 3.
Map 1 C3 (5 C1).
Tel *012 632 46 22.*

Space Gallery
Floriańska 13.
Map 1 C4 (6 D2).
Tel *012 421 89 94.*

Starmach Gallery
Wegierska 5.
Map 4 E3.
Tel *012 656 43 17, 012 656 49 15.*

Stawski Gallery
Miodowa 15.
Map 4 D1 (6 F5).
Tel *012 421 80 46.*

Zderzak
Floriańska 3.
Map 1 C4 (6 D2).
Tel *012 429 67 43.*

CLOTHES AND SHOES

Adidas
Floriańska 14.
Map 1 C4 (6 D2).
Tel *012 429 68 44.*

Diesel
Rynek Główny 13 & 44.
Map 1 C4 (6 D2).
Tel *012 617 02 10, 012 423 26 86.*

House of Carli Gry (Jackpot & Cottonfield)
Rynek Główny 36.
Map 1 C4 (6 D2).
Floriańska 38.
Map 1 C4 (6 D2).
Tel *012 422 61 86.*

Levi Strauss
Floriańska 9.
Map 1 C4 (6 D2).

Mustang
Szewska 14.
Map 1 C4 (5 C2).

Nico
Modlnica 214.
Tel *012 637 03 95.*

Nike
Szewska 20.
Map 1 C4 (5 C2).

Olivier
Szewska 9.
Map 1 C4 (5 C2).
Tel *012 422 28 19.*

Paradise
Floriańska 18.
Map 1 C4 (6 D2).

Pierre Cardin
Św. Jana 12.
Map 1 C4 (6 D2).
Tel *012 423 11 02.*

Puma
Floriańska 7.
Map 1 C4 (6 D2).
Tel *012 423 27 87.*

Ryc-Sport Reebok
Szewska 9.
Map 1 C4 (5 C2).
Tel *012 422 28 08.*

Troll
Floriańska 31.
Map 2 D4 (6 E2).
Tel *012 422 41 42.*

Vistula
Szpitalna 3.
Map 2 D4 (6 E2).
Tel *012 422 09 55.*

Wólczanka
Pl. Mariacki.
Map 1 C4 (6 D2).
Tel *012 421 83 16.*

Wrangler
Sienna 1.
Map 1 C4 (6 D2).
Tel *012 421 92 89.*

Zebra
Szczepańska 7.
Map 1 C4 (5 C2).
Tel *012 422 46 05.*

COSMETICS

Guerlain
Św. Jana 20.
Map 1 C4 (6 D2).
Tel *012 422 39 45.*

INA Center
Szpitalna 34.
Map 2 D4 (6 E2).
Tel *012 421 55 83.*
Szewska 15.
Map 1 C4 (5 C2).

Sephora
Floriańska 19.
Map 1 C4 (6 D2).
Tel *012 421 24 24.*

FOOD SHOPS

Cracovia
Al. Focha 1.
Map 1 A5 (5 A3).
Tel *012 424 56 83.*

Delikatesy
Rynek Główny 34.
Map 1 C4 (6 D2).
Tel *012 428 05 75.*

Dominik
Pl. Dominikański 2.
Map 1 C5 (6 D3).

Hypernova
Witosa 7.
Tel *012 654 58 07.*

Michałek
Krupnicza 6.
Map 1 B4 (5 C2).
Tel *012 422 47 05.*

Pod Aniołami
Grodzka 35.
Map 1 C5 (6 D4).
Tel *012 421 39 99.*

Pożegnanie z Afryką
Św. Tomasza 21.
Map 2 D4 (6 D2).
Tel *012 644 47 45.*

Tesco
Dobrego Pasterza 67.
Tel *012 412 75 34.*
Kapelanka 54.
Map 3 A3.
Tel *012 255 25 00.*
Włoska 2.
Tel *012 655 76 71.*
Wybickiego 10.
Tel *012 633 43 99.*

Wawel
Rynek Główny 33.
Map 1 C4 (6 D2).
Tel *012 423 12 47.*

OFF LICENCES (LIQUOR STORES)

Baryłeczka
Szczepańska 9.
Map 1 C4 (5 C2).
Tel *012 429 62 67.*

Dom Wina
Starowiślna 66.
Map 2 D5 (6 E3).
Tel *012 431 03 68.*

Polmos
Starowiślna 26.
Map 2 D5 (6 E3).
Tel *012 423 11 18.*

Vis-Pol
Lea 90a.
Tel *012 637 95 47.*

PHARMACIES

Dunajewskiego 2.
Map 1 B4 (5 C2).
Tel *012 422 65 04.*

Grodzka 34.
Map 1 C5 (6 D4).
Tel *012 421 85 44.*

Szczepańska 1.
Map 1 C4 (6 D2).
Tel *012 422 92 93.*

Apteka Na Kazimierzu
Krakowska 49.
Map 4 D2.
Tel *012 430 53 46.*

Europa
Karmelicka 56.
Map 1 B3.

Mały Rynek
Mały Rynek 6.
Map 1 C4 (6 E2).
Tel *012 421 90 89.*

Pod Słońcem
Rynek Główny 42.
Map 1 C4 (6 D2).

Pod Świętym Hubertem
Krakowska 1.
Map 4 D2.
Tel *012 422 19 98.*

Pod Złotą Głową
Rynek Główny 13.
Map 1 C4 (6 D2).
Tel *012 422 41 90.*

Pod Złotym Słoniem
Pl. Wszystkich Świętych 11.
Map 1 C5 (6 D3).
Tel *012 422 91 39.*

FLORISTS

BeA
ul. Wrzesińska 6.

Kamelia
Pl. Wszystkich Świętych 11a.
Map 1 C5 (6 D3).
Tel *012 422 76 45.*

Konwalia
Zwierzyniecka 23.
Map 1 B5 (5 B4).
Tel *012 422 93 52.*

Margareta
Długa 74.
Map 1 C2.
Tel *012 633 78 63.*

ENTERTAINMENT IN CRACOW

Cracow is the cultural capital of Poland and visitors may find themselves spoiled for choice. Local theatres are among the best in the country and often host leading international companies. The Szymanowski Philharmonic Orchestra and Choir and the Capella Cracoviensis have high reputations. There are many concerts and festivals of classical music organized in the magnificent interiors of historic houses and churches. The history of Cracow's cabarets goes back some 100 years, attracting both domestic and foreign audiences. The intense nightlife can be compared to that offered by Italian or Spanish cities. You only have to walk a couple of minutes to find a variety of music clubs, discotheques and bars. They are usually housed in Gothic or Renaissance cellars and are open until very late or even till the early hours of the morning. They will leave you with unforgettable memories. Theatre, film, music and ballet festivals take place throughout the year.

Open-air concert

USEFUL INFORMATION

Full listings of cultural events in Cracow appear in the *Karnet – Krakowskie Aktualności Kulturalne* monthly, published by the Centrum Informacji Kulturalnej (Cultural Information Centre) in Polish and English. For the electronic version of the *Karnet* see their website on: http://karnet.euro.net.pl. Current listings and reviews of cinemas, theatres and other events, as well as a guide to restaurants, discos and clubs (live music) are published on Friday in the *Gazeta Wyborcza* supplement entitled *Co jest grane?* (What's on?). Listings also appear in local newpapers on a daily basis. *Kraków, What, Where, When* is published on a monthly basis in English and contains listings in German, French, Spanish and Japanese. *The Kraków Insider* is published solely in English.

A Bücklein Theatre performance

BOOKING TICKETS

Tickets for all major events can be purchased from the Cultural Information Centre. This is the best place to make enquiries how and where to buy tickets or make an advanced booking. Staff at the Centre speak English, French, German and Italian. Booking is also possible through travel agents and hotel receptions. Seats for the Philharmonic Hall and the theatres are available from their respective box offices, which also take advance bookings. Cinema tickets can be booked over the phone. Bear in mind that some performances require booking months in advance.

TICKET PRICES

Ticket prices have increased considerably in recent years but are still cheaper than in the West. Theatre seats are more expensive in Cracow compared to anywhere else in Poland, and in greatest demand. Average prices vary from 25 to 40 zł per person. Cinema tickets cost between 13 and 20 zł. Museum tickets are good value; in some museums the entrance is free on one day of the week.

NIGHT TRANSPORT

Bus and tram day-routes stop around 11pm. Trams do not resume before 5am. Night buses operate according to a timetable displayed at bus stops. Tickets can be purchased from the driver. Taxis are a better option. A radio-taxi booked over the phone is cheaper than one at a taxi-

Musicians wearing costumes of the Cracow region

rank but you can rely on all the taxis waiting at the ranks in the city centre. Most taxi drivers are honest, but it is best to avoid the taxi rank by the main Railway Station. If you require a taxi while in the main Railway Station area, use the radio-taxi rank situated at roof level above the platforms (use the platform stairway).

FESTIVALS

The city plays host to a multitude of cultural festivals; the only problem is to choose the most interesting. The International Festival of Alternative Theatre will appeal to theatre fans, the International Short Film Festival to film lovers, the Cracow Spring Ballet Festival to ballet aficionados, the International Festival of Music in Old Cracow to admirers of classical music, while enthusiasts of brass instruments may attend the International Music Festival of Military Bands.

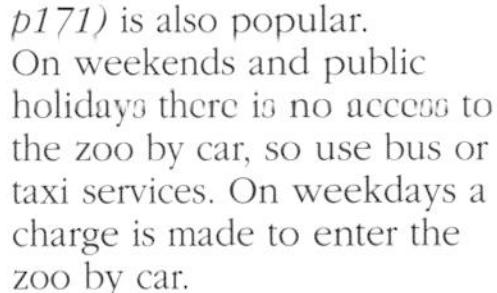

A pillar advertising cultural events

WALKS AND OPEN-AIR EVENTS

The tradition of open-air fairs goes back in Cracow to at least the early part of the 19th century when folk festivals were organized on the Błonia fields, then located out of town. One of the attractions was to try to climb a pole smeared in soap, a flask of alcohol and sausages attached to the top of the pole awaiting the successful climber. The poles have disappeared since but the Błonia are still a venue for public events, of either a national or light entertainment nature. Two great cavalry parades in the inter-war years, attended by Marshals Józef Piłsudski and Edward Rydz Śmigły respectively, took place here. The masses celebrated on these fields by Pope John Paul II, and attended by millions of the faithful, are commemorated by a granite block brought here from the Tatra Mountains. All kinds of concerts, festivals and fairs also take place at the Błonia.

The Jordan Park, situated opposite the Błonia fields, is very popular with mothers with toddlers. Doctor Henryk Jordan, a Cracow physician, introduced the idea of playing fields which are now found throughout the country and are named after this celebrated physician. The Jordan Park in Cracow was the first-ever public playground for small children.

The Wolski Wood (Las Wolski) is not far from Cracow and offers many walking routes *(see pp170–71)*. For Cracovians it is one of the favourite destinations for a day out, but the zoo *(see p171)* is also popular. On weekends and public holidays there is no access to the zoo by car, so use bus or taxi services. On weekdays a charge is made to enter the zoo by car.

Summer concerts in the open air are organized in the Wawel Castle courtyard, in the gardens of the Archaeological Museum and in Radio Kraków's amphitheatre as well as in the courtyard of the Collegium Iuridicum and on a temporary stage in Market Square.

"Pod Baranami" Cinema

OUT OF TOWN TRIPS

A number of appealing sights are located within close proximity of Cracow. A trip to the Ojców National Park *(see p156)*, one of the smallest but most beautiful of Polish national parks, is an unforgettable experience. White limestone rocks, such as Hercules's Club, have most unusual forms; there are many indigenous plants and a fine Renaissance castle in Pieskowa Skała *(see p157)*.

The Salt Mines at Wieliczka *(see p156)* have been included by UNESCO on their World Heritage List. The mines and the underground sanatorium housed here are unique. Niepołomice has a recently restored 14th-century castle and the remnants of an ancient forest where bison are bred. The Benedictine Abbey in Tyniec *(see p157)* is beautifully located on the Vistula and worth visiting.

The Operetta theatre in the former military riding school theatre

Entertainment in Cracow

Cracow is famous for its cultural traditions. The underground Rapsodyczny Theatre was established here during World War II and in 1956 Tadeusz Kantor founded the world-famous Cricot 2 Theatre. The Stary Theatre gained its fame through productions directed by Konrad Swinarski. The Pod Baranami Cabaret and other cabarets in Cracow continue the best of traditions that go back to the Zielony Balonik at the beginning of the 20th century. An evening out in a cabaret or nightclub is highly recommended, and boredom is out of the question in this cultural city.

FOREIGN-LANGUAGE PERFORMANCES

Cracow does not have a theatre performing in a foreign language on a permanent basis. The annual Festival of French-Speaking Theatre takes place in May and attracts many companies from French-speaking countries. The city occasionally hosts foreign theatre companies from all over the world. They perform in their own languages.

A number of bodies, such as the Austrian Consulate, French Institute, Goethe Institute, Italian Cultural Centre and Japanese Centre of Art and Technology, are all actively involved in artistic patronage. They usually organize events in the languages of their countries and information about these events can be obtained from the Cultural Information Centre.

THEATRE

The first professional theatre company was established in Cracow in 1781. Today there are many theatres. The most renowned is **Stary Teatr** (Old Theatre). The best actors, directors and set designers work for the Stary Teatr whose performances are mostly based on Polish classics and Romantic literature.

The **Słowacki Theatre** shares the same traditions and types of plays. The building, modelled on the Opéra Garnier in Paris, opened in 1893. Its splendid Art Nouveau interior features a curtain designed by Siemiradzki. As an added bonus, spectators may watch the performance from the box originally used by the Austro-Hungarian Emperor, Franz Joseph and his wife Sissi.

The **Krakowski Teatr, Scena Stu** gained fame through unconventional performances, sometimes staged in the open air, and other grand productions. In their main venue in Krasiński Avenue classics predominate. Benefit performances celebrating theatre stars are broadcast by television and have became classics in their own right.

The **Ludowy Theatre** in Nowa Huta has had its ups and downs. Today it has a young cast who perform not only in Nowa Huta but also in two other venues in Cracow, namely in the cellars beneath the Town Hall and in Kanonicza Street. The **Bagatela Theatre** specializes in light satirical productions. The **Teatr Lalki i Maski Groteska** generally performs for children but has also staged a number of plays for adults. The productions of the world-famous **Cricot 2** theatre practically ceased following the death of Tadeusz Kantor. The student **Teatr 38** performs only occasionally.

OPERA AND BALLET

The opera of Cracow has no permanent seat and performs in the Słowacki Theatre. This situation is possibly a consequence of the old tradition of attending opera performances in Vienna or the Lemberg (now L'viv) Opera's guest appearances in Cracow.

The **Operetta** is housed rather unusually in the former Austrian riding school. The productions here include Galician all-time favourites by Kalman, Lehar and the Strausses.

The Cracovians have some sort of resistance towards ballet. Even leading foreign companies perform to half-deserted theatres and there is not a single independent ballet company in the city.

Two festivals, namely the annual Cracow Spring Ballet Festival, which takes place in May and June, and the International Ballet Festival, both aim at improving the situation.

CABARET

Cabaret artists are in a much better position in Cracow than ballet dancers and can always rely on good audiences and sell-outs. Following the death of Piotr Skrzynecki, the founder of the **Piwnica pod Baranami**, the future of this cabaret has not yet been decided but the majority of the artists believe it should continue. And this is indeed the case despite the irregularity of performances and often incomplete cast. Individual appearances by the Piwnica's stars are more frequent.

The **Loch Camelot** is artistically affiliated to the Piwnica and also performs in cellars. Very popular is the **Piwnica pod Wyrwigroszem.**

Lovers of classic, satirical texts of the **Jama Michalika** Cabaret may still attend a performance here. In the surroundings of Art Nouveau objects and caricatures dating from the early 20th century, they may listen to Tadeusz Boy-Żeleński's verses. The original decadent ambience of this place is, however, difficult to recreate. The present menu lacks absinthe and there is a total ban on smoking.

CINEMAS

Kijów is the largest cinema in Cracow. Besides its regular programme, it is also a venue for a number of festivals, including the short-film festival and that dedicated to commercials. Food and drinks are available on the first floor. A truly Parisian-style multiplex is situated at the junction of St John's (św. Jana) and St Thomas (św. Tomasza) Streets. It comprises the **Apollo, Sztuka, Aneks Sztuki** and **Reduta Sztuki** cinemas. Cafés can be found in all of them. The Reduta Sztuki is said to be the most prestigious and expensive cinema in Poland.

The small **Pod Baranami** Cinema, housed in the Palace of the Rams, is very popular with those seeking independent and art films from around the world. Its prime location is an added bonus. After a show, walk a few steps to enjoy a drink in the Piwnica pod Baranami bar. Among other cinemas worth recommending are the **Atlantic** and **Mikro.**

CLASSICAL MUSIC

The most prestigious concert hall in Cracow is the **Szymanowski Philharmonic Hall**. Classical music is, however, best enjoyed in the more informal setting of one of the city's many historic houses. Among the many venues are the Wawel Castle, the National Museum in the Cloth Hall and the **Music Academy**, as well as churches, such as St Mary's, St Catherine's and the Holy Cross. In summer, concerts are also organized outside in such open-air venues as the arcades of the Wawel Castle, Collegium Maius's courtyard, in the former prison of St Michael (now the Archaeological Museum), and in the Radio Kraków amphitheatre, housed in the former Tarnowski Palace. For those prepared to travel a little, then there are the renowned organ recitals in the Romanesque Benedictine Abbey in Tyniec near Cracow.

MUSIC CLUBS

Any jazz fan visiting Cracow should have pencilled in his diary the address of the **Jazz Club u Muniaka**. Here on Fridays and Saturdays Janusz Muniak, one of Poland's most celebrated jazzmen, plays to the accompaniment of other musicians. Jazz concerts take place at the **Harris Piano Jazz Bar, Extreme Club, Pod Jaszczurami** and **Jazz Club Kornet** (traditional jazz) as well as Piwnica pod Baranami. Apart from jazz, the **Klub U Louisa** provides blues music and during the break you can surf the Internet using one of several terminals provided.

The **Rotunda-Orlik** and **Pod Jaszczurami** student clubs are also venues for rock groups, blues bands and student cabaret songs. Live music, and rock in particular, can be heard in a number of pubs such as **Klinika 35** or **Jazz Rock Café**.

NIGHTCLUBS AND DISCOS

The best place for techno music, experimental music and drum and bass is the barrel-vaulted **Krzysztofory**, while the **Bar Rózowy Stoń** will attract fans of classic disco. The **Afera Club, Pod Papugami** and **Pasja** discos are also popular.

The **Emergency Club** caters for fans of avant-garde hip hop, grunge and acid jazz music. Lovers of music of the sixties will enjoy the **Bosto** club, which offers a retro atmosphere on its small dance floor. The front end of a Syrena car, mounted in the wall, is a reminder of this unforgettable period.

If you feel exhausted after having a wild time in a disco, the **Roentgen, Free Pub** and **Black Gallery** are good places to relax in.

Cracow's nightclubs do not have any specific hour at which they close. In summer, especially, a club-goer can simply leave a club and go straight to work.

SPORTS

As far as sports facilities are concerned Cracow has much to offer. Two neighbouring sports clubs, **KS Cracovia** and **TS Wisła**, are the oldest and most popular in the city. Both clubs have their own swimming pools, which are open to the public.

The artificial lake in Kryspinów is a good place for both beach lovers and windsurfers. The lake's water is clean. A supervised swimming area can be found in the Nad Zalewem Recreation Centre, however here there is a charge for the use of the centre and the lake's beaches. The sports grounds in the Jordan Park are a good place for badminton players. Other sports clubs include **Korona**, **Olsza** and **Zwierzyniecki**.

Tennis courts are available at **Centrum tenisowe**, **Klub tenisowy "Kosłówek"** and **Hotel Piast**. The courts at the Olza and Zwierzyniecki sports centres are open all year round. Horse-riding facilities are available at the University Riding Club, the **Ewelina Riding Club**, as well as at a number of stables located on the outskirts of the city and further afield. The Korona Club, which is attached to the hotel of the same name, is located in the highlands and offers a covered swimming pool (filled with sea water), fitness centre and sauna facilities.

In recent years, even the Cracovians have shown an interest in healthy living. Sauna, sun bed and health and beauty clinics have been opened in all parts of the city, as have fitness clubs such as **Metamorfoza, Relax Body Club** and **Studio Rekreacji**.

Anyone interested in an active lifestyle can take advantage of Błonia, the expansive field in the middle of the town. Bridge and chess clubs will appeal to those who prefer more cerebral activities. Billiards can be played in a number of places throughout the city.

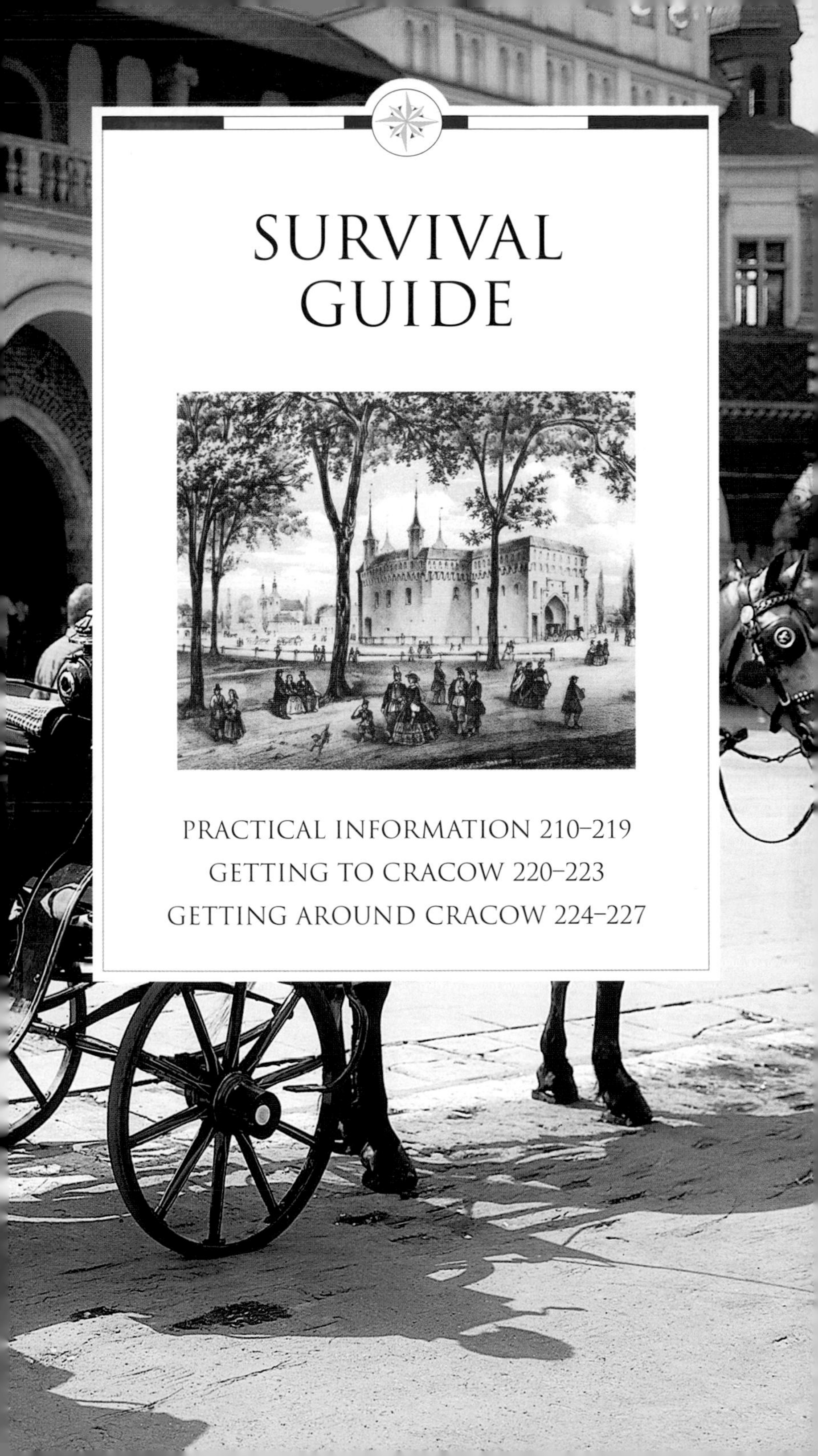

SURVIVAL GUIDE

PRACTICAL INFORMATION

Cracow attracts more tourists than any other Polish city. Much has been done in recent years to improve services for visitors. Balice airport has been modernized and is now second within Poland to Warsaw's Okęcie. The number of hotels has increased substantially both in the city centre and on the outskirts, but is still insufficient to satisfy current requirements. Hundreds of restaurants, bars and nightclubs have opened. The season lasts all year round in Cracow, but summer is particularly busy. Booking a hotel well in advance is necessary, otherwise finding accommodation on arrival may prove extremely difficult. If you intend to go to the theatre, remember to book your ticket early to avoid disappointment. Good performances tend to sell out very quickly.

Polish Tourist Information logo

Orbis Tourist Office sign

TOURIST INFORMATION

The main tourist information office is situated in the Cloth Hall on Market Square. Maps, plans and brochures are available from hotels. Electronic displays with information on the availability of hotels can be found at the main Railway Station and Balice Airport. The PTTK (Polish Tourist Organization) bookshop in Jagiellońska Street specializes in maps and guides to Poland.

The Polish Travel Office, Orbis, has agents in major cities around the world and travel, accommodation and car rental arrangements can be made through them prior to your arrival in Cracow. Enquiries concerning events, their programmes and booking, can be made by phoning, faxing or e-mailing the Cultural Information Centre in Cracow.

TIPS FOR VISITORS

The staff at hotels and restaurants generally speak English and German. Although learning foreign languages is becoming ever more popular in Poland you may experience some difficulty in communicating while in town, at a post office or in shops.

Drivers speaking foreign languages work for radio-taxi companies so you may, for example, request an English-speaking driver. All taxis serving the taxi-rank at the airport accept credit card payment. There is, therefore, no need to exchange money at the airport immediately after your arrival. Spring and summer are the best times to visit Cracow. The city is then transformed into an enormous open-air café.

Cultural Information Centre

Street cafés and restaurants around Market Square do not close until very late at night. You will certainly enjoy eating in the surroundings of Market Square, the largest Gothic and Renaissance square in Europe, and sharing this experience with thousands of others.

OPENING HOURS

The opening hours of the museums and galleries listed in this guide are given individually for each sight. Most state museums and galleries are closed on Mondays. Private galleries of contemporary art are generally closed on Sundays. The opening times vary depending on the day of the week, but late openings are generally on Thursdays. Opening hours are the same throughout the year.

Churches generally remain open from the first to the last service without closing at midday but there are some variations. Visitors are not allowed to sightsee during services. Food stores are generally open between 6 or 7am and 7pm, but there

Street cafés in Market Square

◁ Horse carriage in front of the Sukiennice – view from the Mariacki church

Horse-drawn cab in Market Square

are no strict rules about the opening hours, which are at the owner's discretion. Other shops tend to be open between 10am and 7pm. Many shops are open on Sundays. Enquiries about shops (including pharmacies) and customer services can be made by calling 012 632 34 12 or 012 634 30 20, between 9am and 6pm, Monday to Friday. If you are not certain where to buy a specific item call the above number.

Banks generally open at 8am and close at 6pm on weekdays. The hours are 8am to 1 or 2pm on Saturdays. Banks, shops, restaurants and other public institutions do not close for lunch.

LISTINGS MAGAZINES AND TICKETS

A full listing of Cracow's events appears in the *Karnet* monthly magazine, published by the Cultural Information Centre in English and Polish. The *Kraków Insider* is a good source of information for English-speaking visitors. This magazine, published four times a year, has listings, useful tips, reviews and an excellent food section. The *Kraków. What, Where, When?* and *Miesiąc w Krakowie* are two monthly magazines available from hotels and tourist information desks. Local newspapers list events on a daily basis.

Cracow's listings magazines

Admission charges to museums and galleries' permanent collections are modest but may be increased substantially for a temporary show. Reduced rates are available for children, students and senior citizens. Overseas students should have a valid international student card to qualify for a discount.

SIGHTSEEING

Guided sightseeing tours of Cracow are strongly recommended. A guide who can drive you round in a small electric *meleks* vehicle is a good choice. The *meleks* rank is situated in Market Square by the Church of St Adalbert. The driver-guides speak English, French and German and their best language is indicated by a sticker on the *meleks*. A bike or horse-drawn cab is another option and both these modes of transport have their ranks in Market Square.

The Orbis Travel Office specializes in out of town excursions. Oświęcim (Auschwitz), Zakopane, Wieliczka, Ojców and Pieskowa Skała are among the most popular destinations. An Orbis guide can also be hired for a tour of the town. Out of town excursions are also organized by the PTTK Tourist Organisation. Top sightseeing spots, such as Wawel Castle and Wieliczka, have their own guides.

A number of tourist agents cater for both individual and group visitors, providing all the necessary help for those who wish to stay in and around Cracow.

DIRECTORY

Tourist Information and Accommodation Centre

Pawia 8.
Map 2 D4 (6 F1).
Tel *012 422 60 91.*
www.jordan.pl

Cultural Information Centre

Św. Jana 2.
Map 1 C4 (6 D2).
Tel *012 421 77 87.*
@ *karnet@krakow2000.pl*

Fregata Travel

Szpitalna 32. **Map** 2 D4 (6 E2).
Tel *012 422 41 44.*
www.fregatatravel.pl

Polish Tourist Promotion Agency

Pl. Wszystkich Świętych 8.
Map 1 C5 (6 D3).

Orbis Polish Travel Office

Kremerowska 5. **Map** 1 B3.
Tel *012 421 99 79.*
@ *incoming@orbistravel.krakow.pl*

Rynek Główny 41.
Map 1 C4 (6 D2).
Tel *012 619 24 63.*

PTTK Polish Tourist Organization

Westerplatte 5. **Map** 2 D4 (6 F2).
Tel *012 422 26 76.*

Waweltur

Pawia 8. **Map** C D4 (6 F1).
Tel *012 422 19 21.*
www.waweltur.com.pl

More Practical Information

Telecommunications Centre in Market Square

VISITORS WITH DISABILITIES

Facilities for people with disabilities are still limited in Cracow. Some pedestrian crossings have a low-edge pavement and the number which are equipped with a sound message for the blind is on the increase. Wheelchair access and special lifts are available at the main Railway Station. Such facilities can also be found in a number of museums, including the National Museum's Main Building and the Japanese Centre for Art and Technology, as well as in some cinemas and public institutions. Access to the latter is generally restricted for the disabled, but the Main Post Office and the Telecommunications Centre in Market Square both offer easy access. A number of hotel rooms are available for the disabled. Some buses have low-level entry floors. Moving around Cracow in a wheelchair is not easy owing to the lack of contoured pavements and the number of cars parked in pedestrian areas.

Several organizations which assist the disabled exist in Cracow. However, there is only one taxi company which offers a service to individuals in a wheelchair. Polish people are generally very willing to help, however.

YOUNG PEOPLE AND STUDENTS

Those who are entitled to the ISIC (International Student Identity Card) are advised to apply for it before arriving in Cracow. The card entitles the holder to reduced rates in museums and galleries and at International Youth Hostels.

Students with a valid ISIC card can purchase rail tickets on international routes at a reduced rate, but must buy tickets on public city transport at the normal undiscounted rate. Youth hostels in Cracow accept International Youth Hostel Federation (IYHF) cards.

You will also find that some shops and pizza outlets, as well as places of entertainment and hostels, offer reduced rates to Euro<26 holders. This card is available to those who are 26 years old or younger.

International Student Card (ISIC) and the Euro<26 Card

CUSTOMS REGULATIONS

To enter Poland all visitors require a valid passport. The citizens of most European and many other countries do not reguire a visa. If in doubt, check with your local Polish embassy. There are no restrictions on items for personal use brought into Poland, but a limit applies on the amount of alcohol and cigarettes. It is essential to obtain a certificate before entering Poland with firearms. Gifts up to the value of US$100 are duty free. To export antiques, works of art such as contemporary paintings, permission or licences must be sought from the local authority: Urząd Miasta Krakowa, 3-4 Wszystkich Świętych, Tel: 012 616 12 00, or go to www.bip.krakow.pl.

RELIGIOUS SERVICES

There are nearly 100 Roman Catholic churches in Cracow. Holy Masses are said every Saturday, Sunday and feast day, as well as during the week. There are also churches of other religious denominations in Cracow.

PUBLIC TOILETS

Until recently, the lack of public lavatories used to be a real hindrance. Today, the situation has much improved. The most convenient lavatories are in the Cloth Hall, in the Planty gardens by Sienna and Reformacka streets, and at the coach car park by the Wawel. Toilets are readily available in restaurants, bars and cafés throughout the city.

LOST PROPERTY

To recover lost property is, unfortunately, rarely possible but it is always worth trying the lost property office, which has two outlets. One is situated in the local government (Urząd Miasta) building at 10 Powstania Warszawskiego Street; the other, in the MPK Transport Office at 3 Brozka Street, Tel: 012 254 11 50. To claim an item left behind on a train, try the Main Railway Station, office no. 162.

Cracow's English-language listings magazines

NEWSPAPERS, TV AND RADIO

Foreign papers are available from hotel shops, selected newsagents and bookshops.

National newspapers such as *Gazeta Wyborcza* and *Rzeczpospolita*, the local *Dziennik Polski* and *Gazeta Krakowska*, and the tabloid *Superexpress* are the most popular newspapers in Cracow. The *Dziennik Polski* and *Gazeta Wyborcza* have the best classified sections. The listings magazines *Kraków Insider, Kraków What, Where, When?, Karnet* and *Miesiąc w Krakowie* are published in Polish and English and are available from hotels, newsagents and bookshops.

Polish television offers an ever larger selection of programmes which are broadcast directly, through cable or satellite. The Polish state television, Telewizja Polska, broadcasts on two channels, has a local Cracow channel and the satellite channel Polonia. Private channels include Polsat, Polsat 2, TVN, RTL 7 and TV 4.

The most popular radio stations include RMF FM, Trójka, Radio Kraków and Radio Zet. The following stations and frequencies are available: Radio Alfa – 102.4 FM, Radio Bis – 89.4 FM, Radio Blue – 97.7 FM, Radio TOK FM– 102.9 FM, Jazz Radio – 101 FM, Radio Maryja – 90.6 and 100.7 FM, Radio Plus – 106.1 FM, PR I (Polish Radio One) – 104.8 kHz, PR II – 89.4 FM, PR III (Trójka) – 99.4 FM, Radio Kraków – 101.6 FM, Radio RAK – 100.5 FM, Radio RMF FM – 96 FM, Radio Wanda – 92.5 FM, Radio WaWa – 107 FM, Radio Zet – 104.1 FM.

ELECTRICAL APPLIANCES

The Voltage in Poland is 230 volts. Plugs are the same as in most countries in Europe.

LOCAL TIME

Cracow is one hour ahead of GMT and six hours ahead of Eastern Standard Time. Summer time is observed throughout Poland from late March until late October.

DIRECTORY

INFORMATION FOR THE DISABLED

Polish Association for the Blind
Babińskiego 29, blok 23/3.
Tel *012 262 53 59.*

Polish Association for the Deaf
Św. Jana 18.
Map 1 C4 (6 D2).
Tel *012 422 39 94.*

Polish Society for the Prevention of Disability
Dunajewskiego 5.
Map 1 C4 (5 C1).
Tel *012 422 28 11.*
www.fundacja-sm.malopolska.pl

Taxi Service for the Disabled
Radio Taxi-Partner
Tel *96 33, 96 88.*

CONSULATES

Austria
Cybulskiego 9.
Map 1 B4 (5 A2).
Tel *012 421 97 66.*

France
Stolarska 15.
Map 1 C5 (6 D3).
Tel *012 424 53 00.*

Germany
Stolarska 7.
Map 1 C5 (6 D3).
Tel *012 424 30 00.*

Hungary
Św. Marka 7/9.
Map 2 C4 (6 D1).
Tel *012 422 56 79.*

Russian Federation
Biskupia 7.
Map 1 C3.
Tel *012 422 26 47.*

Ukraine
Krakowska 41.
Map 4 D2.
Tel *012 429 60 66.*

United Kingdom
Św. Anny 9.
Map 1 B4, 5 C2.
Tel *012 421 70 30.*
@ *ukconsul@sonly.pl*

United States of America
Stolarska 9.
Map 1 C5 (6 D3).
Tel *012 424 51 00.*

PLACES OF WORSHIP

Augsburg Evangelical Church of St Martin
Grodzka 58.
Map 3 C1 (6 D4).
Tel *012 423 00 31.*

Baptist Church
Wyspiańskiego 4.
Map 1 A2.
Tel *012 633 23 05.*

Bethlehem Pentecostal Church
Lubomirskiego 7a.
Map 2 E3.

Evangelical Methodist Church
Długa 3. **Map** 4 E1.
Tel *012 633 55 67.*
Przybyszewskiego 36.
Tel *012 637 70 62.*

Polish Autocephalic Church
Szpitalna 24.
Map 1 D4 (6 E2).

Polish-Catholic Church
Friedleina 8. **Map** 1 B1.
Tel *012 633 82 82.*

Remu'h Synagogue
Szeroka 40.
Map 4 D1.

Seventh-Day Adventist Church
Lubelska 25.
Map 1 C2.
Tel *012 633 34 69.*

Personal Security and Health

Logo of the Town Wardens

Cracow is one of the safest cities in Poland. Although the number of reported crimes is generally on the increase, Cracow is a quiet place and visitors can feel safe in all parts of the city. Pollution, a big problem for Cracovians until recently, is showing some signs of improvement. General safety rules apply here as everywhere, so beware of pickpockets, do not leave any property visible in the car, and use guarded car parks. Anyone suffering a minor health problem should seek advice at a pharmacy, while hotels can usually arrange a doctor's visit.

A typical blue and white Police car

PERSONAL SECURITY

During the night the dark, poorly lit Planty gardens in the city centre are a place for occasional crimes. This is despite frequent police patrols in the area. A 24-hour police station is situated next to the Palace of the Rams in Market Square. Due to its large window, it is known as the "police shop". The housing estates in Nowa Huta have a bad reputation and are one source of Cracow's skinheads. Pickpockets tend to operate in the markets. Dishonest gamblers here tempt naive players, promising big wins in card or dice games. To recover money lost through such gambling is practically impossible.

Pickpockets are notorious in trams and buses so keep a close eye on your bag or rucksack, and carry it in a safe way. Passports, ID cards and wallets, car keys and other valuable items should never be carried in a back pocket or the external pockets of a rucksack. A solitary pickpocket is rare. They usually operate in gangs, and a sudden push or other distraction caused by them is hardly ever accidental.

Valuables should never be left unattended in the car. Car break-ins are a big problem in Cracow. If you can remove the radio and take it with you, you may save your windows from being smashed. A car alarm offers no protection against professional thieves, so guarded parking may be a good option. A number of guarded car parks are available in the centre. Figures released by police show that the Polonez, Mercedes, VW Golf, Audi and BMW cars are the most frequent targets.

Policeman

Policewoman

Town warden

POLICJA

Police sign

POLICE AND SECURITY SERVICES

The police are assisted in Cracow by other services that include town wardens and private security guards. Serious crime should be reported to a uniformed policeman at a police station. Major police stations are indicated on the map of Cracow *(see pp232–7)*. The national police force is allowed by law to carry arms and arrest a suspect. Blue and white police cars are used for patrolling the streets. Officers on the beat are also common. City wardens are unarmed and have no power of arrest. They mostly perform traffic wardens' duties and fine the owners of illegally parked vehicles. A traffic policeman will impose a severe fine for exceeding the speed limit and will deal even more severely with a drunken driver. Anyone who drives under the influence

Ambulance

of alcohol within the Cracow region is arrested and charged and will have to appear before a magistrate's court the following day. The court will decide upon the penalty and driving ban period. The level of alcohol in the blood must not exceed 0.02%, so if you drink at all, it is best not to drive. In the event of a serious road accident you are required by law to call an ambulance and the fire brigade. You are also required to contact the traffic police.

Private security agencies are generally responsible for security in large shops and public buildings, as well as during public events. Their security guards wear black uniforms and should always carry identification badges.

A pharmacy window

MEDICAL SERVICES

Both state and private health care are available in Cracow. First aid is provided free of charge. Other treatment may be subject to a fee, which is usually required in advance, along with a passport for identification. It is important to obtain a receipt for any payment made. It is advisable to have insurance cover.

APTEKA

A pharmacy sign

Treatment of the most minor cases is available at the 24-hour pharmacies *(see p201)*. The ambulance service is on call day and night and should be contacted in case of an accident or emergency. Hospital casualty units are shown on the map in the Street Finder Section *(see pp232–7)*.

EU nationals are entitled to state care on production of a valid European Health Insurance Card. In the UK, this can be obtained from the Department of Health or from a post office. It includes a booklet that details what healthcare you are entitled to, and where and how to claim. You still may have to pay in advance to obtain treatment, and then reclaim the money back later.

POLLUTION

The problem of pollution in Cracow was at the top of the local agenda until the late 1980s. The emissions from industrial plants constructed after World War II, of which the Sendzimir, formerly Lenin, Steelworks were the largest, systematically polluted the city. Coal stoves used in heating the old tenement houses in the centre, as well as Cracow's location in a valley, added to the problem. By the 1970s pollution had damaged the gilt dome of the Zygmunt Chapel in the Cathedral. Along with the collapse of Communism, heavy industry fell into decline. New technologies, more concerned with the environment, were introduced. Industrial chimneys were equipped with filters. Thanks to the efforts of George Bush, special funds were designated by the government of the United States to help reduce the low-level pollution caused by domestic stoves. Coal has been replaced by an electric heating system. Coal containing a high level of sulphur is no longer in use. The air is monitored for chemical pollution and information about its current level is displayed electronically above the entrance to 22 Market Square.

DIRECTORY

EMERGENCY SERVICES

Ambulance
Tel *999.*

Police
Tel *997.*

Fire
Tel *998.*

All services, from a mobile telephone
Tel *112.*

MEDICAL ASSISTANCE

Medical information
Tel *012 94 39.*

24-Hour Pharmacies
Galla 26.
Tel *012 636 73 65.*
Nowa Huta
Os. Centrum A, blok 3.
Tel *012 644 17 36.*
Kalwaryjska 94.
Map 4 D4.
Tel *012 656 18 50.*

OTHER SERVICES

Vehicle Assistance
Tel *96 37.*

Wake-Up Service
Tel *94 97.*

Banking and Local Currency

PKO Bank logo

Financial transactions are easy in Cracow. For foreign visitors there are many bureaux de change in the city centre, offering more favourable exchange rates than the banks. Credit cards are accepted by many of Cracow's shops and restaurants. Signs displayed by the entrance to the establishment indicate which cards are accepted.

BANKS AND BUREAUX DE CHANGE

Banks can be found throughout the city, both in and around the centre, as well as in the outskirts. Expect queues. Banks generally open at 8am and close at 6pm. Most banks have their own exchange service but better rates are offered by the independent bureaux de change *(kantor)*, which do not charge commission. Foreign currency can also be changed at hotels (some have a 24-hour service), but rates are poorer. You should never enter into any deal with street "agents" as the money they offer may well be counterfeit. You will just cause a lot of trouble for yourself trying to make any payments with counterfeit bank notes.

Bureau de change sign

Entrance to the PKO Bank in Market Square

Bankomat cashpoint machine

CREDIT CARDS

Credit cards are becoming ever more popular in Poland. These are also issued by Polish banks. Credit card payments are accepted in hotels, the larger clubs and restaurants, car rental outlets and the more exclusive shops. Check with the staff whether credit cards are accepted and what hidden, if any, extras are involved, before entering into any transaction.

Shops, restaurants and hotels normally indicate which cards they accept by displaying appropriate stickers on their windows. Some shops offer minimal discounts for credit card payments. Cards can be used in banks and at cashpoint machines *(bankomat)* to withdraw cash. A listing of cashpoint machines is available from larger banks. The American dollar and the euro are the most popular foreign currency and in emergency payments in dollars or euros can be made at petrol (gas) stations and in private shops.

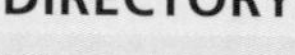

BANKS

Narodowy Bank Polski
Basztowa 20.
Map 2 D3 (6 E5).
Tel *012 618 58 00.*

Bank Polska Kasa Opieki SA
Rynek Główny 31.
Map 1 C4 (6 D2).
Tel *012 422 60 22.*

Powszechna Kasa Oszczędności. Bank Państwowy
Wielopole 19.
Map 2 D5 (6 F4).
Tel *012 421 55 55.*
Rynek Główny 21.
Map 1 C4 (6 D2).
Tel *012 422 40 76.*

Powszechny Bank Kredytowy
Smoleńsk 33.
Map 1 B5 (5 B3).
Tel *012 422 37 48.*

Bank Przemysłowo-Handlowy
Rynek Główny 47.
Map 1 C4 (6 D2).
Tel *012 422 20 66.*

BUREAUX DE CHANGE

Change Office
Sławkowska 14.
Map 1 C4 (6 D2).
Tel *012 421 66 88.*

Dukat
Sienna 14.
Map 1 C4 (6 D2).
Tel *012 421 41 59.*

Euro-Kantor
Szewska 21.
Map 1 C4 (5 C2).
Tel *012 421 55 65.*

J.P.J.
Wielopole 3.
Map 2 D5 (6 E3).
Tel *012 421 74 67.*

Pod Arkadami
Grodzka 40.
Map 1 C5 (6 D5).
Tel *012 421 50 21.*

CURRENCY

The Polish unit of currency is the złoty (meaning golden), which is indicated by the abbreviation zł. One złoty equals 100 groszy, abbreviated gr. Pronounce zł as *zwo-te* and gr as *gro-she*.

10 złoty

20 złoty

50 złoty

100 złoty

200 złoty

Bank Notes
Polish bank notes come in denominations of 10, 20, 50, 100 and 200 zł. They portray Polish sovereigns.

5 zł 2 zł 1 zł 50 gr

20 gr 10 gr 5 gr 2 gr

1 gr

Coins
Polish coins come in denominations of 1, 2, 5, 10, 20, 50 gr and 1, 2, 5 zł. They all feature on one side a crowned eagle, the emblem of Poland.

Communications

In Poland, the telephone service is provided by Telekomunikacja Polska S.A. There are many public telephones in the centre, and these are mainly card-operated. Some phone booths are wheelchair-accessible. Poczta Polska manages the postal service in Poland and has a large office in Cracow.

USING THE TELEPHONE

To make a telephone call you may choose to use a public telephone or go through the operator service at the post office. Note that calling from a hotel room is much more expensive, so it is always better to find a public telephone at the hotel or in its vicinity.

All phones operated by Telekomunikacja Polska offer a multi-lingual facililty, indicated by a button with a flag symbol. These telephones can provide instructions in English, German, Polish, French, Italian or Russian. Although there are still some coin-operated phones in Cracow (run by a company called Netia), the vast majority of public phones are card-operated only. Telephone cards *(karty telefoniczne)* can be purchased from newsagents and post offices. These cards come in units of 15, 30 and 60. There is a uniform tariff for local, long-distance and international calls, but prices do vary within that tariff. A local call will only use up a few units of a phone card, but for long-distance calls a more expensive card is a much better option.

Telekomunikacja Polska – the biggest Polish telecoms company

To make a telephone call lift the receiver and wait for a continuous dialling tone.

Main Post Office

Insert a telephone card and dial the number. A vibrating sound may be heard at first while the connection is being made. If the connection is successful, a longer, intermittent tone will follow. A short, rapidly repeating tone indicates that the number is engaged.

Post office sign

USING A PHONECARD-OPERATED TELEPHONE

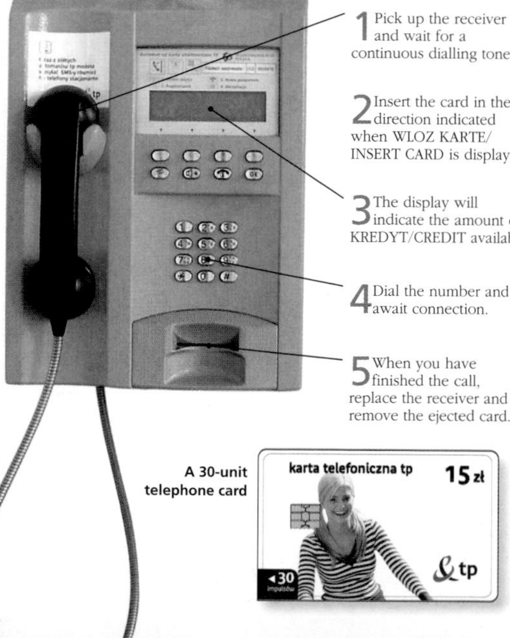

1 Pick up the receiver and wait for a continuous dialling tone.

2 Insert the card in the direction indicated when WLOZ KARTE/ INSERT CARD is displayed.

3 The display will indicate the amount of KREDYT/CREDIT available.

4 Dial the number and await connection.

5 When you have finished the call, replace the receiver and remove the ejected card.

A 30-unit telephone card

ACCESSING THE INTERNET

Cracow has plenty of public access to computers and the Internet. Free Internet access is often available at public libraries, but you may have to book in advance for a slot. Internet cafés *(Kafejki Internetowe)* may charge by the minute for computer use, and charges build up quickly, especially when including the cost of printed pages. To reduce the cost it is worth restricting your Internet access to off-peak times, which are usually cheaper. There are several Internet Cafés in the city including Tera SCFHU (Rynek Główny 9), Café Internet Clarus (ul. Golebia 4), and the Internet Café at the Main Academic Bookshop (Podwale 6).

MOBILE PHONES

Mobile telecommunication is advancing in Poland at a prodigious rate. Poland is well covered and growing in mobile telephone coverage. If you have access to roaming facilities you should have no problem in using your mobile in Cracow. Remember to dial the Cracow area code when making local calls. For other locations in Poland dial the appropriate area code followed by the subscriber's number. Before leaving for Poland check with your service provider, who will be able to give you the latest information.

POSTAL SERVICES

The Polish Post Office offers a wide range of services and has numerous outlets in towns and villages throughout Poland. You will find a large number of postal counters in the centre of Cracow as well as in all the housing estates.

The Main Post Office, situated at the junction of Westerplatte and Wielopole streets, is the most popular. It is open longer than all the others and some counters are open 24 hours a day. You can send letters, telegrams and parcels as well as make national money transfers; use operator initiated calls, and send a fax or telex. Stamp collectors can buy from the philatelic counter. A *poste restante* (mail holding) service is also available. A computerized queue system is in operation. Take a numbered ticket (press the button) from the dispensing machine by the entrance. The electronic display in the main hall indicates the number of people in the queue. Wait for your number to appear then go to the indicated counter.

The Main Post Office has access for the disabled.

A letter box

A post office housed in an old palace by the main Railway Station

SENDING A LETTER

Stamps can be purchased at post office counters and from selected newsagents. Some newspaper kiosks sell stamped envelopes and postcards only. Local letters should be posted in the green boxes, where available, and all other post in the red ones.

Inland letters take from two to three days but international mail takes a week or maybe a little longer. However, mail to some European destinations take less time. Letters sent by express service will arrive sooner. Courier service is the fastest but very expensive. This service is available from the Main Post Office and the Main Railway Station post counter, as well as from DHL and other courier companies.

Urgent letters and small packets can be sent by PKP, the Polish State Railways. Trains which provide this service are indicated in the train timetable by the letter K. To use this service mark your parcel clearly and deliver it to the train conductor who will also take payment. The parcel must be collected from the conductor by the addressee at the destination station.

Inland letter and postcard stamps

DIRECTORY

USEFUL ADDRESSES

Main Post Office
Westerplatte 20.
Map 2 D5 (6 E3).

DHL
Balicka 79.
Tel *0801 345345*

TELEPHONE DIRECTORIES AND DIALLING CODES

- Local (Cracow) directory enquiries in English dial 118 811.
- National (Polish) directory enquiries dial 118 913.
- National and international operator dial 118 912.
- Local calls within Cracow first dial 012, the city's area code. For calls within Poland always include the area code.
- To call overseas dial 0 and wait for the tone, dial 0 again followed by the country code, followed by the area code (omit the initial 0) and the subscriber's number. Country codes: UK 44; Eire 353; Canada and USA 1; Australia 61; South Africa 27; New Zealand 64.

GETTING TO CRACOW

Cracow has good connections with other Polish and European cities. Some Polish roads are, unfortunately, dangerously busy and many require resurfacing or modernizing. There are only a few motorways and the network is growing slowly. Travelling by car may occasionally prove to be tiresome. Cracow is located only 80 km (50 miles) away from the Chyżne crossing point on the Polish-Slovak border, less than 400 km (248 miles) from Budapest and 450 km (280 miles) from Vienna. Direct air routes serve Cracow-John Paul II airport from an ever increasing number of European and American cities, as well as Warsaw. The best connection from Warsaw is by train, with an average journey time of only two and half hours.

A Polish Airlines aeroplane

The logo of Polish Airlines

ARRIVING BY AIR

Cracow's John Paul II Airport at Balice is easily accessible nowadays from anywhere in the world. Apart from flights to Cracow from a number of European capitals, the arrival of a number of low-cost airlines means that there are now direct flights to Cracow on more than 30 routes from all over Europe.

From the UK there's a choice of **British Airways** and **centralwings** (subsidiary of **LOT Polish airlines**) from London Gatwick, **Ryanair** and **skyeurope** from London Stansted and **easyJet** from London Luton. Ryanair also flies from Glasgow and Liverpool (and Dublin), easyJet from Bristol and Liverpool and skyeurope from Birmingham, Edinburgh and Manchester (and also Dublin).

Travellers from North America can arrive direct from Chicago or New York with LOT or via London, Warsaw or other European capitals, while visitors from Australasia can connect via Singapore or Bangkok or London.

The Cracow-Warsaw route is the only domestic flight.

John Paul II Airport sign

LOW-COST AIRLINES

Low-cost airlines offer good deals on flights to Cracow and several other cities in Poland and the number of routes in increasing all the time. For the lowest fares you should book online via the Internet as far in advance as possible. Flights generally do not include in-flight meals, although refreshments are usually sold on board. A useful website for checking the latest low-cost routes is www.flycheapo.com.

Cracow-John Paul II Airport

A LOT Flight Attendant

JOHN PAUL II AIRPORT

John Paul II Airport is small but modern, and the facilities it offers are improving all the time as the amount of traffic it has to accommodate also increases. It is situated west of the city and the journey time to the centre of Cracow is approximately 20 minutes.

The present terminal was built in 1995, at which time the airport changed its name from Balice to John Paul II. The runway has since been lengthened, to permit intercontinental flights to land. In 2004 european flights run by the low-cost airlines began, increasing John Paul II's network of connections within the continent.

Apart from ticket and check-in desks, you have at your disposal a bureau de change, a bank, a small duty-free shop, a restaurant, a café, public phones, a newsagent and tobacco and souvenir shops. There is also a tourist information office and an electronic display which indicates current hotel availability in and around Cracow. Car rental firms have their desks in the main lounge of the terminal.

The lack of a large duty-free shop is a disadvantage, for those travelling outside the European Union, but this situation should improve in the near future.

GETTING INTO TOWN

John Paul II Airport lies approximately 20 km (12.5 miles) west of the city centre. Two bus routes serve the centre and connect with the main Railway Station or John Paul II Airport, or both. The first is bus route 192 which goes from Rondo Mogilskie through to the main Railway Station and then on to Cracovia Hotel.

The 208 route has an hourly schedule, serving the main Railway Station. From here, bus 208 passes via Warszawska Street, Słowacki Street, Mickiewicz Street, Czarnowiejska, Nowojki, Armii Krajowej and Balicka to John Paul II Airport.

A ticket for the bus must be purchased either from a newsagent at the airport or from the driver prior to commencing your journey. Large pieces of luggage are subject to an additional charge. At the terminal's main exit there is a taxi rank. Here you will find radio taxis which accept payment by credit card, so you need not change money at the airport if you do not have enough cash in the correct currency.

The journey into town should not usually take longer than 20 minutes by taxi but in the rush hour may take 30 minutes or even longer. The bus takes half an hour or so to get to town, but you should allow a little longer at rush hour times.

A bus connecting John Paul II Airport and Cracow city centre

DIRECTORY

Cracow-John Paul II Airport
Tel 012 411 19 55.

Cracow Main Railway Station
Pl. Kolejowy 1.
Map 2 D3 (6 F1).

AIRLINES SERVING CRACOW

British Airways
www.ba.com

centralwings
www.centralwings.com

easyJet
www.easyjet.com

LOT Polish Airlines
www.lot.com

Ryanair
www.ryanair.com

skyeurope
www.skyeurope.com

EUROPEAN AIR NETWORK FROM CRACOW
Cracow has good air connections with a number of European cities. All the cities shown on the map are less than 3 hours away by air from Cracow.

Cracow's main Railway Station

ARRIVING BY RAIL

You can get to Cracow by train from almost any Polish city and town, as well as many other European cities. The extensive Polish rail network is operated by the PKP, the Polish National Railways. Trains tend to be faster then either car or coach journeys.

Train tickets are cheaper than in the West. Tickets may be purchased at the main and other rail stations. They are also available in advance from the Orbis Travel Office, 41 Market Square, which charges a small commission. If you intend to purchase your ticket on the day of travel then allow at least half an hour, or more, for possible queues or delays.

A seat reservation must be made for the InterCity and express trains. Trains which require seat reservations are indicated in the timetable by the letter R. Other trains with a stopping service *(osobowy)* and fast service *(pospieszny)* do not offer seat reservations. A place must be reserved in overnight couchettes (*kuszetka*, six persons to a compartment) and sleeping carriages (*sypialny*, two or three persons to a compartment). Any passenger travelling without a valid ticket or reservation is liable to be fined.

You may also buy a ticket from the train conductor but you must tell him that you have no ticket before commencing your journey. A ticket bought from the conductor is subject to a substantial surcharge.

Carriages offering comfortable sleeping facilities are attached to trains on all major long distance domestic routes and on all international connections. When on the train, and especially when boarding or alighting be wary of pickpockets. Do not leave your luggage unattended in the carriage.

Rail Conductor

INTERCITY AND EXPRESS TRAINS

When travelling in Poland the InterCity trains are best. They are modern, fast, clean and comfortable.

There is a wider choice of express trains. Both types of service require a reservation to be made at the time of purchasing the ticket. A seat can also be reserved on the train through the conductor, subject to availability and an additional charge.

The InterCity and express trains have a restaurant or a bar but the cuisine they offer is dull and rather disappointing. A trolley service is in operation, offering hot and cold drinks and snacks. Complimentary coffee, tea or juice and a pastry are offered to passengers on InterCity trains.

RAILWAY STATIONS

Dworzec Główny is Cracow's main railway station and is located in the heart of the city. All international and the majority of domestic trains pass through this station. Trains stop for a couple of minutes or longer and some are ready at the platform well before departure time so there is plenty of time to get comfortable and settled. In the main hall are counters to purchase international and domestic tickets and ticket machines for local destinations, as well as the lost property office and the information desk. Two restaurants and three bars, plus a hairdresser, bank, pharmacy and a number of small shops can be found within the station. A bureau de change is next door and a post office nearby.

The station hall is closed for an hour at night for it to be cleaned. The hall and platforms are monitored by security cameras, which help to keep a check on petty criminals and pickpockets who operate in and around the station.

An InterCity train at Cracow's main Railway Station

A platform at Cracow's main Railway Station

There are other smaller stations in Cracow, including Kraków-Płaszów southeast of the centre. This station is served from the city centre by trams 3, 9, 13 and 34, as well as bus route 502.

ARRIVING BY COACH

Regular coach services operate from Cracow to many European cities. The main coach station, Dworzec Autobusowy, is located in the city centre, opposite the main Railway Station. Local, domestic and most international services operate from this station. When this station originally opened, it soon proved to be too small. It used to be the case that even small provincial towns in Poland had better facilities than Cracow, but this situation has improved since the new coach station opened next to the main Railway Station in 2005, which also under-went modernization.

The coach station is now very inviting, with modern lavatories, shops and other useful facilities. It is usually a good idea to think ahead when travelling in Poland, so buying a ticket in advance or early in the morning are good options. Coach drivers sell tickets if there are unreserved seats. There is no surcharge for this on-board service.

Private international coach operators also use the new bus station, which is in Bosacka Street, on the other side of the railway station. They also use other coach parks. The international coach timetable is on display at the main Coach Station and enquiries can be made at the information desk in the ticket hall. Tickets for domestic services can be purchased in the same hall. Travel agents and coach operators sell tickets for international routes.

The PKS, Polska Komunikacja Samochodowa, is the main national coach operator for inter-city routes within Poland. Sometimes old, mechanically inferior and dirty coaches are used on a few domestic routes, but modern coaches are being introduced at a gradually increasing rate. Alternatively, privately owned companies provide a range of inter-city and long-distance services. However, be aware that a coach journey from Cracow to a distant city may take a very long time, owing to many stops on the way, some requiring a detour from the main road. Travelling by coach is generally cheaper than by rail.

A "Polski Express" coach

ARRIVING BY CAR

Driving licences issued in other countries are generally valid in Poland. If you drive in Poland you must carry on you a valid driving licence and vehicle registration document, as well as the Green Card as confirmation of your international insurance cover. If you drive a hired car, an appropriate document stating this is also obligatory. A national sticker identifying the country in which the car is registered must be displayed on the vehicle. The wearing of seat belts is compulsory. Children under the age of twelve are not allowed to travel in the front of the car. Between 1 October and 1 March headlights must be on, day and night, regardless of the weather conditions.

Cracow's road sign

Road signs at the Polish border indicate speed limits (in kilometres). Speed limits should be strictly observed. Drivers breaking the speed limit risk hefty fines of up to 500 zł. Foreign drivers are required to pay on the spot.

The permitted alcohol content in blood is so low in Poland (two parts per thousand) that drinking and driving should be avoided altogether. Routine checks by police are frequent.

Car thefts are on the increase. Luggage and other property should not be left in the car. It is safer to remove the car radio. Using a guarded car park, even if only for a short stay, is strongly recommended.

GETTING AROUND CRACOW

Central Cracow is small and compact so moving around on foot or by public transport is best. Children in particular will enjoy a sightseeing ride on one of Cracow's blue trams. This guide lists bus and tram routes which you can use to get to the sights described in the *Cracow Area by Area* section. Maps of Cracow's tram and bus systems can be found on the inside back cover. If you require more detailed maps, these can be bought from newsagents, bookshops and tourist information desks. Sightseeing tours in a horse-drawn cab are very popular with visitors. A small electric *meleks* vehicle can also be hired for sightseeing. *Meleks* drivers are qualified guides and speak foreign languages. Both cabs and *Meleks* vehicles await passengers in Cracow's historic Market Square.

A house number

The busy square in front of the local government building

PUBLIC TRANSPORT

Cracow is well covered by an extensive public transport network. Trams and buses are frequent on weekdays but less frequent on Saturdays, Sundays and public holidays. Rush hours are between 7–8am and 2–5pm. At night only buses operate. Many bus routes extend to the suburbs. A number of private firms operate minibus services within the inner and outer city and stop on request. Further information on bus and tram services can be found on pp226–7.

DRIVING IN CRACOW

The historic centre of the city of Cracow is a pedestrian precinct and is divided into three zones. Market Square and the surrounding streets fall within zone A. Access is restricted within this zone to emergency and city services, and between 6pm and 10am also to the city's commercial delivery vans. In zone B, an area which extends to the Planty green belt, access is additionally given to local residents and vehicles displaying a special permit. Zone C extends to the so-called Avenue of the Three Poets (Krasińskiego, Mickiewicza, Słowackiego), Dietla and Westerplatte streets. There is no access restriction to any car within Zone C but you need to purchase a parking permit in order to park. Parking permits are available from most newsagents.

A stop and give way road sign

Long lines of traffic are characteristic of rush hours, especially on Friday afternoons as well as when Cracovians are returning from their holidays.

Road works and temporary road closures are real

TICKETS

One type of ticket is used for trams and buses. Tickets are purchased from newspaper kiosks and MPK ticket outlets. Several types are available: timed, daily, weekly and family tickets. A ticket must be validated after boarding by punching it in a ticket-punching machine. Timed tickets are valid for one hour from the moment of punching and you can change routes as often as necessary within this hour. Daily tickets are valid from the time of punching till midnight. Weekly tickets require the holder to have an ID and are valid for all tram and bus routes, either ordinary or express. A family ticket, not transferable, covers two adults and two children and is valid over the weekend. Children under 4 and senior citizens over 75 travel free of charge. Children between the ages of 4 and 14 years, students, senior citizens and the disabled are entitled to reduced-fare travel, but must carry appropriate identification documents. Foreign visitors to Cracow are not entitled to travel on reduced-fare tickets.

To validate ticket, insert arrow end into punching machine

No vehicles in zone B

hindrances to drivers who have to follow temporary diversion signs set up around the city. Cracow as yet has no ring road. Despite works being undertaken for some time now on a fast ring road round the city, only short stretches are presently in use.

The car is a convenient mode of transport during excursions to the suburbs and out-of-town locations. If you wish to escape the city centre, cars are available for hire from local car-rental firms but this can be a rather expensive option.

pl. Szczepański

P wolny

następny P 400 m ➡

Parking availability ("wolny" means "free")

WALKING IN CRACOW

The majority of historic sights, many museums and other tourist attractions, as well as restaurants and cafés, are located within the very centre of the Old Town, which is a pedestrian precinct. This is a relatively small area and can easily be seen and enjoyed on foot. Signs indicating the directions to major sights are of great help to pedestrian visitors. Information plaques in several languages are displayed on historic buildings and by other sights.

Pedestrain crossing

Map of the old town with the royal route in red

No stopping

PARKING

Finding parking in the city centre may be difficult. Using a guarded car park *(parking strzeżony)* is a safe option. Parking on the pavement is allowed in Cracow but you have to leave at least one metre (3 ft) width free for pedestrians. The guarded car park in Szczepański Square is closest to the historic centre, only a few hundred metres from Market Square. This car park is, therefore, always busy and one of the most expensive. It is always easy to find a space at the large car park situated on the roof above the railway platforms at the Main Station. Other large guarded car parks can be found in Powiśle Street near Wawel, as well as in Rajska, Starowiślna and Straszewskiego streets.

Parking in Cracow is, by Western standards, still relatively easy and finding a guarded car park within walking distance of the historic centre should not be a problem.

WHEEL CLAMPS

Illegally parked vehicles may be clamped by a traffic warden. To have the clamp removed you have to call the warden. The telephone number is given on the penalty notice which you will find attached to the windscreen. The text of this notice is printed in several languages. The warden will arrive and remove the clamp but you will have to pay the fine first.

A clamped, illegally parked car for which a fine is payable

DIRECTORY

CAR RENTAL COMPANIES

Avis Rent a Car
Lubicz 23. **Map** 2 D4 (6 F1).
Tel *012 629 61 08*
or 012 629 61 09

Budget
Lotnisko w Balicach.
Tel *012 285 50 25.*

Eurocar Inter Rent
Krowoderska 58. **Map** 1 B2.

Express Rent a Car
Balice Airport.
Tel *012 254 00 00.*

Hertz Rent a Car
Focha 1. **Map** 1 A5 (5 A3).
Tel *012 429 62 62.*

National Car Rental
Balice Airport.
Tel *012 639 32 86*
Hotel Demel.
Tel *012 636 86 30.*

Travelling by Tram

Horse-drawn trams were introduced to Cracow in 1895. Six years later they were replaced by electric trams. The trams you can see today are made up of either one, two or three carriages. Although they tend to be extremely busy during rush hours, trams are a fast mode of public transport, and are particularly convenient for the city centre. Visitors will find travelling by tram an excellent way to see Cracow. Trams serve the main Railway Station, the centre and all major hotels, as well as residential quarters and many sights of interest.

A Cracow tram

Sign indicating a tram stop

All tram routes which serve the stop, along with a timetable for each, are displayed at each stop.

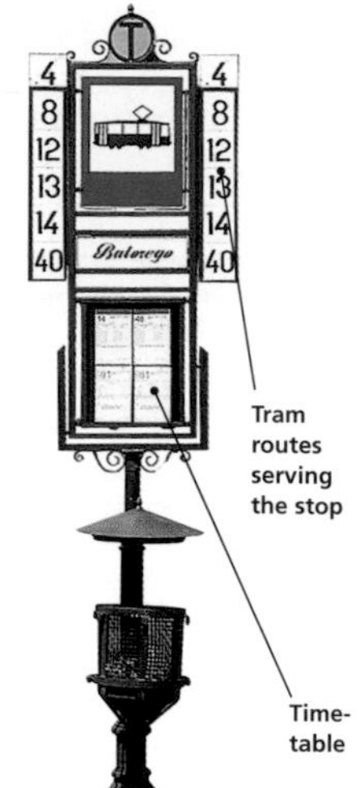

TRAM TICKETS

Tram and bus tickets are the same *(see p224)*. A ticket should be purchased prior to boarding the tram. You may also buy a ticket from the driver when the tram is stationary at a stop and if you have the correct change. Trams are sometimes full and to reach the driver may be difficult. A ticket is a little more expensive if bought from the tram driver.

The ticket must be validated, or punched, immediately after boarding the tram. As on the buses, a ticket which has not been punched is not valid.

A single-fare ticket is valid for an unlimited single journey. A daily ticket should be validated (punched) only once, on your first journey, and is valid on all trams and buses until midnight. Weekly and monthly tickets must not be punched.

A map inside the carriage shows all the stops and connections on the route.

Tram timetables are displayed at all stops. Trams start at 5am and run until 11pm, with a frequency varying from a few minutes to around twenty minutes. There is no night tram service. In some carriages you must press a button to open the door.

TICKET INSPECTORS

On Cracow's trams, tickets are occasionally inspected. The inspectors of MPK, Cracow's transport company, operate in plain clothes but carry an ID with a photograph. A passenger without a valid ticket is liable to a fine which is several times the price of a normal single fare. Travelling with an unpunched ticket can result in a fine, in the same way as travelling without a ticket. You may choose to pay on the spot or get a penalty ticket which must by paid at a post office. In the latter case the fine is higher. Foreign visitors must pay on the spot.

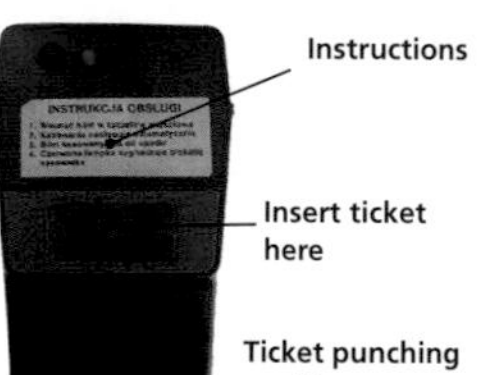

Ticket punching machine

A tram stop

SAFETY TIPS

Pickpockets operate on trams and buses. If you carry money or documents, take precautions. An open handbag or external pockets on a rucksack, coat or trousers are not safe places. Avoid ostentation when carrying a camera or laptop.

DIRECTORY

Bus Information
Tel *91 50.*

Tram Information
Tel *012 260 33 40.*

Train Information
Tel *94 36.*

Travelling by Bus

Cracow is well served by buses which take passengers to all parts of the city and many suburban destinations. A variety of blue, red and multicoloured Ikarus, Jelcz and Scania buses, some modern, some a little bit older, operate on the dozens of different routes. Smoking is forbidden on all the city's buses and trams. Articles of heavy luggage may require a separate ticket.

BUS TICKETS

Bus tickets are the same as those used on trams. If you change buses you need a new ticket for every subsequent leg of your journey, unless you carry a timed, daily or weekly ticket or a monthly pass. A detailed timetable is displayed at every bus stop and generally observed by drivers.

BUS ROUTES

Bus routes indicated by a three-figure number operate a stopping service. Fast routes are operated by buses 501, 502 and 511. They serve selected stops only. The fare on a fast bus is 50 per cent more expensive than on a stopping service.

Bus frequency varies from every few minutes to approximately twenty minutes on weekdays, but buses are less frequent on weekends and public holidays.

Buses indicated by a number above 600 operate a night service. Eight night bus routes link the city centre with the surrounding quarters. A night bus departs every hour and the fare is double the daily stopping fare.

Private minibus services operate on many routes within the city and in the suburbs. You can buy a ticket from the driver and it will cost you twice the fare of the MPK public transport. Most minibuses depart from the main Railway Station. It is a fast and reliable service, especially convenient for Nowa Huta and other quarters outside the centre.

A Cracow bus

Travelling by Taxi

Taxis are a convenient way of getting around Cracow, especially for visitors. To avoid being overcharged, however, it is best to use the services of the reliable radio taxis.

A City Taxi

TYPES OF TAXIS

Taxis in Cracow vary in colour and make, and have different signs, depending on the company to which the drivers belong. All have an identification number clearly marked on the side of the car, as well as an illuminated 'Taxi' sign on the roof with the name of the company. Several taxi companies operate in Cracow; their fares are very similar to each other.

TAXI FARES

On boarding a taxi an initial amount will be displayed on the meter; it will increase at a specified rate with each kilometre travelled. Payment is generally accepted by cash, but radio taxis which serve the Balice airport (and some other taxis) accept credit cards. There are two tariffs in use. The first tariff applies on weekdays from 5am to 11pm, the second comes into effect on Sundays, public holidays and at night. The taxi fare increases as you leave the city limits. Requesting a receipt from the taxi driver will, in most cases, ensure that you will not be overcharged.

DIRECTORY

RADIO TAXI COMPANIES

City Taxi
Tel 96 21.

Express Taxi
Tel 96 29.

Krak Taxi
Tel 012 267 67 67.

Metro Taxi
Tel 96 67.

Radio Taxi
Tel 91 91.

Radio Taxi-Partner
Tel 96 33.

STREET FINDER

Map references, given for each sight within its individual entry in this guide relate to the map on the pages that follow. The same applies to the hotels *(see pp178–181)* and restaurants *(see pp188–193)* listed. The first figure indicates the map number, while the middle letter and the last number refer to the relevant grid. The key map on the right shows Cracow divided into six parts which correspond to the maps that follow. All symbols used are explained in the key. You will find the Street Finder Index on pp230–231. Note that Polish is an inflected language and street names require different name endings (Jan Kowalski but Jana Kowalskiego Street).

Top sights and attractions are indicated on the maps.

Tourists in Cracow

KEY TO STREET FINDER

- Major sight
- Other sight
- Railway station
- Coach terminal
- Tram depot
- Bus stop
- Parking
- Tourist information
- Hospital
- Police station
- Boat pier
- Church
- Synagogue
- Post office
- Railway line
- Pedestrian street
- City wall

A hurdy-gurdy man in Market Square

Stairs leading to the Decius Villa

SCALE OF MAPS 1–4

0 metres 200

0 yards 200

1:13 000

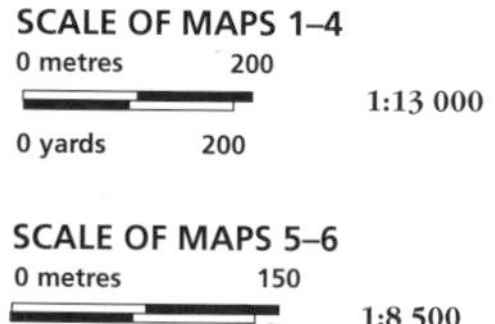

SCALE OF MAPS 5–6

0 metres 150

0 yards 150

1:8 500

0 kilometres 1

0 miles 0.5

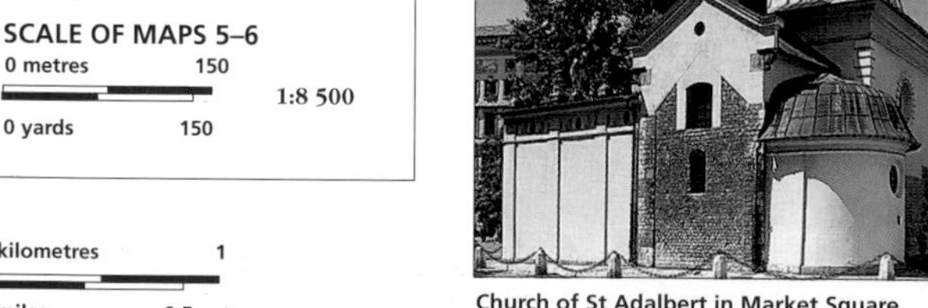

Church of St Adalbert in Market Square

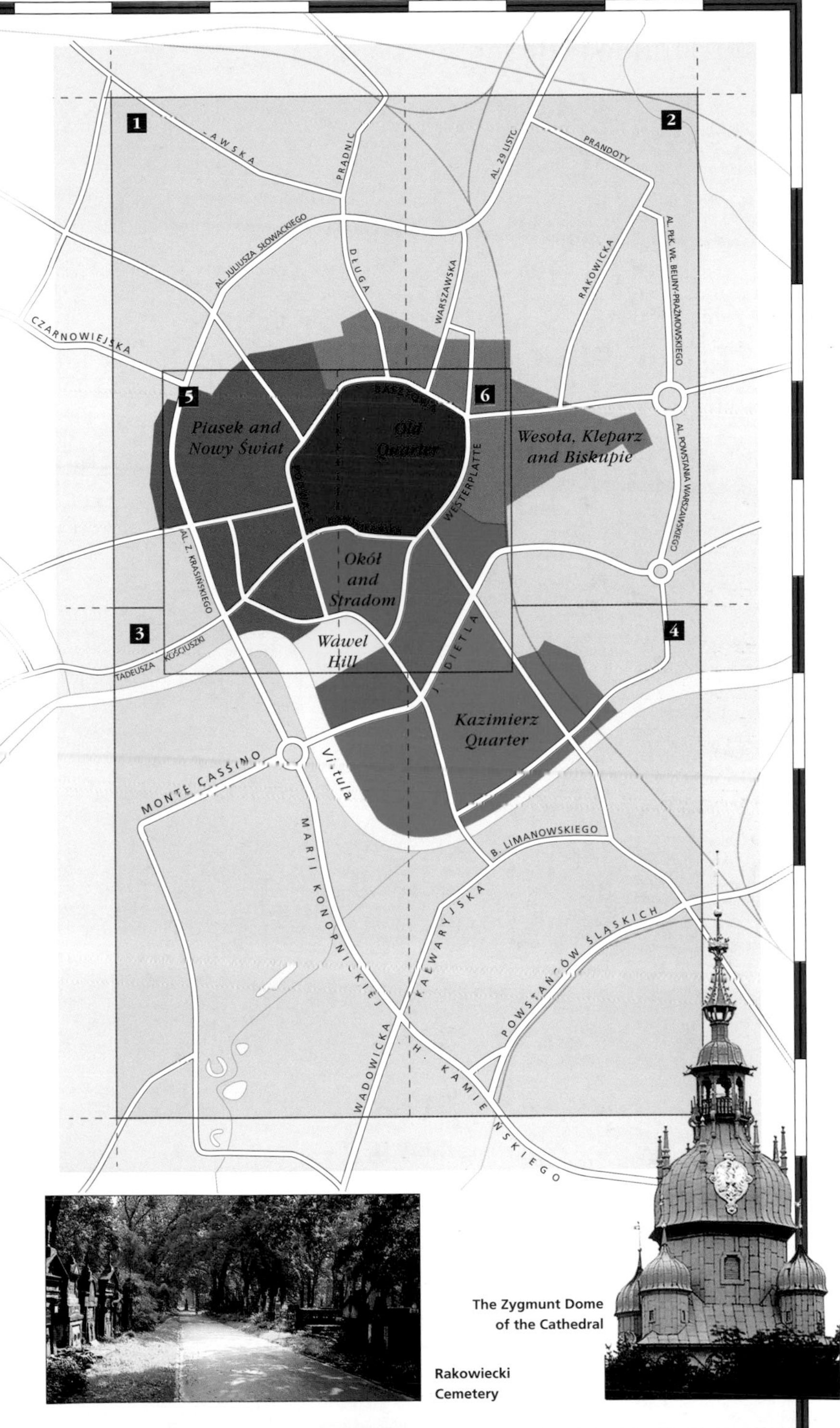

The Zygmunt Dome of the Cathedral

Rakowiecki Cemetery

Street Finder Index

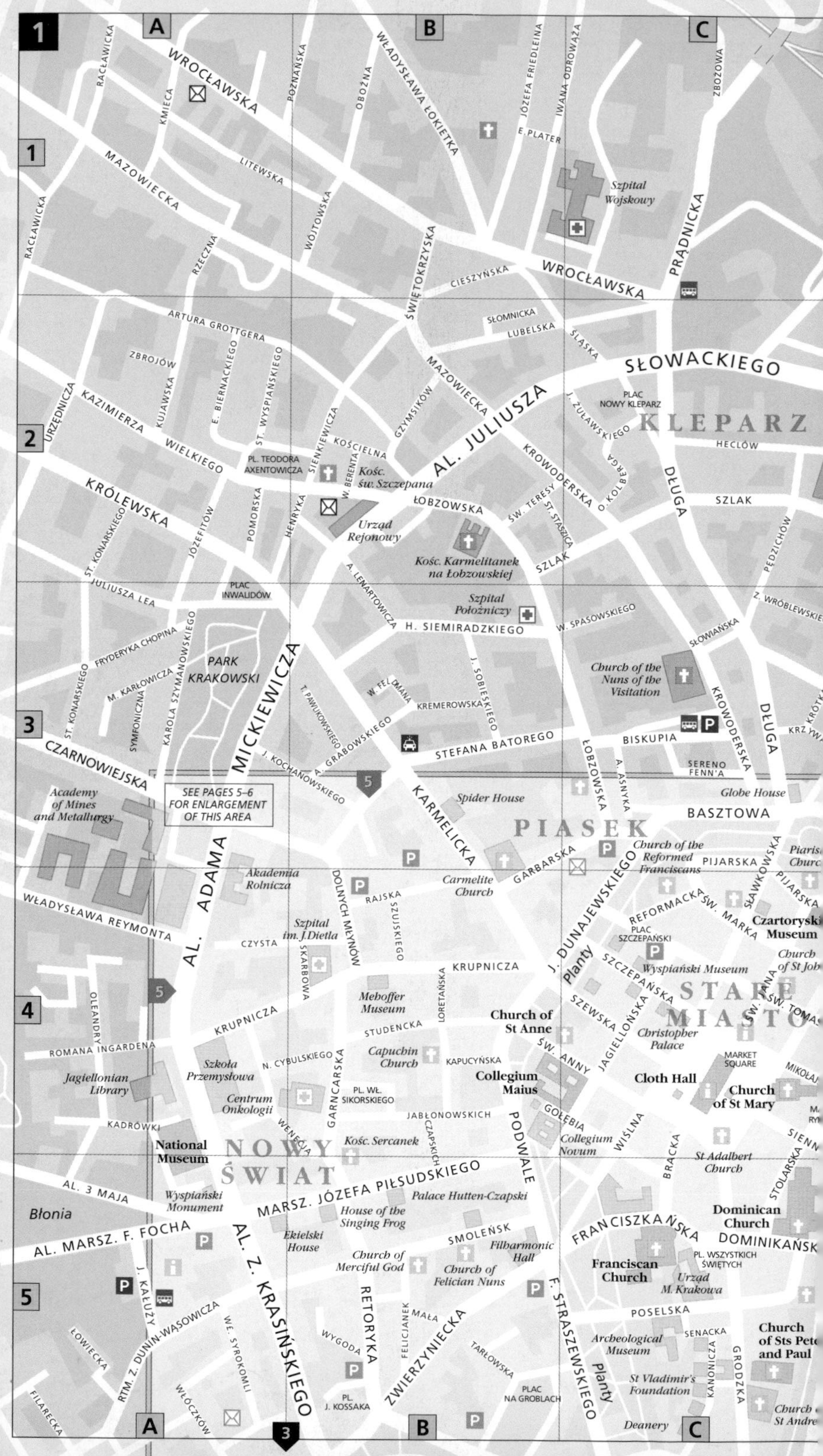
1
A
B
C
1
2
3
4
5
WROCŁAWSKA
MAZOWIECKA
LITEWSKA
PRĄDNICKA
Szpital Wojskowy
SŁOWACKIEGO
AL. JULIUSZA
KLEPARZ
PLAC NOWY KLEPARZ
KRÓLEWSKA
Kośc. św. Szczepana
Urząd Rejonowy
Kośc. Karmelitanek na Łobzowskiej
Szpital Położniczy
PARK KRAKOWSKI
PLAC INWALIDÓW
Church of the Nuns of the Visitation
CZARNOWIEJSKA
Academy of Mines and Metallurgy
SEE PAGES 5–6 FOR ENLARGEMENT OF THIS AREA
AL. ADAMA MICKIEWICZA
KARMELICKA
Spider House
PIASEK
Globe House
BASZTOWA
Church of the Reformed Franciscans
Akademia Rolnicza
Carmelite Church
Czartoryski Museum
Szpital im. J.Dietla
Wyspiański Museum
STARE MIASTO
Meboffer Museum
Church of St Anne
Christopher Palace
Capuchin Church
Szkoła Przemysłowa
Jagiellonian Library
Centrum Onkologii
Collegium Maius
Cloth Hall
MARKET SQUARE
Church of St Mary
National Museum
NOWY ŚWIAT
Kośc. Sercanek
Collegium Novum
St Adalbert Church
Błonia
Wyspiański Monument
MARSZ. JÓZEFA PIŁSUDSKIEGO
Palace Hutten-Czapski
House of the Singing Frog
Ekielski House
Dominican Church
AL. MARSZ. F. FOCHA
AL. Z. KRASIŃSKIEGO
Church of Merciful God
Church of Felician Nuns
Filharmonic Hall
Franciscan Church
Urząd M. Krakowa
Archeological Museum
St Vladimir's Foundation
Church of Sts Peter and Paul
Deanery
PODWALE
F. STRASZEWSKIEGO
Planty
J. DUNAJEWSKIEGO
ZWIERZYNIECKA
RETORYKA
DŁUGA
KROWODERSKA
STEFANA BATOREGO
KRUPNICZA
WŁADYSŁAWA REYMONTA
AL. 3 MAJA
FRANCISZKAŃSKA
GRODZKA

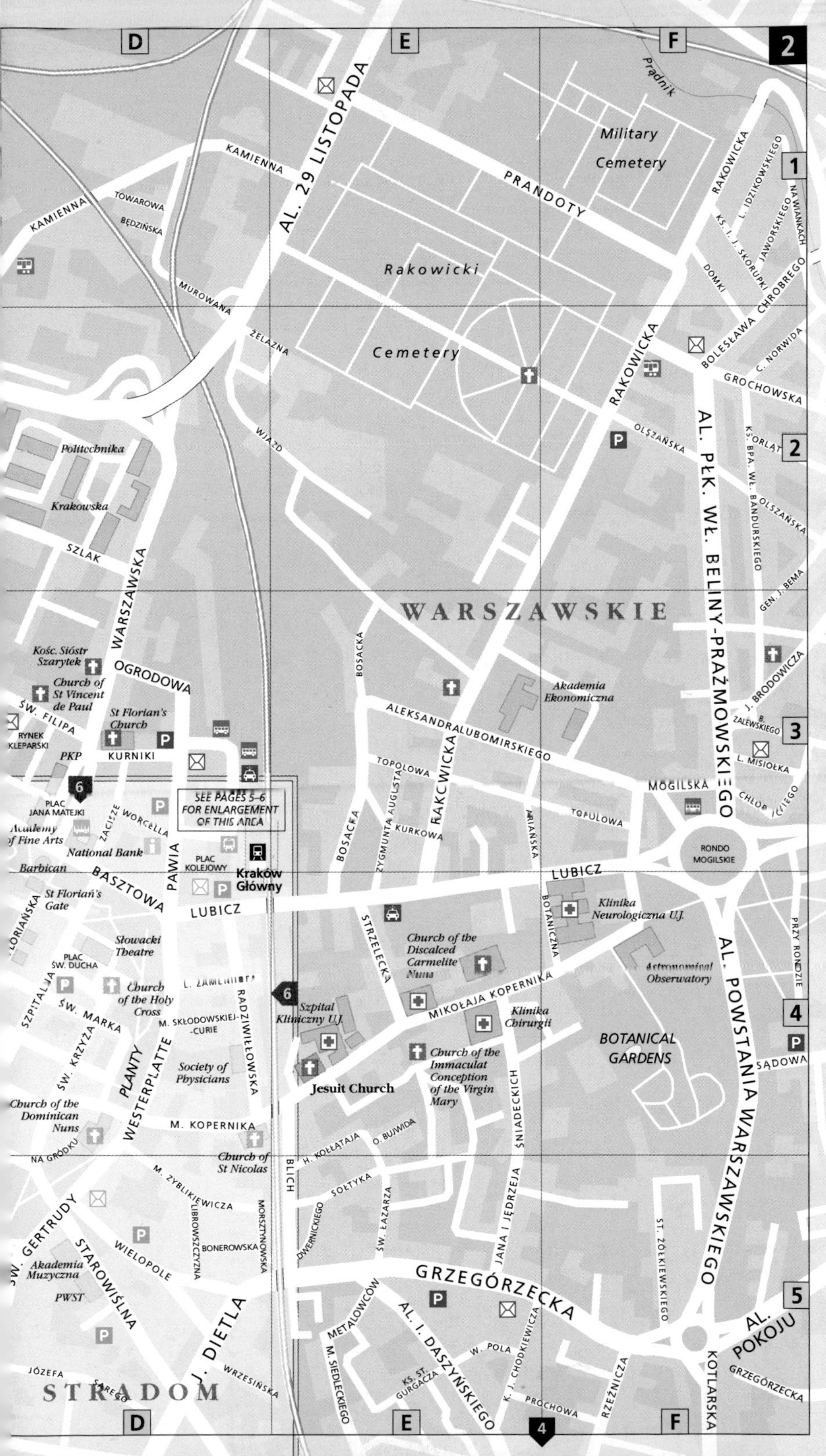

2
D
E
F
1
2
3
4
5
Prądnik
Military Cemetery
Rakowicki Cemetery
AL. 29 LISTOPADA
KAMIENNA
TOWAROWA
BĘDZIŃSKA
MUROWANA
ŻELAZNA
WJAZD
PRANDOTY
RAKOWICKA
BOLESŁAWA CHROBREGO
C. NORWIDA
GROCHOWSKA
OLSZAŃSKA
AL. PŁK. WŁ. BELINY-PRAŻMOWSKIEGO
KS. BPA. WŁ. BANDURSKIEGO
GEN. J. BEMA
L. IDZIKOWSKIEGO
NAWIANKACH
JAWORSKIEGO
KS. I. J. SKORUPKI
DOMKI
Politechnika
Krakowska
SZLAK
WARSZAWSKA
WARSZAWSKIE
Kośc. Sióstr Szarytek
Church of St Vincent de Paul
OGRODOWA
ŚW. FILIPA
St Florian's Church
RYNEK KLEPARSKI
PKP
KURNIKI
PLAC JANA MATEJKI
Academy of Fine Arts
ZACISZE
WORCELLA
SEE PAGES 5–6 FOR ENLARGEMENT OF THIS AREA
National Bank
PLAC KOLEJOWY
Kraków Główny
PAWIA
Barbican
BASZTOWA
LUBICZ
St Florian's Gate
FLORIAŃSKA
Słowacki Theatre
PLAC ŚW. DUCHA
SZPITALNA
Church of the Holy Cross
ŚW. MARKA
ŚW. KRZYŻA
M. SKŁODOWSKIEJ-CURIE
RADZIWIŁŁOWSKA
Society of Physicians
PLANTY
WESTERPLATTE
Church of the Dominican Nuns
M. KOPERNIKA
NA GRODKU
Church of St Nicolas
BOSACKA
ALEKSANDRA LUBOMIRSKIEGO
Akademia Ekonomiczna
J. BRODOWICZA
B. ZALEWSKIEGO
L. MISIOŁKA
TOPOLOWA
ZYGMUNTA AUGUSTA
KURKOWA
RAKOWICKA
ARIAŃSKA
MOGILSKA
CHŁOPICKIEGO
RONDO MOGILSKIE
STRZELECKA
Church of the Discalced Carmelite Nuns
Klinika Neurologiczna U.J.
BOTANICZNA
Astronomical Observatory
PRZY RONDZIE
Szpital Kliniczny U.J.
MIKOŁAJA KOPERNIKA
Klinika Chirurgii
Church of the Immaculat Conception of the Virgin Mary
Jesuit Church
BOTANICAL GARDENS
AL. POWSTANIA WARSZAWSKIEGO
SĄDOWA
ŚNIADECKICH
H. KOŁŁĄTAJA
O. BUJWIDA
BLICH
SOŁTYKA
M. ZYBLIKIEWICZA
LIBROWSZCZYZNA
MORSZTYNOWSKA
BONEROWSKA
ŚW. GERTRUDY
STAROWIŚLNA
WIELOPOLE
Akademia Muzyczna
PWST
DWERNICKIEGO
ŚW. ŁAZARZA
JANA I JĘDRZEJA
ST. ŻÓŁKIEWSKIEGO
GRZEGÓRZECKA
METALOWCÓW
M. SIEDLECKIEGO
AL. I. DASZYŃSKIEGO
KS. ST. GURGACZA
W. POLA
K. J. CHODKIEWICZA
PROCHOWA
RZEŹNICZA
KOTLARSKA
AL. POKOJU
J. DIETLA
WRZESIŃSKA
JÓZEFA
STRADOM
6
4

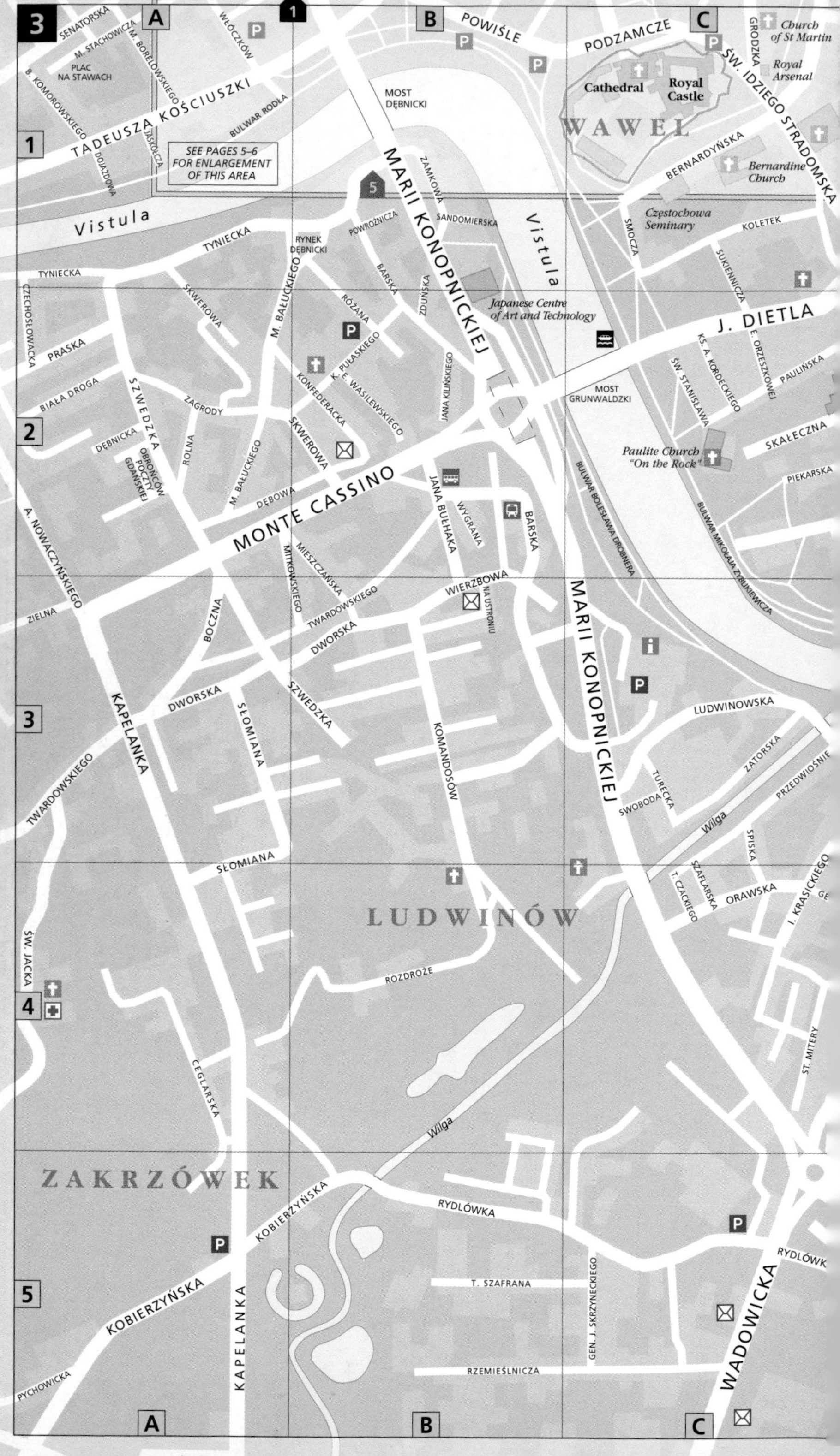
3
A
B
C
1
2
3
4
5
Church of St Martin
Royal Arsenal
Cathedral
Royal Castle
WAWEL
Bernardine Church
Częstochowa Seminary
Japanese Centre of Art and Technology
Paulite Church "On the Rock"
SEE PAGES 5–6 FOR ENLARGEMENT OF THIS AREA
Vistula
LUDWINÓW
ZAKRZÓWEK
TADEUSZA KOŚCIUSZKI
POWIŚLE
PODZAMCZE
ŚW. IDZIEGO STRADOMSKA
GRODZKA
BERNARDYŃSKA
KOLETEK
SMOCZA
SUKIENNICZA
J. DIETLA
MARII KONOPNICKIEJ
MONTE CASSINO
MOST DĘBNICKI
MOST GRUNWALDZKI
BULWAR RODŁA
BULWAR BOLESŁAWA DROBNERA
BULWAR MIKOŁAJA ZYBLIKIEWICZA
SENATORSKA
M. STACHOWICZA
M. BORELOWSKIEGO
WŁÓCZKÓW
PLAC NA STAWACH
B. KOMOROWSKIEGO
JASKÓŁCZA
DOJAZDOWA
TYNIECKA
RYNEK DĘBNICKI
POWROŹNICZA
ZAMKOWA
SANDOMIERSKA
BARSKA
ZDUŃSKA
RÓŻANA
K. PUŁASKIEGO
KONFEDERACKA
E. WASILEWSKIEGO
JANA KILIŃSKIEGO
M. BAŁUCKIEGO
SKWEROWA
CZECHOSŁOWACKA
PRASKA
BIAŁA DROGA
SZWEDZKA
ZAGRODY
ROLNA
DĘBNICKA
OBROŃCÓW POCZTY GDAŃSKIEJ
DĘBOWA
JANA BUŁHAKA
WYGRANA
A. NOWACZYŃSKIEGO
ZIELNA
BOCZNA
MITKOWSKIEGO
MIESZCZAŃSKA
TWARDOWSKIEGO
WIERZBOWA
NA USTRONIU
DWORSKA
KAPELANKA
SŁOMIANA
KOMANDOSÓW
KS. A. KORDECKIEGO
E. ORZESZKOWEJ
ŚW. STANISŁAWA
PAULIŃSKA
SKAŁECZNA
PIEKARSKA
LUDWINOWSKA
ZATORSKA
PRZEDWIOŚNIE
TURECKA
SWOBODA
Wilga
SPISKA
SZAFLARSKA
T. CZACKIEGO
ORAWSKA
I. KRASICKIEGO
ŚW. JACKA
ROZDROŻE
CEGLARSKA
ST. MITERY
RYDLÓWKA
KOBIERZYŃSKA
T. SZAFRANA
GEN. J. SKRZYNECKIEGO
WADOWICKA
RZEMIEŚLNICZA
PYCHOWICKA

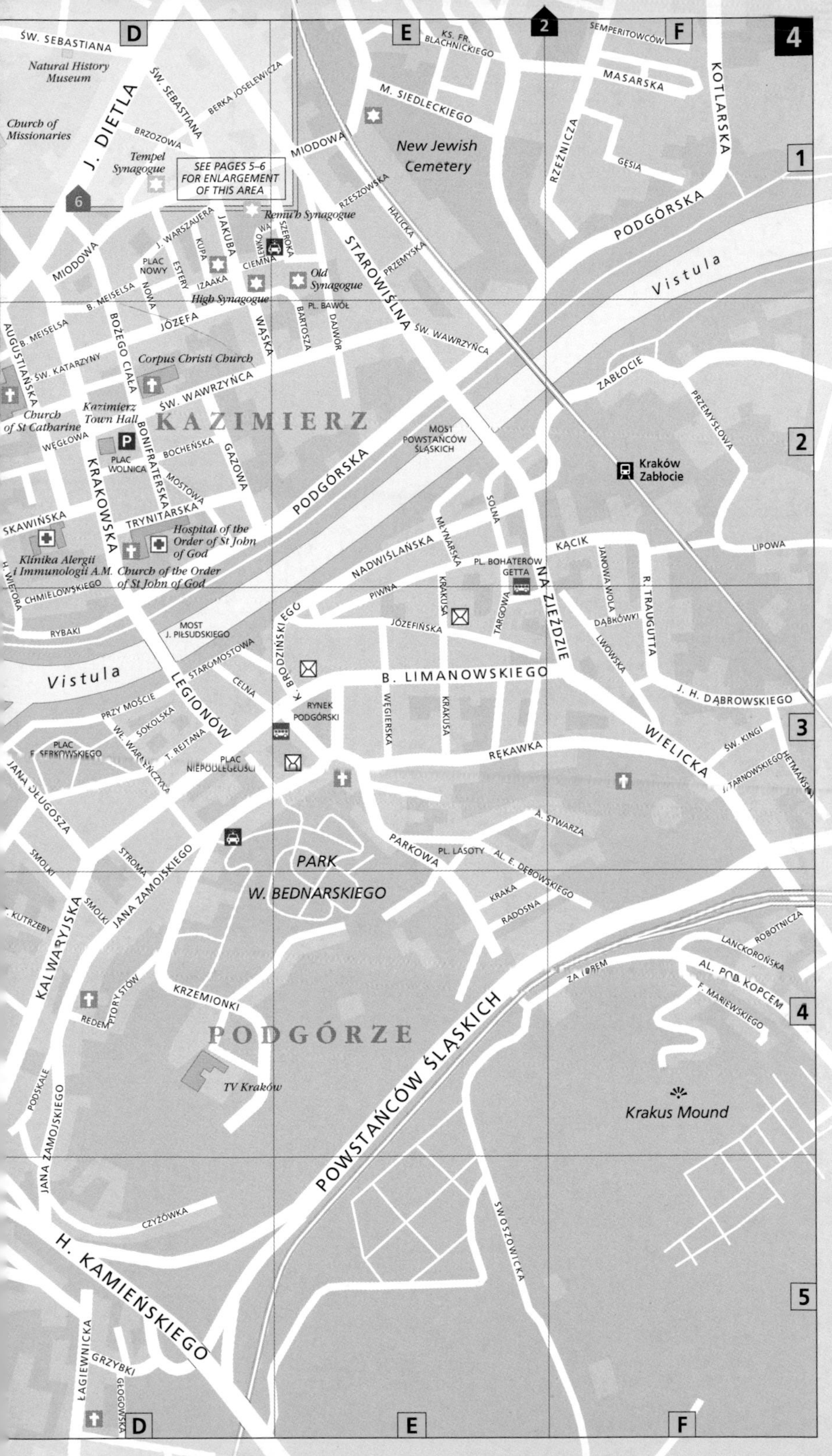

4
D
E
F
2
6
1
2
3
4
5
SEE PAGES 5–6 FOR ENLARGEMENT OF THIS AREA
Natural History Museum
Church of Missionaries
Tempel Synagogue
Remu'h Synagogue
Old Synagogue
High Synagogue
Corpus Christi Church
Church of St Catharine
Kazimierz Town Hall
KAZIMIERZ
Hospital of the Order of St John of God
Church of the Order of St John of God
Klinika Alergii i Immunologii A.M.
New Jewish Cemetery
Vistula
Kraków Zabłocie
MOST POWSTAŃCÓW ŚLĄSKICH
MOST J. PIŁSUDSKIEGO
RYNEK PODGÓRSKI
PLAC NIEPODLEGŁOŚCI
PL. BOHATERÓW GETTA
PARK W. BEDNARSKIEGO
PODGÓRZE
TV Kraków
Krakus Mound
ŚW. SEBASTIANA
J. DIETLA
BERKA JOSELEWICZA
BRZOZOWA
MIODOWA
J. WARSZAUERA
JAKUBA
KUPA
PLAC NOWY
ESTERY
IZAAKA
CIEMNA
SZEROKA
B. MEISELSA
NOWA
JÓZEFA
BOŻEGO CIAŁA
WĄSKA
BARTOSZA
DAJWÓR
PL. BAWÓŁ
AUGUSTIAŃSKA
ŚW. KATARZYNY
ŚW. WAWRZYŃCA
WĘGŁOWA
BONIFRATERSKA
BOCHEŃSKA
PLAC WOLNICA
KRAKOWSKA
MOSTOWA
GAZOWA
TRYNITARSKA
SKAWIŃSKA
H. WIĘTORA
CHMIELOWSKIEGO
RYBAKI
PODGÓRSKA
STAROWIŚLNA
RZESZOWSKA
HALICKA
PRZEMYSKA
ŚW. WAWRZYŃCA
KS. FR. BLACHNICKIEGO
M. SIEDLECKIEGO
SEMPERITOWCÓW
MASARSKA
KOTLARSKA
RZEŹNICZA
GĘSIA
ZABŁOCIE
PRZEMYSŁOWA
SOLNA
MŁYNARSKA
NADWIŚLAŃSKA
KĄCIK
LIPOWA
JANOWA WOLA
R. TRAUGUTTA
DĄBRÓWKI
LWOWSKA
NA ZJEŹDZIE
TARGOWA
KRAKUSA
PIWNA
JÓZEFIŃSKA
K. BRODZIŃSKIEGO
STAROMOSTOWA
CELNA
LEGIONÓW
B. LIMANOWSKIEGO
WĘGIERSKA
J. H. DĄBROWSKIEGO
WIELICKA
PRZY MOŚCIE
SOKOLSKA
WŁ. WARNEŃCZYKA
T. REJTANA
ŚW. KINGI
J. TARNOWSKIEGO
HETMAŃSKA
RĘKAWKA
JANA DŁUGOSZA
A. STWARZA
PARKOWA
PL. LASOTY
AL. E. DĘBOWSKIEGO
KRAKA
RADOSNA
SMOLKI
STROMA
JANA ZAMOJSKIEGO
KUTRZEBY
KALWARYJSKA
ROBOTNICZA
LANCKOROŃSKA
AL. POD KOPCEM
F. MARIEWSKIEGO
KRZEMIONKI
REDEMPTORYSTÓW
POWSTAŃCÓW ŚLĄSKICH
PODSKALE
CZYŻÓWKA
H. KAMIEŃSKIEGO
SWOSZOWICKA
ŁAGIEWNICKA
GRZYBKI
GŁOGOWSKA

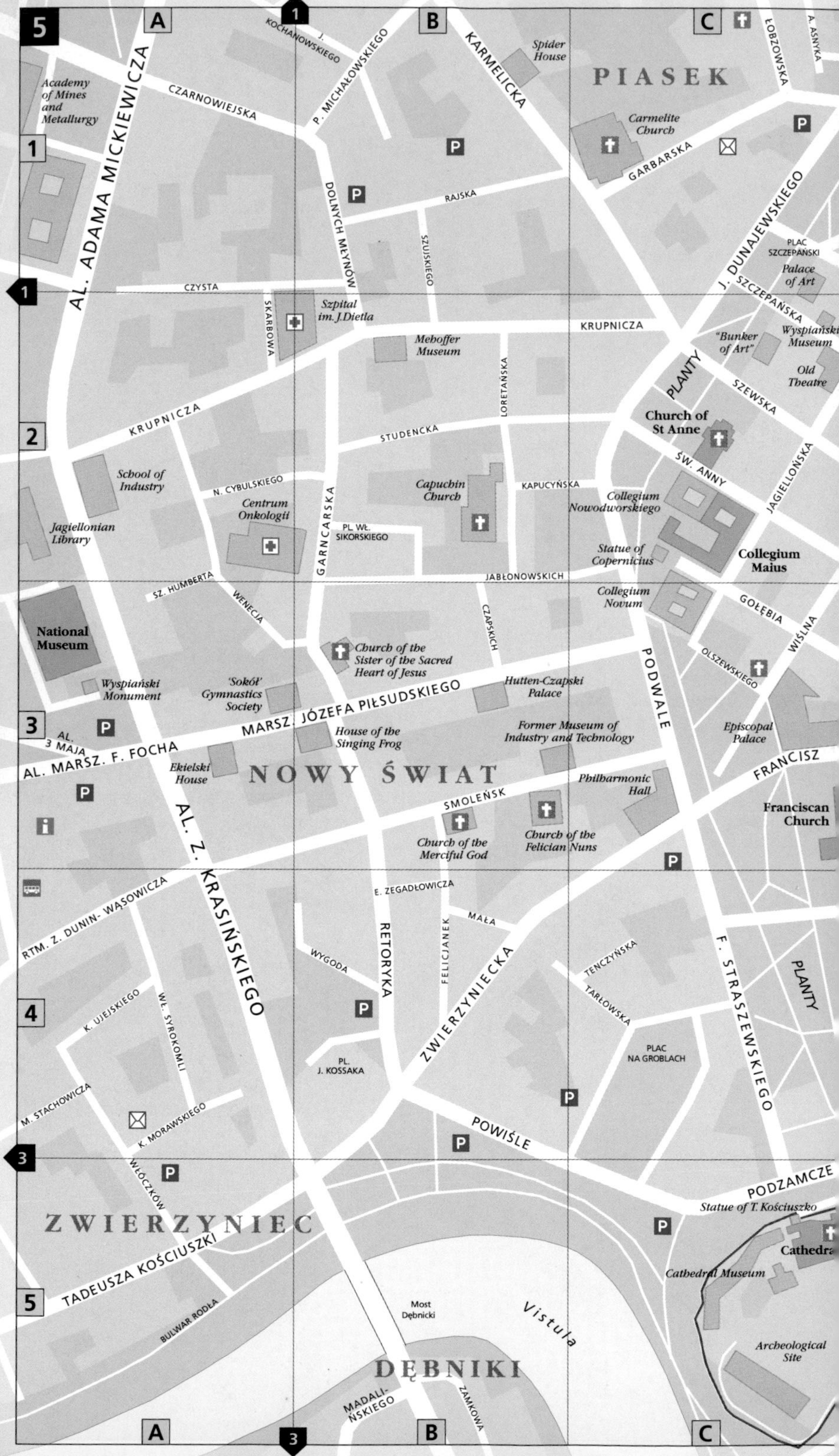
5
A
B
C
1
2
3
4
5
PIASEK
NOWY ŚWIAT
ZWIERZYNIEC
DĘBNIKI
Academy of Mines and Metallurgy
Spider House
Carmelite Church
Szpital im. J.Dietla
Mehoffer Museum
Palace of Art
Wyspiański Museum
"Bunker of Art"
Old Theatre
Church of St Anne
School of Industry
Jagiellonian Library
Centrum Onkologii
Capuchin Church
Collegium Nowodworskiego
Statue of Copernicius
Collegium Maius
Collegium Novum
National Museum
Wyspiański Monument
'Sokół' Gymnastics Society
Church of the Sister of the Sacred Heart of Jesus
Hutten-Czapski Palace
Episcopal Palace
House of the Singing Frog
Former Museum of Industry and Technology
Ekielski House
Philharmonic Hall
Franciscan Church
Church of the Merciful God
Church of the Felician Nuns
Statue of T. Kościuszko
Cathedra
Cathedral Museum
Archeological Site
Most Dębnicki
Vistula
AL. ADAMA MICKIEWICZA
CZARNOWIEJSKA
J. KOCHANOWSKIEGO
P. MICHAŁOWSKIEGO
KARMELICKA
ŁOBZOWSKA
A. ASNYKA
GARBARSKA
DOLNYCH MŁYNÓW
RAJSKA
SZUJSKIEGO
J. DUNAJEWSKIEGO
PLAC SZCZEPAŃSKI
SZCZEPAŃSKA
CZYSTA
SKARBOWA
KRUPNICZA
PLANTY
SZEWSKA
LORETAŃSKA
STUDENCKA
ŚW. ANNY
JAGIELLOŃSKA
N. CYBULSKIEGO
KAPUCYŃSKA
GARNCARSKA
PL. WŁ. SIKORSKIEGO
JABŁONOWSKICH
SZ. HUMBERTA
WENECJA
CZAPSKICH
GOŁĘBIA
WIŚLNA
OLSZEWSKIEGO
PODWALE
MARSZ. JÓZEFA PIŁSUDSKIEGO
AL. 3 MAJA
AL. MARSZ. F. FOCHA
FRANCISZ
SMOLEŃSK
AL. Z. KRASIŃSKIEGO
E. ZEGADŁOWICZA
MAŁA
RTM. Z. DUNIN- WĄSOWICZA
WYGODA
RETORYKA
FELICJANEK
ZWIERZYNIECKA
TENCZYŃSKA
TARŁOWSKA
F. STRASZEWSKIEGO
K. UJEJSKIEGO
WŁ. SYROKOMLI
PL. J. KOSSAKA
PLAC NA GROBLACH
M. STACHOWICZA
K. MORAWSKIEGO
POWIŚLE
WŁÓCZKÓW
PODZAMCZE
TADEUSZA KOŚCIUSZKI
BULWAR RODŁA
MADALIŃSKIEGO
ZAMKOWA

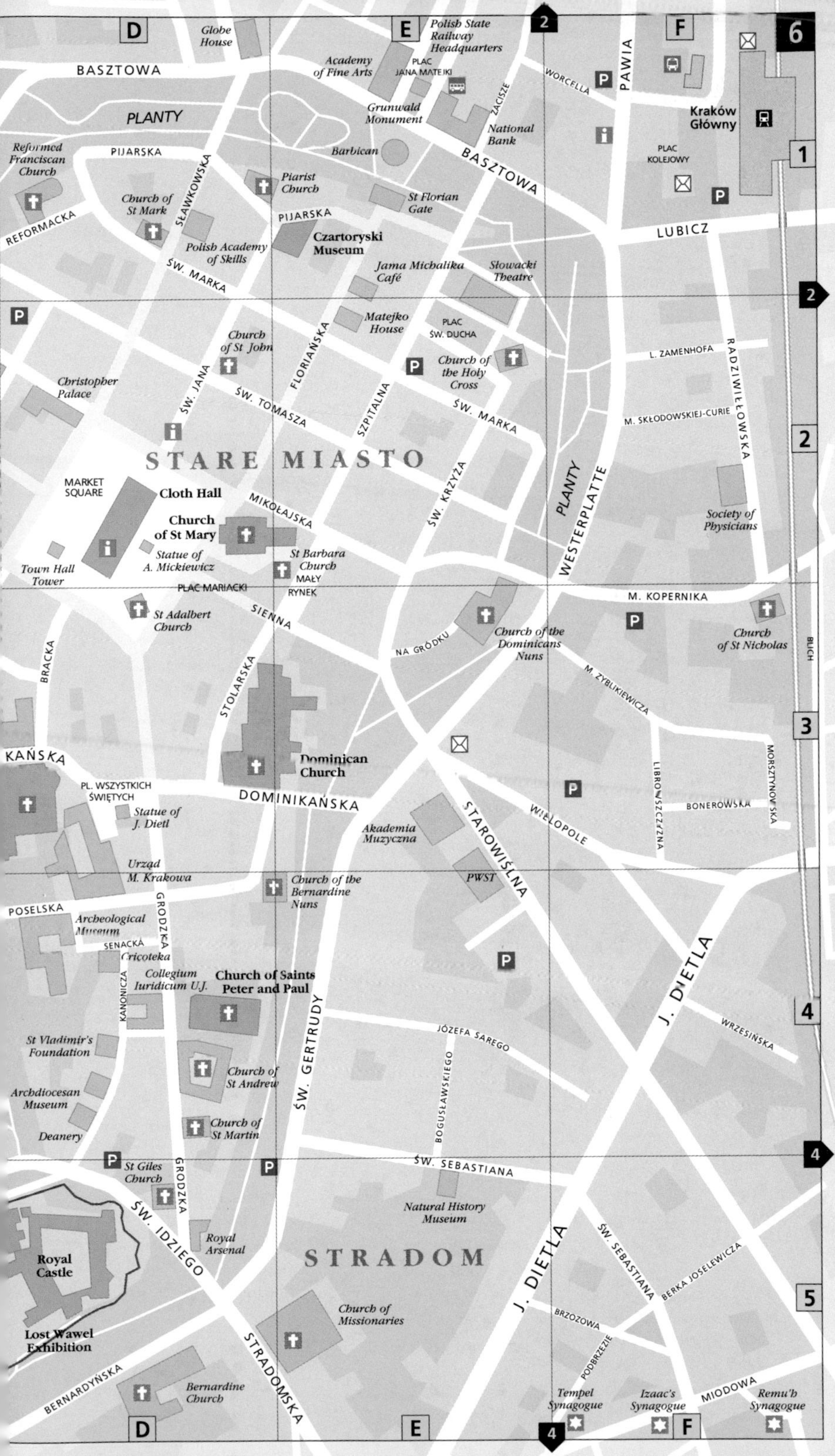

Globe House
Polish State Railway Headquarters
BASZTOWA
Academy of Fine Arts
PLAC JANA MATEJKI
WORCELLA
PAWIA
PLANTY
Grunwald Monument
ZACISZE
Kraków Główny
National Bank
Reformed Franciscan Church
PIJARSKA
Barbican
PLAC KOLEJOWY
BASZTOWA
Piarist Church
Church of St Mark
SŁAWKOWSKA
St Florian Gate
REFORMACKA
PIJARSKA
Czartoryski Museum
LUBICZ
Polish Academy of Skills
Jama Michalika Café
Słowacki Theatre
ŚW. MARKA
Matejko House
PLAC ŚW. DUCHA
Church of St John
FLORIAŃSKA
L. ZAMENHOFA
Church of the Holy Cross
RADZIWIŁŁOWSKA
Christopher Palace
ŚW. JANA
ŚW. TOMASZA
SZPITALNA
ŚW. MARKA
M. SKŁODOWSKIEJ-CURIE
STARE MIASTO
MARKET SQUARE
Cloth Hall
MIKOŁAJSKA
ŚW. KRZYŻA
PLANTY
WESTERPLATTE
Society of Physicians
Church of St Mary
Statue of A. Mickiewicz
St Barbara Church
Town Hall Tower
MAŁY RYNEK
PLAC MARIACKI
M. KOPERNIKA
SIENNA
St Adalbert Church
Church of the Dominicans Nuns
Church of St Nicholas
NA GRÓDKU
BLICH
BRACKA
M. ZYBLIKIEWICZA
STOLARSKA
Dominican Church
KAŃSKA
MORSZTYNOWSKA
LIBROWSZCZYZNA
PL. WSZYSTKICH ŚWIĘTYCH
DOMINIKAŃSKA
STAROWIŚLNA
BONEROWSKA
Statue of J. Dietl
WIELOPOLE
Akademia Muzyczna
Urząd M. Krakowa
PWST
Church of the Bernardine Nuns
POSELSKA
Archeological Museum
GRODZKA
SENACKA
Cricoteka
J. DIETLA
Collegium Iuridicum U.J.
Church of Saints Peter and Paul
KANONICZA
ŚW. GERTRUDY
JÓZEFA SAREGO
WRZESIŃSKA
St Vladimir's Foundation
Church of St Andrew
BOGUSŁAWSKIEGO
Archdiocesan Museum
Church of St Martin
Deanery
St Giles Church
ŚW. SEBASTIANA
GRODZKA
Natural History Museum
ŚW. IDZIEGO
Royal Arsenal
Royal Castle
STRADOM
J. DIETLA
ŚW. SEBASTIANA
BERKA JOSELEWICZA
BRZOZOWA
Church of Missionaries
Lost Wawel Exhibition
STRADOMSKA
PODBRZEZIE
BERNARDYŃSKA
Bernardine Church
Tempel Synagogue
Izaac's Synagogue
MIODOWA
Remu'h Synagogue
D
E
F
6
1
2
3
4
5

General Index

Page numbers in bold type refer to main entries.

G

H

R

Acknowledgments

Dorling Kindersley would like to thank the following people whose assistance has made the preparation of this book possible.

MANAGING EDITOR Helen Townsend

MANAGING ART EDITOR Kate Poole

SENIOR MANAGING EDITOR Louise B. Lang

ART DIRECTOR Gillian Allan

ADDITIONAL PHOTOGRAPHY Ian O'Leary

DESIGN AND EDITORIAL ASSISTANCE Sonal Bhatt, Hilary Bird, Arwen Burnett, Eli Estaugh, Victoria Heyworth-Dunne, Elly King, Ferdie McDonald, Gordon McLachlan, Simon Ryder, Sadie Smith, Leah Tether, Conrad Van Dyk Stewart J. Wild.

Dorling Kindersley wish to thank the following institutions, picture libraries and individuals for their kind permission to reproduce photographs of objects in their care and for the use of other photographic material:

Magdalena Maros the Director, and Krystyna Litewka at the Public Record State Office, Krzysztof Zamorski, Director of the Jagiellonian Library, Stanisław Waltoś the Director, Lucyna Bełtowska and Robert Springwald at the Collegium Maius, Matejko House, St Vladimir Foundation, Katarzyna Bałus, Princes Czartoryski Foundation, Jama Michalika, Prelate Janusz Bielański, Cracow Cathedral and Cathedral Museum, Church of the Bernardine Nuns, Bernardine Church, Father Mirosław Pilśniak, OP, Dominican Church, Sister Wanda Batko, Church of the Felician Nuns, Brother Bogumił Stachowicz, OFM, Franciscan Church, Father Edward Stoch, SJ, Jesuit Church in Wesoła, Capuchin Church, Father Dr Bronisław Fidelus, Church of St Mary, Father Jan Mazur, Paulite Church "On the Rock", Church of St Anne, Father Henryk Dziadosz, Church of St Barbara, Church of St Florian, Church of St Catherine, Church of the Holy Cross, Church of St Mark, Church of St Peter and St Paul, Church of St Vincent, Wieliczka Salt Mine, Father Dr Józef A. Nowobilski, the Metropolitan Curia and Archdiocesan Museum, Balice Airport, Archaeological Museum, Andrzej Szczygieł, Director of the Museum of Cracow, Anna Studnicka, National Museum, Natural History Museum, Zbigniew Święcicki the Director, and Mirosław Ciunowicz at the Polish Military Museum in Warsaw, PAP Polish Press Agency, Society of Physicians, Pieskowa Skała Castle.

Dorling Kindersley are grateful to the following individuals for their kind permission to reproduce their photographs:

Jacek Bednarczyk, Olaf Beer, Maja Florczykowska, Michał Grychowski, Stanisława Jabłońska, Dorota i Mariusz Jarymowiczowie, Beata i Mariusz Kowalewscy, Grzegorz Kozakiewicz, Wojciech Mędrzak, Stanisław Michta, Hanna i Maciej Musiałowie, Tomasz Robaczyński, Maciej Sochor, Jan Zych.

All the dishes whose photographs feature in this guide were prepared in the restaurant Pod Aniołami. We wish to thank the owner, Jacek Łodziński for his help. We are also grateful to Marcin Duszyński, Madropol for his kind assistance.

PICTURE CREDITS t=top; tc=top centre; tr=top right; cla=centre left above; ca=centre above; cra=centre right above; cl=centre left; c=centre; cr=centre right; clb=centre left below; b=bottom; bc=bottom centre; bl=bottom left; br=bottom right; c=centre=below; crb=centre right below;

AKG-IMAGES: 161cr; Ullstein Bild-KPA/HIP/Jewish Chronicle Ltd 125br; ALAMY IMAGES: David Sanger Photography/David Sanger 185tl; Kevin Foy 124tl, 185c; Karolek 10cr; lookGaleria 11bl, 125cb; Paul Springett 70 clb; Peter Svarc 10bl; Krystyna Szulecka 184cl; ARCHAEOLOGICAL MUSEUM: 20clb, 20b, 21cr, 21cb, 21b, 40b; THE ART ARCHIVE: Laurie Platt Winfrey 125cra; AUSCHWITZ-BIRKENAU MEMORIAL & MUSEUM: 160tr, 160cl, 160bl, 160br, 161tc, 162clb, 1§63cr, 163br; Ryszard Domasik 160tl, 161crb, 162cla, 163tl, 163tr; Jarek Mensfelt 162tr.

CATHEDRAL MUSEUM: 22–23c, 24cla, 25cla, 42cl, 60ca, 62c; COLLEGIUM MAIUS: 25cb, 31b, 106–107; CORBIS: Bettmann 125tl; Jon Hicks 72–3; Historical Picture Archive 124tr; CZARTORYSKI MUSEUM: 41t, 43b, 112–113.

EDYTA GAWRON: 124br; Encyclopaedia Judaica 124cl.

JAGIELLONIAN LIBRARY: 20–21c, 24clb, 26tl, 26cra, 26b, 30b, 30crb, 28br, 32cb, 150b; DARIUSZ JEDRZEJEWSKI: 11tr. WOJCIECH KOZŁOWSKI: 212bc, 218clb.

MATEJKO HOUSE: 23cr; MUSEUM OF CRACOW: 18, 19b, 27ca, 29cb, 34b, 35ca, 35cr, 40cr, 41cbr, 42tl, 92tr, 99br; MUZEUM HISTORCZNE MIASTA KRAKOWA: Ignacy Krieger 124clb, 124cb, 124crb.

NATIONAL MUSEUM: 8–9, 22bc, 23tc, 24b, 25cr, 29br, 30bl, 30–31c, 31cr, 32tc, 32–33c, 33t, 33tr, 34cl, 34–35c, 37bl, 40tr, 40cl, 41tcr, 41c, 43t, 50cla, 51tl, 51br, 102tr, 102c, 103, 110cl, 147l, 148–149; NATURAL HISTORY MUSEUM: 43c; NOVOTEL KRAKOW CENTRUM: 175tr.

PUBLIC RECORD STATE OFFICE: 24–25c, 24bl, 24t.

TEL AVIV MUSEUM OF ART: *Jews Praying in the Synagogue on Yom Kippur* by Maurycy Gottlieb, oil on canvas, gift of Sydney Lamon, New York 124-5; TELEKOMUNIKACJA POLSKA: 218c, 218bc; TOPFOTO.CO. UK: Roger-Viollet 162bl.

JACKET
Front – CORBIS: Jon Hicks main image; DK IMAGES: Courtesy of the Public Record State Office, Cracow clb. Back – DK IMAGES: Andrzej Chec cla; Wojciech Czerniewicz clb; Mariusz Kowalewsky bl; Jan Zych, Owls (1964) sculpture by Bronislaw Chromy tl. Spine – CORBIS: Jon Hicks t; DK IMAGES: Jan Zych, Owls (1964) sculpture by Bronislaw Chromy b.